ESTATES and TRUSTS

Gilbert Thomas Stephenson

THIRD EDITION

New York

APPLETON-CENTURY-CROFTS, INC.

Preface

This volume is a completely revised—in fact, largely rewritten—edition of the textbook, *Estates and Trusts,* published in 1949 and revised in 1955 in the light of the Internal Revenue Code of 1954.

Throughout this present edition, an attempt is made to preserve and to present all of the material in the original edition which is regarded as fundamental and basic to the orderly study of estates and trusts. That is, it includes information for the student who, although he, himself, does not expect to be engaged in settling estates or administering trusts, nevertheless, some day (as stated in the preface to the first edition) may have an estate of his own to settle or administer and a family of his own to provide for.

In addition to this basic material carried over from the first edition, new material is included for the student who already is, or who anticipates being, engaged in settling estates and administering trusts or in helping other persons plan the disposition and administration of their property.

In the execution of its enlarged scope, this edition has been divided into four parts.

Part I, on the disposition of property in estates and trusts, is designed to present information which every student, regardless of his anticipated business or profession, should acquire. At this stage of his education his main concern is conceived to be the various dispositive devices that are available to property owners.

Part II, on the administration of property in estates and trusts, is designed for the student who wishes to go further and inquire into the administration of property after it passes into the hands of an executor or administrator, a guardian, a trustee, or an agent.

Part III, on planning the disposition and administration of property, is designed primarily, but not exclusively, for the advanced student who is interested in the practical application of principles and policies of disposition and administration as presented in the two preceding parts. It includes a general, although not technical or detailed, discussion of tax considerations involved in planning such disposition and administration.

Part IV, containing illustrative instruments of disposition and administration, presents a will, a living trust agreement, a personal insurance agreement, and a business insurance trust agreement designed to cover the main points discussed in the three preceding parts.

For the student who wishes to carry his study of a particular topic further, there is appended to each chapter a suggested collateral reading list with abbreviated citations, and at the end of the text there is a comprehensive bibliography in which the citations of collateral reading are given in full.

In an attempt to make the material in this edition adequate, up to date, and adapted to the differing needs of students with various backgrounds and objectives in the field of estates and trusts, the advice and assistance of three main groups and of two individuals have been elicited and obtained.

The first group is composed of instructors in colleges and universities who have used the original or the revised edition as a textbook in their classes. Some of these instructors are full-time members of the faculty, some part-time instructors who are primarily lawyers or insurance men. They, with their connections, are Lewis R. Donelson, III, Donelson and Adams, Attorneys at Law, Memphis, Tennessee; Mark R. Greene, University of Oregon, Eugene, Oregon; Charles L. Kopp, Pacific Fidelity Life Insurance Company, Los Angeles; John T. C. Low, Lincoln National Bank and Trust Company, Syracuse, New York; Louis Maier, Wrought, Grootemaat and Cook, Attorneys at Law, Milwaukee, Wisconsin; Eugene J. Mincks, Indianapolis Life Insurance Company, Houston, Texas; J. E. Mittelman, San Francisco State College, San Francisco; A. S. Moses, Jr., Connecticut General Life Insurance Company, Hartford, Connecticut; C. H. Orr, National Life Insurance Company, Pompano Beach, Florida; Arthur E. Schmauder, The Prudential Life Insurance Company of America, Newark, New Jersey; Stuart Schwarzchild, Georgia State College of Business Administration, Atlanta, Georgia; and Frank J. Schwentker, University of North Carolina, Chapel Hill, North Carolina.

The second group, of which the author has been a member, is the Committee on Trust Education of the Trust Division of the American Bankers Association. This committee, serving in an advisory capacity only, is concerned with every phase of trust education—whether carried on by the American Institute of Banking, The Stonier Graduate School of Banking, the Pacific Coast Banking School, the National Trust School, or by other schools sponsored by state bankers associations either individually or in groups. Members of this committee who have been helpful in the preparation of this edition are Richard P. Chapman, The Merchants National Bank, Boston; Reese H. Harris, Jr., The Hanover Bank, New York; Walter Kennedy, The First National Bank, Montgomery, Alabama; and R. G. Page, Jr., Wachovia Bank and Trust Company, Winston-Salem, North Carolina.

The third group is the staff of The American College of Life Underwriters, Philadelphia, especially Dean Herbert C. Graebner and W. W. Dotterweich, Jr., Director of Educational Publications.

The two individuals who have been especially helpful are Clarence D.

Cowdery, The Boatmen's National Bank, St. Louis, and Robert C. Rogers, The Planters National Bank and Trust Company of Rocky Mount, North Carolina.

Mr. Cowdery, Chairman of the Trust Division Committee on Handling Businesses in Trust, edited Chapter 18, Part II, on investment in businesses.

Mr. Rogers, a lawyer and a trust officer, whose daily work is advising property owners and their lawyers in planning the disposition and administration of property, has read all of the text and made valuable corrections and suggestions.

To all of these the author is deeply grateful; however, he alone assumes responsibility for the accuracy and the propriety of the contents of this edition.

G. T. S.

Warren Place
Pendleton, North Carolina

Contents

PART I

DISPOSITION OF PROPERTY IN ESTATES AND TRUSTS

PART II

ADMINISTRATION OF PROPERTY IN ESTATES AND TRUSTS

PART III

PLANNING DISPOSITION AND ADMINISTRATION
OF PROPERTY

PART IV

ILLUSTRATIVE INSTRUMENTS OF DISPOSITION AND ADMINISTRATION

part I

DISPOSITION OF PROPERTY IN ESTATES AND TRUSTS

A textbook on estates and trusts logically begins with a presentation of the ways by which property in estates and trusts passes from owner to receiver. The principal ways by which property so passes are by operation of law, as where a property owner dies without leaving a valid will; by will; by gift in trust during his lifetime; and by the grant-and-exercise of a power of appointment. The passing of property during the owner's lifetime, except by gift in trust, is beyond the scope of this text.

1

Property and Property Interests

PROPERTY IS THE MATERIAL SUBSTANCE of estates and trusts. It is logical, therefore, that a textbook on estates and trusts begin with a chapter on property and property interests.

What Property Is

Property is whatever a person can own. To own a thing in its full sense is to have the exclusive right to possess, use, and dispose of that thing. But it will be seen that there are many degrees of ownership which affect these rights.

What is property under one set of circumstances may not be property under another set. While no person owns the fish of the seas nor the birds of the air nor the wild animals of the fields and forests, any person may own fish he catches, birds he kills, or animals he captures. While no person owns the free air which we all breathe nor the free light-rays and heat-rays of the sun, any person may own air, heat, and light which he captures, confines, and puts to use. Witness, for example, the hitherto free air captured, confined, compressed, and utilized for the inflation of tires at the modern service station. This compressed air is property. For practical purposes, the best answer to the question, Is it property? may be found in the answer to the counterquestion, Can it be owned?

Kinds of Property

The two main kinds of property are *real* property and *personal* property. Ordinarily, real property is thought of as land and everything else as personal property.

But real property and land are not synonymous. Some property, although dissociated with or disconnected from land, nevertheless is regarded as real property; whereas, other property, although associated or connected with land, is regarded as personal property.

Only reference to the origin of the distinction between real property and personal property will enable a person to reconcile the apparent inconsistencies of treating as real property what, it seems, should be personal property, and vice versa.

Since land itself is immovable and indestructible, whenever one person trespassed upon another person's land or dispossessed him, the person so trespassed upon or dispossessed, seeking redress by an action at law, undertook to have the trespasser removed and to repossess the land itself. That is to say, he undertook to get the thing itself—the land—back into his full possession. The Latin word for *thing* is *res*. An action to recover the thing itself—the land—came to be known as a *real* action and the property involved in the action, as *real* property.

In the case of property that is movable or destructible, the action against a person who damaged, removed, or destroyed it need not be one to recover the property itself but to recover the money-loss resulting from the damage, removal, or destruction of the property. It was an action against the *person* of the wrongdoer to require him to make good the damage. Hence, the property which was the subject matter of the action came to be known as *personal* property.

Keeping in mind this origin of the distinction between real property and personal property will enable the student to understand better why certain interests in land are regarded as personal property and certain interests in movable and destructible things, although dissociated from land, as real property.

Although, as just stated, many of the interests in land are regarded as personal property, it has seemed better to treat all the interests in land together rather than to divide them into real property and personal property.

PROPERTY IN LAND

The term *land* is employed here to include the ground itself and everything in it or growing on it or attached to it with the intent that it shall be regarded as a part of or as going with the ground. Thus, the plat of ground, the trees, shrubs, and lawn growing on it, the house built on the lot, and the furnace attached to the house are regarded as part of the land and in legal contemplation are real property.

Estates in Land

Originally only certain interests in land were known as estates; but at the present time the term *estates* includes all interests in land, and in this broad sense the term is used in this text.

For the origin of our present-day estates in land it is necessary to go back to the Norman Conquest in 1066. After the Battle of Hastings that year, William the Conqueror became, in theory, the owner of all the land. The natives, in surrendering, turned their land over to him, and he let them and his followers retain it on certain terms and conditions. They became his tenants. Thus, in theory, the king became the owner of all the land in the kingdom and the people on the land, his tenants. This, in brief, is known as tenure of land under the feudal system. This system has persisted for nearly 900 years and in modified form still persists throughout the British Commonwealth.

When the American colonies revolted, dissolved their allegiance to the British Crown, and established their own independent government, they, in a measure, substituted the state for the king as the ultimate owner of all the land. That is to say, the owner of land held it subject to the ultimate ownership or dominion of the state. We see a practical application of this theory whenever land escheats to the state because of the failure of heirs.

Thus, it is technically inaccurate to speak of a person as being the *owner* of land or of other *real* property. The state is the ultimate owner. The individual is at most only the tenant, and his interest in the land or other real property is his *estate*. Hence the interchangeable use of the terms *real property* and *real estate*. Technically, the former refers to the land itself and other *real* property; and the latter, to his interest in *real* property. Although in everyday conversation and writing this distinction is not observed, it is well for the student of estates and trusts to be aware of it.

Originally, there were many more estates in land—that is, more kinds and degrees of ownership—than there are now. Yet there still remain in this country different estates in land which the student of estates and trusts must understand and keep in mind.

1. *Fee simple estates.* The largest interest that a person can have in land is known as a fee simple estate. This means that he holds the land for himself and for his heirs forever. He may sell or dispose of the land during his lifetime by deed or at his death devise it (give it by will). He may either pass it on to the person who takes his entire estate in the land or divide his greater estate among two or more takers of lesser estates. If he dies without leaving a valid will, the land descends to his heirs. If he dies without heirs or without having disposed of his land by deed or will, the land escheats—that is, goes back—to the state or a subdivision of the state as the ultimate owner.

Thus, an estate in fee simple is the most nearly absolute ownership of land known to our law. When a person himself has an estate in fee simple and conveys it to another person "and his heirs," the latter takes a fee simple estate. In most states even a conveyance to the person without adding "and his heirs" carries a fee simple estate.

2. *Fee tail estates.* A person who receives land conveyed to himself and the heirs of his body takes what is known as a fee tail estate. Thus, *A*, the

owner of the fee simple estate, conveys the land by deed or will to B and the heirs of his body. *Heirs of his body* means his children or grandchildren or other lineal descendants. If he leaves no heirs of his body, the land goes back to A as the owner of the fee simple estate.

Originally, there were estates tail male—meaning to the male heirs of the body—and estates tail female—meaning female heirs of the body. But in most states these estates no longer exist; and, by operation of law, fee tail estates have become fee simple estates.

3. *Life estates.* A life estate, as the name implies, is an estate in land for the duration of some person's lifetime. It may be for the lifetime of the person who receives the estate or for the lifetime of some other person. For example, A, the owner of a fee simple estate, may convey or devise to B an estate for the life of B, or he may convey or devise to B an estate for the life of C. In the latter case B's would be an estate *pour autre vie* (estate for the life of another person).

The above three estates—fee simple, fee tail, and life—are real property. They are known as *freehold* estates and originally they were the only interests in land which were classified as estates.

In addition to these three freehold estates, there are three other lesser estates in land which, however, are regarded as personal property. Usually they are referred to as *tenancies*—tenancies for years, tenancies at will, and tenancies at sufferance—perhaps to distinguish them from the three freehold estates.

4. *Tenancies for years.* An estate in land that lasts for a definite period is known as a tenancy for years. The period need not be measured in terms of years. It may be for days or months or years or decades or any other unit of time. It is the definiteness of the period that makes it a tenancy for years. The instrument creating such a tenancy frequently is known as a *lease* and the interest itself as a *leasehold*.

5. *Tenancies at will.* An estate in land whose duration is determined by the will of the owner of the larger estate is known as a tenancy at will. For example, A, the owner of the fee simple estate, permits B to occupy and use the land so long as A is willing that he should do so. B's estate is a tenancy at will and B himself, a tenant at will.

6. *Tenancies at sufferance.* An estate in land which results from a lawful tenant's remaining on the land beyond the period of his rightful tenancy is known as a tenancy at sufferance. That is to say, he stays on at the sufferance of the owner of the larger estate. For example, A leases land to B for five years (a tenancy for years). B stays on into the sixth year and A permits him to do so. After the end of the fifth year B has no further lawful estate in the land. He stays on as a tenant at sufferance.

In addition to the foregoing estates in land which a person may own individually—that is, estates in severalty—there are other estates which he may own with one or more other persons: undivided estates,

7. *Tenancies in common*. An undivided estate in land which upon the death of the owner becomes the property of his heirs or devisees, and not of his surviving co-owner or co-owners, is a tenancy in common. For example, *A*, *B*, and *C* each owns an undivided one-third interest in land. Upon the death of *A*, his estate in the land passes to his heirs or devisees and not to *B* and *C*. This is a tenancy in common. If the land is capable of physical division, then *A*, *B*, and *C* may subdivide it or, in case of disagreement, any one of them may petition the court to order a division and each take his part in severalty. If it is not capable of division, then by agreement or, in case of disagreement, by a proceeding in court, the land may be sold and the proceeds of the sale divided.

8. *Joint tenancies*. Upon the death of a joint tenant his interest passes, not to his heirs or devisees, but to his co-owner or co-owners. For example, *A*, *B*, and *C* jointly own land. Upon the death of *A*, the whole, not just a share, of the land becomes the property of *B* and *C*; upon the death of *B* later, it becomes the sole property of *C*; and upon the death of *C*, the property of *C's* heirs or devisees. The characteristic of a joint tenancy is that the surviving tenant or tenants, not the heirs or devisees, succeed to the estate of a deceased tenant, until there is one surviving tenant who then becomes the sole owner.

At the present time the law favors tenancy in common over joint tenancy. If *A* conveys land to *B* and *C* without specifying whether or not they take as joint tenants or without adding the phrase "with right of survivorship," they take as tenants in common and not as joint tenants.

9. *Tenancies by the entirety*. In those states in which tenancy by the entirety still is recognized, a conveyance of land to a husband and wife makes them tenants by the entirety and not tenants in common nor joint tenants. Tenancy by the entirety resembles a joint tenancy to the extent that upon the death of either the husband or the wife the land passes to the survivor. It is confined to husband and wife. It cannot be terminated except by consent of both parties as joint tenancy can be. These are the basic differences between the two.

Even in those states in which tenancy by the entirety never existed or has been abolished, it is possible for a husband and wife, the same as any other two persons, to receive and to hold land as joint tenants with right of survivorship with the result that upon the death of either the land passes to the survivor.

10. *Community property*. In those states which inherited their legal system from the French or Spanish rather than from the British and in a few states by statute there exists an interest in land known as *community property*. The states which inherited their legal system from the French or Spanish are Louisiana and some states of the West and Southwest. Reduced to its simplest terms, in a community-property state the property that a husband or wife owns at the time of the marriage and the property that each

individually inherits or purchases with individual funds afterwards remain separate property, whereas the property that they acquire during their married life becomes community property in which each has an undivided one-half interest. Either can dispose of separate property without the consent or joinder of the other. Although the husband may control and even dispose of the community property during the continuance of the marriage, he cannot dispose of more than one-half of it by will; nor can the wife, by will, dispose of more than one-half of the community property.

PROPERTY OTHER THAN LAND

Sometimes it is said rather loosely that the earth and everything of a permanent nature attached to it and improvements of a permanent nature placed upon it, with the intent that they shall remain attached to the earth, are real property and that everything else is personal property. But, as already indicated, this definition is inadequate because some interests in land are personal property and some interests in other things than land are treated as though they were real property.

Furthermore, the conversion of real property into personal property and vice versa are everyday occurrences. For example, the tree standing in the forest is real property; the same tree when felled becomes personal property. The water pipes in the plumber's shop are personal property; the same pipes installed in the house as a part of the water system are real property.

Although many of the words or phrases which apply to the ownership of property other than land are found only or mainly in legal literature, nevertheless it is essential that the student of estates and trusts understand their technical meaning. Such terms, among others that will appear from place to place in the text, are *chattels, tangibles* and *intangibles, choses,* and *mixed.*

Chattels

There are two kinds of chattels—chattels *real* and chattels *personal.* A chattel *real* is one of the minor estates in land—a tenancy for years, at will, or at sufferance. A chattel *personal* is an item of goods—for example, a piece of jewelry, silverware, or an automobile. The common phrase, *goods and chattels,* includes both these interests in land and in goods themselves.

Tangibles and Intangibles

Property which has physical substance—which may be touched, seen, felt—is known as *tangible* (touchable) *property,* or as tangibles. The ground itself, the house, the tree, the book, the typewriter—such items as these are tangible property or tangibles. There is no difficulty in distinguishing or characterizing tangibles.

Difficulty does arise with regard to intangible property or intangibles. *Intangible property* may be defined as property which does not have physical substance or which cannot be seen, touched, or felt. A certificate of stock, a bond, or a mortgage is classified as intangible property. The ad valorem (meaning based on value) tax on stocks, bonds, and mortgages frequently is referred to as the intangibles tax or as the tax on intangibles. Does not the certificate of stock, the bond, or the mortgage have physical substance? No, the real value is what the paper-writing known as the certificate of stock or the bond or the mortgage stands for and not the paper-writing itself. Destroy the paper-writing and the property itself is not destroyed nor the ownership affected; only evidence of the property is affected.

For practical purposes it may be said that, if the thing itself has value, it is tangible property; if the thing—the certificate of stock, for example—is only evidence of value, it is intangible property. Furthermore, there is much intangible property which is not evidenced by any paper-writing nor other tangible thing—for example, a right based upon an oral contract.

Choses

In legal literature or in the company of lawyers a person frequently comes across the term *chose in action* and, less frequently, *chose in possession*. *Chose* means *thing* and is pronounced *shōz* which sounds very much like *shows*.

1. *In possession*. A chose in possession, to mention the easier one first, is a thing in a person's physical possession—such as a watch, a horse, or an automobile. It is almost, if not quite, synonymous with tangible property.

2. *In action*. A chose in action is a right in property which has not been reduced to possession and which is recoverable only by an action at law. This does not mean that an action at law is necessary in all cases to recover the property but that such an action is the only way of asserting the right to the property.

Among the commonest types of choses in action are debts, patent rights, copyrights, royalty rights, rights growing out of damages to person or property, rights under life insurance contracts, and rights under property insurance contracts. All these are rights to property in the exercise of which rights, through an action at law, the owner can recover the property itself.

Mixed

Property which partakes of the nature of both real property and personal property sometimes is referred to as *mixed property*. A key to a house, a tombstone, an heirloom—these are typical examples of mixed property. They are like real property in that they pass to the heirs or devisees; but like personal property in that they are movable and destructible.

Undivided Interests

Also there are undivided interests in property other than land.

1. *Interests in common.* It is possible and quite common for two or more persons to own property other than land as owners in common, so that upon the death of any one of them his share passes to his own next of kin or passes under his will and not to his co-owners. For example, A, B, and C may own in common shares of stock, bonds, or mortgages so that upon the death of A, his share will pass to his next of kin or under his will and not to B and C.

2. *Joint interests.* It is quite common also for two or more people to hold property other than land in joint ownership. For example, in most states, if A and B purchase shares of stock and have the certificates made out to A and B "as joint owners with right of survivorship and not as owners in common," upon the death of A, the ownership of the shares would pass to B or, upon the death of B, to A by right of survivorship.

But this is not a universal rule. In some states—North Carolina, for example—joint ownership of personal property, with right of survivorship, applies only if there is a contract between or among the owners that it shall apply—that is, based upon such a contract, upon the death of any one of the owners, the property will pass to the survivor or survivors and not to the next of kin or legatees of the deceased owner.

3. *Interests by the entirety.* Under the common law, tenancy by the entirety was confined to real property. But in some states it is said that tenancy by the entirety exists also as to property other than land. What this means, perhaps, is that in these states a transfer of personal property to a husband and wife makes them joint owners with right of survivorship even though in the instrument of transfer they are not described as husband and wife. For example, in those states, a certificate of stock issued to "A and B" would make them joint owners with right of survivorship if they were, in fact, husband and wife, even though they were not described as such on the certificate and even though there was no mention of their being joint owners with right of survivorship.

As to both joint interests and interests by the entirety in personal property, states statutes and decisions vary so widely that the student must not rely upon any general statement but must consult the laws of the state involved.

4. *Interests in community property.* In the community-property states provisions for separate property and for community property apply both to real property and to personal property.

OTHER PROPERTY INTERESTS

There are still other interests in property which the student of estates and trusts should understand. There are legal interests, equitable interests, present interests, future interests, vested interests, contingent interests, and uses. A clear understanding of legal interests and equitable interests is essential to an understanding of this text.

Legal

The legal owner of property is the person who has the legal title to the property. The property itself may not be in his possession. It may be real or personal, tangible or intangible. If a person can say rightfully, "That is my property, I have the legal title to it," he is the legal owner of that property. In every country which has the institution of private property, as distinct from that of state ownership, it is not difficult, in practice, to understand what legal ownership means.

Equitable or Legal

But in all the common-law countries, sometimes called the English-speaking countries (the British Commonwealth and the United States of America), there is the interest known as equitable ownership of, or equitable interest in, property. The system of law prevailing in these countries is known as the *common* law, as distinct from the *civil*-law system that prevails in the other civilized countries. In these countries it is common for one person to be the legal owner and for another person to be the equitable owner of the same property. This is what confuses some lawyers, as well as laymen, in other countries. They do not understand, they say, how there can be two ownerships of the same property. Equitable ownership exists only in the British Commonwealth and the United States, except in a few countries, such as Panama, Puerto Rico, and Mexico, in which it has been introduced by statute and grafted to their own legal system.

In the countries of the British Commonwealth and in the United States, equitable ownership is common and is almost as well known as legal ownership. For example, *A*, who is the husband of *B* and the father of *C*, by his will leaves his land, his securities, and his cash to *D* (his friend or his bank) in trust to pay the income from the property to *B* during her lifetime and after her death to pay, transfer, or convey, the property itself to *C*. The creation of such an arrangement as this is a typical, everyday occurrence. Upon the death of *A* and the settlement of his estate, *D* becomes the legal owner of all the property—land, securities, and cash—and *B* and *C* each becomes an equitable owner. *B* becomes the equitable owner of the right to the income from the property during her lifetime, and *C* becomes the equitable owner of the property itself, subject to *B's* life right to the income. Since *B*, during her lifetime, is entitled to all the benefits of the property—that is, the income from it—and C is entitled to the property itself, including the income, after B's death—they frequently are referred to as the beneficial owners of the property or as the beneficiaries. The terms *equitable owner* and *beneficial owner* are used interchangeably.

Present or Future

A person's ownership of an interest in property, whether legal or equitable, may be either a present interest or a future interest. It is present if he has a present right of use or enjoyment of the property; future, if the use or enjoyment is postponed to some future time. In the illustration above, upon A's death, B's became a present interest and C's a future interest in that B came into immediate enjoyment of her right to the income, whereas C's right to possession or enjoyment of the property itself was postponed to the time of B's death.

Vested or Contingent

A person's interest in property may be either vested or contingent.

It is vested if he has a present, already determined right to either the present or the future enjoyment of the property. In the illustration, upon A's death, both B's and C's interests will be vested. B will have the present, already determined right to the immediate enjoyment of the income from the property and C will have the present, already determined right to the property itself upon B's death. The postonement of C's right to possession and enjoyment of the property until B's death does not keep it from being a vested interest. Future interests and contingent interests must not be confused.

The interest is contingent if the right itself is dependent upon the happening of some future, uncertain event. Suppose, in the illustration, A had provided in his will that, after B's death, C would receive the property if he were living at that time but that, if he had died before B, the property at B's death would go to E (A's college). Both C's and E's interest in the property would be a contingent interest—C's upon his outliving B, E's upon his not doing so. At no time up until B's death would it be possible to tell whether C or E ever would have any interest in the property.

Use

Occasionally, a person has the right to the use of property without being the owner.

The student is warned against confusing the word *use* as employed here with the same word employed in connection with trusts—as, for example, in the Statute of Uses. In the Middle Ages, property frequently was conveyed by *A* to *B for the use of C*. This arrangement was the forerunner of the modern practice of conveying property to *B in trust for C*. Conveying land to *B* for the use of *C* led to such abuses that in 1536 the Statute of Uses was enacted to abolish *uses*. But it was through loopholes left in that statute that the modern trust has evolved. This, however, is not the sense in which the term *use* is employed in this section.

A, for example, may leave his land to *B*, his wife, for her use and occupancy during her lifetime and then to his son *C*. This is, in effect, leaving her a life estate in the land.

Or *A* leaves shares of stocks and bonds to *B* for her use during her lifetime and then to his son *C*, in which case *B* would receive the dividends and interest during her lifetime and at her death the stocks and bonds would be transferred to *C*.

In practice, perhaps the most frequent employment of the use instead of the trust is in connection with household furniture and other items of a personal or domestic nature. *A* leaves specified items of furniture, for example, to the use of *B*, his wife, during her lifetime and then to *C*, his son.

It is not so common now as it was before the development of the trust to give or leave people the use of property. However, this arrangement still is employed frequently enough to make it advisable for the student to understand what the term *use* means here and to distinguish it from the same term which was the forerunner of the modern trust.

Power

There is still another interest regarding property which, mainly due to recent tax legislation, has come into much prominence. This is the power of appointment. For example, *A* leaves property to or in trust for *B*, his wife, with power granted to her by deed or will to appoint the property to or for whomsoever she desires. He thus gives her a *general* power of appointment. He might have restricted her power to appointment by deed or by will and it still would have been a general power. But if he had left her the power to appoint, either by deed or will, only to their children, for example, it would have been a *limited* or *special* power.

ACQUISITION OF PROPERTY

All methods of acquiring property are grouped under two headings—acquisition by descent and acquisition by purchase.

Descent

Property is acquired by descent when it comes by inheritance from someone related by blood or adoption; that is, when the person receives it because he is kin by blood or adoption to someone else.

Purchase

Acquisition by purchase is a broad term that covers all methods of acquisition except that by descent.

1. *Escheat.* The state or a subdivision thereof acquires property by escheat when it receives it because of failure of heirs or next of kin of the owner. In some states all escheated property passes to the state university, to some other designated state institution, or for some specified objects, such as the support of common schools.

2. *Occupancy.* Property is acquired by occupancy when, having no owner, it is possessed or captured. In the early days homesteaders acquired land by occupancy. At the present time hunters acquire wild game by capture. This applies only to property that has no owner other than the state and to property thus possessed or captured with the intent of reducing it to private ownership.

3. *Prescription.* Property is acquired by prescription when a person has held property in his possession the length of time required under the law for it to become his property. At common law the term *prescription* applies only to intangible interests in land, such as easements. For example, *A*, in order to get to and from his own land, has passed back and forth over *B's* land for the length of time required to give him an easement by prescription over *B's* land.

4. *Adverse possession.* The real property itself, as distinct from the easement, is acquired by adverse possession when a person has occupied it without molestation or without anyone else claiming it for a specified length of time. In some states the length of time is seven years where the person is holding the property under "color of title"—that is, having some sort of paper-title to the property—or twenty years if he does not claim to have title. In former times, more than at the present time, a person might live on, occupy, use, and to all appearances own a parcel of land—perhaps himself thinking and other people thinking that he was the owner of the land—only to learn later that he had no legal title to the land or, if he did, that his title was defective. In order to "quiet the title" in such cases the states provide by statute for the acquisition of title by adverse possession after the person has been in unmolested possession of the property the specified length of time.

5. *Gift.* The foregoing—escheat, occupancy, prescription, and adverse possession—are the less common methods of acquisition of property. The two common methods—other than by descent—are by gift and by purchase. The acquisition of both real property and personal property by gift is so much an everyday occurrence as not to call for further comment.

6. *Bargain-and-sale.* Using the term *purchase* now in its everyday sense of bargain-and-sale, the acquisition of property by purchase is, by far, the most common method of acquisition.

DISPOSITION OF PROPERTY

Some of the methods of disposing of property are counterparts of the methods of acquiring property. One person devises and another person inherits; what one person gives, another person receives; what one person sells, another person buys. There are, however, several methods of disposing of property or of its being disposed of which deserve special mention.

Gift

As mentioned above, one of the most common methods of disposing of property is by the owner giving it outright during his lifetime to some other person with intent on the part of the one to give and of the other to receive. In the case of real property, this is accomplished by a deed of gift; intangible property, by transfer; tangible property, by delivery.

Gift in Contemplation of Death

Sometimes a person, conscious of approaching death, makes gifts of personal property—furniture, jewelry, portraits, and the like—to some other person, actually delivers the property to that person and then dies. This is a gift *causa mortis* (in contemplation of death) and, if the method employed satisfies the legal requirements, the gift is valid.

Trust

There are several ways by which a person can dispose of the legal or equitable ownership of property or both through the medium of a trust.

1. *Living trust.* During his lifetime A can convey, transfer, or deliver property to B in trust for A himself; in which case he disposes of the legal but not the equitable ownership of the property. Or A can convey, transfer, or deliver property to B in trust for C; in which case he disposes of both the legal and the equitable ownership of the property—legal to B, equitable to C.

2. *Declaration of trust.* A can declare himself trustee of property for B; in which case A retains the legal but disposes of the equitable ownership of the property. Or A can convey, transfer, or deliver property to B and B, in turn, can declare himself trustee of the property for C. This method of disposition sometimes is employed to keep C from ever knowing that A is the person who created the trust for C's benefit.

3. *Trust under will.* A, under his will, can leave property to B in trust for C.

Will

The final method of disposition of property is through a valid will. This may be an outright disposition of both the legal and the equitable ownership;

or it may be a disposition of the legal ownership to a trustee and the equitable or beneficial ownership to another person.

Operation of Law

There are several methods of disposition of property by operation of law rather than by act of the owners.

1. *Right of survivorship.* *A* and *B*, husband and wife, own their home as tenants by the entirety. *A* dies; without any action on *A's* part but by operation of law, *B* becomes the sole owner of the home.

A and *B* purchase shares of stock and have the certificate made out to them as joint owners with right of survivorship and not as owners in common. *A* dies; by operation of law in some states, but not in all, as already pointed out, *B* becomes the sole owner of the shares.

2. *Intestacy.* *A* dies without leaving a valid will. By operation of law, the real property passes to his heirs and his personal property, to his next of kin. In many states the difference between the passing of real property and of personal property and the distinction between heirs and next of kin have been abolished.

As a general proposition of law, if *A* conveys, transfers, or delivers property outright to *B*, *B* becomes the owner of a fee simple estate in real property and the absolute owner of personal property, and *A* cannot impose any restrictions upon *B's* right to dispose of the property.

1. *In trust.* However, if *A* conveys, transfers, or delivers property to *B* in trust for *C*, then *A* can impose upon *B* certain restrictions upon the disposition of either the legal or the equitable ownership of the property. For example, *A* can convey land to *B* in trust to hold it for *C* until *C* shall become twenty-one years of age; and *B*, having accepted the land in trust, cannot dispose of it during the period of the trust. This would be a restraint upon the alienation of the legal ownership of the property. Or, in those states in which the spendthrift trust is recognized, *A* can convey, transfer, or deliver property to *B* in trust for *C* and provide that *C* cannot assign or otherwise dispose of the income or the principal of the property and that creditors cannot reach the property by any legal process. This would be a restraint upon the alienation of the equitable ownership of the property.

2. *Contingent interests.* In order to keep property in the channels of trade, it is the policy of the law to cut off contingent, as distinct from vested, interests in property after they have run for what the makers of the common law, over the centuries, have come to regard as long enough. Consequently, a general principle of the law, subject to many statutory modifications, is that, generally speaking, no interest in property is good unless it must vest, if at all, not later than twenty-one years after some life in being at the time of the creation of the interest plus the time between the conception and the birth of a child, known as the period of gestation. The time of creation of

an interest under a will is the date of the death of the testator; under an irrevocable living trust, the date of creation of the trust; under a revocable trust, it is the date when the trust is made irrevocable or, if never made irrevocable, the date of the death of the settlor. This limitation commonly is known as the *rule against perpetuities*. According to this rule, *A* can will property to *B* for life and then to such of *B's children* as shall reach the age of twenty-one years plus the period of gestation because the interests of *B's* children would have to vest within *B's* lifetime and twenty-one years plus the period of gestation thereafter. But *A* cannot trustee property to *B* for life and then to *B's grandchildren* who shall reach the age of twenty-one years because *B* conceivably might have grandchildren born after the creation of the trust who would not be lives in being at the time of the creation of the interest.

3. *Accumulation of income*. The law looks askance also upon the long or indefinite accumulation of income. Suppose *A*, trying to look two or more generations ahead, should convey, transfer, deliver, or will property to *B* in trust to manage and invest the property and to accumulate and invest the income and add it to the principal until all *A's* grandchildren were twenty-one years of age and then divide the property and all the accumulations equally among the grandchildren. This might mean the accumulation of income for seventy-five or one hundred years. The law would not permit such an accumulation. In most states income may accumulate for the same period as that within which a contingent interest must vest. That is to say, the period under the rule against perpetuities and that under the rule against accumulations are the same. But in a few states permissible accumulation is for a still shorter period. In charitable trusts there are some exceptions to the rule against accumulations.

4. *Duration of private trusts*. It sometimes is stated that a private trust, as distinct from a charitable trust, can last only for the same period that the rule against perpetuities permits an interest in property to remain a contingent interest—that is, in most states during a life in being and twenty-one years after the creation of the interest plus the period of gestation. But this is not quite an accurate statement in that, if the interest vests within the period, the trust itself may continue even though it be beyond the period prescribed by the rule. But for all practical purposes the safe course in creating a private trust is to see that the trust itself terminates by the time the interests in the property must vest.

COLLATERAL READING

Note: For complete citations, see Bibliography, pp. 417–428.
American Jurisprudence, 42, *Property*.
CASNER, *American Law of Property*.

Corpus Juris, 50, *Property*.
Powell, *Real Property*.
Ruling Case Law, 22, *Property*.

In any of these legal treatises, one or more of which will be found in most law libraries, the student will find the point of law of property in which he is particularly interested discussed in detail.

2

Intestate Distribution

𝕴 NTESTATE MEANS "without having made a valid will." Intestate distribution of property means the distribution at his death of the property of a person who has died without leaving a valid will. It is one of the common methods of disposing of property, not by act of the owner, but by operation of law.

Wherever the institution of private property exists, it is a practical necessity that there be laws providing for the intestate distribution of property. It exists throughout the common-law world and, to a greater or less degree, in all of the other civilized countries of the world. If it were not for these laws, all property not disposed of by will either would escheat to the state or some subdivision thereof or else would become the property of the taker which, in the latter case, would lead to confusion, if not to the jeopardy of civilization itself.

The sources of authority for the intestate distribution of property are the statutes of the several states. Each state makes its own laws of intestate distribution and changes them from time to time at the pleasure of its legislature.

This chapter will show wherein the difference between real property and personal property, which in the first chapter may have seemed somewhat academic, is intensely practical. Generally speaking, the distribution—usually called descent—of real property is governed by the laws of the state in which the property is located—called the law of the *situs*; whereas the distribution of personal property is governed by the laws of the state in which the owner was domiciled (that is, his home state). Real property descends to heirs, and personal property is distributed among next of kin. In some states heirs and next of kin constitute separate, although overlapping, groups.

For the purposes of this chapter, imagine that a person dies without a valid will, leaving property, called his *estate*, and a family. His estate consists of all the usual kinds of property: houses and land; businesses and business interests; stocks, bonds, and mortgages; rights of various kinds, such as royalty rights and patent rights; life insurance policy contracts; and cash in hand and on deposit in bank. His family consists of parents; of husband or wife, as the case may be; of children of all kinds known to the law: legitimate, illegitimate; by birth, adopted; whole-blood, half-blood; already born, posthumous; adult, minor; of grandchildren; of brothers and sisters; of uncles and aunts; and of cousins to the nth degree. The question, the answer to which is the subject matter of this chapter, is, Who gets what property?

The statutes, as a rule, employ the term *spouse* in referring to either husband or wife. But throughout this text, except in quoting a statute, the terms *husband* and *wife* and *widower* and *widow* will be used instead of *spouse*. Children of the same parents sometimes are referred to as *siblings*; and children, grandchildren, great-grandchildren and on down the line of direct descent, as *issue*. While these terms will not be employed in this text except in quotations, the student should know their meanings.

Before entering the discussion of the intestate distribution of property, it may be well to call attention to two situations related to intestate distribution to the surviving widow or widower. One is antenuptial agreements or property settlements; the other, the signing away of property rights by the husband or wife during his or her lifetime.

Antenuptial Agreements

It is not uncommon for a man and woman—particularly if it is a second marriage for either of them with surviving children by a first marriage—to enter an antenuptial agreement regarding each other's property or to make a property settlement. By such an agreement or settlement either may waive or otherwise affect his or her right to share in the intestate property of the deceased wife or husband. The terms of antenuptial agreements and property settlements are far too varied to permit generalizations about them. But in considering the survivor's share in the deceased's intestate property the student must have them in mind.

Signing Away Dower or Curtesy

A surviving widow or widower shares not only in the real property that the deceased husband or wife owned at the time of death but also in that which he or she may have owned and disposed of during their married life without her signing away her dower or his signing away his curtesy. This explains why in many states it is necessary for the wife to join in the execution of a deed and be examined by a notary public or other officer "separate and apart from her husband as to her voluntary execution thereof," even though the title to the property stands in the name of the husband alone.

By joining in the execution of the deed, she signs away her dower right and the law is careful that it be her voluntary act and not under the compulsion of her husband. Likewise, in order to sign away his right of curtesy, it is necessary for the husband to join in the execution of a deed to his wife's real property. While both of them are alive, the wife's right in his real property is known as her *inchoate dower;* and his right in her real property, as his *inchoate curtesy.*

In many states, just as the distinction between the passage of real property and that of personal property from generation to generation and, as a consequence, the distinction between heirs and next of kin have been abolished, so, as a consequence in those states, dower and curtesy as such have been abolished. On all these points the student must acquaint himself with the laws of the state in question.

We pass now to a consideration of the steps in the distribution of the property of a person who dies without a will.

FAMILY ALLOWANCES

After the head of a family has died without a will and an administrator has been appointed to settle and distribute his estate, one of the first steps in the distribution of his property is having the family allowances—sometimes called the widow's and children's allowances or year's support—set aside for the widow and minor children. In some states the allowances apply to a widow only; in others, to either a widow or a widower.

The family allowance is the property the family is allowed to retain. This property is not regarded as a part of the distributable estate. It does not pass through the hands of the administrator. It usually consists of intimate personal effects, supplies on hand, and a small amount of cash or productive property.

Homestead Exemptions and Family Allowances

It is necessary to distinguish between family allowances and homestead exemptions.

1. *Homestead exemptions.* In nearly every state, by statute, a property owner is entitled to have a specified amount of real property and, in some states, of personal property set aside for him as a *homestead.* This property thus is placed beyond the reach of his creditors—that is, it is exempt property.

In some states the homestead passes on to his family and is exempt from the claims of creditors of his estate. In other states, if the property owner does not have his homestead laid off and set aside during his lifetime, his family may have it done after his death and thus may enjoy the exemption.

2. *Family allowances.* Thus, in a broad sense in these states the home-

stead exemption becomes a part of the family allowance. But in the more restricted sense in which the term is used in this chapter, *family allowance* means the property, apart from whatever may be included in the homestead exemption, that the law sets aside for and makes available to the deceased person's family for their support during the time his estate is being settled and until it is distributed.

Illustration of Family Allowances

Whereas every state makes some statutory provision for family allowances, scarcely any two of them make similar provisions. In *Wills, Estates, and Trusts* loose-leaf service, Section 2734, there is a state-by-state collection of these statutes. It is not practicable to quote any of them in full, for most of them are several pages long. Besides, any statute that is the law at the moment may be changed during the next or any subsequent session of the state legislature and, consequently, any quotation or summarization of the present statute of any state might be misleading and confusing rather than informative and helpful. The only recourse seems to be to give in this text the substance of the statutes of one state—the State of Maine, in this instance—and send the student to the statutes of any state in which he is interested for authoritative and dependable information.

Maine. The judge may allow the widow as much of the personal estate, besides her ornaments and wearing apparel, as he deems necessary, according to the degree and estate of her husband, and the state of the family under her care. He may allow her also any one pew in a meeting-house of which her husband "died seized." She shall have reasonable sustenance out of the estate for ninety days after her husband's death and she may remain in the family residence ninety days rent-free. Upon the death of a wife whose estate is solvent, he may make a reasonable allowance to the widower. Also, if the estate is solvent and if the income from their distributive share would not be sufficient for their support and education, the judge may make an allowance from the personal estate to minor children under fourteen years of age. Even if the estate is insolvent, he may make an allowance for children under fourteen years of age and for children between fourteen and twenty-one who, because of ill health, cannot labor.[1]

DOWER AND CURTESY

In the intestate distribution of property, following the family allowance comes the laying off of the widow's dower or the husband's curtesy or the statutory substitute for dower or curtesy.

At common law, which still is the law in some states, a widow's dower consisted of a life estate in one-third of her husband's real property. A

---

[1] Revised Statutes, 1954, Ch. 156; *Wills, Estates, and Trusts,* Sec. 2734.

widower's curtesy consisted of a life estate in all his wife's real property if, but only if, they had a child born alive capable of inheriting from them.

Common-Law Dower and Curtesy

In many states common-law dower and curtesy have been abolished or have been modified by statute to such an extent that the only way to give a student a true picture of the present-day interest of a wife or husband in the other's real property is by selecting for illustration the present laws of one state in which common-law dower and curtesy still persist and of another state in which there are statutory substitutes for dower and curtesy. First, an illustration of common-law dower and curtesy is presented.

New Hampshire. 1. Dower. The widow of every person deceased shall be entitled to her dower in the real estate of which her husband died seized, to be assigned to her by the court of probate, in one or more parcels thereof, as may be convenient.

No widow shall be entitled to dower in any lands, unless the same were during the marriage and seizing of the husband in a state of cultivation, or were used or kept as a wood or timber lot and occupied with some farm or tenement owned by the husband.

Every widow having right of dower shall be endowed of so much of any real estate of the husband as will produce a yearly income equal to one third of the yearly income thereof at the time the husband died or parted with his title.

When the dower of a widow cannot be conveniently and equitably assigned by metes and bounds she will be endowed thereof in a special manner, as of the third of the rents and profits thereof, to be estimated as aforesaid.

No widow shall commit or suffer any waste of the land or real estate of which she is endowed, but shall maintain the same in good repair during her estate therein, and shall be answerable to the owner of the reversion for any waste done or suffered thereupon; but the consumption of necessary fuel, taken therefrom, at her residence, when she shall not reside on her dower, shall not be deemed waste.

The widow shall be entitled to receive one undivided net one-third part of the rents and profits of the estate of which her husband died seized, until her dower is assigned.

If a settlement was made upon the wife before marriage, which was stipulated to be in lieu of her right of dower, homestead right, distributive share, or either of them, in her husband's estate, it shall be enforced by the court of probate, and the widow shall not be entitled to any right or rights in lieu of which the settlement was made. A settlement made upon the husband before marriage shall have a like effect and be enforced in like manner.[2]

While common-law dower is preserved in principle, statutory protection is thrown around the widow in the laying off her dower and around the

---

[2] Revised Laws, 1942, Sec. 560; *Wills, Estates, and Trusts*, Sec. 2731.

remainderman who is to come into possession after her death and in regard
to marriage settlements.

2. Curtesy. The husband of a person deceased, holding property in her own
right, shall be entitled to his estate by the curtesy in all lands and tenements
owned by her when he would be entitled to hold as tenant by the curtesy at
common law.

If a husband has willingly abandoned his wife and has absented himself
from her, or has willfully neglected to support her, or has not been heard from,
in consequence of his own neglect, for the term of three years next preceding
her death, he shall not be entitled to any interest or portion of her estate, real
or personal, except such as she may have given to him in her will.[3]

Statutory Substitutes for Dower and Curtesy

Indiana. 1. For dower. The estates of dower and curtesy are hereby
abolished. Any interest acquired by a widow in the decedent's real estate, including contracts for the purchase of real estate, whether by descent or devise,
not exceeding one-third of said decedent's real estate, shall be received by her,
free from all demands of creditors: Provided, however, that where the real
estate exceeds in value ten thousand dollars, the widow shall have one-fourth
only, and where the real estate exceeds twenty thousand dollars, one fifth only,
as against creditors.[4]

2. For curtesy. As regards the husband's substitute for curtesy, unless he
has waived his right thereto and estopped himself to assert it, he is entitled to
one-third of his deceased wife's real estate subject only to its proportion of her
debts contracted before marriage. If he abandons his wife, he is not entitled to
any part of her estate.[5]

DESCENT OF REAL PROPERTY

Assume that the widow or, in some states, the widower and children
have been left in the family home undisturbed and rent-free for a short
period of time and that the widow's dower or the widower's curtesy or the
statutory substitute for dower or curtesy has been laid off. We then come
to the first of the two main steps in the distribution of intestate property—
namely, the descent of real property.

At common law the rules governing the descent of real property were
known as the *canons* (laws or rules) *of descent.*

Generally speaking, the descent of real property, other than the
widow's or the widower's share, appears in most cases in substantially the
following order: children, grandchildren, great-grandchildren, and down
the line of lineal descendants; parents; brothers and sisters; nephews and
nieces; uncles and aunts; and cousins.

[3] *Wills, Estates, and Trusts,* Sec. 2732.
[4] Probate Code, 1953, Sec. 202; *Wills, Estates, and Trusts,* Sec. 2701.
[5] *Wills, Estates, and Trusts,* Sec. 2702.

Canons of Descent

In most states the canons of descent of real property and the rules of distribution of personal property have been merged and both kinds of property pass to the same persons.

Illustrative of the few remaining states in which the distinction between the descent of real property and the distribution of personal property still is in effect is the State of Delaware in which the canons of descent are as follows:

Delaware. When any person having title or right, legal or equitable, to any lands, tenements, or hereditaments, in fee simple, shall die intestate as to the same, such lands, tenements, or hereditaments shall descend, in fee simple, unless herein otherwise provided, to his kindred, in coparcenary, according to the following course or order:

1. In equal shares to the children of the intestate, and the lawful issue of any deceased child, by right of representation;
2. If there be no lawful child or issue of the intestate, then to his father and mother as tenants by the entirety, if both be living; provided, if the father and mother shall have been divorced, and be divorced at the time of the death of the intestate, then they shall hold as tenants in common, and not as tenants by the entirety; or, if only one be living, to the survivor in fee simple;
3. If there be no father or mother, then in equal shares to his brothers and sisters, and the lawful issue of any deceased brother or sister, by right of representation; provided, any brothers or sisters of the whole blood and their issue shall be preferred to brothers and sisters of the half-blood and their issue, and further, that any lands, tenements, or hereditaments, to which the intestate shall have title by descent or devise from his parent or ancestor, shall first descend to his brothers and sisters of the blood of such parent or ancestor, and the lawful issue of such brothers and sisters, by right of representation;
4. If there be no brother or sister of the intestate, or lawful issue of such brother or sister, then to the next of kin in equal degree, and the lawful issue of such next of kin, by right of representation; provided, that the collateral kindred claiming through a nearer common ancestor shall be preferred to collateral kindred claiming through a more remote common ancestor;
5. The descent of intestate real estate, in all cases, shall be subject to the rights of the surviving husband or widow; that is to say, if the intestate leaves a husband and issue, the husband shall have one-half part of the real estate for the term of his life, and if the intestate leaves a husband and no issue the husband shall have all of the real estate, for the term of his life, as tenant by the curtesy;
6. If the intestate leaves a widow and issue, the widow shall have one-half part of the real estate for the term of her life, and if the intestate leaves a widow and no issue the widow shall have all of the real estate, for the term of her life, as tenant in dower;

7. If the intestate leaves a husband or widow, and if there be no kin, or heir of the intestate, to the husband or widow in fee simple.[6]

For the sake of the student who has not studied the law of property, some of the terms in the foregoing statute should be defined and explained. *Coparcenary* means partnership in inherited property; the coparceners are tenants in common, not joint tenants, as explained in Chapter I. *Hereditaments* means any kind of property that may be inherited: real, personal, or mixed. *By right of representation* means that a person inherits property because he is the child of someone else who himself would inherit the property if he were living; the legal term for this right of representation is *per stirpes*. *Issue* means the descendants of a person: children, grandchildren, and on down the line of descent. Brothers and sisters of the *whole blood* had or have the same parents; of the *half-blood*, only one parent in common; and, therefore, the latter are known as *half-brothers* and *half-sisters*.

DISTRIBUTION OF PERSONAL PROPERTY

Order of Distribution

Instead of using for illustration the statutory order of distribution of personal property of some other state than Delaware, it will be better to use Delaware again so that the differences in inheriting real or personal property become apparent. The Delaware statute on distribution of intestate personal property follows:

Delaware. When any person having title or right, legal or equitable, to any personal estate shall die intestate as to the same, the residue of such personal estate after the payment of all legal demands and charges, shall be distributed by the personal representative of the descendant according to the following course or order:

1. To the children of the intestate and the lawful issue of such children who shall have died before the intestate;
2. If there be no child or lawful issue of the intestate, then to the father and mother of the intestate in equal shares; or if only one parent be living, all to such parent;
3. If there be no father or mother, then to the intestate's brothers and sisters of the whole blood and the lawful issue of such of them as shall have died before the intestate;
4. If there be no brothers or sisters of the whole blood or issue of a deceased brother or sister of the whole blood, then to the intestate's brothers and sisters of the half-blood and the lawful issue of such of them as shall have died before the intestate;
5. If there be no brother or sister of the intestate, or lawful issue of such brother or sister, then to the next of kin of the intestate, in equal degree, and the lawful issue of such kin as shall have died before the intestate;

[6] Delaware Code, 1953, Title 12, Sec. 502; *Wills, Estates, and Trusts,* Sec. 2701.

Provided that if the intestate is married at the time of his or her death and leaves no child nor descendants of a child living, the surviving spouse shall be entitled to the residue of the intestate's personal estate absolutely; and provided further that if the intestate is married at the time of his or her death and leaves a child or children living or issue of a child living, the residue of the intestate's personal estate shall be divided among the surviving spouse and such child or children, one-third to the surviving spouse and the remaining two-thirds to the child or children share and share alike, and if any such child or children being dead shall have left issue, such issue shall be entitled to the share of the parent.[7]

The main difference between the Delaware canons of descent and order of distribution is in the last paragraph of the latter statute relative to the husband's or the wife's share of the personal property.

Personal representative is a general term that means either executor or administrator; in this statute it means administrator (the one who settles the estate of a person who dies without a valid will). *Next of kin* means, literally, the person or persons in the nearest degree of relationship by blood to a person who, in the case of his death intestate, would receive his personal property in contradistinction to his *heirs* who would take his real property. In some states this natural order of kinship by blood has been changed by statute, and we encounter the term *statutory next of kin*.

Next of Kin

This immediately brings on the question: Who is one's next of kin? In a large number of states the statute simply provides that the degree of kinship must be computed according to the rules of the civil law; in a few (Arkansas, for example) "according to the course of the common law, but without distinction of sex;" but in other states, by statute. A typical statute is that of California:

1. *California.* The degree of kinship is established by the number of generations, and each generation is called a degree.

Lineal consanguinity, or the direct line of consanguinity, is the relationship between persons, one of whom is the descendant of the other. The direct line is divided into a direct line descending, which connects a person with those who descend from him, and a direct line ascending, which connects a person with those from whom he descends. In the direct line there are as many degrees as there are generations. Thus, the child is, with regard to the parent, in the first degree; the grandchild, with regard to the grandparent, in the second degree; and vice versa as to the parent and grandparent with regard to their respective children and grandchildren.

Collateral consanguinity is the relationship between people who spring from a common ancestor, but are not in a direct line. The degree is established by counting the generations from one relative up to the common ancestor and from

[7] Delaware Code, 1953, Title 12, Sec. 512, as amended by Laws, 1955, 372; *Wills Estates and Trusts,* Sec. 2702.

the common ancestor to the other relative. In such computation the first relative is excluded, the other included, and the ancestor counted but once. Thus, brothers are related in the second degree, uncle and nephew in the third degree, cousins germane in the fourth, and so on.[8]

The student will find the civil-law and the common-law methods of computing kinship in Richard Henry Nolan's *Universal Chart, Showing Relationships and Degrees of Kindred according to the Civil, Canon, and Common Laws* published in West Roxbury, Boston, by the Dawn Publishing Company in 1945. The state-by-state collection of statutory methods of computing kinship may be found in *Wills, Estates, and Trusts*, Section 2723.

MERGER OF DESCENT AND DISTRIBUTION

In most states the canons of descent of real property and the order of distribution of personal property have been merged and, in the case of intestacy, the two kinds of property now pass on to the same persons. In the early days, when real property constituted the bulk of economic wealth, there was reason for making this distinction between real property and personal property; but, under present-day economy, need for this distinction no longer obtains.

For purpose of illustration of states in which the distinction between descent of real property and distribution of personal property has been abolished, the statutes of Pennsylvania and of California are selected.

1. *Pennsylvania.* Under a statute that became effective January 1, 1948, the order of descent of real property and that of distribution of personal property are the same. The order is as follows: The surviving husband or wife shall be entitled to the following share or shares: One-third if the decedent is survived by more than one child, or by one or more children and the issue of a deceased child or children, or by the issue of more than one deceased child; or one-half if the decedent is survived by one child only, or by no child but by the issue of one deceased child; or the first $10,000 in value and one-half of the balance of the estate if the deceased is survived by no issue; or all of the estate if the decedent is survived by no issue, parent, brother, sister, child of a brother or sister, grandparent, uncle, or aunt. The share of the estate, if any, to which the surviving husband or wife is not entitled, and the entire estate if there is no surviving husband or wife, shall descend in the following order: To the issue of the decedent; if no issue survives the decedent, then to the parents or parent of the decedent; if no parent survives the decedent, then to the issue of each of the decedent's parents; if no issue of either of the decedent's parents but at least one grandparent survives the decedent, then half to the paternal grandparents or grandparent, or, if both are dead, to the children of each of them and the children of the deceased children of each of them, and half to the maternal grandparents or grandparent, or, if both are dead, to the children of each of them and the children

[8] Probate Code, 1949, Secs. 252–253; *Wills, Estates, and Trusts*, Sec. 2723.

of the deceased children of each of them. If both of the paternal grandparents or both of the maternal grandparents are dead, leaving no child or grandchild to survive the decedent, the half which would have passed to them or to their children and grandchildren shall be added to the half passing to the grandparents or grandparent on the other side. If no grandparent survives the decedent, then to the uncles and aunts and the children of deceased uncles and aunts of the decedent.

The provisions of the act are applied to both real and personal estate in accordance with the following rules: The shares descending under this act to the issue of the decedent, to the issue of his parents or grandparents or to his uncles or aunts or to their children, shall descend to them as follows: The part of the estate descending to any such persons shall be divided into as many equal shares as there shall be persons in the nearest degree of consanguinity to the decedent living and taking shares therein and persons in that degree who have died before the decedent and have left issue to survive him who take shares therein. One equal share shall descend to each such living person in the nearest degree and one equal share shall descend by representation to the issue of each such deceased person, except that no issue of a child of an uncle or aunt of the decedent shall be entitled to any share of the estate.[9]

2. *California.* Dower and curtesy are not recognized. Since California is a community-property state, a deceased husband or wife usually leaves for disposition both separate property and his or her interest in the community property. Either may will his or her separate property and one-half of the community property. But if he or she fails to will the interest in the community real property, it goes to the survivor. The following is the order of descent of separate property. If the deceased left: (a) widow or widower and only one child or issue of one deceased child, the estate goes one-half to the surviving widow or widower and the other one-half to the child or issue of the deceased child; (b) widow or widower and two or more children or one child and issue of one or more deceased children, one-third to the surviving widow or widower and the remainder to and among the children and the issue, the latter taking by right of representation; (c) no widow or widower but child or children, to child or children and issue of deceased child or children; (d) widow or widower but no child or issue of deceased child, one-half to widow or widower and other half to parents in equal shares, the issue of a deceased parent taking by right of representation; (e) widow or widower but no issue, parent, brother or sister or descendant of one, to widow or widower; (f) no widow or widower, no child or issue of deceased child, to parents in equal shares, or to the survivor, or, if both parents dead, to brothers and sisters in equal shares or their issue by right of representation; (g) no widow or widower, no child or issue of deceased child, no parent, no brother or sister, no descendant of deceased brother or sister, to next of kin in equal degrees except that, where they claim under different ancestors, the ones claiming under the nearest ancestor are given the preference; (h) neither widow nor widower nor issue, property inherited from a previous wife or husband goes to the issue of the deceased wife or husband or, if no issue, to her or his brothers and sisters and their descendants. [10]

[9] Intestate Act of 1947; *Wills, Estates, and Trusts,* Sec. 2701.
[10] Probate Code, 1949, Secs. 220–230; *Wills, Estates, and Trusts,* Secs. 2701–2702.

SPECIAL GROUPS OF HEIRS AND NEXT OF KIN

There remains for consideration the status of several groups of persons as heirs and next of kin, namely, husbands and wives, adopted children, illegitimate children, posthumous children, divorced persons, half-bloods, criminals, and aliens.

Technically, it is inaccurate to refer to either a husband or a wife as an heir or as next of kin of the other. Their relationship has been defined as one of affinity and not one of consanguinity. One takes from the other not by virtue of blood kinship but by virtue of their marital status.

Adopted Children

Generally speaking, a legally adopted child inherits from the adopting parent or parents precisely as a child of their own blood inherits. Also, the child inherits from his natural parents or other kin. Furthermore, the terms *heir* and *issue* include an adopted child unless a contrary intent appears. In most cases the adopting parent inherits from the adopted child.[11]

The problem of descent and distribution of intestate property arises, not with respect to formally, legally adopted children, but with respect to informally and those never legally adopted. An orphaned child, for example, is taken into the family, accepted as a member of the family, reared and educated along with the other children of the family, regarding himself, and regarded by everyone else, including the adopting parents, as a fully adopted child. Then the parent dies without a will, or even with a will referring to his or her "children." An administrator or executor is appointed, and then only is it discovered that the child never had been legally adopted and, therefore, was not entitled to share in the estate as one of the children.

Illegitimate Children

The general rule is that an illegitimate child inherits from his mother but not from his father unless the latter either (1) marries the mother later, or (2) acknowledges in writing, before witnesses, that he is the father of the child. In all cases the mother inherits from the child and, if the father and mother marry later, either or both of them may inherit from the child.[12]

Posthumous Children

A *posthumous* child must be distinguished from an *after-born* child. A posthumous child is one born after the death of the parent; an after-born child, one born after the making of the parent's will. The status of the after-born child will be discussed in the next chapter. A child born after the

[11] *Wills, Estates, and Trusts,* Sec. 2711.
[12] *Ibid.,* Sec. 2712.

father's death usually inherits along with the other children. Should a child be born after its mother's death, presumably the same rule would apply. There is a recently reported case of a child born alive and surviving a mother who just had died of infantile paralysis.

The rights of a posthumous child are assured by this one-sentence statute which is found in several states and presumably is the law in all the other states. "Posthumous children are considered as living at the death of their parents."[13]

Children of the Half-Blood

In some states the child of only one of the parents inherits along with and the same as the children of both the parents. In other states he inherits along with the children of both parents except as to inherited property of the stepparent, in which case he does not share as to this property with his brothers and sisters of the whole blood. In several states collateral relatives of the half-blood inherit only one-half as much as those of the whole blood.[14]

Divorced Persons

It is impossible to generalize about the effect of divorce upon the right of the erstwhile husband and wife to inherit from each other. In most cases there would be a property settlement before or in connection with the decree of divorce. But let us assume for the moment that the divorce is absolute and that there is no property settlement. What, if any, right of inheritance has either of the divorced persons in the other's property should one of them die without a valid will?

Under the Alabama statute, for example: ". . . a divorce from the bonds of matrimony bars the wife of her dower and of any distributive share of the personal estate of her husband," but makes no mention of its barring the husband of any share of her estate.[15]

Under the New York statute, "no distributive share of the estate of a decedent shall be allowed under the provisions of this article, either (a) to a spouse against whom or in whose favor a final decree or judgment of divorce recognized as valid by the law of this state has been rendered; or (b) to a spouse who has procured without the State of New York a final decree or judgment dissolving the marriage with the decedent, where such decree or judgment is not recognized as valid by the law of this state." [16]

An Oregon statute provides that: "Whenever a marriage is declared void or dissolved, the court shall make such division or other disposition

13 *Ibid.,* Sec. 2713.
14 *Ibid.,* Sec. 2715.
15 *Ibid.,* Sec. 2731; Code of 1940, Title 34, Sec. 44.
16 Decedent Estate Law, Sec. 87; *Wills, Estates, and Trusts,* Sec. 2714.

between the parties of the real or personal property, or both, of either or both of the parties as may be just and proper in all the circumstances, in addition to any further relief decreed. . . ." [17]

The variations in these three statutes show the impossibility of making generalizations; consequently, the student must consult the statutes of the states in which he is interested.

Criminals

Only one crime—that, the murder of the intestate—affects the criminal's right of inheritance. The following are three typical statutes on the subject:

Illinois. A person who is convicted of the murder of another shall not inherit from the murdered person or acquire as surviving spouse or otherwise under this Act any interest in the estate of the decedent by reason of the death, but the estate of the decedent descends and shall be distributed in the same manner as if the person who murdered the decedent died before the decedent.[18]

Minnesota. No person who feloniously takes or causes or procures another so to take the life of another shall inherit from such person or receive any interest in the estate of the decedent or take by devise or bequest from him any portion of his estate.[19]

Washington has a long, sixteen-section, 1955 statute which goes into great detail about the descent and distribution of the estate of a murdered decedent, two pertinent passages of which, as regards the murdered himself, are as follows:

Washington. No slayer shall in any way acquire any property or receive any benefit as the result of the death of the decedent, but such property shall pass as provided in the sections following.

The slayer shall be deemed to have predeceased the decedent as to property which would have passed from the decedent or his estate to the slayer under the statutes of descent and distribution or have been acquired by statutory right as surviving spouse or under any agreement made with the decedent . . ." [20]

Aliens

The states are, as a general rule, lenient towards aliens acquiring, holding, and passing on property, both real and personal, in this country. The following statutes illustrate this fact:

[17] Revised Statutes, Sec. 107.100; *Wills, Estates, and Trusts, loc. cit.*
[18] Smith-Hurd Annotated Statutes, Ch. 3, Sec. 167; *Wills, Estates, and Trusts,* Sec. 2741.
[19] Statutes, 1949, Sec. 525.87; *Wills, Estates, and Trusts,* Sec. 2741.
[20] Laws, 1955, Ch. 141; *Wills, Estates, and Trusts,* Sec. 2741.

Alabama. An alien, resident or nonresident, may take and hold property, real and personal, in this state, either by purchase, descent, or devise, and may dispose of and transmit the same by sale, descent, or devise, as a native citizen.[21]

Utah. Aliens as well as citizens may in all cases take by succession; and no person capable of succeeding under the provisions of this title is precluded from such succession by reason of the alienage of any relatives.[22]

California. (California has separate statutes for the descent of real property and the distribution of personal property to aliens.)

    a. Real property. Aliens are empowered to take, hold, transmit, and dispose of property, real or personal, within this state.[23]

    b. Personal property. Foreigners eligible to become citizens of the United States under the naturalization laws thereof, while bona fide residents of this State, shall have the same rights in respect to the acquisition, possession, enjoyment, transmission, and inheritance of all property other than real estate, as native-born citizens.[24]

However, the student is warned not to accept these three statutes without examining the limiting provisos accompanying them.

AN ILLUSTRATIVE ORDER OF INTESTATE SUCCESSION

The foregoing items of intestate succession of various kinds of property to persons of different relationships or degrees of kinship to the property owner who dies without a valid will have, of necessity, been presented piecemeal, without generalization, and with repeated warnings against accepting them as statements of current law for any state, even the state whose statute is quoted. It may be helpful to the student, but still only by way of illustration, to give the order provided for in the Intestate Succession Act adopted at the 1959 session of the General Assembly of North Carolina to become effective July 1, 1960.[25]

Distinctions Abolished

So far as intestate succession is concerned, the statute abolishes the distinctions between (1) real and personal property, (2) ancestral (that is, of "the blood of the first purchaser") and nonancestral property, and (3) relations of the whole blood and of the half-blood. It abolishes estates of curtesy and of dower.

Where the distributees of the property are in equal degree of kinship to the deceased property owner, they take per capita and not per stirpes. *Per capita* (by the head) is distribution to persons as individuals and not as

[21] Code, 1940, Title 47, Sec. 1; *Wills, Estates, and Trusts,* Sec. 1001.
[22] Code Annotated, 1953, Sec. 74-4-24; *Wills, Estates, and Trusts,* Sec. 2742.
[23] Real Property Law, Sec. 10; *Wills, Estates, and Trusts,* Sec. 2742.
[24] Constitution, Art. I, Sec. 17; Laws, 1953, No. 10; *Wills, Estates, and Trusts,* Sec. 1001.
[25] General Statutes, Ch. 29; *Wills, Estates, and Trusts,* Secs. 2701 *et seq.*

members of a family. *Per stirpes* (by the branch) means distribution to persons as members of a family.

The distinction between per capita and per stirpes distribution can be easily illustrated. *A*, the property owner, dying without a valid will, leaves (1) *B*, a surviving brother; (2) *C*, the only son of a deceased brother, and (3) *D*, *E*, and *F*, the children of another deceased brother. The net estate is $90,000. Under the old law, *B* would receive one-third or $30,000; *C*, representing his deceased father, $30,000; and *D*, *E*, and *F*, representing, per stirpes, their deceased father, $10,000 each. Under the new law, *B* will receive $30,000 and the remaining $60,000 will be divided equally among *C*, *D*, *E*, and *F*, each of them receiving $15,000, taking per capita and not per stirpes.

Share of Widow or Widower

The share of the widow in her deceased husband's estate and that of the widower in his deceased wife's estate are similar. Her share in his estate will be used for illustration.

If he left:

1. Widow and one child or lineal descendant or descendants of one child, she would take one-half of the estate;

2. Widow and two or more children or descendants of deceased children, she would take one-third of the estate;

3. Widow, no child or descendant of deceased child, but one or both parents, she would take one-half of the real property, the first $10,000 of personal property, and one-half of the remainder of personal property;

4. Widow but no child, descendant of deceased child, or parent, she would take all of the estate.

Shares of Other Persons

After the widow's share had been taken out or if the deceased left no widow, the rest of the estate would go as follows:

If he left:

1. One child or descendants of one child, the child or the descendants would take all of the estate;

2. Two or more children or descendants of deceased children, the estate would be divided among the children and the descendants, the descendants receiving their respective shares per capita as illlustrated above;

3. No children or descendants of deceased child, but one or both parents, the estate would be divided between the parents or would all go to the surviving parent;

4. No child, descendant of deceased child, or parent, but brothers and sisters or descendants of deceased brothers or sisters, the estate would go to the

brothers and sisters and descendants of deceased brothers and sisters, the descendants taking per capita;

5. No child, descendant of deceased child, brother, or sister, or descendant or deceased brother or sister, but one or more grandparents, one-half of estate would go to the paternal grandparents or surviving grandparent or their descendants and the other half to the maternal grandparents or surviving grandparent or their descendants.

The statute goes on to state the circumstances under which great-grandchildren, great-great-grandchildren, grandnephews and grandnieces, and great-grandnephews and great-grandnieces would take. It also covers adopted children, legitimated children, and illegitimate children.

The bill, as introduced in the General Assembly and as adopted with only slight modification, consists of fifteen sections and covers twenty-five pages. The foregoing outline of just a few of the sections, does no more than illustrate how the property of a person who dies without a valid will will be distributed in this one state under its 1959 statute.

It is suggested that the student, using the headings and subheadings of this chapter, look up and write out for himself the order of intestate succession of his native state at the present time, keeping in mind that the order may be changed, as it was changed in North Carolina in 1959, by any succeeding session of the state legislature.

COLLATERAL READING

Note: For complete citations, see Bibliography, pp. 417–428.
ATKINSON on *Wills and Administration.*
Wills, Estates, and Trusts, Secs. 1001, 2701–2742.

For his collateral reading on this chapter the student very well may go to one of the other loose-leaf services such as *Wills, Estates, and Trusts,* which he will find in law libraries, the libraries of lawyers who specialize in estate planning, and the libraries of many banks and trust companies. He must keep in mind that any statement of the law or quotation from a statute may be changed during any subsequent session of the state legislature.

3

Distribution by Will

ISTRIBUTION OF PROPERTY BY WILL is the counterpart of intestate distribution as discussed in the preceding chapter. One method is distribution by will under the law; the other, distribution without a will by operation of law. This chapter well might be entitled Testate Distribution.

Definition of a Will

A *will* is a legally enforceable declaration of a person's instructions as to matters to be attended to after his death and is inoperative until his death. It is not accurate to define a will as a legal instrument for the disposition of a person's property after his death, for, as will be seen, one type of will may be made by word of mouth and not reduced to writing until after the maker's death. Nor is it accurate to define a will as a disposition of property, for the sole purpose of a will may be to leave instructions as to the person's burial or to name an executor, leaving the property itself to be disposed of as though there were no will. It is accurate to define a will as a declaration that remains inoperative until the person's death, for a person may change or destroy his will up to the moment of his death. This is why a will is said to be "ambulatory" (walking) until the death of the maker.

POWER OF DISTRIBUTION BY WILL

One of the characteristics of common-law countries is the power they give their citizens to distribute their property by will. This power is called freedom of testation. Yet even in these countries there are some restrictions upon this power.

Source of Power

The power to dispose of property by will is a power granted by the state and not a power inherent in the citizen himself. The legislature that grants the power to the citizen to dispose of his property by will may, and to some degree does, restrict that power and conceivably might withdraw it altogether. The disposition of property by will is a privilege and not an inalienable right.

Freedom of Distribution by Will

Only in common-law countries is there broad freedom of disposition of property by will. In other countries a person is free to dispose by will of only a small part of his property. Most of it goes by operation of law to persons who are called his "forced heirs." In common-law countries, by contrast, subject to only a few restrictions, which will be mentioned next, a person may will all his property to whomsoever he pleases.

Restrictions upon Distribution by Will

One restriction upon the freedom of distribution of property by will is that the will itself, in order to be effective to dispose of the property, must satisfy the legal requirements of a valid will.

Another restriction in most states is that a husband cannot by will deprive his wife of her share or a wife, her husband of his share, of the property. In a few states—North Carolina, for example—a wife could, until July 1, 1960, but not after that, "disinherit" her husband, but he could not "disinherit" her.

Still another is that in some states a person cannot give more than a specified portion of his property to charitable objects to the deprivation of his own family.

1. *After-born children.* In the preceding chapter there was a discussion of the position of posthumous children in the intestate distribution of property but a discussion of the position of after-born children in the testate distribution of property was postponed until this chapter.

An after-born child is one born after the parent has made his will. The parent may and usually does provide for all his children whether born before or after the making of the will. But suppose, for example, *A*, the father, wills his entire estate, in equal shares, to his wife, *B*, and to his children, *C*, *D*, and *E* by name, making no provision for any other child, and that later two other children, *F* and *G*, are born. At *A's* death he leaves two after-born children, *F* and *G*, for whom his will makes no provision and of whom it makes no mention. In most states the will stands so far as *B*, *C*, *D*, and *E* are concerned, except that *F* and *G* receive the share of *A's* estate they each would have received had *A* died intestate, and *B's*, *C's*, and *E's* respective shares are reduced accordingly. The practical effect of this is that, although the after-born children receive their full share of the estate in quantity, they do not receive the benefit of the judgment of their parent as regards special provision for them. Inasmuch as after-born children are, naturally, younger members of the family, they are likely all the more to need special provision for their protection and for the management of their share of the estate.[1]

CAPACITY FOR DISTRIBUTION BY WILL

Any person who owns property can dispose of it by will provided he has the requisite age and legal capacity to make a valid will. The latter is known as *testamentary capacity*.

Age

In every state a person 21 years of age is of the legal age to make a valid will. In some states the legal age is 18 for personal property and 21 for real property; in other states, 21 for men, 18 for women; in others, 21 if unmarried, 18 if married; in still others, 21 for men and for unmarried women, and 18 for married women. Since the legal age for making a valid will is statutory and varies among the states, the student should turn to the statutes of the state in which he is interested in for information on this point.[2]

Testamentary Capacity

While a person must be of sound mind (which is the common term) in order to make a valid will, he need not be of a high order of intelligence nor even be able to read or write. Since the law favors the testate, rather than the intestate, distribution of property, the courts in general go as far as, in good conscience, they can go in finding that a person who tried to make a will had the capacity to make and did make one.

The general rule is that a person is regarded as having the capacity to make a valid will if (1) he comprehends the fact that he is making a will, (2) realizes the property which he undertakes to dispose of by his will, (3) realizes the persons who naturally will be expected to have claims upon him, and (4) comprehends the manner in which his will will distribute his property.

This capacity is determined as of the date of the making of the will and not of the death of the person who made it. If a person had the capacity to make a valid will at the time he made it, then his will is valid although later he ceased to have that capacity and at the time of his death did not have it.

KINDS OF WILLS

In this country every will belongs in one of three classes—attested wills, holographic wills, and nuncupative wills.

[1] *Wills, Estates, and Trusts,* Sec. 1010.
[2] *Ibid.,* Sec. 1001.

Testament

Legal literature abounds in the phrase *will and testament*, as though a will and a testament were two different instruments. "I declare the following to be my last will and testament" is a common beginning for a will. Originally, in early English law, a will and a testament did mean different things. A testament disposed of chattels only; whereas a will disposed of all kinds of property. But this distinction has been abolished long since and *will* has become the comprehensive term.

Although the term *testament* itself has gone out of vogue, its derivatives still exist and are in common use—for example, *testate* (with a will), *intestate* (without a will), *testamentary capacity* (ability to make a valid will), *testamentary disposition* (disposition of property by will), *testator* (maker of a will), *letters testamentary* (evidence of authority to act as executor of a will), *testamentary trust* (a trust under will).

Attested Wills

An attested will is one written, signed, and witnessed. It may be handwritten, typewritten, or partly one and partly the other and on any kind of material that will take writing or typing; but it must be written and not oral. It may be signed by the testator himself or by someone for him; but it must be signed by or for the testator and, if signed for him, he must acknowledge the name or symbol as his signature. The signature of the testator must be witnessed either at the time of the execution or at the time of probate of the will.

Holographic Wills

A holographic will is one written altogether—every part of it—by the testator himself and not witnessed. If a will, altogether in the handwriting of the testator, is witnessed, it is classified as an attested and not as a holographic will. It contemplates handwriting. Whether a will altogether typewritten by the testator would be valid is not known. However, since 1895, Pennsylvania has had the following statute about typewriting:

That all typewriting heretofore executed or done, and all typewriting which may be hereafter executed or done, for any purpose, and in any instrument whatsoever, shall have the same legal force, meaning and effect as writing, and writing shall be held to include typewriting; provided, this act shall not be construed as to in any manner affect or change the law as it now is respecting signatures.[3]

Nor is it known yet whether a will spoken into a machine, recorded, and reproduced would be valid. In only about one-third of the states is a holographic will valid.

[3] Purdon's Statutes, Title 28, Sec. 281; *Wills, Estates, and Trusts*, Sec. 1005.

Nuncupative Wills

A nuncupative will is one expressed by word of mouth in the presence of witnesses called for the purpose and made by a person in his last illness or under circumstances making it impossible for him to make an attested will or a holographic will. In practice, this kind of will is made only by persons during their last illness or by persons in military service.

EXECUTION OF WILLS

Each kind of will, to be valid, must be executed according to the legal requirements for its kind; and the requirements for each kind are different.

Attested Wills

Execution of an attested will involves signing and, except in Pennsylvania, witnessing at the time of execution.

1. *Signing*. The testator must sign in the presence of his witnesses or, if he actually has signed beforehand, he must acknowledge his signature in their presence. He may sign by his own hand, or he may sign by making his mark, or he may adopt a name or a symbol as his signature, or he may have his name signed by the hand of someone else. But, whatever way is adopted, it must be *his* acknowledged signature.

2. *Witnessing*. In most states only two witnesses are required; in a few states, three. To be valid to pass title to real property a will must be witnessed as required by the law of the state in which the real property is located. Thus a two-witness will, although valid to pass real property in the testator's state, would not be valid to pass title to real property in a three-witness state.

The witnesses must be informed that it is the testator's will, and not some other kind of document, they are being requested to witness; but they need not read nor be told the contents of the will.

They must sign as witnesses in the presence of the testator and, as already stated, he must sign or have signed the will and must himself acknowledge his signature in their presence. But the laws vary as to whether the witnesses must sign in one another's presence. In some states a will is not properly executed and, therefore, is not valid unless the testator and the witnesses are in one another's presence and each signs in the presence of the others. In other states, while the witnesses must sign in the presence of the testator, they need not sign in each other's presence. In the latter group of states, it is permissible for the testator and the first witness to sign the will in each other's presence and then, at a different time and place, for the testator to acknowledge his signature and the other witness or witnesses to sign.

Only in Pennsylvania, so far as is known, the valid execution of a will does not require the witnessing or the signing of the witnesses at the time of the execution of the will. In that state the testator may write his own will (handwritten or typewritten) and sign it but not have it witnessed at the time. Then, after his death, the will may be admitted to probate upon two witnesses swearing to the signature of the testator. These are known as *attesting* witnesses to distinguish them from *subscribing* witnesses who, in other states, sign at the time of the execution of the will.[4] The Pennsylvania method would not apply if the signature of the testator was by the hand of someone else.

Holographic Wills

Two characteristic features of the execution of a holographic will relate to the writing and the safekeeping of it among valuable papers.

1. *Writing.* The will must be altogether in the handwriting of the testator. It must contain the signature of the testator and, in some states, the date, but there is no special place required for them; they may be at the top, at the bottom, or in the body of the instrument.

2. *Among valuable papers.* As a general rule, a holographic will, to be valid, must be found among the valuable papers of the testator. What valuable papers consist of and where the testator kept his valuable papers are questions of fact. In one state that recognizes holographic wills one probate court held that a holographic will found in the testator's safe deposit box in his bank was not valid because it was the only thing in the box and, therefore, was not found *among* his valuable papers. Another court in the same state held that a holographic will found in the pocket of the testator's coat which was hanging in his bedroom closet was found among his valuable papers and, therefore, valid, because that was where he kept his valuable papers.

Nuncupative Wills

Two characteristic features of the execution of a nuncupative will are its expression to the witnesses and its reduction to writing.

1. *Expression to witnesses.* The testator, conscious of approaching death or of what he thinks is approaching or probable death (as in the case of a soldier or sailor or airman on duty), must call witnesses for the purpose and tell them what disposition he wishes made of his property. In some states this applies to personal property only and in some of these to personal property of a limited amount or value only; in other states it applies to both real property and personal property without restriction as to amount or value.

2. *Reduction to writing.* If the testator dies within a specified number of days thereafter or never regains his ability to make an attested will or holographic will and if the oral will is reduced to writing and presented to

[4] Purdon's Statutes, Title 20, Par. 191; *Wills, Estates, and Trusts*, Sec. 1005.

the proper court within a specified number of days after the death of the testator, the will is valid to pass the property covered by the will which, under the laws of that state, may be passed by a nuncupative will.

Nuncupative wills usually are resorted to only in cases of emergency, and in the aggregate only a comparatively small volume of property passes under them. Holographic wills, being valid in only about one-third of the states, are not employed even in those states to any great extent and usually only to pass comparatively small estates. This leaves the attested will as the vehicle for the distribution of most of the property that passes by will.

CONTENTS OF WILLS

The contents of wills range all the way from the one-sentence, holographic will, "I leave everything to Mother, (signed) Son," dated, and left among his valuable papers to an elaborate document of many pages disposing of many kinds of property to many people and institutions upon many different terms and conditions. Facing such a diversity of contents, about all that one can do is to take a usual will, such as Form I in Part IV of this volume, and trace its contents step by step.

Beginning

Many of the older wills began: "In the Name of God, Amen!" This phrase may have added solemnity but it did not add validity to the will.

Not a few wills still begin with a statement to the effect that the testator is of sound mind and memory, but being conscious of the uncertainty of life and the certainty of approaching death, declares what follows to be his last will. Nor does this add anything to the validity of the will. Instead, such a funereal note in the wills they read may have deterred younger people from making wills.

The beginning of the will usually carries the name and domicile of the testator. If he goes by more than one name, the will first may give his legal name in full and his nickname or his other name in parentheses. If there is any likelihood of there being a question about his domicile (the place he regards as home), the beginning usually contains a definite statement as to what the testator himself regards as his domicile. For example: "I, John William Jones (usually known as J. W. Jones) now temporarily residing in the City of X, State of Y, but a citizen of the State of Z, declare this to be my will."

Revocation of Former Wills

Next comes a phrase or a sentence revoking former wills. This phrase or sentence will do no harm even though the present will be his first one; it may be essential to the desired disposition of his property if he should have made an earlier will and not destroyed it. Should two or more wills of the same testator coexist unrevoked, then each of them may be valid to pass property except in the respects in which the former will or wills may be inconsistent with the last will.

The revocation of former wills may be effected either by a phrase, usually added to the first sentence, "revoking any previous will made by me," or by a sentence following the first sentence or in a separate paragraph, "I hereby revoke any and all former wills made by me."

Debts

Many of the older wills mentioned next debts and funeral expenses. For example: "After the payment of all my just debts and funeral expenses, I dispose of my estate as follows." Unless the testator has something specific in mind about his debts in general—as, how they are to be paid—or about certain debts—what he wishes done about them—or about his funeral expenses—how much he wishes expended for this purpose or what provision he has made for them—these references to debts and funeral expenses do not add to the will, for they would have to be paid anyway.

Personal Effects

Usually the first property a testator disposes of by his will is his personal effects. These include clothes, jewelry, household furniture, books, portraits and pictures, and all other items of property of a similar character which naturally would be considered as belonging to him or his family for personal or family use as distinct from his business or profession. In some states most of these items would be included in the family allowances, and in those states the personal items, unless specifically mentioned in the will, would go to the widow or widower and minor children. Personal effects, if they are mentioned in the will, sometimes are itemized, and named items given to certain persons, sometimes they are given as one item to the surviving head of the family with the thought that the family home will be kept intact. In a well-drawn will care is taken that a public sale of these items is avoided, that they are disposed of in such a way as, so far as possible, to avoid family dissension or misunderstanding over them, and that they are not included in the property left in the trust.

Token Gifts

Next after the disposition of intimate personal effects frequently come token gifts. These are gifts that, the testator anticipates, will be received and appreciated not for their intrinsic value but for their sentimental value—

tokens of friendship or gratitude. Such gifts include heirlooms, keepsakes, and small amounts of money.

Next, in the usual order, come legacies and devises which are given and are received not only for their sentimental value but for their substantive value as well. *Legacies* are gifts of personal property, the gift being known as a bequest or legacy and the person who receives it, as a legatee. *Devises* are gifts of real property, the gift being known as a devise and the person receiving it, as a devisee.

Legacies

There are many different types of legacies the technical names of which the student should recognize.

1. *General.* A general legacy is a gift, not of a particular thing, but of a specified amount of a thing—as one hundred dollars or fifty barrels of corn. This is not a gift of any particular bills or coins but of an amount of money, not of any barrels of corn already measured and set aside but of a specified number of barrels out of the mass.

2. *Specific.* A specific legacy is a gift of a particular thing—as of a specified portrait of the testator's father or of the corn in a described crib. Only that particular portrait or that particular corn satisfies the gift.

3. *Demonstrative.* A demonstrative legacy is a gift of a specified amount to be derived from a specified source but with the intent manifest that, if that source should fail, the gift is to be satisfied out of the general estate. For example, a gift of one thousand dollars payable out of the proceeds of a named insurance policy. Unless the will is worded so that, if the gift cannot be satisfied out of the specified source, it is to be satisfied out of the general estate, it is not a demonstrative legacy.

4. *Pecuniary.* A pecuniary legacy is a gift of money. It may be a general, specific, or demonstrative legacy; the subject matter of the gift being money is what counts.

Devises

Most gifts of real property (other than that included in the residue) are specific devises. It is conceivable that a person might give a son a specified number of acres of farmland out of a much larger acreage or a lot of specified dimensions out of an undeveloped suburban subdivision, the acres or the lot to be selected either by the son or by someone designated by the testator. A person can also devise all of his real property, wherever situate, which would be a *general* devise. But ordinarily the testator would devise specific real property or an undivided interest in specific real property, in either of which cases it is a *specific* devise.

Fractional Gifts

Where legacies or devises are substantial in value or amount and especially where the testator intends to make the main provision for his family through his residuary gift, it is becoming increasingly important for him to make his other legacies and devises in fractions instead of amounts. For example, estimating the value of his estate at the time he was making his will at $100,000, instead of making a legacy of $10,000 to some friend or collateral kinsman, he would make a legacy of one-tenth of his estate. If between then and his death his estate should shrink to $50,000, his friend or kinsman would receive $5,000 instead of $10,000 and the gift would not reduce by too much the provision for the testator's family through the residuary estate. If his estate should increase to $200,000, his legacy to his friend or collateral kinsman might be the more generous without disfurnishing or perhaps disserving his family. On account of inevitable fluctuation in the size of estates and in the purchasing power of money between the making of the will and the death of the testator, estate-planners strongly urge heads of families to make fractional instead of lump-sum gifts.

Residuary Gifts

After all the other legacies and devises have been made, then comes the gift of the residue—that is, of all that is left over. The residue may consist of any and all kinds of interests in real property and personal property, including powers of appointment, wherever the property may be located. It may include *lapsed gifts*—that is, gifts that fail because of the death of the legatee or devisee prior to that of the testator. If, for example, the personal effects, as mentioned above, have not been disposed of by the will or are not included in the family allowances, they pass as a part of the residue.

Since a will is said to "speak from the date of the death of the testator," it covers, not the property he owned at the time he made the will, but the property he owned at his death. If a person makes his will a considerable time before his death and does not change it afterwards, and especially if, when he made his will, he had in mind only the property he then owned, he is likely to throw into his residuary estate property he did not own nor expect to own when he made his will. Thus the residuary gift may assume an importance and a character not contemplated by the testator when he made his will.

Some testators undertake to dispose of practically all of their estate by specific or general legacies or devises and to leave in their residuary estate only the left-overs of their property. Other testators—and this is especially true of heads of families—dispose of only comparatively small parts of their estate by means of legacies or devises and leave the bulk of their estate in the residue. The latter group of testators should be cautioned against the possibility of disposing of the cream of their estate, both in quantity and in quality, in legacies and devises, and leaving in the residue for their family only the less desirable property and, possibly, not enough of that.

The gifts of the residue, the same as any other gift, may be either outright or in trust. For example, the testator may leave his entire residuary estate in one trust or he may direct that his residuary estate shall be divided into shares and certain of the shares distributed outright to specified legatees and devisees and other shares put in trust.

Executor

Next in the usual order after the disposition of all the property comes the naming of an executor to settle and distribute the estate according to the terms of the will. The executor named may be an individual or it may be a bank or trust company. The testator may name two or more individuals or a bank or trust company and one or more individuals or, conceivably, two or more banks or trust companies coexecutors.

Although the testator names or, to be technically more accurate, nominates, the executor or coexecutors of his will, the probate court actually makes the appointment. Although the court would, in the vast majority of cases, appoint the executor or coexecutors named in the will, it would have the power to make a different appointment if that seemed necessary or advisable.

The paragraph or section of the will naming the executor or coexecutors frequently covers two other points—namely, the executor's bond and the executor's powers.

1. *Executor's bond.* In most states a testator, by express provision, may relieve the executor of his will of the necessity of giving a bond *with surety* which in some states is known as a "justified" bond. In other states he may relieve the executor of giving bond with surety to cover the legacies but not the debts. It is the *surety* feature, not the bond itself, from which relief may be given; a bond *without surety* adds nothing to the legal obligation of the executor. In most states a bank or trust company named executor or coexecutor is not required to give bond with surety.

2. *Executor's powers.* Under the statutes of every state an executor has certain powers which he or it can and must exercise in the settlement of the estate. But experience has demonstrated that under present-day conditions the proper settlement of an estate—particularly a large or involved estate—requires the exercise of powers which the statutes themselves do not grant. In order to supply this lack, the draftsmen of modern wills usually have the testator grant the executor additional powers.[5]

[5] See the list of executor's powers in the illustrative will, Form I, Part IV.

Compensation

Although the will makes no reference to the executor's or, if there are trusts under the will, the trustee's compensation, the executor or trustee, as the case may be, will receive what the statute provides for or what the court regards as reasonable compensation for the services. In some states the statute fixes the compensation as a percentage of the property; in others, it fixes a minimum; in others, a minimum and a maximum; but in most states the compensation both of the executor and of the trustee is left to the sound discretion of the court. Some testators prefer to leave it to the court to fix the compensation when the times comes in the light of the service rendered. Others prefer to name an amount or percentage. One difficulty in naming an amount or percentage at the time a will is made is that at the time it becomes operative it may not fit the case. Another is that, since the excutor named in the will is not under any legal obligation to accept the appointment, he may decline to accept it if the provision for compensation is not satisfactory.

Taxes

Since taxes—estate, inheritance, income, gift—now consume such a large portion of even medium-sized estates, it is highly desirable that the will contain specific tax provisions, covering such points as these: Out of what property are the inheritance taxes to be paid? the federal estate tax? the tax on property in taxable living trusts or on property given in contemplation of death? How is the money to be raised to pay the taxes? These questions will be raised again and discussed in Chapter 22, Part III.

End

A common form for the end of a will is: "In witness whereof, I have hereunto set my hand and affixed my seal the —— day of ——, ——," followed by the signature and seal of the testator.

The date either at the end or somewhere in the will is essential; otherwise it may be impossible to prove that it is the *last* will, and therefore the effective will, of the testator.

Seal

The seal is not essential unless it is required by the statutes of the state of residence of the testator or the state in which real property is located or unless, as more frequently is coming to be the case, the will is itself the execution of a power of appointment which must be under seal. No harm can come of executing the will under seal and, for the reasons just stated, it may be important for the testator to do so.

Attestation

In most states the law would be satisfied if the two or three witnesses, according to the required number, signed as witnesses without any attestation clause. But one seldom sees a modern, well-drawn will without an attestation clause. A common wording of this clause is: "Signed, sealed, published, and declared by the said (name of testator) as and for his last will in the presence of us who at his request and in his presence and in the presence of each other (or one another) hereto each subscribed his name as a witness." Subscribing to such a statement not only adds solemnity to the execution of the will but also serves to call attention to the requisites of a valid execution of an attested will—namely, signature of the testator, his declaration that it is his will, his signing in their presence, their signing in his presence, and their signing in one another's presence.

Address of Witness

In New York State, and possibly in some other states, the law requires that each witness must write opposite his name his place of residence or run the risk of a penalty of fifty dollars, but his failure to state his address will not invalidate the will.[6] Whether required by statute or not, the difficulty often experienced in locating witnesses to old wills makes it advisable in all cases to note on the will itself the present address of each witness.

PAPERS ASSOCIATED WITH WILLS

The foregoing information regarding the contents of wills appertains to a fairly simple will. There may be, and, in practice, there frequently are, papers associated with wills which themselves are not part of a will. If a paper is not intended to be a part of the will, it should be so stated in the paper and it should not be excuted as a will.

Funeral Instructions

Funeral instructions usually should be given in a separate paper. If the envelope containing the will should not be opened until after the funeral, then it would be too late to carry out instructions contained in the will; and there frequently is reluctance to open the will before the funeral.

Other People's Property

It is not uncommon for one person, as an accommodation to a friend or kinsman, to keep another person's property—a coupon bond, for example—

---

[6] Decedent's Estate Law, Sec. 22; *Wills, Estates, and Trusts*, Sec. 1006.

in his safe or safe deposit box. To avoid confusion, he should attach a paper or make a notation on the property stating to whom such property belongs.

Business

A testator who owns a business or a controlling interest in a business may wish to leave suggestions or recommendations as to the carrying on, sale, or liquidation of it as distinct from directions or instructions. If he intends them as directions or instructions, he should incorporate them in his will. But if he intends them to be nothing more than suggestions or recommendations, he may express them in a memorandum separate and apart from his will. In such a memorandum he can express his ideas about the continuance or disposition of the business or business interest a great deal more freely that he would in a will. By putting his ideas about the business in his will which, after his death, would become a matter of record, he might deprive his executor of any advantage regarding the sale of the business which he otherwise might have had.

Personal Matters

A testator may wish to convey to his executor information about members of his family that would be signally helpful to the executor but which the testator would prefer not to publicize through his will. It might be about a prodigal son or an extravagant wife or a credulous daughter. Many statements on personal or family matters which, if set forth in a will, would sound unkind or inconsiderate, would prove of great value to the executor or trustee if set forth in an informal memorandum prefaced by an explanation.

Legal Service

It is a general principle of law that an executor is free to select his own attorney at law and that not even the testator can select one for him. Yet in many cases the executor would like to know whom the testator himself would prefer to do the legal work involved in the settlement of his estate. In many cases also the testator would like to express a preference as to the attorney of the executor of his will. Since the mention of an attorney of the executor would be effective only as a recommendation and not binding as an instruction, it is advisable to make this recommendation in a separate paper and not in the will itself in that it may save embarrassment should the attorney mentioned not be acceptable to the executor or vice versa.

SAFEKEEPING FOR WILLS

Let us assume that the will, whether it is an attested will or a holographic will, having been drawn and executed properly, is ready to be filed away for safekeeping. The next question is: What is to be done with the will?

Among Valuable Papers

If it is a holographic will, then, as a matter of law, to be valid it must be found among the testator's valuable papers. Presumably in any state the testator's personal safe or his business safe or his safe deposit box in his bank would satisfy the requirement as to the place; and deeds, contracts, birth certificates, and the like would satisfy the requirements as to valuable papers. But, as is well known, many persons with a sizable estate who write their own wills do not have safes or safe deposit boxes and keep their deeds, contracts, certificates, and other papers that would come under the classification *valuable papers* in a desk, a trunk, or a bureau drawer. What are valuable papers and what is the place of safekeeping of a person's valuable papers are questions of fact which must be decided for each case if such questions arise.

In Probate Court

In a few states there is statutory provision for the filing and safekeeping of wills in the office of the probate court. In these states this solves the problem of the safekeeping of the wills of living persons.

In Private Custody

In some states there is a statute imposing a penalty upon the safekeeper of another person's will who does not file it in court within a specified number of days after he has knowledge of the death of the testator. Under such a statute the safekeeping of a will involves a legal responsibility.

Safeguarding

Since a person's will is a document of first-rate importance both to himself and to the beneficiaries under his will, its proper safeguarding becomes a matter of corresponding importance. The term *safeguarding* means keeping the will from being changed or tampered with during the lifetime of the testator insofar as is humanly possible. One common safeguard is to have each page of the will signed or initialed by both the testator and the witnesses. For all practical purposes this prevents the removal and insertion of sheets.

REVISION OF WILLS

Next after the making, execution, and safekeeping of a will, there comes, after an interval of greater or less duration, the revision of the will.

Within a comparatively short time after a person has made a will which he thought and which in fact at that time was ideally suited to his case, his entire estate (by sales or purchases or losses or gains) or his family (by births or deaths or marriages) or both may have changed to such an extent that his will no longer suits his case at all. Or changes in the tax laws may have made it advisable for him to change his will. Experience has shown that for a man with a family, or with dependents, or having a sizable estate not many years pass without need for changes in his will. When this time comes and however it is brought to his attention, the question for him to answer, upon the advice and only upon the advice of his attorney, is: Shall I make a codicil to my will or shall I make a new will?

Codicil

A codicil is a modification of an existing will. It must be executed in accordance with all the requirements of the execution of a will. However, the codicil and the will it modifies need not be executed in the same way. The codicil to a holographic will may be typed, signed, and witnessed as would be required of an attested will; or a codicil to an attested will may be holographic.

If a will needs to be modified in only a few minor respects, then a codicil may serve every purpose. This might be true if the only change were the elimination or the addition of a gift or the change of the amount or fraction. If the will as it stands is substantially satisfactory and if the testator is aging in body and mind so that there possibly may be some question of his testamentary capacity at the time he wishes to change his will, it may be better to have him make a codicil than a new will.

New Will

If there are major or substantial changes to be made in the will, a new will is preferable to a codicil. Furthermore, if the desired changes would mean striking out or reducing a substantial gift in the will, which change would be likely to offend or hurt the beneficiary, it would be better to make a new will.

However, even though a new will be made, it is not always advisable to destroy the old one. If the testator is aging or ailing and, if on account of the family situation, there is any probability of dissatisfaction in the family over the changes in his will, it may be advisable for two reasons to keep the former will or wills.

First, if the general plan of distribution under his last will was not fundamentally different from the plan under his former wills, the series of wills considered together would show a continuity of testamentary purpose. For example, suppose all the wills contained a gift to a charitable institution and the last will contained a larger gift to that institution or a gift to an institution of the same general type. The former wills would show that such a gift was not an afterthought or that he had not been unduly influenced after he had become feeble-minded.

Second, if the last will should fail because of the testator's lack of testamentary capacity, then one of the former wills, made when he was younger and of sound mind, might be probated.

REVOCATION OF WILLS

Since a will speaks only from the death of the testator, until that time or until he loses testamentary capacity, he can revoke it—that is, rescind it, make it have no effect as though it never had been made. Furthermore, in some cases the law itself steps in and revokes a person's will.

Act of Testator

A testator himself may revoke his will by (1) making a later will in which he declares that he revokes any former will, (2) making a codicil expressly revoking his will, (3) making a later will which is wholly inconsistent with the former will, and (4) physically destroying or mutilating the will with the intention of revoking it. The unintentional, accidental destruction or mutilation of a will would not revoke it, if its contents can be proved otherwise. Cutting off the signature of the testator is a common way of revoking a will by mutilation.

Operation of Law

In some states a subsequent marriage of the testator revokes a will. In some states the marriage of the man revokes his prior will while that of a woman does not revoke hers. In a few states the birth of a first child used to revoke the will of the parent. And possibly still does. In these states note the difference in the effect upon the parent's will between the birth of a first child and of a posthumous child. Whereas the birth of a first child may revoke the will in its entirety, the birth of a posthumous child simply "opens" the will for the child to receive what it would have received had the parent died intestate, and in all other respects the will stands.

CONTESTING WILLS

Let us suppose now that the will was made, was not revoked, and, so, was in existence at and after the death of the testator. This may not be the end of the story, for even then, when or after the will is offered for probate, someone may appear to contest the will—that is, to claim that it is not a valid will.

Grounds for Contesting

There are six grounds on one or more of which a will may be contested. The first is that it was not executed properly; for example, that it does not have the requisite number of witnesses or, in the case of a holographic will, that it is not altogether in the handwriting of the testator or was not found among the testator's valuable papers. The second is that the testator did not have testamentary capacity at the time he made or tried to make the will. What constitutes testamentary capacity has been discussed earlier in the chapter. The third is that he was unduly influenced to make the will, that he really was not a free agent and was not carrying out his own desires but someone else's in making his will as he did. The fourth is that he was defrauded into making his will as he did, that some one misled him into doing so. The fifth is that the will or what purports to be the will is itself a forgery. The sixth is that the will has been revoked either by the testator himself or by operation of law.

Penalty for Contesting

Not infrequently a testator who may be suspicious of the attitude of one or more of his heirs or next of kin undertakes to prevent a contest of his will by including in it a provision to the effect that any person who contests or joins with others in contesting or tries to contest his will shall lose any interest he might have had under his will or in his estate. As a general rule of law, such a provision is not effectual as regards a person named in the will unless there is provision in the will for a gift-over to someone else should the gift to the beneficiary contesting or trying to contest the will fail.

COLLATERAL READING

Note: For complete citations, see Bibliography, pp. 417–428.

REMSEN, BURTON-SMITH, and REMSEN, on *The Preparation of Wills and Trusts.*

STEPHENSON, *Drafting Wills and Trust Agreements*–I. Administrative Provisions.

———, *Drafting Wills and Trust Agreements*–II. Dispositive Provisions.

WORMSER, *Your Will and What Not to Do About It.*

American Jurisprudence, 57, *Wills.*

Corpus Juris, 68, 69.

Ruling Case Law, 28.

Wills, Estates and Trusts, Secs. 201–495; 1001–1040.

4

Property Under Guardianship

$\mathcal{T}$HIS CHAPTER MARKS THE FIRST MAJOR turn in the development of the subject, *estates and trusts*. The two immediately preceding chapters have dealt with the distribution of the estates of deceased persons; this chapter and several that follow deal with the distribution of the property of living persons.

A chapter on guardianship is in logical sequence to the preceding chapters because a guardianship usually, but not always, is a sequel to the distribution of an intestate estate, and, logically, it precedes the chapters on trusts because a guardianship partakes of the nature of, but is not, a trust.

Definition of Guardian

A guardian is a person appointed (or whose appointment is confirmed by the court) and charged with the duty of taking care of and managing the property or person or both of another person who on account of his youthfulness in years (minority) or his mental incompetence (temporary or permanent) is unable to take care of or manage his property or to take care of himself. Such a person, whether a minor or an incompetent person, is said to be under legal disability.

Guardian and Trustee Distinguished

A guardian is not a trustee because he, unlike a trustee, does not have title to the property. He is appointed or, at any rate, his appointment is confirmed by the court and he derives his powers from the statutes or from the court; whereas a trustee may be and in many cases is appointed by the creator of the trust and derives his powers, in part at least, from the trust instrument. Otherwise, as will be seen, there are many similarities between a guardian and a trustee and a guardianship and a trust.

KINDS OF GUARDIANSHIP'

A person who is known as a guardian in one state may be known by a different name in another state. Among the other names are: committee, conservator, curator, tutor, and receiver. In some states the guardian of the property or of the person of a minor is known as a guardian or conservator, whereas the person who takes care of and manages the property of a mentally incompetent person is known as a trustee or committee. Since *guardian* is the most common term, it is the one that will be used throughout this text for all kinds of guardianship of property or of person.

Under the feudal system in Great Britain there were many kinds of guardianship—such as, guardianship by nature, for nurture or by nurture, by socage, by custom—which are not in use in this country at the present time, and to discuss them would be confusing rather than helpful.

Ad Litem

Furthermore, there is a type of guardianship which, although well known and in common use in this country at the present time, is not included in this discussion. It is guardianship *ad litem*. A guardian *ad litem* is a person appointed by the court to conduct or to defend a particular suit or legal proceeding on behalf of a minor or incompetent person, and he is not in charge of the property of that minor or incompetent person except as regards that suit or proceeding. Appointed for a specific and temporary purpose, he sometimes is known as a special guardian.

In this chapter only those kinds of guardianship will be discussed with which the student is likely to come in contact.

The main classification of guardianships in this country at the present time is guardianships of property and guardianships of person.

Of Property

A guardianship of property is, as the name implies, that of the property, as distinct from the person, of a minor or incompetent person. It is purely a business relationship.

Of Person

A guardianship of the person, also as the name implies, is that of the person, as distinct from the property, of the minor or incompetent person. A guardian of the person takes care of the minor or incompetent person himself, out of funds provided by the guardian of the property. This may include providing a home for him and supplying food, clothes, shelter, and, in the case of a minor, schooling. It is substantially accurate to say that a guardian of the person takes the place, so far as that may be possible, of a parent.

Another classification is based mainly on the method of selection of the guardian.

By Will

In some states a parent, by will, may name a guardian of a minor child and, unless there is good reason to the contrary, the court will appoint the guardian whom the parent names. The common name for this kind of guardian is *testamentary guardian.*

By Parenthood

A parent is recognized as the natural guardian of the person of his or her minor child. In some states the courts are less disposed to name a parent guardian of the property than of the person.

By Election

In some states a minor over fourteen years of age is permitted to "elect" his own guardian and, unless there is good reason to the contrary, the court will appoint whom he elects.

By Judicial Act

In a broad sense every guardian is a guardian by judicial act. Even in the case of a guardian elected by the youth of fourteen years or over or of one named in the will, the court confirms the appointment. But there are many cases in which the court makes the appointment of its own selection, and in such cases the appointee is said to be a *guardian by judical act.*

By His Own Wrong

A person who, without court appointment or confirmation, takes over, takes care of, and manages the property of a minor or incompetent person is said to be guardian *de son tort* (of his own wrong). He, like an administrator *de son tort,* is held to full responsibility for the proper handling of the property.

Ancillary

If the minor or incompetent person should own property in more than one state—real property, for example—the court of the state of residence of the minor or incompetent person would appoint the principal guardian and the court of the state of location of the other property would appoint an ancillary guardian—one to administer the property in that state and account to the local court and to the principal guardian.

KINDS OF GUARDIANS

Any person who himself is of legal age and mentally competent or any corporation which is authorized by law to serve as guardian may be appointed guardian. Seldom, if ever, would the court appoint a nonresident individual or corporation for the reason that, if it did so, it would not have jurisdiction over the guardian, to supervise and control the administration of the guardianship.

It is possible to have as coguardians two or more individuals or a bank or trust company and one or more individuals, just as it is possible to have coadministrators and coexecutors; but coguardianships are less frequent than coadministrators or coexecutors, possibly due to the provision for separate guardians, of the property and of the person.

Individuals

An individual may be guardian of the property or of the person or of both. In many cases he is appointed general guardian, without specifying whether he is the guardian of the property or of the person, and in those cases he serves in both capacities.

Banks or Trust Companies

With respect to banks or trust companies which are appointed guardian, there is a sharper distinction between guardian of the property and guardian of the person. While in every state, so far as known, a bank or trust company may be authorized by law to serve as guardian of the property, in some states it cannot serve as guardian of the person. In the latter group of states it is not an uncommon practice to appoint a bank or trust company guardian of the property and an individual guardian of the person. In those states in which a bank or trust company may serve in either capacity, it is customary for it to be appointed guardian "of the estate," which presumably means the same as guardian of the property, and for it then, without the formal appointment of a guardian of the person, to recognize and deal with the surviving parent or with the person who takes care of the child as if he or she were the formally appointed guardian of the person.

WARDS

Persons for whom guardians are appointed fall into two classes—minors and incompetent persons. They are known as *wards*.

Minors

In any given state it is not difficult to determine who are minors. They are persons who are under legal age. Legal age itself varies by states. In most states it is 21 years for both men and women and for both unmarried and married persons. In some states it is 21 years for men and 18 for women. In some states it is 21 years for unmarried persons but 18 for married persons. In these latter states it is said that marriage emancipates the minor. When a person has attained legal age, whether by lapse of time or by marriage, he or she is said to have attained maturity or "come of age."

Incompetent Persons

The determination of mental incompetence offers a great deal more difficulty.

In the first place, it is *mental* and not *physical* incompetence to manage one's own affairs or to take care of one's self that counts. No matter how incompetent physically a person may be—he may be bedridden, paralyzed, blind, deaf, mute—if he is mentally capable of attending to his own affairs, he is not a subject for guardianship.

In this respect some of the other common-law countries seem to have been more progressive and, possibly, more humane than the United States has been thus far. In Australia and New Zealand, for example, provision is made by statute for the protection, care, and management of the property of persons who, although mentally competent, are physically incapable of attending to their own affairs. These persons include the aged and infirm; in law they are known as protected persons and the statute under which they are protected as The Aged and Infirm Persons Protection Act.[1]

In 1957, the State of California took a major step in the direction of the more humane laws of Australia and New Zealand, which well may be and perhaps will be emulated by other states. It created the office of conservator in addition to, not as a substitute for, guardian and coined the term *conservatee*. It defined a *conservatee* as a "person, whether insane or not, who by reason of old age, disease, weakness of mind, or other cause, is unable, unassisted, properly to manage and take care of himself or his property, and by reason thereof is likely to be deceived or imposed upon by artful or designing persons." The test is not mental incompetence but either mental or physical inability properly to take care of himself or his property.[2]

[1] Stephenson, *Trust Business in Common-Law Countries*, pp. 333–418.
[2] Deering's Probate Code 1949, Sec. 1460, Laws 1957, 1701–1705; *Wills, Estates, and Trusts*, Sec. 13,502.

Included in the group of persons who are classed as incompetent for the purposes of guardianship are not only insane persons, imbeciles, lunatics, and feeble-minded persons but also spendthrifts and habitual drunkards. While it may be comparatively easy in most cases, but not in all, to tell whether a person is insane or an imbecile or a lunatic, the common term being *non compos mentis* (of unsound mind), it may become a baffling question of fact whether a person is feeble-minded, a spendthrift, or an habitual drunkard.

Guardianship for incompetent persons, as distinct from minors, is complicated further by the fact that, before a guardian can be appointed for an incompetent person, the incompetence actually must be determined by a legal proceeding. The members of the family cannot have the court appoint a guardian because *they* think the person is a subject for guardianship. Nor can the court itself appoint a guardian merely upon the petition of the family or on its own initiative. Instead, according to the varying laws of the different states, a jury or commission must conduct a formal proceeding. Notice must be served on all interested parties. There must be a hearing, with legal representation and possibly arguments for and against declaring the person incompetent. The jury or commission must find as a fact and render a verdict that the person is or is not mentally incompetent. The embarrassment to the family, as well as to the person himself in some cases, of having a hearing to declare him incompetent is so great that in many cases members of the family will go to extreme lengths to avoid such embarrassment. In some cases this avoidance of embarrassment has led to the dissipation or misuse of the incompetent person's property while he tried unsuccessfully to take care of it himself and while there was no one who was legally responsible for taking care of him or his property.

NEEDS FOR GUARDIANSHIP

The needs for guardianship arise mainly, but not only, in connection with inherited property.

Inherited Property

Regarding inherited property, the need for a guardianship frequently, perhaps usually, results from some parent's or grandparent's failure to make a will or from his failure in his will to make special provision for beneficiaries who would be the subjects for guardianship.

For example, a father, having failed to make a will, leaves property to a child who, because of his minority or who, even though of legal age, because of mental incompetence, cannot receive or manage the property. Thus the father, by his failure to make a will, forces a guardianship upon his minor or incompetent child as a condition precedent to his receiving and enjoying his inheritance.

Or, the father, although he makes a valid will, leaves property outright to, instead of in trust for, a minor or incompetent child. Again, the appointment of a guardian is prerequisite to his receipt of his inheritance.

In either case guardianship might have been avoided by the father's making a will and leaving his minor or incompetent child's share of the estate in trust instead of outright. The advantages of a trust over a guardianship in dealing with such a situation will be the subject of later discussion.

Accumulated Property

The need for guardianship applies also to accumulated property. Occasionally it is property accumulated by a minor himself through his own effort or by gift; more often, it is property accumulated by an adult person before he becomes incompetent.

For example, a parent makes a gift of shares of stock or bonds to a minor and has the certificate of stock or the bond registered in the name of the minor without disclosing that he is a minor. In course of time, while he still is a minor, occasion arises to transfer the stock or the bond. Then, before the transfer can be made, it may be necessary to have a guardian appointed. In many states a statute, commonly known as the Uniform Gifts to Minors Act, has been adopted recently which obviates the necessity of appointment of a guardian to make the transfer by having the stock or bond registered in the first instance "in the name of ———— (parent, grandparent, or some third person) as custodian for ———— (name of minor) under the ———— (name of state) Uniform Gifts to Minors Act.[3] However, the parent's naming himself custodian of his minor child's stock or bond may have unexpected and undesirable tax consequences.

Or, what is more often the case, a person accumulates property while he is of sound mind and later becomes mentally incompetent, which necessitates the appointment of a guardian. This is especially true following a war, when men and women return from military service mentally ill and unable to care for either the property they themselves may have owned or that provided for them by the government. Veterans' guardianships are administered under a Uniform Veterans Guardianship Act of 1938, revised in 1942, which already has been adopted by a large number of states.

In case of both the inherited and the accumulated property of a minor, a guardianship might have been avoided by leaving or putting the property in trust. But in case of an incompetent person, it may have been impossible to avoid guardianship as to property accumulated by him, because by the time he came to need a trust he was not mentally competent to create one.

---

[3] *Wills, Estates, and Trusts,* Sec. 5222.

PROPERTY INVOLVED

Every kind of property will, sooner or later, pass under guardianship. This, in the nature of things, has to be so, for a minor or incompetent person inherits his share of every kind of property that passes by inheritance. A guardian handles a greater miscellany of property than a trustee ordinarily does. The creator of a trust usually pays some attention to the kind of property adaptable to trust administration and, so far as possible, avoids putting in trust property that is ill-adapted to trust administration. But a guardian takes over whatever the minor or incompetent person owns and administers it as best he can. A few types of property call for special mention.

Life Insurance

Life insurance may be purchased on the life of a minor and made payable to his estate, and the proceeds of insurance on someone else's life may be made payable to a person who is a minor. If it is purchased on the life of a minor, provision should be made for the continued payment of the premiums during his minority, for under the laws of a given state a life insurance contract may not be a legal investment for either a trustee or a guardian. If it is made payable to a person who is a minor, the purchaser should be made aware of the fact that the insurance company could not pay over the proceeds direct to the beneficiary who is a minor and that a guardian would have to be appointed.

Stocks and Bonds

As brought out in the preceding section, when a person, often for sentiment's sake, makes gifts of shares of stock or registered bonds to a minor, he should understand that he may be creating a situation whereby an otherwise unnecessary guardianship might have to be created in order to effect a transfer of the securities.

This discussion of property under guardianship will be continued in Chapter 15. In this chapter we have been concerned only with guardianship as a means of disposing of property.

COLLATERAL READING

Note: For complete citations, see Bibliography, pp. 417–428.
American Jurisprudence, 25, *Guardian and Ward,* p. 1137.
Corpus Juris Secundum, 33, pp. 3–404.
Ruling Case Law, 12, pp. 1101–1175.
Wills, Estates, and Trusts, Secs. 13,001–13,072.

5

The Trust as a Dispositive Device

𝕿HIS CHAPTER and the six which follow are devoted to a discussion of trusts, trusts of all kinds; trusts under will, living trusts, insurance trusts, employees trusts, charitable trusts, and corporate trusts.

There are so many characteristics that are common to all kinds of trusts that it is deemed wise to introduce the entire subject of the trust as a dispositive device in one chapter, then pass on to the characteristics that are common to personal trusts, and, finally, to those that are, more or less, peculiar to each kind of trust.

Definition of a Trust

A *trust* is defined as follows:

A fiduciary relationship with respect to property, subjecting the person by whom the property is held to equitable duties to deal with the property for the benefit of another person, which arises as a result of a manifestation of an intention to create it.[1]

It is an arrangement whereby one person has the legal title to property which he holds for the benefit of someone else who has the equitable title to the property. The holder of the legal title may be also one of two or more holders of the equitable title; but, should he become the sole holder of both the legal title and the equitable title to the same property, he would become the outright owner of the property and the trust would cease to exist.

Prevalence of the Trust

The trust seems to be indigenous to the common-law countries and to exist in the civil-law countries only by adoption.

1. *In common-law countries.* The trust as a dispositive device is well

[1] *Restatement of Law of Trusts*, Sec. 2.

known and in general use throughout the English-speaking countries of the world.

2. *In civil-law countries.* There are, to be sure, trusts of a kind in some of the more advanced civil-law countries; but they are not indigenous to those countries and only by legislation have they been grafted onto their civil-law system. These countries have been driven by necessity either to adopt the common-law trust by statute or to devise statutory substitutes for the trust. (Should, perchance, any student ever be interested in the trust adopted or substituted for in civil-law countries, he will find an introduction to the subject in the author's typescript volume, *Notes on Trust Business in Civil-Law Countries*, in the libraries of the American Bankers Association and of its Trust Division.)

In the common-law countries the trust, in the modern sense of the term, has been in process of evolution at least since the adoption of the Statute of Uses by the British Parliament in 1536. So our colonial ancestors brought the idea of the trust with them. (The student who wishes to go into the history of the common-law trust is referred to Scott on *Trusts*, Sec. 1, and to the author's *Trust Business in the Common-Law Countries*.)

CHARACTERISTICS COMMON TO ALL TRUSTS

There are five characteristics common to all trusts and essential to their validity, namely, a creator, a trustee, a beneficiary, property, and terms of the trust.

Creator

A trust cannot exist without there having been a creator of the trust. However, a person frequently creates a trust without realizing that he has done so. Furthermore, in order to create a trust, it is not necessary for him to use the word *trust* provided another word or phrase clearly shows his intent to create a trust.

Only a natural person can create a trust under will, for only he can make a will. But a corporation, an association, a unit of government, or any other group or organization of natural persons which as such can hold legal title to property can create a living trust.

Trustee

There cannot be a trust without a trustee. However, a person can create a trust without naming a trustee or without using the term *trustee;* but the trust does not become operative until a trustee is named. Should a person originally named or later appointed trustee fail or refuse to serve or be removed as trustee, the trust itself would not be terminated; it would remain inactive until another trustee was named. One of the basic principles of the law of trusts is that a trust does not fail for want of a trustee. If the trustee originally named or later appointed does not serve, the court appoints one to take over and execute the trust.

There may be one trustee or two or more cotrustees. The trustee may be an individual or a corporation or any other group or organization of individuals capable of owning property. An individual or a corporation may be a trustee even though, because of some legal disability, he or it cannot execute the trust. The capacity of a corporation to be a trustee and its authority to serve as trustee are not the same. A corporation and one or more individuals can serve as cotrustees, and two or more corporations as well as two or more individuals can serve as cotrustees.

Beneficiary

There cannot be a trust without a beneficiary—that is, a person for whose benefit the trust was created and exists. The beneficiary may be a natural person, a corporation, an association, a unit of government, or any other organization or group of individuals capable of owning property. Because a person is himself under legal disability—as a minor or incompetent person—and, therefore, incapable of serving as trustee is no reason why he cannot be beneficiary of a trust. In fact, it is all the more reason for his being a beneficiary. Trusts for persons under legal disability are the ones created most often and they perhaps are of the greatest individual and social good.

Another name for beneficiary is *cestui que trust* (pronounced seti-kee-trust; plural, *cestui que trustent*) or, as frequently shortened, *cestui*.

Property

Since a trust is a property arrangement, there cannot be a trust without property. The property in the trust is called the trust *res* (thing) or the trust estate or the trust property. The property may be either a legal interest or an equitable interest. The lawyer's name for the property in trust, which the student should know, although it is unfamiliar to laymen, is *corpus* (body).

As will be brought out in the chapter on insurance trusts, the essentiality of a trust *res* becomes a matter of practical importance in connection with the proceeds of life insurance left with the insurance company.

Any kind of property which can be owned *can*, as a matter of law, be put in trust. Whether or not it should be is another matter.

Terms of Trust

There cannot be a trust except that it be created for some purpose. That is to say, a person cannot create a trust by will or otherwise by simply declaring, "I leave such-and-such property in trust," or "I create a trust for So-and-so." He must go further and declare for what purpose or purposes he creates the trust and for whose benefit he creates it. This information is obviously necessary. How would a trustee know how to administer a trust unless he knew for whom and for what purpose he was to administer it? The duties and powers of the trustee and the rights of the beneficiaries, whether based upon the law of trusts or upon the terms of the trust instrument, or both, constitute the terms of the trust.

DUTIES COMMON TO ALL TRUSTEES

The duties of a trustee *as trustee* run to the beneficiaries of the trust. He may have and he usually does have contractual duties to the creator of the trust (although not a beneficiary) or to third parties (such as creditors), but his fiduciary duties run to the beneficiaries alone.

The duties of all trustees to all beneficiaries, except as modified by the terms of the trust, have been classified in the *Restatement of the Law of Trusts* (Sec. 169–185) under seventeen heads. One cannot do better than quote the *Restatement* with a minimum of explanatory comment.

Administer the Trust

Upon acceptance of the trust by the trustee, he is under a duty to the beneficiary to administer the trust.

He cannot be forced to accept the trust but, once he has accepted it, he must administer it unless, or until, he is relieved of that duty. This is one of the basic principles of trusteeship which will be discussed at more length in Part II, Chapter 14.

Of Loyalty

The trustee is under a duty to the beneficiary to administer the trust solely in the interest of the beneficiary.

The trustee, in dealing with the beneficiary on the trustee's own account, is under a duty to the beneficiary to deal fairly with him and to communicate to him all material facts in connection with the transaction which the trustee knows or should know.

This duty of loyalty Professor Scott calls "the most fundamental duty by the trustee to the beneficiaries of the trust." It truly is the most fundamental because it is the one on which the other duties of a trustee to the beneficiary are based. The many and varied applications of this duty will be discussed at length in Part II, Chapter 15.

Not to Delegate

The trustee is under a duty to the beneficiary not to delegate to others the doing of acts which the trustee can reasonably be required personally to perform.

This does not mean at all that the trustee cannot employ servants, agents, and other representatives. But it does mean that he is under a duty not to delegate to others the doing of what he himself reasonably can be expected to do—the exercise of discretion, for example.

Keep and Render Accounts

The trustee is under a duty to the beneficiary to keep and render clear and accurate accounts with respect to the administration of the trust.

The duty to keep and render clear and accurate accounts really is a branch of the duty, to be discussed next, to furnish information. The form of the keeping and rendering of the accounts will be determined by the nature and requirements of the terms of the trust.

Furnish Information

The trustee is under a duty to the beneficiary to give him upon his request at reasonable times complete and accurate information as to the amount and nature of the trust property, and to permit him or a person duly authorized by him to inspect the subject matter of the trust and the accounts and vouchers and other documents relating to the trust.

While the trustee is under a duty to keep information about the trust confidential as to all the rest of the world, he is under a duty to furnish the beneficiary or his accredited representative complete and accurate information as to the nature and amount of the trust property. It is not easy always for a third person to understand why a trustee is so informative when dealing with a beneficiary and yet so secretive about the trust when dealing with everyone else.

Exercise Reasonable Care and Skill

The trustee is under a duty to the beneficiary in administering the trust to exercise such care and skill as a man of ordinary prudence would exercise in dealing with his own property; and if the trustee has greater skill than that of a man of ordinary prudence, he is under a duty to exercise such skill as he has.

There is some disposition to hold a trustee to the standard of care and skill, not of the man of ordinary prudence dealing with his own property, but to that of the man of ordinary prudence serving as trustee of other people's property. And in their Statement of Principles the trust institutions of the United States commit themselves to this higher standard by declaring it to be one of the fundamental duties of a trustee, "in administering the trust, to exercise the care a prudent man familiar with such matters would exercise as trustee of the property of others." [2]

If the trustee actually does have greater skill than that of the man of ordinary prudence, he must exercise all the skill that he has. This makes the standard of skill required of a trust institution and a professional individual trustee higher than that of a person who does not make a business or profession of serving as trustee.

Whether a trustee is held to the standard of care and skill that he *claims* to have, and whether or not he actually has it, still are open questions in law, if not in ethics; in ethics, it would seem clear, he should be held to the standard he claims.

Take and Keep Control

The trustee is under a duty to the beneficiary to take reasonable steps to take and keep control of the trust property.

This means that the trustee must not neglect the trust property by leaving it in the possession or under the control of anyone other than his own agent or representative for whom he is responsible. By the terms of the trust the property can be left in the possession and under the control of the beneficiary or of some third person, but this is true only if the terms of the trust so provide.

Preserve the Trust Property

The trustee is under a duty to the beneficiary to use reasonable care and skill to preserve the trust property.

This means that the trustee must protect and preserve the trust property as the man of ordinary prudence would protect and preserve that kind of property. He would protect and preserve a diamond or a ton of coal in quite different ways.

Enforce Claims

The trustee is under a duty to the beneficiary to take reasonable steps to realize on claims which he holds in trust.

An enforceable claim is property. Such a claim may be one against a predecessor trustee. It may be one against a member of the family of the creator of the trust. If it is an enforceable claim it is the trustee's duty to realize on it, no matter how embarrassing it may be to do so, unless expressly relieved of the duty by the terms of the trust. For example, a physician in

[2] *A Statement of Principles of Trust Institutions*, Art. III, Sec. 3.

his will may relieve his executor and trustee of the duty to realize on claims he holds against patients of limited means.

Defend Actions

The trustee is under a duty to the beneficiary to defend actions which may result in a loss to the estate, unless under all the circumstances it is reasonable not to make such defense.

This duty is the companion of the duty to enforce claims. If it is the duty of the trustee to enforce claims in favor of the trust, it must, in reason, be his corresponding duty to defend claims against the trust. And in the one case as in the other, it is the duty of the trustee not to throw good money after bad by trying to enforce worthless claims nor to contest actions in which the trustee has no real defense.

Keep Property Separate

The trustee is under a duty to the beneficiary to keep the trust property separate from his individual property, and, so far as it is reasonable that he should do so, to keep it separate from other property not subject to the trust and to see that the property is designated as property of the trust.

In discharge of the duty of separateness the trustee must not mingle property of which he is trustee with property of which he is outright owner. He must not deposit trust funds in his individual bank account. Furthermore, he must keep the property in each trust separate from that in every other trust. Two apparent exceptions to this are (1) that a corporate trustee can deposit the funds of different trusts in one bank account and (2) that it can purchase participations for its trusts in a single common trust fund.

By the terms of the trust the trustee may be permitted to mingle property of one trust with that of another trust. But in any case the books of account of the trust must show its part-ownership of the bank deposit or the common trust fund.

With Respect to Bank Deposits

The draftsmen of the *Restatement of the Law of Trusts* felt justified in making a special statement of the duty of a trustee as regards bank deposits.

While a trustee can properly make general deposits of trust money in a bank, it is his duty to the beneficiary in making such a deposit (*a*) to use reasonable care in selecting the bank; and (*b*) properly to earmark the deposit as a deposit by him as trustee; (*c*) not to leave the money on deposit for an unreasonably long time; and (*d*) not to make any agreement which would prevent him from withdrawing the money at any time.

The trustee must not deposit trust funds in a bank as to the solvency of which he has any reasonable doubt. He must show on his books the amount of the funds of each trust so deposited. He must not leave the funds on deposit an unreasonable length of time. What would be an unreasonable length of time would depend upon the terms of the trust and might be influenced by general economic conditions. He must not deposit trust funds in a savings account or on certificate of deposit whereunder prior notice of withdrawal is required.

Make the Trust Property Productive

The trustee is under a duty to the beneficiary to use reasonable care and skill to make the trust property productive.

Although this is the general duty, it is by no means the universal one, of a trustee. By the terms of the trust the trustee may be under a duty to keep trust funds uninvested, to keep houses untenanted, and to keep land and mines unworked. But, unless otherwise provided by the terms of the trust, the trustee is under a duty to make and keep the trust property reasonably productive.

Pay Income to Beneficiaries

Where a trust is created to pay the income to a beneficiary for a designated period, the trustee is under a duty to the beneficiary to pay to him at reasonable intervals the net income of the trust.

This general duty is subject to certain limitations. Of his own motion and without express power to do so, the trustee can withhold a reasonable amount of the income to meet present or anticipated expenses which are chargeable to income. By the terms of the trust, he may be authorized or directed to accumulate income.

Deal Impartially with Beneficiaries

Where there are two or more beneficiaries of a trust, the trustee is under a duty to deal impartially with them.

This duty applies to two kinds of beneficiaries—cobeneficiaries and successive beneficiaries. *A* and *B* may be income cobeneficiaries or *A* may be the immediate, income beneficiary, and *B*, the ultimate, principal beneficiary. In either case, the trustee must deal impartially as between or among the beneficiaries of the trust.

With Respect to Cotrustees

If there are several trustees, each trustee is under a duty to the beneficiary to participate in the administration of the trust and to use reasonable care to prevent a cotrustee from committing a breach of trust or to compel a cotrustee to redress a breach of trust.

As to this duty the draftsmen of the *Restatement* make this comment: "Where there are several trustees, action by all of them is necessary to the exercise of powers conferred upon them."

This statement of duty should serve as a warning to property owners who would like to name one trustee to do the work and assume the responsibility and another trustee as a compliment, not expecting him to do any of the real work. It has given rise to the practice of naming advisers to the trustee and of naming separate trustees instead of cotrustees, as discussed in Part II, Chapter 13

With Respect to Person Holding Power of Control

If under the terms of the trust a person has power to control the action of the trustee in certain respects, the trustee is under a duty to act in accordance with the exercise of such power, unless the attempted exercise of the power violates the terms of the trust or is a violation of a fiduciary duty to which such person is subject in the exercise of the power.

There is far more to this statement of a trustee's duty than meets the eye. It is the two "unless" clauses that count. The trustee is under a duty *not* to follow directions, if doing so would be in violation of the terms of the trust, of which violation the trustee, not the director, would make the decision. The trustee would be under a duty *not* to follow direction if to do so would involve a violation of the fiduciary duty that the *director* owes the beneficiary of the trust. When faced with a charge of breach of trust, the trustee cannot excuse himself by saying, "I was following directions." Really, the trustee and the director are cofiduciaries and are jointly responsible for obeying the terms of the trust. It is the anomalous relation between trustee and director that makes many experienced trustees hesitate to accept *direction trusts*, as they are called.

POWERS OF A TRUSTEE

If a trustee is under a duty to do or to refrain from doing a thing, he is under a duty to obtain the power to do or to refrain from doing that thing. Stated another way, a trustee is not and cannot be placed under a duty to do or not do what he has not or cannot get the power to do or not do. However, as will be brought out in detail in Part II, Chapter 16, a trustee is not under a duty, by any means, to do everything that he has the power to do. In modern wills and trust agreements there are many express powers which the trustee never may need to exercise.

The *Restatement* lists a few powers which, is says, a trustee is privileged to exercise without violating his duty to the beneficiary.

Extent of Powers

(Except for impossibility, illegality, or major change of circumstances of which the court would be judge) the trustee can properly exercise such powers and only such powers as (*a*) are conferred upon him by specific words by the terms of the trust, or (*b*) are necessary or appropriate to carry out the purposes of the trust and are not forbidden by the terms of the trust.

For his powers the trustee must look to the specific terms of the trust and, for additional powers, to the law of the jurisdiction in which the trust is being administered for powers necessary or appropriate to carry out the purpose of the trust. The powers of the trustee, as stated above, are as extensive as his duties.

Control of Discretionary Powers

Where discretion is conferred upon the trustee with respect to the exercise of a power, its exercise is not subject to control by the court, except to prevent an abuse by the trustee of his discretion.

When the creator of a trust gives his trustee power to exercise his discretion about a matter, he means for the trustee and no one else, not even the court, to exercise that discretion. Yet sometimes a trustee will ask the court to tell him how to exercise his discretion and the court may, in error, tell him. This is contrary to the law of trusts.

Incur Expenses

The trustee can properly incur expenses which are necessary or appropriate to carry out the purposes of the trust and are not forbidden by the terms of the trust, and such other expenses as are authorized by the terms of the trust.

The trustee has power to incur expenses and charge them to the trust for such things as: collecting in the trust property, preserving it, making it productive; court costs; employment of servants, agents, and other representatives to do what the trustee cannot be expected reasonably himself to do; expenses of managing, repairing, and improving the trust property.

Lease

Except as otherwise provided by the terms of the trust, the trustee can properly lease trust property for such periods and with such provisions as are reasonable.

But for this power the trustee might not be able to make real property productive. But in the absence of express power by statute or in the trust instrument, a trustee cannot lease property for a period that will extend beyond the duration of the trust. This point is discussed further in Chapter 16, and illustrated in Part IV, Form I.

Sell

The trustee can properly sell trust property if (*a*) a power of sale is conferred in specific words, or (*b*) such sale is necessary or appropriate to enable the trustee to carry out the purposes of the trust, unless such sale is forbidden in specific words by the terms of the trust or it appears from the terms of the trust that the property was to be retained *in specie* in the trust.

In a word, there is a presumption that the trustee has the power to sell trust property which may be rebutted by showing that sale is forbidden or unless it appears clearly that the property was to be retained in kind.

Mortgage, Pledge, or Borrow

(Except in case of major change in circumstance and then only under order of court) the trustee cannot properly mortgage or pledge trust property unless a power to mortgage or pledge is conferred by the terms of the trust.

(With the same exception as named under the preceding power) the trustee cannot properly borrow money on the credit of the trust estate and charge the trust estate therefor unless a power to do so is conferred by the terms of the trust.

In the light of this restriction upon the right of a trustee to mortgage or pledge trust property or to borrow on the credit of the trust estate, the common practice at the present time, as illustrated in Form I in Part IV, is to give the trustee express power in the will or trust agreement to borrow and secure by mortgage or pledge. But for this power in many cases good trust administration would be a practical impossibility.

Compromise, Arbitrate, or Abandon Claims

The trustee can properly compromise, submit to arbitration, or abandon claims affecting the trust property, provided that in so doing he exercises reasonable prudence.

But for this power a trustee might feel impelled to throw good money after bad in not compromising, arbitrating, nor even abandoning claims by or against the trust estate.

Vote Shares of Stock

Unless it is otherwise provided by the terms of the trust, the trustee of shares of stock or other securities can properly vote and exercise the other powers of holders of such shares or other securities.

Although it is clear that the trustee has the power to vote shares in person, it is not so clear that he has the power to vote them by proxy. If it is a case where the trustee is under a duty to exercise personal judgment as to voting or not voting, it may be a breach of trust for him not to vote in person or for him to vote by proxy and thus delegate to someone the exercise of judgment which the trustee himself is under a duty to exercise.

Several Trustees

If there are two or more trustees, the powers conferred upon them can properly be exercised only by all the trustees, unless it is otherwise provided by the terms of the trust.

Under the preceding topic we discussed the duty of each of several trustees to participate in the administration of the trust. Now we are saying that the powers must be exercised by *all*, not by less than all, of them unless otherwise provided by the terms of the trust.

Surviving Trustees

If two or more persons are named as trustees and one or more of them fails to become trustee or dies, resigns, is removed, or otherwise ceases to be trustee, the powers conferred upon the trustees can properly be exercised by the remaining trustee or trustees, unless it is otherwise provided by the terms of the trust.

This is in aid of practical trust administration. Otherwise, upon the failure of any one of the two or more trustees to be or to remain trustee, the surviving trustee or trustees would have no other recourse than to go to court for needed powers.

Successor Trustees

The powers conferred upon a trustee can properly be exercised by his successors, unless it is otherwise provided by the terms of the trust.

This power may not be as broad as it appears to be. If there should be anything in the terms of the trust that would indicate that the creator of the trust meant that a given power should be personal to the original trustee, that power might not survive in a successor. Suppose, for example, the mother, as individual trustee, was given broad powers regarding the support, schooling, and care of their children. Such a power might not survive in a corporate successor trustee. Consequently, it is highly advisable that the will or trust agreement say whether powers in the original trustee shall survive in a successor trustee and, if not all of them, which of them shall survive and which die with the original trustee.

DURATION OF A TRUST

"How long can I keep my property in trust for my children and grandchildren?" This is the common question family-conscious or family-proud property owners put to their lawyers, trustmen, and other estate-planning counselors. The only ready answer is, "It depends." "Upon what?" they persist.

For Charitable Objects

For charitable objects, as discussed in Chapter 10, there is no time limit upon the duration of the trust. A property owner can create a trust in perpetuity for the benefit of a college, a hospital, or a community foundation. Harvard University, for example, still is the beneficiary of a gift by will from John Harvard over three hundred and twenty years ago.

For Individuals

The duration of a trust for an individual beneficiary is quite a different story. There is a classic common-law rule known as the rule against perpetuities which is to the effect that "no interest is good unless it must vest, if at all, not later than twenty-one years after some life in being at the creation of the interest." To this twenty-one-year period is added the period of gestation (pregnancy) should that be needed to protect the interest of a child conceived but not yet born. How does this rule apply to the duration of a trust?

"If," says Professor Scott, "a trust is created under which no interest is to vest in any beneficiary within the period of the rule, the trust fails altogether. . . . If a trust is created for several beneficiaries, and the interests of one or more of them will not vest within the period, the trust fails as those interests. Whether in such a case the trust fails altogether depends upon whether the provision which fails can be separated from the other provisions without defeating the purpose of the settlor in creating the trust. . . . If the interests under a trust vest within the period of the rule against perpetuities, the fact that the trust may continue beyond the period does not invalidate it." [3]

Let us take for an example Joseph Henry Barnes whose will and trust agreements constitute Part IV. Mr. Barnes is 53; his wife, 50; their children, 26, 24, 21, 18, and 15 respectively; their two grandchildren are two and one, respectively; they are not likely to have any more children unless adopted; they are more than likely to have many more grandchildren, new ones up to Mr. Barnes's death; and he even may have great-grandchildren. Let us say that Mr. Barnes lives until he is 75 and that by that time he has two great-grandchildren, the grandchildren of his son, Thomas.

By his will, Mr. Barnes can create a trust that will last as long as any of his children, grandchildren, and great-grandchildren is living at his death, plus 21 years, and, if need be, plus the period of pregnancy to protect the

[3] Scott on *Trusts*, Sec. 62.10.

interest of a person conceived but not born. If by that time a given interest has vested, the trust may continue throughout the lifetime of the beneficiary in whom the interest has vested. Suppose one of Mr. Barnes's great-grandchildren, an infant at the time of Mr. Barnes's death, should live to be 75. Mr. Barnes, then, by will could create a trust that would continue the 75 years (lifetime of the great-grandchild), plus 21 years, and plus the period of pregnancy if that additional period were needed for the sake of a child conceived but not born.

Suppose Mr. Barnes decided not to wait to create a trust under will but to create a living trust now. If he created a revocable trust, as will be explained in Chapter 7 of and illustrated in Form II in Part IV, his trust can be made to continue during any life in being at the time the trust was converted into an irrevocable trust or, if he never converted it, at the time of his death plus the 21 years and the period of pregnancy, and plus the period that the trust ran after the interest of the beneficiary had vested.

If Mr. Barnes decided to make his living trust irrevocable from the beginning, it could continue during any life in being at the time he created the trust, plus the 21 years and the period of pregnancy and plus the period that the trust ran after the interest of the beneficiary had vested.

For a trust under will the period begins to run from the death of the testator; for a revocable trust, from the time it is converted into an irrevocable trust or, if never converted, the death of the creator; and for an irrevocable trust, from the date of its creation.

So, all in all, Mr. Barnes can keep his property in trust for the life of his children, his grandchildren, and the youngest of his great-grandchildren living at the time of his death plus 21 years, plus the gestation period. This, to be sure, is long enough to keep property in trust for individual beneficiaries.

The student who wishes to study the duration of trusts for individuals further will do well to make a special study of Part 24,[4] Part 25,[5] and Part 26,[6] of *American Law of Property*. The common-law rule against perpetuities has been changed in so many states by statute that one must not rely upon any statement about the duration of trusts based upon the common-law rule. He will find in Part 25 of *American Law of Property* mentioned above the statutory rule for his own state up to the time of the publication in 1952, since when, however, there already have been several statutory changes.

Having laid the foundation by discussion of characteristics common to all kinds of trusts, we should be able now better to understand the characteristics peculiar or specially adapted to certain kinds of trusts.

[4] Leach and Tudor, *The Common-Law Rule against Perpetuities*.
[5] Whiteside, Statutory Rules Against Perpetuities and Accumulations.
[6] Schnebly, Restraints upon Alienation of Property, *American Law of Property*, Vol. VI.

COLLATERAL READING

Note: For complete citations, see Bibliography, pp. 417–428.
BOGERT's *Handbook.*
BOGERT on *Trusts and Trustees.*
LORING's *Trustee's Handbook*, Shattuck rev.
Restatement of Law of Trusts.
SCOTT on *Trusts.*

6

Trusts Under Will

𝕵N THE PRECEDING CHAPTER we discussed the characteristics that are common to all kinds of trusts—the trustee's duties, the trustee's powers, and the duration of the trust. We pass on now to consider characteristics that are common to personal, as distinguished from employees, charitable, and corporate, trusts and then to characteristics that are, more or less, peculiar to each of the six kinds of trusts.

Projecting One's Self into the Future

One feature that is characteristic of trusts under will is that the testator in making his will must, of necessity, project himself into the future. Making his will today, he may live on another twenty or twenty-five years and see his children through infancy, youth, young manhood or womanhood, and into marriage and parenthood. His lawyer, sensing that his client is trying to dispose of his property as though he knew he would live out his expectancy and as though he knew what the condition of his estate and of his family will be then, must remind him, in the most diplomatic language he can command, that he should make his will "as though he knew he would die tonight." Thereupon, the man sets himself to the task of having his will drawn in the light of things as they are now, not as they may be, nor as he hopes they will be fifteen or twenty years or longer hence. To be sure, he can make a new will or add codicil after codicil to his present will as long as he lives and retains his legal capacity to make a valid will; but his lawyers will remind him to make his will now as though he would not have the right or capacity to change it later.

Trusts under will share this characteristic with revocable living trusts and insurance trusts which will be discussed in the next two chapters.

77

Characteristics Common to Personal Trusts

There are three characteristics that are common to personal trusts, that is, to trusts under will, living trusts, and personal insurance trusts. They are brought under discussion by these three questions: (1) Should the property be left outright to or in trust for the beneficiary? (2) If left in trust, how long should the trust continue? (3) If left in trust, what right, if any, should the beneficiary have to demand principal and what power, if any, should the trustee have to pay over or apply principal?

OUTRIGHT OR IN TRUST?

Setting tax consequences and even tax considerations aside for the moment—they will be the subject matter of Chapter 22—the property owner comes to grips at once with the question: Should I leave the property outright to, or in trust for, the persons whom I wish to share in the disposition of my estate? It is at this point that he first needs an adviser.

Dispositive Alternatives

1. *Personal property*. As to his personal property, he has two alternatives: outright legacies or trusts. As pointed out in Chapter 1, he might, conceivably, leave personal property to the "use" of one person and then outright to another. But this is a rather anomalous dispositive device; and, instead of leaving it "to the use of" he had better leave it "in trust for."

2. *Real Property*. As to his real property, he has three alternatives: outright devises, life estates or other limited estates or interests with remainder over, and trusts. If he makes an outright devise, the devisee can do what he pleases with the property he receives. If he leaves the property for life or years with remainder over, he creates two estates or interests in the same real property—one a life estate or a tenancy for years, the other a future estate which will become effective only upon the termination of the immediate estate for life or years. Or he may leave the real property in trust upon such terms (within the law) as he thinks will serve the best interests of the persons for whom he wishes to provide.

There are advantages and disadvantages as regards each of these dispositive arrangements; but let us concentrate now upon the trust as one of these devices.

NEED FOR A TRUST

If the property owner is a family man with a wife and children, he must decide, upon advice, whether to leave property in trust for his family as a unit or separate trusts for his wife and children. As will be brought out in Chapter 22, there may be tax considerations that would make him create individual trusts instead of a family trust; but, for the moment, we are not taking possible tax consequences into consideration.

For Family as Unit

The head of a family, in making his will, should consider whether he should leave his family's share of the estate outright to them as individuals, in trust for them as individuals, or in trust for them as a group. Consider first a trust for the family as a unit.

There may be several overlapping reasons why he should decide to hold the family intact by creating a family trust under his will. Among these reasons may be the following: (1) to preserve the family home; (2) to enable the mother to devote her time and energy to homemaking; (3) to supply her the income necessary for the support of the family and the maintenance of the family life; and (4) to enable her to exercise her own judgment in making special provision for the different children. While the needs for a family trust usually are considered in connection with the will of the husband and father, there are situations in which a widowed mother who owns an estate would have fully as much need for creating a family trust.

1. *Family home.* In many cases the family home already is owned jointly or as tenants by the entirety by the husband and wife, so that at the death of the husband-and-father it is the property of the surviving widow-and-mother. In this case, a trust of the family home would be appropriate only under the will of the survivor of the husband and wife. However, if title to the family home is in the husband-and-father, he can will it outright to his wife alone, or to his wife and children as tenants in common, or to his wife for her life, remainder to their children as tenants in common. By doing any one of these things he would avoid creating a trust of the family home. But analysis of each of these possibilities may show that in a given case it is not the best way to dispose of the family home.

If the husband-and-father wills it outright to his wife and if it constitutes a considerable part of the estate, he may leave his wife overloaded with an expensive residence and without enough income from his estate to keep the residence up and support the family.

If he wills it to her and the children as tenants in common and, if some of the children are minors or incompetent persons, she and they or their guardians may have difficulty in keeping up the property or selling it to advantage. As the children marry and make homes of their own, they may desire to get their share of the value of the family home and put it into a new home of their own.

If he leaves the family home in trust and authorizes his trustee to permit his family to use and occupy it as a home so long as they desire it for that purpose, he makes it possible for the trustee to come as nearly as is humanly possible to making a home for the family. Then should the time come when the house was not needed or desired any longer for a family home, the trustee could dispose of it or convert it as the best interests of the estate seemed to require. See the family-home provision in Form I in Part IV.

2. *Release of the mother from business and financial responsibilities.* A family trust makes the trustee responsible for the safekeeping, safeguarding, investment, and management of the property of the estate and releases the widow-and-mother's time and energy to be devoted to the family home and the children. If she receives the estate in whole or in part outright, she may be obliged to assume business, financial, and investment responsibilities at the time when, as the surviving head of the family, her time and energy are needed all the more for her home and children.

3. *Supply necessary family income.* One of the basic duties of a trustee of a family trust is to make the property reasonably productive and, if it is not so at the time it is turned over to the trustee, to put it on a productive basis as soon as it can be done. Thus the widow-and-mother comes to look to the trustee for the funds with which to maintain the home and pay the family expenses as she had looked to the husband-and-father during his lifetime.

4. *Make special provisions for children.* In a family of several children, nearly always one or more of them need to be treated somewhat differently from the others—special schools, special medical or surgical attention, special provision of one sort or another. By creating a family trust and giving the mother broad powers to use the income or principal or both, not necessarily equally for each child, but according to each one's needs, the mother is able to meet the special requirements of each child.

For the surviving head of a family, a family trust may be the arrangement that will serve the best interests of every member of the family.

For Individuals

We come now to trusts for the benefit, not of a family as a unit, but of individual human beings whether or not they are members of the property owner's family.

A trust is designed to supply one or more elements lacking in a given person's character or ability or taste which are essential to the proper care, management, and use of property. These elements are physical capacity, mental competence, thrift, interest, maturity, experience, and prudence. If a testator decides that any individual to whom he would make a gift under his will lacks any one of these elements, he should consider putting that gift in trust instead of making it outright.

1. *Physical capacity*. This refers to the physical capacity of a person properly to care for, manage, and use his property. Incapacity may result from illness, accident, old age, or some physical defect or infirmity. Whatever the origin, if the incapacity exists, a trust, instead of an outright gift, should be considered.

2. *Mental competence*. Mental competence means actual, not merely legal, ability to take care of, manage, and use one's property. Many a person actually is mentally incompetent who never has been and perhaps never will be declared a mentally incompetent person. If the testator decides that any individual for whom he would provide by his will, whether or not a member of his immediate family, does not have the mental capacity properly to take care of, manage, and use his property, he should consider a trust instead of an outright gift.

3. *Thrift*. There are more than a few individuals who, although physically capable and mentally competent by every test of sanity, nevertheless cannot and would not take care of, manage well, nor use wisely any property that might be left to them by will. They do not know the value of a dollar, or they cannot say *no*, or they have little or no judgment about the use of money. Such an individual must receive his gift in trust and not outright, if it really is to serve the best purpose.

4. *Interest*. In this group are included a host of individuals who, although physically capable, mentally competent, and endowed with a sense of money values, nevertheless should receive inherited property in trust instead of outright. This is so because they are not interested in the management of property. They are interested primarily in other, eminently worthwhile things. This group includes men and women who are at the forefront of every good work. They are lawyers, physicians, educators, scientists, artists, social workers, and many others whose lives are devoted to interests far removed from the management of property. Testators who are leaving property to such individuals, whether members of their family or friends, should consider leaving their gifts in trust and relieving their beneficiaries of the necessity of managing property.

5. *Maturity*. If the property owner makes his will while any of his children is a minor and if he plans to leave a share of his estate to his wife and to each of his children, instead of leaving it in a family trust, he should consider leaving each minor child's share in trust. If he does not leave it in trust and if he dies while the child still is a minor, it will be necessary, as explained in Chapter 4, for the court to appoint a guardian to take over and manage the property until the child comes of age.

A question that arises at this juncture is: Cannot a guardian manage a minor's or incompetent person's property as well as a trustee? A guardian must manage the property and care for his ward according to the laws of guardianship prevailing in the state, and these laws must, of necessity, be more or less inflexible; whereas a trustee can be given the power to use his own discretion to manage the property and care for the child or incompetent person as the special needs of that particular minor or incompetent person seem to the trustee to require. It is like the difference between ready-made suits made in quantity to fit average-sized human bodies and the one suit made to fit the body of a specific person.

6. *Experience.* If the property owner decides that any one of the proposed beneficiaries under his will does not have experience in the care, management, and use of property sufficient to enable him to make good use of it, he should consider leaving the property in trust.

Perhaps the best illustration of this type of beneficiary is the testator's own mother or wife or daughter. Any one of these may have spent her life with domestic affairs and have paid practically no attention to business, financial, or property matters. She may have had no experience regarding her son's, husband's, or father's business or with respect to investments, the management of property, or anything of that nature. Her lack of experience in property management should make the property owner consider leaving her share of his estate in trust.

7. *Prudence.* There are persons who from their youth on seem to be natural-born risk-takers, and civilization owes a great deal of its progress to them. Nonetheless, the parent of a person who already has demonstrated his lack of prudence or caution in business or money matters may be well advised to leave a portion, at least, of that child's share in trust instead of outright.

Only where a trustee is needed to supply one of the elements essential to the proper care, management, and use of property is a trust under will instead of an outright gift to be considered with respect to an individual beneficiary.

DURATION OF TRUST

Having decided, upon sound advice, that for one good reason or another or, perhaps more nearly accurately, for a combination of reasons, he should leave property in trust for instead of outright to the given beneficiary or class of beneficiaries, the property owner comes face-to-face upon the next question: How long should the trust continue? Again, the only general answer is, "It depends." "Upon what?" "Upon the needs of the beneficiary."

As we have seen in the preceding chapter, the trust *can* continue throughout the lifetime of the longest liver of any person in being at the time of the death of the property owner, plus 21 years, plus the period of pregnancy, if that much more time is needed for the protection of a child conceived but not yet born. In Mr. Barnes's case, as we have seen, it can continue throughout the lifetime of the longest liver of any child, grandchild, or great-grandchild living at the time of his death plus 21 years, plus the period of gestation. Or he might have selected any other group or class of persons and said that the trust would continue throughout the lifetime of the longest liver in that group or class who was alive at the time of his death plus the 21 years, and plus, if need be, the period of pregnancy.

But to say how long a trust *can* continue is quite a different matter from saying how long it *should* continue. Again, the easy answer is: as long and only as long as there is need for separating the burdens and the benefits of property ownership. But the question remains: How long is that? For some trusts the answer is easy; for others, this question is practically unanswerable.

Family Trusts

A trust for the property owner's family as a unit should continue as long and only as long as there shall be need for holding the family as a unit intact. This, normally, would be until the children are adults and married and have homes of their own and the time has come in due course for breaking up the old family home. After that, the trusts, if continued, should be for the members of the family as individuals and not for the family as a unit.

For Minors and Incompetent Persons

A trust for a minor should be continued at least until he has attained his majority. If it should be continued, and how much longer will be discussed later.

A trust for an incompetent person should continue until he has regained his mental competence. This may be, but is not necessarily, for his lifetime. Whether he has regained his competence it may be for the court, not the trustee, to decide.

For Physically Incapable or Incapacitated Persons

If the person needs a trust because of physical, as distinguished from mental, incapacity to manage property properly, the trust should continue as long and only as long as the physical condition continues. Normally, but not always, this means throughout the lifetime of the beneficiary.

For Thriftless, Indifferent, or Imprudent Persons

A trust for a chronically thriftless, improvident person should be continued through the lifetime of that person. One for a person indifferent to property management because he is much more interested, adept, and useful in other occupations should continue for life. One for a person who already has shown himself to be incautious and imprudent in the management of property should, in most cases, continue throughout that person's lifetime, for his incaution and imprudence are likely to be chronic and incurable.

For Inexperienced Persons

Here we must draw a sharp line of distinction between the person inexperienced because of youthfulness and, consequently, due to the lack of opportunity to acquire experience and the person who, although of mature years, has had little experience in the management of property. Typical of the first is the son or daughter still in school; of the latter, the mother of that son or daughter. The duration of a trust for the son or daughter will be discussed under the next heading. If the mother is not a businesswoman by nature and aptitude, she is likely never to acquire experience in the management of property and, if that be the case, her inexperience will be lifelong and the trust should continue throughout her lifetime.

This leaves for consideration only normal young persons who have attained their legal majority. How long should a trust for one of these continue? This is a question to which no definitive answer can be given.

For Normal Young Persons

The following are some of the conventional times set for the termination of trusts for normal young persons. And with each of them one can find fault without being overly critical.

1. *At twenty-one.* In every state a young person can take over the ownership and management of property upon the attainment of 21 years of age. In some states it is 21 for boys; 18 for girls. But at 18 or at 21 the young person may be in school still and, whether or not in school, may not be experienced enough to take over his inheritance.

2. *At twenty-one and through school.* Realizing the inadvisability of jeopardizing an heir's schooling by having him take over his inheritance while still in school, some draftsmen, including the author himself, have provided for him to receive his inheritance outright as soon as he is "of age and through school," only to find that he had put himself "through school" by dropping out before graduation in order to take over his inheritance.

3. *In installments.* Some property owners provide for their beneficiaries to receive their inheritance, discharged of trust, in installments. These installments may be one-third each at 21, 25, and 30, or one-third each at 25, 30, and 35; or one-half each at 25 and 30, or at 28 and 35.

The reasoning in favor of installment distribution is that, if the beneficiary should waste his first or even his second installment, he would have learned enough to take care of his second or his third installment and that an early installment or installments might help him to get established in his business or profession.

The reasoning against installment distributions is that, if he should play fast and loose with his first installment, he would be likely to do the same with his second, then with his third and final installment and to acquire lifelong habits of improvidence and extravagance. Persons who are dubious of the wisdom of installment distribution say that the beneficiary is likely to reason, perhaps subconsciously, that, even if he should waste his first or his second installment, he still would have a third one to fall back upon.

4. *For life.* Some property owners leave property in trust for their children and grandchildren for life. Others make a distinction between their daughters and granddaughters on the one hand and their sons and grandsons on the other, leaving property in trust for the life of the former and for less than life for the latter.

Those who oppose lifetime trusts for normal young people say that such a trust is likely to have an enervating effect upon the beneficiary, that it is likely to rob him or her of initiative, that it is likely to make him or her the victim of designing persons due to lack of knowledge of how to protect himself or herself. They are opposed to the endowment of normal individuals. They are ready to admit that, if the young person has manifested talent in some worthwhile field of endeavor that is foreign to the management of property, the property owner may be justified in creating a trust under will for the lifetime of such a beneficiary and leave him or her free to develop his or her special talent and to make a signally valuable contribution to society.

5. *In discretion of trustee.* The question as to how long a trust for a normal son or daughter should continue baffles all testators, and some of them have tried to shift the responsibility for deciding to the trustee. But placing the responsibility upon the trustee to determine the duration of the trust puts the trustee into almost as difficult a position as the one in which the testator found himself. In addition, giving the trustee authority to terminate the trust by paying over all the principal to the beneficiary may subject the trustee to two opposite criticisms. If he declines to terminate the trust, he may be accused of retaining the trust for selfish purposes. If he terminates it early, he may be accused of shirking his responsibility. Experienced trustees, as a rule, are loath to accept trusts under which they themselves have uncontrolled discretion to terminate the trust when they think it has served its purpose.

DISPOSITIVE TERMS OF TRUSTS

In addition to the duration of the trusts under his will the property owner must consider and decide what rights he will give the beneficiary and what powers he will grant the trustee over the property, income, and principal, in the trust, for the individual and the social value of the trust may depend largely upon these rights and powers.

We are not considering now the administrative powers of the trustee, for they will be discussed in due course in Part II but, rather, the powers of the trustee over the property—the dispositive powers.

Income

The testator should give consideration to the terms of the payment or the application of the income.

1. *Payment.* He may provide that the income shall be paid over to the beneficiary as and when received, as and when called for by the beneficiary, as and when the trustee thinks it should be paid over, or periodically— weekly, monthly, quarterly, semiannually, annually, or at any other period. Each of these methods of payment has both advantages and disadvantages and may be good for one type of beneficiary and bad for another.

a. As and when received. If the income is payable to the beneficiary as and when received by the trustee, it is likely to be received and paid in irregular amounts at irregular times, which will increase greatly the expense to the trustee of administering the trusts, and to make it all the more difficult for the beneficiary to budget his living expenses. On the other hand, the nature of the trust property may be such that the trustee would, as a matter of course, pay over the income as and when received. Suppose, for example, the trust property was a farm or a business house leased for an annual rental payable the same day each year. In that case it might not be amiss to provide that the income be paid to the beneficiary as and when received.

b. As and when called for. If the income is to be paid to the beneficiary as and when called for by him and if the beneficiary himself is a thrifty person and if a rule against accumulations does not interfere, it may be a good plan to permit the beneficiary to have the trustee accumulate the income temporarily or even invest it. But if the beneficiary is not a thrifty person and particularly if he is inclined to be importunate, a provision that the income shall be payable to him as and when called for by him is likely to cause no end of trouble to the trustee and, besides, not to serve the best interests of the beneficiary.

c. As and when trustee decides. If the income is to be paid to the beneficiary as and when the trustee decides, it enables the trustee to pay it over when he thinks it will be of the most good to the beneficiary. The trustee can withhold income for a period when the beneficiary does not need it and build up a reserve of income for some later period. Suppose, for example, one of the main purposes of the trust is to provide for the education of a beneficiary who at the time the trust becomes operative is still in high school and living at home. During the time the school expenses of the beneficiary are comparatively light the trustee can build up a reserve for the college, university, or professional education of the beneficiary. But such a provision puts an inexperienced, an inconsiderate, or a more or less indifferent trustee into a position to do the beneficiary a disservice by not using good conscience or good judgment in paying over the income.

d. Periodically. If the income is payable periodically, it enables the beneficiary to budget and regularize his expenses and to make commitments because he knows when his income check will be received. Whether the period should be a week, month, quarter, half-year, or year would depend upon the circumstances of the particular beneficiary or of the trust itself. But a disadvantage of periodic payment is that it does not provide for emergencies; this would be particularly true if the period were as long as a year or even a half-year.

2. *Application.* The testator would understand that, if the beneficiary were a minor or incompetent person, the income would be applied for his benefit and not paid direct to him; that is, unless, in the case of a minor, the will contained a provision authorizing the trustee to make payments of income direct to the beneficiary. Such a provision might be advisable in the case of a minor in his teens who is normal and thrifty. If, for example, he were in college, it might be better for the trustee to make payments direct to him than to undertake to pay his college bills.

In the case of beneficiaries who were of legal age and mentally competent, the normal plan would be for the trustee to make payments direct to the beneficiary. But, even then, in view of the ever-present possibility that a competent beneficiary may in course of time, by illness, accident, or old age, become actually, if not legally incompetent, it may be advisable to include in the terms of the trust a provision that the trustee may apply the income for the use of the beneficiary instead of paying it to him.

Principal

In formulating the terms of his trust, the testator should face the question and decide definitely whether he would want principal as well as income paid to or applied for the beneficiary. Here, as in the case of the payment or application of income, he has a wide variety of choices.

1. Right of beneficiary to demand. He may authorize the beneficiary himself to call for all of the principal, which in effect would terminate the trust, or to call for not over a stated percentage of the principal or for a stated amount or not over a stated amount for each period—for example, each year.

2. Power of trustee to pay or apply. Or he may place authority for the payment or application of principal entirely in the hands of the trustee; and in so doing he may authorize the trustee to pay over or apply all of the principal, thus terminating the trust, or a stated percentage or a stated amount within any given period.

3. Right of beneficiary to demand and of trustee to advance. Or he may authorize the beneficiary himself to call for a stated percentage or amount of principal and at the same time authorize the trustee to pay over or apply part or all of the principal remaining in the trust. In a word, the terms about the payment or application of both income and principal can be made almost as flexible as any testator cares to make them.

By giving the beneficiary himself authority to call for principal the testator may create in the mind of the beneficiary a better attitude toward the trust itself than by restricting him to income only. He also may enable the beneficiary to acquire business and financial experience and judgment sooner. And particularly in the case of a family trust and a careful, thrifty, provident widow-and-mother, it may enable her to use the trust as a whole, principal as well as income, for the best interests of herself and her children.

On the other hand, giving the beneficiary authority to call for principal makes it possible for him, by too frequent calls, to defeat in whole, or in part, the purposes of the trust. This would be particularly true in the case of a trust in which the ultimate beneficiaries—that is, those who are to receive the principal after the trust has served its purpose—were the chief objects of the testator's provision. Suppose, for example, the widow-and-mother had an independent income and the husband-and-father was more concerned about conserving his estate for his children than providing for their immediate needs. In such a case he might prefer not to give any beneficiary the right to call for any principal. Furthermore, if the widow-and-mother should marry again and come under the influence of an inconsiderate or improvident second husband, right in her to call for principal might lead to a depletion of the trust and, consequently, a disservice to the beneficiaries, including the wife herself.

By giving the trustee himself the authority to pay over or apply principal—whether a stated percentage or amount or the whole of it—the testator enables the trustee to do what he thinks is for the best interest of the beneficiaries as and when needs arise. The wisdom of such a provision becomes especially impressive during a period of rising living expenses. The testator, for example, leaves a trust estate of $100,000 yielding $3,000 a year and at the time of the testator's death that much income is sufficient for the living expenses of the family. But within a few years living costs have advanced to the point where $3,000 will purchase only one-half the goods or services it would have purchased when the trust was created. This means that, in terms of purchasing power, the husband has left his family an annual income of only $1,500 when he thought he was leaving them $3,000. Then, if the trustee has authority to use principal, he can supplement income with principal to the extent of restoring the purchasing power as contemplated by the testator. The fluctuations in purchasing power of money have led planners of disposition of property in recent years strongly to urge the inclusion of a provision for using principal, as well as income, to meet the needs of beneficiaries.

But there is another side to this matter. Giving the trustee authority to pay over or apply principal, in addition to income, enables the trustee himself to defeat the purposes of the trust. He may be unable or unwilling to resist the importunities of the beneficiary. He may misjudge the needs of the beneficiary. He may misjudge the length of the trust or the earning power of the trust property. He may deplete the trust before it has served its purpose.

A combination of power in the beneficiary and in the trustee to use principal has worked well in a great many cases. The testator, for example, gives his wife authority to call for a stated amount or percentage of principal each year and also gives his trustee authority to pay over or apply a stated amount or percentage of the principal each year. If the amounts or percentages are not too much, the needs of the beneficiary may be served under varying conditions without depleting the trust before it has served its purpose. The disadvantage of this arrangement is that, if both beneficiary and trustee go to the limit of the use of principal every year, the two calls together may prove to be too much of a drain upon the trust and exhaust the principal too soon.

In any case the trustee should have power to apply as well as pay over principal as well as income, and for the same reason which is that any day the beneficiary may be physically or mentally incapacitated to receive and use either income or principal.

These, then, are the characteristics common to all personal trusts: trusts under will, living trusts, and insurance trusts. Now let us consider the characteristics that are, more or less, peculiar to living trusts and, after that, to insurance trusts.

COLLATERAL READING

Note: For complete citations, see Bibliography, pp. 417–428.
ATKINSON on *Wills and Administration.*
BOGERT's *Handbook.*
LORING's *Trustee's Handbook,* Shattuck rev.

7

Living Trusts

$\mathfrak{M}$OST OF THE ELEMENTS of a trust as set forth in Chapter 5 apply to a living trust. It will be necessary, therefore, to call attention only to the characteristic features of a living trust.

Definition of a Living Trust

The broad definition of a living trust—a trust created and made operative during the lifetime of the creator—includes many types of trusts, such as employees trusts, charitable trusts, and corporate trusts, which are outside the scope of this chapter. But in practice and in this text the term *living trust* is restricted to a personal trust created by an individual during his lifetime for the benefit of himself or of some other person or object.

1. *Other names for living trusts.* Other names for living trusts are *voluntary trusts, immediate trusts,* and *inter vivos* (between living persons) *trusts. Voluntary* emphasizes the fact that it is a trust created voluntarily by a person during his lifetime as distinct from a trust under will that can become operative only upon the creator's death, which event presumably would be involuntary. Or the term *voluntary* may be used to distinguish this type of trust from one imposed by operation of law, such as a *resulting trust*—that is, one resulting from the relationship of the parties to the transaction,—or a *constructive* trust—that is, one growing out of a fraudulent transaction in which the law holds the fraudulent party to the transaction *as if he were* trustee. *Immediate* emphasizes the fact that the trust becomes operative immediately and is not postponed to the death of the testator. *Inter vivos,* which is the lawyers' name for this type of trust, emphasizes the fact that it is a transaction between living persons.

DISTINGUISHING FEATURES OF A LIVING TRUST

All of the elements which are essential to a trust as set forth in Chapter 5, —a creator, a trustee, a beneficiary, property, and terms of the trust—are no less essential to a living trust. To avoid repetition, only those features of each of these elements which are distinctive to living trusts will be discussed here.

Settlor

The creator of a living trust is known in this text as the *settlor* but settlor is not the only name for the creator of a living trust. Others are *grantor* (usually, but not always applied to a living trust involving real property), *donor*, and *trustor*. The adoption and use of the term *settlor* throughout the *Restatement of the Law of Trusts* for all creators of trusts assures the continued employment of *settlor* in preference to any of the other terms.

Trustee

The settlor himself may be the trustee. He can declare himself trustee for some other person's benefit. He can be one of the trustees for his own benefit. He can create a trust with another person as trustee for the benefit of himself and another person. But he cannot create a trust with himself as sole trustee and sole beneficiary.

Property

There is nothing legally distinctive about the property in a living trust. A settlor can put into a living trust any kind of property that he as testator can leave in a trust under will. But, as a matter of fact, a settlor is more likely than a testator to be selective regarding the trust property. The settlor has the privilege of selecting for his living trust property which he and his trustee think will be well adapted to trust administration; whereas, a testator, particularly in a trust of the residue of his estate, leaves in trust whatever property he owns at the time of his death, which may or may not be well adapted to trust administration.

Terms of Trust

With respect to the terms of the trust, the main differences between a living trust and a trust under will relate to the settlor himself as the beneficiary and to the duration of the trust.

1. *Settlor as beneficiary*. In the nature of things, a person cannot create a trust under his will for his own benefit. A settlor can create a living trust for his own benefit, and the terms of a trust so created may be and are likely to be different from the terms of a trust created by him for the benefit of some other person.

2. *Duration of trust*. As brought out in Chapter 5, the duration of a trust is governed by the rule against perpetuities as it exists in the law governing the administration of the trust. In a trust under will the time at which

the period begins to run is the death of the testator. In an irrevocable living trust it begins to run from the date of creation of the trust; in a revocable trust, from the date it is converted into an irrevocable trust and, if it never is converted into an irrevocable trust, it begins to run from the date of death of the settlor when, of course, it does become irrevocable. As in a trust under will, so here, a person can create a trust to continue throughout the lifetime of a person or persons in being at the time the period begins, plus twenty-one years, plus the period of gestation thereafter which, conceivably, may be a duration of over a century.

METHODS OF CREATING A LIVING TRUST

A living trust can be created by a person in any one of three ways—by agreement, by declaration, and by agreement and declaration combined.

By Agreement

This is by far the most common way of creating a living trust. *A* and *B* enter into an agreement with each other by which *A* delivers or agrees to deliver property to *B*, and *B* agrees to hold it in trust and administer it for the benefit of *A* or of *C* according to the terms set forth in the agreement. Where real property is involved, the agreement frequently is called a *deed of trust*.

By Declaration

A less common, but still not an uncommon, way of creating a living trust is by declaration. *A* declares himself trustee of his own property for the benefit of *B*; whereupon *A* remains the legal owner but *B* becomes the equitable owner of the property.

By Agreement and Declaration

A combination method of creating a living trust has proved to be useful where, for one reason or another, it is desirable that the beneficiary should not know the real creator of the trust. For example, *B* agrees with *A* for *B* to serve as trustee of property turned over to him by *A* to be held in trust for the benefit of *C*. In accordance with this agreement the property is turned over to *B*, not as trustee, but, so far as the record would show, as absolute owner. *B* forthwith declares himself trustee for the benefit of *C*, and *C* need never know that *A* was, in fact, the creator of the trust.

The following is an illustration of how agreement and declaration can be combined effectively and considerately: A woman who had spent her mature life conducting a school for girls came to the end of her teaching career without having accumulated a sufficiency for her old age. Some of her former pupils, by then mature and affluent women, knew that their former teacher would not accept from them money she would regard as charity. So they found a person who agreed to serve as trustee and turned over to him the necessary amount for their former teacher's support in comfort the balance of her life. He thereupon declared himself trustee and began making regular payments to her. She never knew who her benefactors were. The whole affair was handled in such a way as to save everyone embarrassment.

PURPOSES SERVED BY A LIVING TRUST

In the discussion of trusts under will it was stated that a trust is designed to supply one or more elements lacking in a given person's character, ability, or taste which are essential to the proper care, management, and use of property. Living trusts likewise are designed to supply one or more of these elements.

Living trusts, according to their main purpose, fall into three classes— (1) those primarily for the benefit of the settlor himself; (2) those primarily for the benefit of members of the settlor's family; and (3) those for the benefit of other persons. This suggests several questions: (1) Why should any person create a trust for himself? (2) Why should any person create a trust for the members of any member of his family while he himself is alive and head of his family? (3) Why should he create a living trust for any other person during his own lifetime, rather than wait until his death and create the trust under his will?

For the Settlor

The following are some of the purposes served by living trusts primarily for the settlor's own benefit:

1. *To build up his estate.* A young person, whose profession or business does not involve investment of funds or the management of property, creates a living trust, perhaps very small in the beginning, and adds to it by installments as he saves money out of his business or profession and in this way builds up an estate.

2. *To free himself of burden of property management.* A young person or even an older one desires to devote himself without interruption or distraction to his profession or business. He is inexperienced and he does not expect ever to become experienced in the investment of funds or the management of property. So, he creates a living trust and puts into it all of his surplus earnings, shifts to his trustee the burdens of investment and property management, and frees himself of those burdens while he pursues his occupation.

3. *To build up an independent estate.* A person actively engaged in

business decides that, instead of putting all of his profits back into his business, he should build up an estate which, in the event of any casualty to his business, would provide for himself and his family. So, he creates a living trust and gradually builds up an estate separate and apart from and independent of his business.

4. *To safeguard himself against effects of misadventure.* A person who already has accumulated some estate decides to enter a business or an undertaking of some kind which, he realizes, is fraught with risks. So, he creates a living trust and puts into it as much of his accumulations as he feels that he can spare and then launches forth on his venture or adventure, having the satisfaction of realizing that, should his new undertaking come to naught, he would not have jeopardized his entire estate or the actual needs of his family.

5. *To be free during years of retirement.* As brought out in the second paragraph, a young person may create a living trust in order to shift the burden of investment or property management to a trustee so as to be free to go ahead with his profession or business. But an older person may create a living trust because he is approaching or has reached the age of retirement and he does not feel competent longer to continue the investment and management of his property; or, although still for the time being as competent as ever, he wishes to be relieved of the burdens and responsibilities incident to the investment of funds and the management of property so as to be free to pursue his avocation or hobby during his period of retirement. So he creates a living trust for the dual purpose of obtaining good investment service and property management and release from the burdens incident thereto.

For Members of Settlor's Family

Seldom would a person create a living trust, as he would a trust under will, for the benefit of his family as a unit. Usually it would be a trust for the members of his family as individuals. But sometimes even in creating a living trust he might be thinking more of his family as a whole than of his wife and sons and daughters as individuals. For example, he might have in mind bringing the members of his family and his trustee together and familiarizing them with his affairs and his plans and getting them accustomed to working with one another while he still is alive and able to smooth over any rough spots that might show up in the process of adjustment. Sometimes one of the most difficult problems that a trustee has to solve is the adjustment of his relations with the beneficiaries whom he had not known and who had not known him until after the death of the creator of the trust. In many cases lasting and perplexing maladjustments might be avoided altogether by the settlor creating a living trust and bringing the trustee into contact with the beneficiaries and they with him during his lifetime.

Considering the members of the family as individuals, why should a person create a living trust for his wife, for his son, or for his daughter?

1. *For his wife.* A wife, as the head of the home, naturally desires a steady, dependable, and ample income with which to meet the living expenses of the family. Her husband can give her a regular weekly or monthly allowance; but this term *allowance* is itself offensive to some wives who regard themselves as partners with their husband in a joint enterprise and not as recipients of an allowance from his gracious hands. Furthermore, allowances themselves are not always regular or prompt. Where the husband is able to create a living trust and put into it at one time, or by installments, property enough to yield income sufficient for the family expenses and his wife's own personal expenses, he is likely to establish a much more satisfactory family atmosphere than when the wife has to depend upon a sometimes hit-or-miss allowance.

2. *For his son.* Just as a father makes outright gifts to his son for various purposes and various reasons, so he may make gifts in trust for his son. If his son is physically incapable or mentally incompetent or thriftless, he may create a living trust for him solely or primarily for his protection, to make sure that, no matter what may happen to the father's business or his professional earnings, his unfortunate son will be provided for.

But as often a father creates a living trust, not so much for his son's protection as for his son's relief from the burdens and responsibilities of investment and property management. Suppose the son is headed toward or already is engaged in a profession or business that is foreign to the investment of funds or the management of property. Suppose he is an artist or writer or social welfare worker or is planning to devote his life to public service. By creating a living trust for his benefit, the father can release the time, energy, and talent of his son for the pursuit of these eminently worthwhile but more or less unremunerative occupations.

3. *For his daughter.* In the case of an unmarried daughter, particularly one headed toward or already engaged in some professional career, there might be as many reasons for creating a living trust for her as there would be for creating one for a son.

In the case of a daughter already married or soon to be married there may be still another reason for creating a living trust for her. Even in a country, such as the United States, in which dowries or marriage settlements as such are not common, it is quite common for a father or mother to make a substantial gift, wholly apart from a conventional wedding gift, to a daughter upon her marriage. This gift may be outright or in trust. If it is an outright gift, its conservation and its use for good or ill will be at the mercy not only of the daughter but also of her husband. If either of them is improvident, the property may be dissipated. Even though the daughter may be provident, if her husband is not so, he may deprive her of the benefits of her parent's gift. Should the marriage not be successful and result in divorce, the gift from her parents may be lost to her forever. Whereas, if the gift is in trust for her benefit alone or for the benefit of herself and her children or even for the benefit of herself, of her husband so long as he is her husband, and of her children, the property is protected and is administered for the benefit of the persons designated, no matter what the fate of the marriage may be. Thus in the case of a substantial marriage gift, there would seem to be many sound reasons for making it in trust rather than outright.

For Other Persons

We come now to the purposes served by living trusts for persons other than the settlor himself and members of his immediate family. These would include parents, brothers and sisters, other kinsmen, and friends. The following are some of the main reasons for putting gifts to such persons in trust rather than making them outright:

1. *To supply lacking element of ability, or character, or taste.* When a person decides that he should make a substantial immediate gift to or for any of the groups of persons just mentioned, he next must decide whether that person can or will use the gift properly. Is the person physically capable? Is he mentally competent? Is he thrifty or economical or conscious of the value of money? Is he experienced in handling property? Is he interested in making investments or managing property? Is he reasonably prudent? If the answer to any of these questions clearly is *no*, then a living trust, rather than an outright gift, should be considered.

2. *To serve as a go-between.* In some cases a living trust serves in a pleasant way (in others, in a way that may not be so pleasant) the purpose of providing a go-between in the person of the trustee.

An illustration of the pleasant way was given earlier in this chapter in the section on methods of creating living trusts—that of the pupils who used a trustee to be their go-between in providing for their former teacher.

The following case illustrates a less pleasant way of using the trustee as a go-between. A widowed mother has a profligate or spendthrift son who bedevils her for advances or allowances or gifts. She creates a living trust and puts into it practically all her estate; makes the trust irrevocable; makes the income payable to herself for life, with some provision for the use of principal in the trustee's, not her own, discretion; and after her death makes the income payable to or for her son with some kind of protective provision and with some provision for the use of principal in the trustee's discretion. Then, when her son begins to importune her for money, she can answer him truly that her estate is in trust and that not even she can get it out of trust. Such an arrangement not only protects the settlor from unreasonable importunities but also protects the estate both for the settlor and for the beneficiary.

3. *To familiarize trustee with settlor's estate and family.* Sometimes it is said that one of the purposes of creating a living trust is to try out the trustee before the executorship and trusteeship under the will are entrusted to him. *A*, having decided to make *B* executor and trustee under his will and having

made his will to that effect, creates a revocable living trust of a portion of his estate for the benefit of himself for life and then for his wife and children or other persons under terms substantially the same as those under his will. In this way he can try out his trustee during his lifetime and, if he does not like the way the trustee administers his living trust, he can change his will and name another executor and trustee. This, no doubt, is one of the motives for creating some living trusts.

But perhaps more often the primary motive is not so much to try out the trustee as it is to help the trustee to become familiar with the estate and the beneficiaries of the settlor. In the administration of a living trust for the benefit of the settlor for life, the trustee and the settlor-beneficiary come into frequent contact with each other. The settlor acquaints the trustee not only with the property in the trust but with his general estate as well. He helps the trustee to understand what he has in mind for his beneficiaries after his death both under his living trust and under his trust under will. He explains to his trustee the characteristics of each of his beneficiaries and tells him how each of them must be dealt with in order to get the best results with the least unpleasantness.

Furthermore, a living trust may be used as a means of getting the trustee and the beneficiaries acquainted with each other, pending the time when the settlor no longer will be present to serve as a go-between for the trustee and the beneficiaries. It is quite a shock sometimes for the beneficiaries of an estate or a trust under will never to have had any acquaintance or dealings with the executor and trustee until after the testator's death and suddenly be made to realize that from then on for the balance of their lifetime they must look to a trustee who until then had been a stranger to them, instead of their husband or father. If only the husband or father had put a portion of his estate in trust with the same trustee during his lifetime and through that trust had brought them in contact with the trustee, the living trust would have served as a bridge over the chasm between their life before and their life after the death of her husband or father, and he himself would have been present to help them cross that bridge.

The foregoing only partially illustrate the purposes served by living trusts. There are many others. One of the others that already must have occurred to the student relates to the economy of putting property into a living trust instead of leaving it outright or in trust under will.

If a person puts property into a living trust, does that not take it out of his general estate and save his beneficiaries the expenses and costs incident to the settlement of his estate at his death? The answer is *yes;* but whether it will be a saving in the long run will depend upon the relation that the compensation of the trustee under the living trust bears to the expense of settling the estate minus the property put in trust.

If a person puts property into a living trust, may he not save estate taxes, inheritance taxes, and income taxes? The answer is: "Maybe so, maybe not." It depends upon the terms of the trust and the state of the tax laws at the time.

Both these points are mentioned here only to show that they have not been overlooked in the development of the needs for, or purposes served by, living trusts.

TRUSTEE OF A LIVING TRUST

The wide choice the settlor has in the selection of his trustee already has been shown. The question now arises: What are some of the practical considerations the settlor should have in mind in selecting his trustee or trustees? Many of the same considerations obtain here as obtain in the selection of the trustee under his will; but there are some which apply only or mainly to a living trust.

Settlor

As already stated, the settlor may declare himself sole trustee or he may enter a trust agreement under which he is one of the trustees. While this is permissible legally, it would seem that in most cases he would prefer to dissociate himself more completely from his trust and to make the line of demarcation between his trust estate and his general estate more clear-cut and unmistakable. While it is not, by any means, true in all cases, nevertheless when a settlor names himself trustee or one of the trustees, it looks as though he were trying to have his cake and eat it too.

Member of Family

A settlor may name his wife or son or daughter or any other person trustee of his living trust, just as he can name him trustee under his will. But then, is it usually wise to name a member of the family?

Experience and competence aside, a member of the family as trustee may find himself in an unenviable position in dealing with beneficiaries who themselves are members of the family. Where the mother or brother or sister, for example, is trustee, it is difficult for the other members of the family who are beneficiaries to realize that the trust is a legal arrangement that must be carried out to the letter and not merely a family arrangement that can be upset or changed at the pleasure of the trustee or the beneficiaries. When such a trustee, well advised, refrains from doing what the beneficiaries wish him to do or in the way they wish him to do it, they are likely to charge it to his obstinacy or unreasonableness or prejudice or some other unworthy motive and subject him to wholly undeserved criticism.

Succession of Trustees

If the living trust is to continue beyond the lifetime of the settlor, in naming his trustee he should give consideration to a succession of trustees that will provide for a competent trustee throughout the entire period of the trust which, as in the case of a trust under will, may last through two generations and over into the third. In providing for this succession of trustees, the settlor may employ either an individual or a bank or trust company or both. That is to say, he may name an individual the original trustee to be succeeded by a bank or trust company in the event of the death or incapacity or removal of the original trustee. Or he may name a bank or trust company in the first instance, in which case either the law or the trust instrument would provide for a successor to the original trustee in case of the loss of identity of the original trustee resulting from merger or consolidation. Or he may name a self-perpetuating board of trustees.

Adviser to Trustee

During his lifetime the settlor himself could and perhaps would serve as adviser to his trustee not only on investment matters but on other matters as well, including the personal problems of his beneficiaries. In the event of his incapacity or death, he may wish to provide for another adviser or for other advisers to his trustee. He may wish to appoint his wife, if living, an older son or daughter, an intimate friend, or a business or professional associate adviser to his trustee on the problems relating to the beneficiaries themselves. This might be especially true in the case of a physically or mentally defective beneficiary who requires special care and attention either in the home or in an institution.

Furthermore, in addition to an adviser on personal problems of his beneficiary, the settlor may desire to appoint an adviser to his trustee on business or investment matters. Instead of appointing cotrustees, he may appoint a sole trustee and make him solely responsible for administering the trust and yet name an adviser to him on problems connected with a business or business interest which the settlor has put in trust during his lifetime to be carried on and held intact until it could be turned over to, say, a son too young or too inexperienced in the business to take it over and run it on his own responsibility. Or he may appoint an adviser on investment problems and so word the provision in the trust instrument as not to undermine the responsibility of the trustee for the investment management of the trust.[1]

The selection of the trustee is one of the most important steps in the creation of a living trust. No single element of the trust nor combination of all of the others can make up for an incompetent trustee.

[1] Stephenson, "Cofiduciary or Consultant?" 741.

TERMS OF A LIVING TRUST

Under a living trust the settlor, the same as the testator under a will, can provide for the payment or application of income, for the advancement or use of principal, for the duration of the trust or for any length of time permitted by the applicable rule against perpetuities, and for the protective provisions of spendthrift trusts, discretionary trusts, trusts for support, and protective trusts as discussed in Chapter 23. But there are other items which, in the nature of things, are peculiar to living trusts. Two of these distinctive terms are: the *revocability* and the *amendability* of the trust.

Revocable

One of the questions that every settlor must face and which he should answer in the trust instrument itself with an unequivocal *yes* or *no* is: Shall my living trust be revocable or irrevocable. He should ask himself: If I decide later that I should like to do away with—revoke—my trust and take back my property, shall I reserve the right to do so? Or shall I deliberately and intentionally part with the right ever to do away with the trust and take back my property once I have established the trust?

From the usual discussion of the revocability of a living trust, a person would get the impression that the only or certainly the chief reason for making a trust irrevocable would be in the hope of saving taxes—estate taxes, inheritance taxes, or income taxes. But there are valid reasons, entirely apart from any possible tax savings, for making a trust irrevocable. Under the present tax law (1960) there are certain tax advantages in making a living trust irrevocable for a stated period of time—not less than ten years—but for the moment we are considering revocability without regard to tax consequences.

1. *Instruments silent as to revocability.* Suppose the trust agreement or the declaration of trust is silent as to the revocability of the trust. In a few states by statute a trust is presumed to be revocable unless it is declared expressly in the instrument to be irrevocable; but in most states it is presumed to be irrevocable unless declared expressly to be revocable. So, the settlor and the draftsman of a trust instrument should ascertain first what the law of the state is regarding revocability and in the light of that decide what to say in the instrument about revocability.

2. *Termination by consent of beneficiaries.* Suppose *A* creates a living trust for the benefit of *B* and *C* for life and after the death of the survivor to the heirs of *B* and *C* in equal shares and says nothing about revocability. Could *A*, *B*, and *C* by agreement terminate—not revoke—the trust? Here also the law varies. In Great Britain the law favors the termination of a trust by the consent of all the beneficiaries when all of them are of legal age and are competent and all their interests are vested. In some states in this country, on

the contrary, the law looks with disfavor upon terminating a trust even under these circumstances.

Suppose *A* creates a living trust for his sole benefit for life, after his death the property in trust to revert to his estate, and says nothing in the instrument about the revocation of the trust. Later he decides to revoke or terminate the trust. It would seem on first impression that, without question, he should be permitted to do so. But suppose he was a periodic drunkard, spendthrift, or even a lunatic with extended periods of sanity and, having realized his condition during his lucid periods, had created the living trust for his own protection against the time when he realized that he might go on a spree, spend his money unwisely, or experience a period of insanity. In a few states, the courts already have decided that in such cases the settlor will not be permitted to terminate his own trust even if he is the sole beneficiary of the trust. But, even in those states, if the settlor and the trustee should agree, however unwisely, to terminate the trust, it would seem that no other person would have any standing in court, as an interested party, to object to the termination.

Having called attention to these two legal points about the revocability or termination of a trust when the trust instrument is silent as to revocation, we may pass on to discuss a few of the situations in which a trust well may be expressly irrevocable entirely apart from tax-saving considerations.

Irrevocable

1. *Importunities of dependent beneficiaries.* One illustration of the usefulness of an irrevocable trust to resist the importunities of dependent beneficiaries already has been given earlier in this chapter—that of the widowed mother and her profligate son. There are not a few cases in which it would be a comfort and relief, as well as a protection, to a person to make his trust irrevocable so as to be able to say to the importunate, profligate, spendthrift beneficiary: "My affairs are in the hands of my trustee; go to see him."

2. *Infirmities of one's old age.* Suppose a person, having accumulated during his active business or professional career a sufficiency for himself and his dependents during his and their old age and infirmity, realizes that he is approaching the period of life in which not only will he not be able much longer properly to care for his property but also the period in which he may not be able to trust himself to make wise decisions with respect to the disposition of his property. He is afraid that, even though he puts his property in trust, if he makes his trust revocable, he may, unwisely, in an unguarded moment, perhaps under some undue influence or overpersuasion, revoke the trust. So, he deliberately and intentionally makes his trust irrevocable to protect himself and his dependents—perhaps his wife or an incapacitated or in-

competent son or daughter—against the weaknesses of his own senility or infirmity.

3. *Protection against one's defects of character or habits.* As brought out earlier in this chapter, a young person, realizing his addiction to drink, his extravagance, or his periodically unsound mind, may make his trust irrevocable in order to protect himself against his own defects and weaknesses. Even though he is in a state in which a trust for the settlor's sole benefit is terminable by consent of the trustee and the beneficiary, a prudent trustee would hesitate to permit such a settlor to terminate his trust in the face of an express provision that the trust is irrevocable.

Amendable

Amendability is different from revocability. It means the power to change the terms of the trust without revoking the trust itself. *A* creates a living trust for the benefit of *B* and *C* for life and then outright to *B's* and *C's* children in equal shares and declares the trust amendable by designating another or other beneficiaries than himself should *B* or *C* die without any surviving children.

The power to amend a revocable trust is not so important, for, although a power to revoke does not include the power to amend, nevertheless, if the settlor desires to change the terms of the trust, he can revoke the trust and immediately thereafter create a new trust with the terms changed as he desires.

But the power to amend an irrevocable trust is a point of vast importance. In the first place, the power to amend may have fully as great an effect on taxes as the power to revoke. But, in the second place, tax considerations aside, a person who for good reason decides that he should make his trust irrevocable should consider also the advisability of reserving the power to amend by changing the ultimate beneficiaries and possibly the terms of distribution to the immediate beneficiaries. For example, suppose a father creates a living trust for his profligate son for life, then outright to his son's children, thinking that his son's wife had been provided for from some other source, and realizes or finds out later that his son's wife has not been provided for properly. He might desire to change the terms of the trust by making her one of the beneficiaries. Or suppose the terms of the trust required the trustee to make payments direct to the beneficiary and the settlor learned later that the beneficiary was wasting the direct payments he received and that for his own protection the income should be applied for the benefit of himself and his family. This irrevocable trust should be amended to a protective trust as well.

This chapter, like the preceding one, deals only with the distribution of property in trust. The administration of that property after it is put into the hands of the trustee will be discussed in Chapters 15, 16 and 17.

COLLATERAL READING

Note: For complete citations, see Bibliography, pp. 417–428.

BLAKE, "Trusts and the Family."

KING, "Reappraisal of the Revocable Trust—Cautions in Face of Spouse's Rights."

SHATTUCK and FARR, *An Estate Planner's Handbook*, Ch. IV, p. 84.

SHATTUCK, Mayo Adams, "The Revocable Trust: Its Manifold Uses in Times of War and Peace."

STEPHENSON, "Trusts in the Everyday Affairs of People;" *Studies*, 3d ser., 1.

8

Insurance Trusts

INSURANCE TRUSTS are a type of living trust. But they have so many distinctive features that they have acquired their own name and have won separate treatment for themselves in texts on estates and trusts.

Definition of an Insurance Trust

An insurance trust is any living trust of which the trust property is wholly or partly life insurance policy contracts during the lifetime of the insured and insurance proceeds after the death of the insured. It would be possible—sometimes it is done—to make insurance payable to the estate of the insured and then provide by will for the proceeds to be held in trust; but such an arrangement would be classified as a trust under will and not as an insurance trust.

KINDS OF INSURANCE TRUSTS

All insurance trusts fall under two main heads—personal insurance trusts and business insurance trusts—and each of these main heads, in turn, is divided into several subheads.

Insurance trusts, like other living trusts, may be revocable or irrevocable, amendable or unamendable; but revocability and amendability seldom are used as a basis of classification of insurance trusts.

Personal Insurance Trusts

Personal insurance trusts are those created by individuals for individuals, institutions, or other groups capable of being beneficiaries but in which no provision regarding a business or business interest is involved. For example, *A*, the insured, has insurance made payable to *B*, trustee, for the benefit of *C* (*A's* wife).

Personal insurance trusts are subdivided into unfunded, funded, and installment insurance trusts.

1. *Unfunded.* An unfunded insurance trust is one in which the trustee is not charged with the duty of paying the premiums on the insurance. The insured or the creator of the trust himself continues to pay the premiums. In most cases it is the insured who creates the trust and continues to keep the insurance in force; but it is possible for one person to trustee insurance on the life of another person and pay the premiums.

2. *Funded.* A funded insurance trust is one in which the trustee is supplied funds with which, or property out of which, to pay the premiums and is charged with the duty of paying them so long as he has the available funds or property for that purpose. For example, *A*, the insured, trustees $100,000 in securities and $100,000 of insurance and charges his trustee with the duty of paying the premiums out of the income or principal of the $100,000 in securities.

It would be possible for *A* to put the securities and the insurance in trust and yet himself continue to pay the premiums. This would not be a funded insurance trust, because the trustee had not been placed under any duty with regard to the premiums, although he has the funds which, had the creator of the trust desired, might be used for that purpose.

3. *Installment.* An installment insurance trust—sometimes called an accumulating or cumulative insurance trust—is one in which the trustee is charged with the duty of paying the premiums and is supplied with some, but not with sufficient, funds and property, for paying them. For example, *A* trustees $50,000 of insurance, the annual premiums on which amount to $1,500. It would take $50,000 of securities yielding 3 per cent to produce enough income to pay the premiums. But *A* has only $25,000 in securities. So he puts the $25,000 in securities, along with the $50,000 insurance, in trust and arranges to add cash to the trust at the rate of $100 a month or $1,200 a year. Of the $1,200, $750, added to the $750 from securities, would be used to pay the premiums on the insurance. This would leave $450 a year to be added to the principal of the trust and invested. The installment insurance trust, taking its name from the periodic installment additions to the trust, usually is a trust on its way to becoming a funded insurance trust and is adapted to the requirements of a young person whose estate still is in the making.

Business Insurance Trusts

Business insurance trusts, as the name implies, are those connected with a business. They are subdivided into (1) insurance trusts created by the business and (2) those created by individuals for the liquidation of a business or business interest. The former usually are called *key-man insurance trusts.* The latter are subdivided still further into proprietorship insurance trusts, partnership insurance trusts, and stock-purchase insurance trusts. There are still other names by which business insurance trusts sometimes are known, but this classification will serve the purpose of this text.

1. *Key-man*. A key-man insurance trust is one in which a business—a proprietorship, a partnership, or a corporation—purchases insurance on the life of one or more of its key-men, puts the insurance in trust, either pays the premiums itself (in which case it would be an unfunded trust) or puts in trust, along with the insurance, cash or securities out of which to pay the premiums (in which case it would be a funded trust), and sets out in the trust agreement instructions on what is to be done with the proceeds of the insurance at the death of the insured. This kind of insurance trust is for the benefit of the business and, naturally, the business should pay the premiums. Partnerships and corporations likewise may insure their key-men, pay the premiums, and at the death of the insured use the proceeds for the purposes of the business.

2. *Liquidation*. Here the term *liquidation* is employed in the sense, not of liquidating (closing out) the business itself, but in the sense of cashing in on the owner's business or interest in the business. Perhaps, in the beginning, a better word than *liquidation* might have been found, but by this time it has become too firmly embedded in insurance-trust literature to be uprooted easily.

This type of business insurance trust, as already stated, falls under three subheads—proprietorship, partnership, and stock-purchase.

a. Proprietorship. A proprietorship insurance trust can be illustrated more easily and simply than it can be defined. For an example, A is the sole proprietor of a prosperous $100,000 manufacturing business which after his death he especially desires to be carried on for the benefit of his family. Yet he has no son to carry it on. But he does have associated with him in the business a promising young man, B, with very limited capital. So, A insures his own life for $25,000, pays the premiums out of the business, and makes the insurance payable to a trustee. Upon B's agreeing to remain in his employment and carry on the business after A's death, A provides that at his death the trustee shall use the proceeds to purchase for B a $25,000 interest in the business. At A's death B receives a $25,000 interest in the business. A reasons that by keeping B in his employment and at his death making him a part-owner of the business, the remaining 75 per cent will be worth more to A's family than 100 per cent would be without B's help. Although it is, in effect, a gift of $25,000 by A to B, it is a gift in trust that will assure B's continued interest and participation in the business.

b. Partnership. A partnership insurance trust is a much more common arrangement than a proprietorship trust. Suppose A and B are equal partners in a business that is worth $100,000. Each desires that his half-interest in the business be liquidated as soon as possible after his death and that, should he survive longer, he buy out the other's half-interest in the business and become sole proprietor. So, *A* and *B* insure each other's life for $50,000, make the insurance payable to *C*, trustee, and by the terms of the trust provide that upon the death of the insured and the collection of the insurance the proceeds be used to purchase the deceased partner's interest in the business. The proceeds of the insurance supply the ready cash for the purchase of the deceased partner's interest in the business and supply the deceased partner's estate with ready cash which it may need for debts, taxes, and expenses.

c. Stock-purchase. A stock-purchase insurance trust serves for the stockholders of a close corporation the same purpose as a partnership insurance trust serves for partners. For example, *A*, *B*, and *C* are the only stockholders of *X* Company, each owning one-third of the outstanding stock. They desire that, should one of them die, the survivors purchase the stock from his estate, reissue it to a stockholder of their own choice, and carry on the business. So *A* purchases insurance on the life of both *B* and *C; B*, on the life of *A* and *C* each; and *C*, on the life of both *A* and *B;* and each of the three makes the insurance he purchases payable to *D*, trustee, to use the insurance proceeds on the life of a deceased stockholder to purchase the deceased stockholder's stock for the accounts of the surviving stockholders. The proceeds of the insurance would furnish the ready cash for the purchase of the stock and the ready cash that might be needed in connection with the settlement of the estate of the deceased stockholder.

PURPOSES SERVED BY INSURANCE TRUSTS

Why should life insurance ever be made payable to a trustee instead of payable in lump sum to a named beneficiary or to the insured's estate or left with the insurance company under one of the options of settlement it offers its policyholders? To answer this question is to state the purposes served by insurance trusts.

Personal Insurance Trusts

The purposes served by personal insurance trusts may be grouped under four heads, namely: (1) to unify the insured's estate, (2) to provide for flexibility of administration and exercise of discretion, (3) to provide a local personal adviser for the beneficiary, and (4) to prevent or reduce the shrinkage of the estate by providing the ready cash for the debts, taxes, and expenses of settlement of the estate.

1. *Unify insured's estate.* This means, first, unifying his insurance estate alone. The average person's insurance estate consists of several different policies in different companies under different terms and conditions, some payable in lump-sum, some left with the insurance companies but under different options of settlement. By means of an insurance trust, the insured can bring all of his policies together under a single plan of administration

and distribution and thus adapt his whole insurance estate to the different needs of his beneficiaries. In the case of the medium-sized estate or one in which the insured is depending largely upon his insurance to provide for his family or other dependents, this use of the insurance trust to unify his insurance estate may be one of its most practically useful purposes.

But the unifying process does not stop here. The insurance trust is used also as a means of unifying and integrating the insured's general estate and his insurance estate so as to make them do teamwork for the beneficiaries. This is accomplished by authorizing the executor under the insured's will to make sales to or obtain loans from the trustee of his insurance and by authorizing the trustee to make purchases from or loans to the executor. Thus by preventing sacrifice sales in a period of economic depression, the estate as a whole may be protected, preserved, and made to serve the needs of the beneficiaries. Since the beneficiaries of a family-man's will and those of his insurance trust usually are the same persons and since the terms of the two trusts usually are substantially alike, the beneficiaries themselves will scarcely be aware of any difference or care whether the payments they receive are from the insurance trust or from the trust under will or from a living trust. This use of the insurance trust as a means of consolidating and integrating the insured's entire estate for his beneficiaries may prove, and, in fact, many times has proved, one of the most beneficent purposes of the insurance trust.

2. *Flexibility and discretion.* If the insurance is purchased for the support, maintenance, and, in the case of children, education of the members of the insured's family, or for the support or maintenance of some other person for whom the insured has or feels a moral, if not legal, obligation to provide, the chances are that there will be continuing need for support and maintenance and, in the case of children, several years' need for school expenses in different types of schools. During this period of years or, perhaps, of a lifetime, needs will develop which the insured cannot foresee to provide for or provide against. The best way, it would seem, to meet such a situation would be by providing in some way for flexibility of administration of the insurance proceeds and by giving some person the power to meet unforeseen needs and emergencies that are likely to arise in the life of any beneficiary.

Flexibility of administration means ability and authority to change the method of handling without changing the underlying purpose to be served by the insurance proceeds. For example, at one time in his life a beneficiary may be competent to use direct payments made to him wisely and economically. Later in his life, physical or mental illness might render him totally unable to do so. The administration of the proceeds should be flexible enough to permit some person to make direct payments so long as that would be the wise thing to do but to withhold direct payments and apply the funds for the benefit of the beneficiary should that ever be the wise thing to do.

Exercise of discretion means that, instead of the insured's saying what shall or what shall not be done regarding the proceeds of his insurance, he clothes some person, who probably would survive him, with power to use his own discretion in meeting the needs of the beneficiaries as those needs arise. For example, to revert to an illustration already used, the insured has an insurance estate of $100,000. At the time of his death an income of $3,000—representing a 3 per cent yield on the insurance proceeds—would be ample for the requirements of his beneficiaries—say, his widow and children. But ten years from his death the purchasing power of the income is only one-half what it was at the insured's death and in terms of purchasing power it now amounts to only $1,500. If the insured has authorized some person who survived him to exercise his discretion to the extent of supplementing income with principal out of the insurance proceeds to provide for the living expenses of the beneficiaries, then that person, in the exercise of his discretion, can meet the changing living-expense requirements of the insured's beneficiaries.

Only by means of a trust can such flexibility of administration and exercise of discretion be provided. The insured himself cannot do so, for he will not be present to administer the proceeds of his insurance to meet the changing and unpredictable needs of his beneficiaries. The insurance company cannot do so, for under the terms of its contract with the insured, it is not permitted to exercise *its own* discretion with regard to the payment or application of the proceeds of the insurance. It is obligated to pay and it will pay only according to the terms of the contract. While the beneficiary himself can be and frequently is given very wide discretion as to the terms of the payment of the proceeds, it is *his* discretion and, if he is not capable of exercising his discretion wisely or prudently, the placing of the discretion in him may not be for his own best interest.

By putting the insurance in trust and, by the terms of the trust agreement, giving the trustee power in his discretion to meet the changing and unpredictable needs of the beneficiaries, the proceeds of the insurance may be used to serve the needs and best interests of the beneficiary as they materialize over the years.

3. *Local adviser.* Usually a person begins to receive the benefits of insurance only after the death of the insured. The insured may have been his father, mother, brother, sister, or some other person who has felt a moral obligation to provide for his material welfare by means of insurance. At and after the death of the insured the beneficiary may need a local, personal adviser almost as much as he is in need of the material provision made for him through the insurance.

The insurance company itself is not in a position, either through its home office or its local representative, to furnish such a local adviser; first, because its home office usually is not in the same community as the beneficiary and, second, because the function of its local representative is not to render personal, as distinct from insurance, advisory service to the beneficiaries.

A trustee is adapted to the giving of such personal, advisory service. In the first place, the trustee usually is a local bank or trust company and its trust officer is experienced in the rendering of personal advisory service to beneficiaries of its trusts. While an individual can serve as trustee of an insurance trust the same as he can serve as trustee of any other type of trust, in the evolution of the insurance trust, banks and trust companies have come to be the trustee in the vast majority of cases.

4. *Estate shrinkage.* A fourth purpose served by personal insurance trusts is the prevention or reduction of estate shrinkage through debts, taxes, and expenses. This purpose is accomplished not only by providing through insurance proceeds for paying these charges but also for paying them with the least possible sacrifice of the general assets of the estate. If the insurance is payable direct to the estate, it becomes subject to all the charges against the estate and, besides, it may not be used for the defrayment of those expenses to the best advantage; whereas, if the insurance is put in trust, by the terms of the trust the insured may leave specific instructions, based upon his own experience with the affairs of his estate, about using the proceeds of the insurance for the protection of the estate from needless shrinkage. For example, suppose *A*, the insured, has $100,000 in insurance payable to a trustee, $100,000 in securities, and owes $50,000 in debts, taxes, and expenses at the time of his death—that is, he should have a net estate of $150,000. He dies in the midst of an economic depression when the market value of his securities had dropped to $50,000 and a sale for them, if they are local securities, scarcely can be found at any price. Under his insurance trust *A* has authorized his trustee to make purchases from or loans to the executor under his will and has authorized the executor under his will to make sales to or obtain loans from the trustee of his insurance. In the exercise of their respective powers, the trustee of the insurance purchases the securities for $50,000 and takes them over into the insurance trust and the executor under *A's* will realizes the funds with which to pay off the charges against the estate. Thus, the shrinkage that would have resulted from a sacrifice sale of the securities is avoided.

Business Insurance Trusts

The main purpose served by a business insurance trust is to provide a person who will carry out to the letter the insured's plan with regard to the insurance and who will serve as a prompt, impartial, and, if need be, courageous paymaster of the insurance proceeds.

Note first the basic difference between a personal insurance trust and a business insurance trust. One of the main purposes of a personal insurance trust is to provide a trustee who will exercise discretion; whereas one of the main purposes of a business insurance trust is to provide a trustee who will live up to, and insist upon all others living up to, the letter of the terms of the insurance trust agreement. This is true of every type of business insurance trust. For example, a sole proprietor or a partnership or a corporation decides to insure the life of a key-man in the business for a special purpose. That purpose may be to provide ready cash for the business, to bolster the credit of the business, to absorb the shock and loss by the death of the key-man, or for some other purpose equally important to the business and its owner or owners. Or partners or stockholders insure the life of each other so as to provide the funds with which to liquidate the interest of a deceased partner or stockholder. In all these cases what the insured and his associates desire is that the plan, as conceived by them, be carried out to the letter. But for an impartial and responsible trustee, the best-laid plans of proprietors, partners, or stockholders regarding the insurance might miscarry to the detriment of the business and its owners. A trust offers assurance that the plans made and entered into by the owners of the business will be carried out to the letter.

Insurance Company as Trustee

If all the foregoing purposes are served by insurance trusts, if there is so great a need for them in the ways indicated, the question at once arises in the mind of the student: Can the insurance company itself serve as trustee? If not, why not? If so, why does it not do so?

Originally in this country life insurance companies did serve as trustee; and in England they still do serve. Beginning with the New York Life Insurance and Trust Company in 1830, insurance companies, far more than banks, served as trustee until about 1850. It was not until 1922 that the Provident Life and Trust Company of Philadelphia was separated into the Provident Mutual Insurance Company and the Provident Trust Company (a new corporation, now the Provident Tradesmens Bank and Trust Company), the former carrying on the insurance business and the latter, the trust business.

The difficulty about the insurance company serving as trustee of the proceeds of the policies it issues is not legal; it is practical.

Legally, an insurance company, the same as any other corporation, can be authorized to serve as trustee. In fact, the first corporations in the United States authorized to serve as trustee were insurance companies. There still are a few insurance companies in the United States which, under their charters, are authorized to serve as trustee. And by statute in several states any insurance company chartered under the laws of the state is authorized to serve as trustee of the proceeds of its own policies and to do so without segregating the assets of any trust.

But the practical difficulty arises from the facts (1) that there cannot be a trust without trust property and (2) that an insurance company cannot be trustee of the proceeds of its policies without segregating and setting aside the proceeds and administering them separate and apart from its own funds. Such segregation would mean the establishment of hundreds of thousands of trusts, small and large, for beneficiaries scattered not only over this country but also over other countries in which beneficiaries of its insurance policies have established their residence.[1]

The relationship between an insurance company and a beneficiary of one of its policies is that of a debtor and a creditor. The insurance company owes the beneficiary so much money under certain terms and conditions set forth in the policy contract. Its entire assets stand to make good its obligations under its policies. If it violates its contract in any respect, it can be sued for damages in a court of law.

The relationship between a trustee and a beneficiary is not that of creditor and debtor. The trustee is the legal owner and the beneficiary, the equitable owner of property. There must be specific property as to which the trustee can say to the beneficiary, "This is your property," and the beneficiary to the trustee, "This is my property." If the trustee misbehaves, he is surcharged for the amount of loss his misbehavior has caused the beneficiary. His misbehavior is called a breach of trust; whereas an insurance company's failure to live up to the terms and conditions of its policy is a breach of contract.

So, while it is legally possible for an insurance company to become and serve as trustee of the proceeds of its policies for the beneficiaries under those policies, it is doubtful that any insurance company at the present time would find it practicable to segregate its assets into a multitude of trusts and administer them in trust as separate entities.

DISTINCTIVE FEATURES OF INSURANCE TRUSTS

There are certain distinctive features of insurance trusts which it is appropriate to discuss in this chapter.

Methods of Making Insurance Payable to Trustee

There are two methods of making insurance payable to a trustee—by designation or change of beneficiary and by assignment.

1. *Designation or change of beneficiary.* The insured can have new insurance made payable to his trustee or can have the beneficiary of existing insurance changed to his trustee. The insured usually—in some cases, how-

[1] Griswold, *Spendthrift Trusts,* Sec. 112.

ever, only with the consent of the named beneficiary—has the right under his policy to change the beneficiary time and again, which means that, having once made it payable to his trustee, he can change the beneficiary again and make it payable to some other beneficiary. It follows, therefore, that designation or change of beneficiary is the appropriate method of making insurance payable to a trustee under a revocable insurance trust agreement.

2. *Assignment.* The insured can make insurance payable to his trustee by assigning to him all his right, title, and interest in and to the policy. There is a finality about an assignment that is not true of a designation or change of beneficiary. It follows, as a matter of course, that assignment is the appropriate method of making the insurance payable to a trustee under an irrevocable trust agreement.

In the drafting of an insurance trust agreement, it is important that the method of making the insurance payable to the trustee in the trust agreement and that under the contract with the insurance company be consistent with each other. Take, for example, an irrevocable insurance trust. In the agreement it is declared that the policy has been assigned to the trustee; but, in fact, it has been made payable to the trustee by designation or change of beneficiary. Under the agreement the insured has parted with his rights under the policy; in the contract with the insurance company he has reserved his rights. This inconsistency is likely to produce confusion and possible litigation.

Rights Reserved by Insured

The insured has certain rights under his insurance policy contract, some of which are: (1) to receive or apply dividends or distributive shares of surplus, disability benefits, surrender values, proceeds of matured endowments; (2) to obtain advances or loans; (3) to sell, assign, or pledge the policy; and (4) to change the beneficiary. When he creates a revocable trust and makes the insurance payable to the trustee by designation or change of beneficiary, he should spell out in the trust agreement an express reservation of all of the above rights and any others that he may have under the policy, so that there can be no question in the mind of the insurance company, the trustee, of the beneficiary as to the insured's right during his lifetime to exercise any and all of his rights under the policy.

Payment of Premiums

If it is to be an unfunded insurance trust, the trust agreement should declare expressly that the trustee is not under any duty regarding the premiums.

But if, on the other hand, it is to be a funded or installment trust and the trustee is charged with the duty to pay the premiums, there are several points that must be covered. If the income is insufficient, can the trustee use principal? If both principal and income are exhausted, can the trustee use loan values or other cash values to keep the insurance in force? If income, principal, and loan or other cash values are exhausted, what is the duty of the trustee about notifying the insured or the beneficiary of the trust so that one of them may supply additional funds? If funds are not forthcoming from any of these sources, what must the trustee do to divest itself of any further responsibility with respect to the policy? If the trustee should advance its own funds to keep the insurance in force, what right of recoupment or recovery would it have out of the proceeds of the policies? These points should be covered in the trust agreement.

Should the trustee negligently fail, when it had the funds available, to pay the premiums and let the insurance lapse, what would be the measure of his liability? Would *it* become the insurer itself? Could it insist upon the insured's reinstating the insurance if he still was insurable? What remedy would the trustee have if the insured had become uninsurable in the meantime? No attempt is made to answer these questions because, as yet, they have not arisen and, so, any attempts to answer them would be guesswork and, possibly, misleading.

Collection of Insurance

When the trustee comes to the collection of the insurance after the maturity of the policy, there is no difference between a funded and an unfunded trust, except that in case of the funded trust the trustee will have on hand funds with which, if necessary, to take steps to enforce the collection. In either case the trustee is under a duty to collect the insurance and has the same rights regarding the collection as any other beneficiary has.

But suppose there is a question about the liability of the insurance company and the issue comes to compromise or litigation. The first question to be decided is whether the trustee has the right to compromise the claim. Most insurance trust agreements give the trustee this power, and it is one of the points to be considered by the draftsman of the instrument. If the claim cannot be compromised, the next question relates to the expenses of the litigation. If it is a funded trust, the trustee will have funds for that purpose. But if it is an unfunded trust, the trustee may call upon the beneficiaries to advance the costs. Only under extraordinary conditions would the trustee be justified in advancing and never would it be under an obligation to advance its own funds for the purpose.

Protection of Insurance Company

In the early stages of the development of insurance trusts, insurance companies took opposite positions regarding knowledge or notice of the terms of the trust. Some companies refused to receive or consider the terms of the trust as set forth in the trust agreement on the ground that, if they knew them, they might have some responsibility regarding the administration of the trust by the trustee. Other insurance companies insisted upon receiving a copy of the trust agreement and refused to make the insurance payable to the trustee unless or until they had received, considered, and passed upon the agreement and all later amendments to it. In these early days the latter group of insurance companies were helpful in improving the quality of insurance trust agreements, particularly the administrative provisions.

At the present time it is customary to incorporate in an insurance trust agreement a provision relieving the insurance company of any and all responsibility regarding the administration of the proceeds put in trust. Under such a provision the insurance company has no more responsibility for following the proceeds of insurance paid to a trustee than those paid to any other beneficiary.

Exercise of Options of Settlement by Trustee

Is a trustee-beneficiary entitled to exercise options of settlement under the trusteed policies the same as any other beneficiary?

This question came to issue in 1939 in Minnesota, and the Supreme Court of that state held that a trustee has the same rights as any other beneficiary to exercise such options.[2]

Following this decision, a number of insurance companies wrote into their policies a provision to the effect that their options were available only to an individual, noncorporate, or nonfiduciary beneficiary.

Later, one insurance company after another began to extend the privilege of exercising options to trustee-beneficiaries as well as other beneficiaries, some of the companies making no distinction in this respect between trustee-beneficiaries and others, and other companies extending the privilege to trustee-beneficiaries only to a limited extent. At the present time a majority of the insurance companies generally or with restrictions extend this privilege to trustee-beneficiaries.

But this liberalization by the insurance companies is not the end of the matter. Although the insurance company may give the trustee the right to exercise any of the options, still the trustee cannot exercise it unless it is authorized by the terms of the trust to do so. The insured may have desired that the proceeds be administered by the trustee for the purposes set out in the trust instrument and not left with the insurance company under any of the options of settlement. Or he may have desired that the matter be left to the discretion of his trustee. If there is any likelihood that the insured may, under any circumstances, desire his trustee to leave the proceeds with the insurance company instead of administering them himself, he should include a provision to this effect in his trust agreement.

[2] *First Trust Company of St. Paul v. Northwestern Mutual Life Insurance Company*, 204 Minn. 244, 283 N.W. 236 (1939).

Purchase of Annuities by Trustee

Should the trustee be authorized to purchase for the beneficiary annuity contracts from an insurance company?

This question arises in connection with living trusts as well as with insurance trusts. For example, *A*, having no children nor other dependents except his wife *B*, creates a living trust or an insurance trust with *C*, trustee, to pay *B* the income and principal, if need be, for life and then to pay over any remainder to *D*, a charity. His primary purpose in creating the trust is to provide for *B*. After *A's* death *C* decides that the best interests of *B* will be served by purchasing an annuity for her. Then *C* faces the question: Do I have the power to purchase an annuity, or must I continue the administration of the trust myself? The answer depends on the terms of the trust. In creating either a living trust or an insurance trust primarily for the support of one individual—as a wife or mother—the creator of the trust very well may consider authorizing—not directing—the trustee to use the trust property for the purchase of an annuity, if the trustee decides that that will be for the best interest of the beneficiary.

Purchase of Insurance on Life of Beneficiary or of Person in Whom Beneficiary Has Insurable Interest

Where the beneficiary of the insurance trust is a young person and, presumably, is insurable, it may be advisable for the creator of the trust to give the trustee power to purchase insurance on the life of the beneficiary and carry the policy contract as a trust investment. In some states a life insurance policy contract is an authorized trust investment; in other states it is not. The draftsman will, of course, be governed by the law of the jurisdiction.

Furthermore, in some cases it may be advisable to authorize the trustee to purchase, as a trust investment, insurance on the life of any person in whose life the beneficiary has an insurable interest. For example, *A*, the widow-and-mother, is life beneficiary of her husband's insurance trust; and after her death the property is to be held in trust for their son, *B*, until he shall attain a specified age and then delivered to him outright. It may be advisable for the trustee to purchase out of *A's* surplus income insurance on *A's* life payable to or for her son, *B*.

Both these points should be brought to the attention of the creator of the insurance trust while the trust agreement is being drafted.

Some of the foregoing features apply equally to personal insurance trusts and to business insurance trusts. This is true of the methods of making the insurance payable to the trustee, of the rights reserved by the insured, of the payment of the premiums, of the collection of the insurance, and of the protection of the insurance company. But there are other provisions that apply only to personal insurance trusts—for example, those about the exercise of option of settlement by a trustee and the purchase of annuities—and still others, which will be discussed next, that apply only to business insurance trusts.

Valuation of Business or Business Interest

A, *B*, and *C*, whether partners or stockholders, insure one another's life in order to provide funds for the purchase of a deceased partner's or stockholder's interest in the business. But what is the value of his interest in the business, or how is it to be arrived at? Any number of ways have been worked out. In some cases the value of each partner's or stockholder's interest is fixed arbitrarily at a specified amount; in others, it is fixed periodically by appraisement; in others, it is determined by the book value of the business at the end of the last calendar or fiscal year before the death; in still others, it is fixed by an appraisement of the assets within a specified time before or after the death of the partner or stockholder. Each type of business probably would have its own preferred method of arriving at the value of an interest. The only pertinent point is that the insurance trust agreement must set out some definite and workable method of arriving at the value of the deceased partner's or stockholder's interest.

Insurance on Life of Surviving Partners or Stockholders

Again, *A*, *B*, and *C*, partners or stockholders, insure one another's life and put the policies in trust. Then *A* dies and *B* and *C*, according to the terms of the trust, acquire *A's* interest in the business. But, if it is a partnership, with the death of *A* the partnership is terminated; a new partnership may be formed and the business continue as though there had been no break, but, just the same, it is a new partnership and not the old one. *A's* estate finds itself the owner of insurance on the life of *B* and *C*, and *B* and *C* each finds himself the owner of insurance on the life of the other. They no longer need the insurance in connection with the old partnership, although *B* and *C* may desire to create a new insurance trust in connection with the new partnership.

The insurance trust agreement should provide for the disposition of the insurance on the life of a surviving partner or stockholder. The provision may be to offer the policy to the insured for its cash value at the time of the death of the deceased partner. Should he not exercise such an option to take over the policy, then perhaps the purchaser of the insurance would take its cash value and let the policy lapse. The only point is that the trust agreement should contain a definite and workable provision about the disposition of the policies on the life of the surviving partners or stockholders.

TRUST AS A MODE OF SETTLEMENT

It will be helpful in putting the insurance trust into proper perspective with both trusteeship and life insurance if the trust is regarded simply as an additional mode of settlement of insurance proceeds.

The modes of settlement of insurance proceeds fall under three main heads—namely, lump-sum settlement, trust settlement, and optional settlement.

Lump Sum

The insured has the privilege of making his insurance payable in lump sum to some named beneficiary—his estate, his wife, his child, his business associate, or anyone else capable of owning property. In many cases the lump-sum settlement is the mode that will serve the best interest of the beneficiary and, if so, that is the mode which should be adopted.

Trust

The insured has the privilege also of having his insurance made payable to a trustee and setting forth in a trust agreement how and for what purposes he desires that the proceeds of the insurance shall be used. As already pointed out, whether he should put his insurance in trust depends, first, upon whether he can obtain the services of a competent trustee and, second, upon whether his beneficiaries need to be relieved of the burdens and responsibilities of the legal ownership and management of the property in which the proceeds would be invested or whether, in the case of a family, the insured concludes that the proceeds of his insurance should be held intact and administered for the benefit of his family as a unit.

Options of Settlement

Again, the insured has the privilege of leaving the proceeds of his insurance under one of the options of settlement offered by the insurance company. Although there are many variations in the details of these options, all of them fall into three main groups as follows:

1. *Interest options.* The insurance company retains the insurance proceeds and at regular intervals pays interest at not less than a specified rate until the principal is withdrawn or paid out in accordance with the terms of the policy contract.

2. *Installment options.* The insurance company retains the proceeds and pays them out in regular installments, principal and income combined, either (*a*) for a fixed period with the amount of each installment determined by the number of years or (*b*) with the amount of each installment fixed and the payments continued until the principal and interest are exhausted.

3. *Annuity options.* The insurance company retains the proceeds and pays installments at a guaranteed amount to a named beneficiary for the remainder of his life. In addition, the option may provide that, if the beneficiary dies before a stated number of payments have been made, payments will be continued after his death until the stated number of payments have been made.

There is no occasion for competition among the various modes of settlement. Under one state of facts one mode is preferable; under another state, another mode. That mode should be employed which, in the judgment of the insured upon the best advice obtainable, will be most likely to be for the best interest of his beneficiaries. Their welfare is the supreme consideration alike of the insured, of the insurance company, and, if there is a trust, of the trustee.

Once the life insurance policy has matured by lapse of time or by the death of the insured and the proceeds are in the hands of the trustee, the administration of the proceeds in trust is not different from that of other trust funds, as will be discussed in Chapters 16 and 17.

COLLATERAL READING

Note: For complete citations, see Bibliography, pp. 417–428.
COLLINS, *The ABC of Business Insurance Trusts.*
HORTON, *Some Legal Aspects of Life Insurance Trusts.*
————, *Life Insurance Trusts—A Handbook for the Draftsman.*
————, *Making the Best Use of Your Life Insurance.*
LLOYD, "CREF and TIAA—A Variable Annuity Plan in Action."
SHATTUCK and FARR, *An Estate Planner's Handbook,* III, 36.
SMITH, *Insurance Trusts.*
ZUBER, *Life Insurance Trusts.*

9

Employees Trusts

$\mathfrak{W}$ E COME NOW TO DISCUSSION of three types of trusts which are different from the three types we have discussed already. They are employees trusts, charitable trusts, and corporate trusts. One of the main differences is in the beneficiaries of these groups of trusts. In a trust under will, a living trust, or any insurance trust, the beneficiaries are few in number and are treated as individuals or as a small class of individuals (as the children of the same parents). In an employees trust, a charitable trust, or a corporate trust, on the contrary, the beneficiaries may, in one case, be tens of thousands of employees of the same employer; hundreds of charitable objects, institutions, or agencies, in another case; or tens of thousands of bondholders of the same corporation, in the third case. The differences in beneficiaries lead to vast differences in the terms of these types of trusts whether compared with one another or with the types of trusts already discussed.

In this part of our text only the dispositive aspects of these types of trusts will be included; discussion of the administrative aspects will be postponed until Chapter 19.

Definition of Employees Trust

An employees trust, as the name implies, is one created for employees of the same enterprise. The enterprise may be a business corporation, a group of related corporations, a charitable institution, or a unit of government. The creator of the trust may be the employer alone or the employer and employees. The employees may be salaried officers or wage earners. The trustee may be an individual, a board, or a bank or trust company. The trust property consists of contributions made by the employer alone or by the employer and employees. The making of these contributions is known as the *funding* of the trust.

Growth of Employees Trusts

Although employee-benefit plans, including employees trusts, are a comparatively recent development, the growth of them in recent years has been phenomenal.

The first industrial pension plan of which we have any record was created by the American Express Company in 1875. By 1929, over a half-century later, in the United States and Canada there were only four hundred private pension plans in operation.[1] Yet, by way of contrast, in December, 1958, it was reported that retirement plans alone were being established in the United States at the rate of about 25 a day, 600 a month, or 7,000 a year; that corporations already had set aside $35 billion for funding retirement plans for employees; and that 60 per cent of this amount was being administered by banks and trust companies as trustees.[2] Pension trusts alone constitute a large part of this business.

In both the volume of trust property and the number of beneficiaries, employees trusts constitute one of the main classifications of trusts. However, even with this phenomenal growth, of the 40 million salaried and wage-earning employees in the United States there still are 25 million who are not covered by any nongovernmental retirement plan.[3]

EMPLOYEE-BENEFIT PLANS

Since an employees trust is only one of many employee-benefit plans, many of them overlapping or supplementing one another, it is necessary to place and consider it in perspective with other plans.

Employee Benefits

The common characteristic of all employee-benefit plans is that they shall be for the benefit of employees. A recent statutory definition of an employees trust is:

Any fund established for employees of one or more employers for providing employees, their families or dependents medical or hospital care, disability benefits, death benefits, retirement benefits, annuity benefits, health care services which meets certain statutory requirements.[4]

Self-Administered Plans

Out of its current earnings or reserves an employer may have a definite plan under which one or more or all of the employee-benefits listed above

[1] Zaugg, "Recent Developments in the Pension Trust Field," 32 at 33.

[2] Bethel, "The Case for the Trustee in Funding Pension and Profit-Sharing Trusts," 23 at 23, 55.

[3] Swain, "Retirement Trusts—A Challenge to the Smaller Trust Departments," 40.

[4] Washington State, Laws, 1955, Ch. 8, Sec. 2.

are provided for. If the employer itself provides the funds and administers the plan, without calling to its aid a life insurance company or a trustee, it is a *self-administered* plan.

Insured Plans

If, under the terms of the plan, the employer itself or its trustee purchases insurance on the life of employees or annuity contracts for them, it is known as an *insured* plan.

Trusteed Plans

If, under the terms of a trust, the employer delivers cash or other property to a trustee to provide employee benefits, it is known as a *trusteed* plan. Under the terms of the trust, the trustee itself may hold and invest the funds received in trust and make payments to employees or their families or dependents, or it may, just as the employer itself, purchase insurance on the life of employees or annuity contracts for them. In the latter case it would be a combination of an insured plan and a trusteed plan and is an illustration of the overlapping mentioned above.

Contributory and Noncontributory Plans

If the employer and the employees contribute to the funding of the plan, it is known as a *contributory* plan; if the employees do not contribute, as a *noncontributory* plan. Employees' contributions usually are in the form of moneys withheld from salaries or wages.

Negotiated Plans

A plan worked out and agreed upon between an employer or employers of the same industry and employees who are members of the same labor union is known as a *negotiated* plan. It provides for employees' fringe benefits. It may or may not be a trusteed plan. Banks and trust companies are called in more often to serve as custodian than as trustee of the employee-benefit funds. Under these plans, when employees move from employer to employer in the same industry, they take with them the benefits under the plan, which has led to the term, *multiemployer* plan.

Qualified Plans

A plan which, under the current Internal Revenue Code, relieves the employer and the employee (if it is a contributory plan) of federal income taxes on the contributions is known as a *qualified* plan. The tax-saving feature makes most employers eager to "qualify" their plans. However, a case can be made out for nonqualified plans which do not enjoy these tax-savings.[5]

1. *Required of all qualified plans.* The following, presented in summary form only, are the requirements for qualification of all employee-benefit plans, whether or not trusteed:

a. The plan must be established by the employer for the exclusive benefit of its employees or their beneficiaries; it must not discriminate in favor of highly paid employees, executives, officers, or stockholders; it must be operated and administered in a nondiscriminatory fashion;

b. It must cover a sufficient, specified proportion of employees or their beneficiaries or a nondiscriminatory classification of employees;

c. The purpose of the plan must be to offer employees or their beneficiaries either (*a*) a share of the profits or (*b*) an income after retirement;

d. It must be established with the bona fide intention of its being a permanent plan, although it may be amended or even terminated; but, if it is terminated within a few years after establishment, that will be regarded as evidence that it never was intended to be permanent;

e. It must be in writing; if a trusteed plan, a trust instrument; if an insured plan, by insurance policies or annuity contracts; and

f. It must be communicated formally to the employees.

2. *Additional requirements of trusteed plans.* If it is a trusteed plan, that is, if it is an employees trust, to be qualified it must satisfy these four additional requirements:

a. Under the terms of the trust instrument it must be impossible for any of the trust principal or income at any time to be used for any purpose other than the exclusive benefit of the employees or their beneficiaries;

b. The contributions to the trust must be for the purpose of accumulating funds for distribution to employees or their beneficiaries according to a qualified plan;

c. The trust must be valid and existing under controlling local law; and

d. It must be created within the United States of America.

We shall confine our discussion to employees trusts as the one of the employee-benefit plans that is within the scope of this text.

Purposes Served by Employees Trusts

The over-all purposes served by employees trusts may be summarized as follows:

1. To provide for employees who become incapacitated before reaching the normal age for retirement;

2. To provide for them after they reach that age;

3. To enable them to share in the profits of the enterprise;

4. To enable them to become part-owners of the enterprise;

[5] Young, "Individual Deferred Compensation," p. 705.

5. To reward employees for especially meritorious service or for distinctive contributions to the welfare of the enterprise;

6. To encourage the application of economies of both personnel and materiel in carrying on the business of the enterprise and to stimulate creative activities;

7. To reduce turnover and attract new employees; and

8. To encourage habits of thrift and economy on the part of employees.

Kinds of Employees Trusts

For the accomplishment of these purposes, employees trusts are classified under these five heads: pension trusts, profit-sharing trusts, stock-acquisition trusts, thrift trusts, and unemployment-benefit trusts.

PENSION TRUSTS

Pension trusts are designed to provide funds for employees who have reached the age of retirement or have become incapacitated before reaching that age.

Kinds of Pension Trusts

Pension trusts have been classified under these three heads:

1. *Immediate purchase of annuity contract.* Under this plan, the employer (together with the employees under a salary- or wage-withholding plan) makes contributions directly to the trustee, and the trustee, in turn, immediately purchases an individual deferred annuity contract for each of the participating employees.

2. *Deferred purchase of annuity contract.* Under this plan, the employer (together with employees if it is contributory) makes contributions to the trustee and the trustee holds and invests the funds until the employee's retirement and then purchases an annuity for him to become operative forthwith.

In either of these cases the annuity may be for the employee alone or for a surviving beneficiary also, usually his wife. Furthermore, the annuity contracts may be either individual or group.

3. *Distribution by trustee.* Under the third plan, the employer (or employer-employees) makes the contributions, as in the other two plans, direct to the trustee, and the trustee itself, instead of using the funds to purchase annuity contracts, invests them and makes payments to the incapacitated or retired employee according to the terms of the trust. This well might be called the trustee-administered type of pension trust, except for the fact

that the purchase of the annuity contracts under the other two types is part of the administration of the trust.

Actuarial Calculations

No matter which of the three plans is adopted, there must be actuarial calculations and, if need be, recalculations to determine the amount of contributions necessary to provide funds for the purchase of annuity contracts or for direct payments by the trustee to the beneficiaries or their dependents according to the terms of the trust. The actuary may be one in the employment of the employer or of the trustee or he may be a professional, outside actuary. The success of the trust depends in no small measure upon the accuracy of the actuarial calculations.[6]

Advantages of Trusteed Plans

There should be no competition among the different kinds of pension plans. In some cases the employer itself should make its own payments out of its current earnings or out of its reserves to or for its incapacitated or retired employees.

In other cases the employer should deal directly and exclusively with the life insurance company without the intervention of a trustee, and, out of its profits or reserves, purchase the type of annuity contract best suited to the needs of the given beneficiary.

In still other cases the employer should create a pension trust and, in so doing, should select the type of pension trust best suited to the needs of its beneficiaries.

The plan selected should be the one that is regarded by specialists in the pension-trust field as being the one best suited to the needs of the employer and the employees alike. The selection of the plan is, definitely, the work of the specialist in that field.

Among the advantages of the trusteed plan over other plans in a given case the following have been suggested:

1. *Flexibility*. Within certain reasonable limitations to prevent discrimination and tax avoidance, a trusteed plan can be made so flexible and so amendable as to meet future, now unpredictable, needs of the employer and its employees alike. Since the employer's enterprise is or should be dynamic and the employees' needs are, unavoidably, variable, the elements of flexibility and amendability of the plan would in many cases be determined in the selection of the plan.

2. *Integration of Social Security benefits*. The trusteed plan can be integrated with Social Security benefits so that increase in the latter will reduce the payments made by the trustee out of the trust funds in its hands.

[6] Luick, "The Actuary's Functions in Trusteed Pension Plans," Seal, "Pension Trusts—Some Current Aspects."

Since increase in the Social Security benefits may involve increase in taxes payable by the employer, this integration may aid the employer without doing disservice to the employees.

3. *Full amount of trust income applicable to benefits*. The full amount of income earned by the trustee on investment of the employer's contributions is applied to payments to the employees. This tax-free income, compounded through reinvestment, will pay a very substantial part of the benefits to employees.

4. *Higher income-yield*. The income-yield under a trusteed plan is likely to be somewhat greater than that under a nontrusteed plan. Even if it were only one-half of one per cent greater, it might result in a saving to the employer of ten per cent of the cost of the plan.

5. *Absence of extra charges*. It is pointed out by those who favor a trusteed plan that it avoids extra charges, such as loading charges, severance charges, lapse charges, or state taxes on premiums. The only inescapable charges are the attorney's fee for drawing the documents and setting up the plan and the trustee's compensation for administering the plan.

6. *Availability of early-retirement benefits*. Under a trusteed plan early retirement or disability of an employee may be provided for. If the payments to these employees are actuarily equivalent to the service credits accrued to the time of the early retirement or disability, the additional cost to the employer will be negligible.

7. *Variable contributions to plan*. Again, within certain limits, the employer can let its annual contributions to the plan fluctuate or it may even omit payments in a given year without disqualifying the plan. This enables the employer, in a measure, to adjust its contributions to current economic conditions.

Regarding the limits, on the minimum side the trustee must, as a matter of course, at all times have funds adequate to meet the employer's commitment to employees. Although one of the stated requirements of qualification of the plan taxwise is that it must be intended as a permanent plan, nonetheless, business conditions may justify a suspension of all or of a portion of the normal contributions for one or more years, which may be done without disqualifying the plan. On the maximum side, the most income-tax free contribution that can be made during any given year is one year's current-service cost plus one-tenth of the past-service cost. Furthermore, within the minimum and maximum, the employer can make above-normal contributions any given year without incurring income-tax liability on its contributions for that year.

8. *Reversion of overcontribution to fund*. If the amounts contributed to the fund by the employer should prove to be more than the amounts required for payments to employees or their survivors, the surplus may accrue to the benefit of the employer, through reduction of subsequent employer contributions.

The foregoing statement of the advantages of trusteed over nontrusteed plans is presented here with such brevity and without illustration that the student may not grasp the full import of some of the points. Therefore, he is referred to several recent discussions at more length and with illustrations of these and other advantages claimed for trusteed plans.[7] In each of these articles by a specialist in the field of trusteed plans the author is presenting the case for trusteed plans and, incidentally, some of the disadvantages of some other plans without attempting to balance the advantages and disadvantages of the various plans.

PROFIT-SHARING TRUSTS

Although it is, clearly and commendably, the growing practice of employers to have their employees share in the profits of the enterprise, not all, perhaps not even a majority, of the profit-sharing plans are trusts. At the end of the calendar or the fiscal year, after the employer's profits or losses for the year have been determined, the employer, then and there, may pay to the employees a percentage of that year's profits. It may vary the payments according to its estimates of the merits of the individual employee. This, of course, does not involve a trust; it is only direct dealing between employer and employees.

Purposes of Profit-Sharing Plans

The purposes of profit-sharing plans, whether or not they are trusteed, may be summarized as follows:

1. To induce employees, realizing that they will be sharers in the profits of the enterprise, to reduce waste of both time and material;

2. To increase productivity; and

3. To make employees feel (and to *feel* is fully as important as to know) that they have a proprietary interest in the enterprise.

A predetermined profit-sharing plan, whatever it is, appeals especially to younger employees in that they feel that they will participate in current profits and will not be merely ultimate, perhaps long-postponed beneficiaries of some far-off retirement plan.

Characteristics of Profit-Sharing Trusts

Two of the characteristics of profit-sharing plans, including trusts, are that the employee-benefits are based on profits and that special provision must be made for older employees.

1. *Based on profits.* The main difference between a pension trust, on

[7] Bethel, "The Case for the Trustee in Funding Pension and Profit-Sharing Trusts," 23; Howes, "Employee Benefit Plans," 717; Thorp, "The ABC's of Pension and Profit-Sharing Plans," 16; Warner, "Superiority of Trusteed over Insured Pension Plans," 28.

the one hand, and a profit-sharing trust, on the other, is that, in the former, the employer sets aside and adds to the trust a predetermined amount, whereas, in the latter, the employer's contribution to the trust is determined by the current profits of the enterprise. In the pension trust, calculability and dependability of payments at retirement are main attractions to employees. In profit-sharing trusts the possibility, in an expanding economy, of larger payments from year to year and the satisfaction of having had a part in the increased payments are attractive items to consider.

Pension trusts and profit-sharing trusts are not mutually exclusive employee-benefit plans. It is not unusual for an employer to have both kinds of trusts. The pension trust with its calculable and dependable payments may be regarded as the employee's main source of support during his years of retirement, while the profit-sharing trust, with its variable and incalculable payments, may be looked to for more of the comforts and even some of the luxuries of those years of retirement.

2. *Provision for older employees.* The older employees offer a special problem in the establishment and administration of profit-sharing trusts. Suppose the age for retirement is sixty-five, and that at the time the trust is established there are employees in their late fifties or early sixties, at best they will have only a few years to participate in the profits of the enterprise. For these a profit-sharing trust cannot be a substitute for a pension trust.

Realizing this disadvantage of the profit-sharing trusts employers have introduced the technique of "weighting," whereunder the older, late-coming employees receive payments more nearly, if not absolutely, in line with those of younger employees with longer prospective terms of service.

STOCK-ACQUISITION TRUSTS

Many of the larger industrial corporations are establishing plans whereby their employees become stockholders and, for the accomplishment of this objective, are establishing trusts. The common name for them is stock-bonus trusts, but that term is not quite inclusive enough because it does not include stock acquired by purchase as well as that given as a reward for service—a *bonus*. Hence, the broader term, *stock-acquisition* trusts.

Stock-Bonus Trusts

The employer corporation may set aside and turn over to a trustee shares of its stock to be delivered by the trustee to certain of its employees as rewards for especially meritorious service to the corporation and its customers.

One of these corporations, for example, has three stock-bonus plans. One, known as *Plan A*, is for "conspicuous service of any nature, regardless of the company's earnings." This bonus is paid partly in cash and partly in company stock. The part-cash payment instead of all-stock feature is designed to enable the employee to meet his cash requirements for income-tax purposes without having to sell any of his stock. Under *Plan B*, awards are granted "to employees who have contributed most in a general way to the company's success by their ability, efficiency, and loyalty." The maximum amount available for these awards depends upon the company's earnings. These awards also are made partly in cash and partly in stock and are delivered directly to the employees and not through a trust. Under *Plan C*, awards may be made to "employees who concurrently are, or otherwise would be, recommended for *B* bonus." The awards under *Plan C*, which are substitutes for a part of the awards under *Plan B*, are granted in the form of "dividend units" which may be accompanied by an option to purchase the company's common stock.

While the student would need much more than the above outline to understand fully these three stock-bonus plans in all their details, the outline alone does show the care with which corporate employers are endeavoring to bring their employees into merited stock-ownership of the company.

Stock-Purchase Trusts

Some corporations create stock-purchase trusts for the benefit of their employees. They place shares of their own stock in trust to be purchased by and delivered to their employees under the terms of a trust instrument. In some cases they issue for their employees a special class of stock from that offered the public. In other cases, they provide for their employees an opportunity to purchase the stock of the company at a discount. In still other cases, they, themselves, contribute to the purchase-price of the stock for their employees.

While the terms of stock-purchase trusts vary widely, the objective of all of them is the same; namely, to encourage and help their employees to become part-owners of the enterprise.

The main difference between a profit-sharing trust and a stock-acquisition trust is that, in the former, the stock of the company may or may not constitute all or even part of the trust property; whereas, in the latter, the stock of the company does constitute all of the trust property.

THRIFT TRUSTS

Another type of employees trust which seems to be growing in favor with both employers and employees is one we will call *thrift trusts*. We state it this way because this kind of employees trust goes by other names, such as *savings-and-investment* trust. Although there are many variations in the plans of this kind of trust, they all have the common objective of encouraging and helping employees to be thrifty. They are not substitutes for any of the other types of employees trusts.

Payroll Deductions

The employee's contribution to the plan is in the form of payroll deductions. These deductions range in amount between 2 per cent and 10 per cent of the employee's salary or wages.

Employer's Contribution

The employer's contribution to the trust ranges between 25 per cent and 100 per cent of the employee's payroll deduction. Under the terms of the trust, this percentage may be based upon the net earnings of the employer.

Trustee's Function

The employees' payroll deductions and the employer's contributions are delivered to the trustee and by it invested under the terms of the trust. In many cases the employees' deductions are invested in Government bonds and the employer's contributions, in common stock. In some cases it is the other way around: employees' deductions in common stock, employer's contributions in government bonds.

Vesting of Employee's Interest

1. *Payroll deductions.* Upon the employee's retirement or severance his own contributions to the trust through payroll deductions are delivered to him or to his designated beneficiary. They are his property at all times.

2. *Employer's contributions.* His share of the employer's contribution depends, as a rule, upon the length of his term of service. A not uncommon arrangement is for 20 per cent of the employer's contribution to vest in the employee after five years of service and an additional 20 per cent each year thereafter until the ninth year of service, at which time all employer contributions and earnings become vested.

Distribution

There are two types of distribution to employees: short-term and long-term.

1. *Short-term.* Under the short-term plan, the employee can withdraw his own salary or wage deductions and all, or a specified portion, of the employer's contributions after three or five years. Under some plans the employee does not receive all of his share of the employer's contribution

unless the fund remains intact the specified length of time. This allows employees to withdraw their savings at the stipulated intervals.

2. *Long-term.* Under the long-term plan, the distribution is not made to the employee until his retirement, severance, or to his beneficiary at his death. In case of his death before severance or retirement, his share goes to his designated beneficiary.

UNEMPLOYMENT-BENEFIT TRUSTS

This is a comparatively new kind of employees trust and frequently is known as a supplemental unemployment-benefit trust. It is designed, not to take the place of, but, as the name implies, to supplement the governmental unemployment-compensation benefits.

Under one of these plans, which perhaps may be taken as typical or, at least, illustrative, the employer contributes five cents per hour for each participating employee for each hour of the employee's employment. Upon qualification of the plan the employer is required to create a trust with a bank or trust company and to deposit the contributions with the trustee. Under this particular plan the minimum supplemental weekly benefit is $2, the maximum $25.

Under this type of trust the administrative duties of the trustee are quite exacting, but they are beyond the scope of this part of the text and will be discussed in Chapter 19.[8]

Anyone who analyzes and studies the thousands of employee-benefit plans, including employees trusts, will be impressed by the extent to which present-day industrial corporations, each with its hundreds or thousands of employees, are taxing the ingenuity of their policy-makers and planners in devising plans that will be for the benefit of their employees and, in connection with negotiated plans, how highly organized labor appraises the fringe benefits resulting from these plans. These plans are a demonstration of industrial democracy in action, and the trustee seems to be an increasingly important party to the development.

COLLATERAL READING

Note: For complete citations, see Bibliography, pp. 417–428.

ACKERMAN, "Financing Pension Benefits."

BETHEL, "The Case for the Trustee in Funding Pension and Profit-Sharing Trusts."

GORDON, *Profit-Sharing in Business and Estate Planning.*

HARVEY, "Supplemental Unemployment Benefit Plans."

HEALY, "Corporate Services—Multiemployer—Employee Benefit Plans."

HINES, "The Changing Role of Insurance Companies in the Pension Field,"

[8] Harvey, "Supplemental Unemployment Benefit Plans," 57.

McGILL, *Fundamentals of Private Pensions.*

SWAIM, "Recent Developments in Employee Benefit Funds."

———, "Retirement Trusts—A Challenge to the Smaller Trust Departments."

TORP, "The ABC's of Pension and Profit-Sharing Plans."

WARNER, "Superiority of Trusteed over Insured Pension Plans."

ZAUGG, "Recent Developments in the Pension Trust Field."

"Pension and Profit-Sharing Digest," a monthly feature of *Trusts and Estates.*

"Report of Committee on Pension and Profit-Sharing Trusts of Probate and Trust Law Division," American Bar Association, appearing annually in *Trusts and Estates,* as well as in *Proceedings of the Division.*

Because employees trusts are such a recent and rapidly growing development in the field of trusts, the student is given an unusually wide selection of collateral reading so that he can find material on that phase of the subject in which he may be especially interested.

10

Charitable Trusts

WE COME NOW TO THE DISCUSSION of a large group of many and varied types of trusts which, because of certain basic characteristics in common, are known as *charitable trusts*.

Definition of a Charitable Trust

A *charitable trust* is one created for the benefit of a legal charity.

A *legal charity* is "an agency, institution, or organization in existence and operation for the benefit of an indefinite number of persons and conducted for educational, religious, scientific, medical, or other beneficent purposes." [1]

A term more common than *legal charity*, which will be employed in this chapter, is *charitable object*.

CHARACTERISTICS OF A CHARITABLE TRUST

The characteristics of a charitable trust are: (1) it must be for the benefit of an indefinite number of persons, as distinct from specified individuals; (2) it must be for a charitable object within the legal meaning of that term; (3) it may be for an unlimited duration; and (4) it has tax advantages over other kinds of trusts.

Indefinite Number of Persons

A trust under will, a living trust, or an insurance trust is for the benefit of one person, such as a wife, parent, son, daughter, friend, or for a small number of persons, such as the sons and daughters or brothers and sisters of the same family. A charitable trust, on the contrary, must be for an indefinite number of persons who fall into certain categories, such as

[1] American Bankers Association, *Glossary of Fiduciary Terms*, 1959.

students, patients, or persons in need, of a large enough group for the community to be interested in the enforcement of the trust.

Charitable Object

A charitable trust must be administered for educational, religious, scientific, or medical purposes, for the relief of poverty, or for other beneficent purposes. The term, *beneficent purposes,* is not as all-embracive, however, as it sounds.

One definition or description of a charitable object is in the Internal Revenue Code of 1954 [2] which is as follows:

1. The United States, any State, Territory, or any political subdivision thereof, of the District of Columbia, for exclusively public purposes;

2. A corporation, or trust, or community chest, fund, or foundation, organized and operated exclusively for religious, charitable, scientific, literary, or educational purposes, including the encouragement of art and the prevention of cruelty to children or animals, no part of the net earnings of which inures to the benefit of any private shareholder or individual, and no substantial part of the activities of which is carrying on propaganda, or otherwise attempting to influence legislation;

3. A fraternal society, order, or association, operating under the lodge system, but only if such gifts are to be used exclusively for religious, charitable, scientific, literary, or educational purposes, including the encouragement of art and the prevention of cruelty to children or animals;

4. Posts or organizations of war veterans, or auxiliary units or societies of such posts or organizations, if such posts, organizations, units, or societies are organized in the United States or any of its possessions, and if no part of their net earnings inures to the benefit of any private shareholder or individual.

A charitable object, then, is a nonprofit corporation, association, trust, or fraternal order devoted exclusively to religious, charitable, scientific, literary, or educational purposes, or the encouragement of art or the prevention of cruelty to children or animals and is not engaged substantially in carrying on propaganda or otherwise attempting to influence legislation.

Unlimited Duration

Whereas a trust for individual, specified beneficiaries has limited duration, a charitable trust may have unlimited duration. The common-law rule against perpetuities or against remoteness of vesting, as we have seen, is that property must vest within a life in being at the time of creation of the estate or interest, and twenty-one years, and the period of pregnancy thereafter (should it be necessary to invoke the additional period). Once the estate or interest has vested, the trust itself may continue awhile longer—say, during the remaining period of minority or incompetency of the beneficiary.

[2] Sec. 2522 (a).

No such time limit applies to a charitable trust. As the law now stands and has stood for generations, the trust may continue as long as the beneficiaries are and remain charitable objects under the then prevailing law. It is not essential, however, that it continue indefinitely.

Tax Advantages

Within prescribed limits a property owner who makes gifts to charitable objects is relieved of both federal and state taxes and the objects themselves are relieved of taxes. For example, under present tax laws he can give, free of federal income taxes, 30 per cent of his adjusted gross income to religious, educational, hospital, or medical-research objects and 20 per cent to other charitable objects. If he makes gifts to charitable objects during his lifetime, he is relieved of federal and state gift taxes; so is the object. If he makes such gifts by will, his estate will be free of federal and state estate taxes and state inheritance taxes. If he creates an irrevocable living trust for one of the enumerated charitable objects to run not less than two years, he will be relieved of federal income taxes on that income.

KINDS OF GIFTS TO CHARITABLE OBJECTS

Not all gifts to charitable objects, by any means, are gifts in trust. A property owner can make a direct, immediate, outright gift to a charitable object of any kind of property. He can make his gift during his lifetime or under his will. He can make it a vested, future, or contingent gift. He can give a sum of money or an item of property, real or personal, or a fraction or percentage of his estate. He can give the proceeds of life insurance.

The three kinds of gifts that call for some further comment are direct gifts, gifts *to* the charitable object in trust, and gifts in trust *for* the charitable object.

Direct Gifts

While the following comments apply to direct gifts, they apply no less to gifts in trust for charitable objects. One relates to the limitations upon such gifts; the other, to the legal name of the charitable object.

1. *Limitations upon gifts.* In some states there is a statutory limit upon the part of his estate that a family man can give or leave to a charitable object. The New York statute, for example, provides:

No person having a husband, wife, child, or descendant or parent, shall by his or her last will and testament devise or bequeath to any benevolent, charitable, literary, scientific, religious or missionary society, association, corporation or purpose, in trust or otherwise, more than one-half part of his or her estate, after the payment of his or her debts, and such devise or bequest shall be valid to the extent of one-half and no more.[3]

Another limitation in some states is that the gift, to be effective, must have been made a stated time—one month, three months, six months, a year—before the death of the testator.

In *Wills, Estates and Trusts*, Sec. 1020, the student will find the limitations, if any, upon gifts to charitable objects in individual states.

2. *Legal name of charitable object.* One of the problems of making an effective gift, particularly a gift by will or a future or contingent gift, is that of making sure that the object receiving the gift is designated by its legal name. An object—a school, for example—may be called by a name quite different from its legal name. Any substantial difference between the name used and the legal name may lead to the contest of a will or to other litigation.

In some, but not all states, in case of such a difference, the court will apply the cy pres doctrine. By this doctrine, where a person makes a gift to or for a charitable object that cannot be carried out to the letter, and in so doing manifests a general intention to devote the property to a charitable purpose, the court will direct that the gift be made as nearly as possible, in its judgment, in conformity with the intention of the giver.

Again, in *Wills, Estates, and Trusts*, Sections 9013–9020, the student will find a discussion of the cy pres doctrine with state-by-state citation of cases.

Some draftsmen of wills and trust agreements, in an effort to cure the defect in the naming of the object, incorporate in the instrument a provision to this effect:

In the event that I have not designated by its correct name any of the charitable objects named as beneficiaries above or if any of said objects is not incorporated, the executor or trustee, as the case may be, is authorized to make distributions of any of the gifts hereinbefore made to the governing body of the object which in the executor's or trustee's judgment I have intended to designate as the beneficiary of such gift, and the receipt of the officers of such object shall be complete discharge of the executor or the trustee for such distribution.

Such a provision is intended to shift the responsibility for applying the cy pres doctrine from the court to the fiduciary, and by so doing may prevent contests of wills and other litigation over gifts to charitable objects. Even then, if the executor or trustee should fail or refuse to make the selection, the court still might apply the cy pres doctrine.

Gifts to Object in Trust

A property owner can make his gift direct to a charitable object and earmark it for some specified purpose. In such case the charitable object

[3] Decedents Estate Law, Sec. 17, as amended, Laws 1936, Ch. 288; *Wills, Estates, and Trusts*, Sec. 1020.

itself becomes the trustee and the specified object the beneficiary of the trust. This point will be developed in the discussion on institutional trusts.

Gifts in Trust for Object

The property owner also can make his gift to an outside trustee for a named charitable object and either state or leave unstated the purpose or purposes for which he wishes his gift used.

If he does not state the purpose, the trustee will hold and invest the property and pay over the income to the governing board of the object to be used by it for the purposes of that object as its own judgment dictates.

If he states the purpose for which he wishes his gift used, both the trustee and the governing board of the object are under a legal, as well as moral, duty to see that the income or the principal or both, according to the terms of the trust, are used for, and only for, the purpose or purposes specified.

Of the different kinds of gifts to or for charitable objects, gifts in trust only will be the subject matter of this chapter. These may be divided into individual trusts and foundations.

INDIVIDUAL TRUSTS

Let us assume that the property owner and his lawyer know the legal name of the charitable object or objects to receive gifts in trust; that they have selected the property to be given and decided when the gift is to become effective. One of the points to be decided is whether the gift shall be direct or in trust.

Advantages of a Trust

Two advantages of a trust present themselves. One is the unified administration of the estate; the other, the business and financial management of the property.

1. *Unified administration of estate.* Some property owners prefer that the same trustee that administers the family trust also administer the charitable trust. They say that they prefer to keep all their affairs under one roof.

2. *Business and financial management.* If the charitable object is young or not yet well established, or if there is any doubt in the mind of the property owner as to the experience or efficiency of the governing board of the charitable object in the investment and management of property, he may prefer to channel his gift to the object through a responsible outside trustee. This may not be due to lack of confidence in the object nor in the ability of the governing board and the administration to carry out the

purposes of the object but only to doubt as to the aptitude or experience of the board or of the administration in business and financial affairs.

As a consequence of this misgiving many property owners create an individual charitable trust and leave the property in trust with the same trustee that is to administer the family or other private trusts.

FOUNDATIONS

The general term, *foundations*, is employed to include the great number and variety of larger charitable trusts, the size and nature of which require more organization than individual charitable trusts ordinarily do.

Most of these organized trusts now are known as foundations and, in deference to the prevailing terminology, that is what they will be called in this chapter. But they are actually charitable trusts.

The principal foundations may be classified as follows: individual, family, professional, religious, civic club, institutional, special-object, corporation, and community.

Individual

There are no basic differences between an individual foundation and an individual trust, as already discussed, for a charitable object, except one of size and administrative requirements on account of the size and variety of objects served.

Persons of large wealth create their own individual foundations. Under this head we think of the Carnegie, the Rockefeller, the Russell Sage, and the Kress foundations, and so on. There are now thousands of such foundations. Most urban communities have one or more of them.

The huge sums or amount of property involved call for two staffs—one to administer the property; the other, to select the purposes and make the distributions. The trustee of such a foundation is likely to be a board of trustees, rather than a single trustee, with appropriate provision for keeping the board intact as time goes on.

Family

Family foundations are a comparatively new kind of charitable trust. They seem to be growing in favor among individuals who for one reason or another prefer to make it a family rather than an individual foundation.

For example, one member of a family or several members of the same family create a foundation. They give it the name of the family, or they give it the name of the father, or mother, or both. Usually they make it a memorial to their parent or parents or to their spouse or some member of the family.

The charitable objects may be specified or they may include all legal charities. If the person to be memorialized was interested or active in some particular charitable object—religion, education, hospital, or medical-research—the objects of the foundation may be limited to the one or the few in which he was especially interested.

Professional

Professional foundations also are growing in favor. Members of the same profession, usually initiated by their professional organization—such as a medical society or bar association—create such a foundation.

There are medical foundations to promote progress in the medical profession; legal foundations to do the same for the legal profession; architectural foundations; and so on, in all of the leading professions.

The purposes of these foundations are as broad as the needs of the professions, provided that these needs come within the legal limits of a charitable object. Foundation funds—income, principal, or both, according to the terms of the trust—may be used for scholarships, for loans, for research, or for any other purpose of the profession involved.

Religious

Similarly the members of a given religious denomination, order, or even those of an individual church or synagogue or other religious body may create a foundation for the promotion of the interests and activities of that organization, association, or body. There are Baptist, Methodist, and Presbyterian foundations, and so on through the long list of the most numerous and active religious bodies. These foundations receive support from friends as well as from communicants of these denominations.

Civic Club

In this country the civic-club movement started in 1904 with the organization of the Rotary Club of Chicago. At the present time there are over 10,000 Rotary clubs with a membership of about 500,000 in every civilized country of the world. Rotary was followed by Kiwanis, Lions, Exchange, Optimist, and a long list of other civic clubs. These clubs are creating foundations to receive, administer, and distribute gifts of their members and friends for international (such as scholarships for students from other countries) as well as national and local activities.

Institutional

The friends and promoters of a given charitable institution may establish a foundation to receive, administer, and distribute gifts for that institution. For example, there is the University of Nebraska Foundation for the benefit of that institution.

At this point we must revert to the distinction between gifts *to* such an institution in trust, and gifts in trust *for* that institution. For an illustration of the institution we may use a college.

1. *General endowment.* A college, let us say, is trying to build up its general endowment. In so doing it encourages its alumni and friends either to make gifts *to* it earmarked for its general endowment, or to an outside trustee *for* its general endowment. If the gift is to the college for its general endowment, the college itself becomes trustee. If the gift is to an outside trustee for the general endowment of the college, the trustee receives, invests, and manages the property, and pays over the income to the governing board of the college. Whether the gift is to the college in trust for general endowment or to an outside trustee in trust for the general endowment of the college, the income, paid over to the governing board of the college, may be used for any college purpose as determined by the governing board.

2. *Special endowment.* Or the alumni and friends of a college may make their gifts to the college or to an outside trustee earmarked for specified college purpose, such as scholarships, loans funds, laboratory or library equipment, chairs of instruction. In such case, if the gift is to the college for the specified purpose, the college is under a legal as well as moral duty to use the income—not the principal, unless so specified by the terms of the trust—for the named purpose. If the gift is to an outside trustee for a specified college purpose, the trustee cannot deliver the income or the principal to the college and ignore what the college does with it. If the trustee has reason to believe that the college is not using the income or principal received for the specified purpose, it is under a moral obligation, and in some cases a legal one as well, to see that the college does not commit a breach of duty.

The appeal of general-endowment trusts it that the needs of charitable institutions change from time to time and the governing board should be free to use endowment income to meet current needs.

The appeal of special-endowment trusts it that some potential donors are interested in a special object and others in another object. Thus, by catering to the preferences of donors, it is thought, more gifts in the aggregate will be received.

Special-Object

There are numerous special-object foundations, for example: textile, engineering, dairy, agricultural, business, architectural, pharmaceutical research, medical, dental, journalist, home economics, forestry, and educational to mention the names of only a few of the foundations created to promote specified activities of a single state university. Among the better known national special-object foundations are: Nutrition Foundation, Sugar Research Foundation, American Foundation for Pharmaceutical Education, and National Vitamin Foundation. At the University of Pennsylvania there is the S. S. Huebner Foundation for Insurance Education. There are foundations to fight cancer, tuberculosis, heart disease, polio, and most of the other prevalent crippling or invaliding diseases. There is even a National Park Trust Fund held and invested by the United States Treasury Department for our national park system.[4]

The number of these foundations and of the special objects served by them is great, and they are increasing in number and in volume of assets at a phenomenal rate.

Corporation

Industrial corporations are creating their foundations. Since 1935 such a corporation has been permitted to deduct from its taxable income 5 per cent thereof for charitable objects; but instead of making distributions direct to these objects itself the corporation creates its foundation, makes its gifts to it, and the foundation has a special staff to make investigations and distributions.

The advantages of this device for distributing a corporation's gift to charitable objects have been summarized as follows by Ralph Hayes, Executive Director, New York Community Trust:

Company contributions and their custody and investment receive centralized and responsible handling and accounting. The foundation office provides a convenient instrument for the selection of future donees or the review of prior grants. The level of the "foundation reservoir" can be raised in good years, allowed to fall in others. The tax-free status of gifts continues to apply to their proceeds if they become investments of the foundation. The precise purpose of outpayments can be decided subsequently to the time when gifts are made to the foundation. Some corporations, obliged to refuse many more applications than they can approve, feel that a foundation's declination can be made to seem less lethal than rejections sent direct from the company.[5]

Other corporations, instead of creating their own foundation, channel their gifts to charitable objects through a community foundation which now is to be described at more length because, in a way, it has set the pattern for most of the other foundations.

COMMUNITY FOUNDATIONS

The original name of this type of charitable trust was community trust; however, now such trusts are known generally as *foundations*.

[4] Wirth, "Trusts for Public and Civic Uses," 748.
[5] Corporate "Charitable Giving—Community Trusts as Solution of Dilemma," 492 at 493.

Origin

The father of the idea for the community trust, or community foundation, was Frederick H. Goff of Cleveland, Ohio. Both as a lawyer and as
president of a trust company he had been impressed by the number of gifts
to charitable objects that failed because of the inaccuracy of the designation
of the object or the failure of the object itself. He set himself to the task
of working out a practicable device that would prevent the failure of such
gifts and at the same time would encourage gifts to charitable objects. In
1914, this resulted in the organization of the Cleveland Foundation by the
Cleveland Trust Company of which Mr. Goff was president.

Although each of these community foundations has one or more distinctive features and differs as to details, they all have certain features in
common which class them as community trusts.

Community

The term *community* applied to community foundations is employed
in a very broad sense. The community may be a city, a county, a region,
or an entire state. There are the New York Community Trust for New York
City; the Roanoke-Chowan Foundation for four counties between or
adjoining the Roanoke and Chowan Rivers in North Carolina; the Delaware
Foundation for the entire State of Delaware. The boundaries for community
foundations are common interests and needs, not geographical lines.

Contributors

One of the characteristics of the community foundation is that anyone
so minded can contribute any amount of money or any kind of property
to the foundation. It makes a special appeal to people of modest or even
limited means who wish to leave something to their community either
generally or for some specified object and yet do not feel that their gift
will be enough to justify the setting up of a separate trust for their gift.
This appeal to all the people of the community makes it, indeed, a *community* trust.

Instrument of Creation

The instrument of creation may be either the charter of a corporation
or a declaration of trust.

1. *Charter.* Comparatively few of the community foundations are
corporations. As a corporation it can receive gifts in its corporate name and
have the property administered by a board or by an outside trustee.

2. *Declaration of trust.* Most of the community foundations are unincorporated. The first step is the making of a declaration of trust by the

board of directors of a bank or trust company that it will receive and administer gifts for the foundation. The declaration sets forth the terms of the trust.

Trustee

One bank or trust company may be the only trustee, or most or all of the active trust institutions of the community may be trustees (separate trustees, not cotrustees).

1. *Single*. In the early years of the community foundation, while it still was in the experimental stage, the trustee was a single bank or trust company. In time it was learned by experience that single trusteeships did not work out to anyone's advantage if there were other active trust institutions in the community. A foundation created by one bank or trust company was regarded as an exclusive, competitive device of that institution. Customers of other banks or trust companies hesitated to make gifts to this device of a rival institution. Other banks and trust companies hesitated to promote or even to encourage gifts to be administered by their competitor. The community itself hesitated to advertise or otherwise promote the foundation lest it be favoring a particular institution at the expense of the others.

2. *Multiple*. Sensing these disadvantages of single trusteeship, banks and trust companies that had begun as a single trustee began to invite other banks and trust companies to join with them in developing their community foundation. In other communities, multiple trusteeship was adopted in the beginning. Each of the participating trustees adopted identical declarations of trust except for dates and names. Then each donor channeled his gift to his community through the trustee of his choice. Thereupon all the trustees felt free to participate in co-operative advertising. The foundation itself felt free to advertise. The foundation became, in fact, a *community* enterprise.

Purposes

Illustrative but not exclusive of the purposes served by community foundations are the following, taken from the charter of a recently incorporated foundation:

1. For the care and assistance of the sick, aged, needy, and disabled;
2. For the assistance and guidance of youth;
3. For providing scholarships or otherwise assisting in the education of deserving young persons;
4. For the promotion of public recreation and character-building;
5. For the improvement of physical, moral, social, and domestic conditions;
6. For the promotion of sanitation and physical hygiene;

7. For the improvement of living and working conditions;

8. For promoting scientific research for the advancement of human knowledge and the alleviation of human suffering;

9. For research into the causes of ignorance, poverty, crime, and vice, for preventing the operation of such causes, and for remedying or ameliorating the conditions resulting therefrom; and

10. For assisting individuals, associations, corporations, and institutions engaged in any of the above purposes.

Types of Gifts

The two types of gifts to community foundations are undesignated and designated.

1. *Undesignated.* If the gift is to the trustee for the foundation without any designation of the purpose for which it is to be used, the distribution committee of the foundation will use the property, principal or income, for any authorized purpose that its own judgment dictates. Notice, the gift is not *to* the foundation, for an unincorporated foundation is not a legal entity, but to the trustee *for* the foundation.

2. *Designated.* If the person who makes the gift specifies the purpose for which his gift is to be used and states whether principal as well as income is to be used, the distribution committee must follow the terms of the gift so long as it is practicable to do so. But should it be or become "unnecessary, undesirable, impracticable, or impossible"—to quote one declaration of trust—to carry out the designated purpose, the distribution committee, in the exercise of its own judgment, will be free to use the property remaining in the trust for other purposes within the stated objects of the foundation. This is the attendant condition upon which one makes a designated gift to the foundation. This is the feature that makes it impossible for a gift to a community foundation to fail either because of the impossibility of carrying out the terms of the gift or the failure of the designated object.

Since the trustee of a designated gift must keep the property separate from that of other gifts, undesignated or designated, the designated gift lends itself to use as a memorial as it can be given the name of the person or of the family to be memorialized.

Distribution Committee

The repeated reference to the distribution committee brings us to a discussion of the committee itself which is really the keystone of the community-foundation arch.

1. *Composition.* So far as is humanly possible, the distribution committee is composed of only top-level men and women of the community—persons who, it is thought, will be judicious, farsighted, and impartial in

the exercise of their broad dispositive powers. The method of selection of the members is indicative of the regard in which they are held. The following is, perhaps, a typical method of selection: one member, appointed by the mayor of the city; another, by the resident state judge; a third, by the judge of the federal district court of the district in which the community is located; and one, by the trustee or, if there are several trustees, two or more members. Care is taken that the trustee-appointed members always constitute a minority of the committee. The terms of the members are staggered so that one or more leave the committee and one or more new members join it each year.

2. *Powers and duties.* The powers and duties of the committee are exclusively dispositive—that is, selecting the objects and ordering the distributions to be made by the trustee or trustees. The committee has no responsibility with respect to the investment of funds, management of property, or the administrative bookkeeping and accounting; these are the functions of the trustee or trustees.

But, as already indicated, the committee has full, unshared responsibility for distribution to or among the objects of the foundation; for carrying out faithfully the terms of designated gifts as long as it is practicable or possible to do so; for diverting such gifts to other objects of the foundation should it be impossible or impracticable longer to adhere to the designation; and to use the principal or the income of undesignated gifts, according to its own judgment, for the objects of the foundation.

In most cases the distribution committee makes its distributions to existing charitable institutions or agencies for them to make the final distributions to the beneficiaries of the institution or agency. If the foundation should see fit to do so, its distribution committee itself has the power to select and make distributions to individual beneficiaries.

COLLATERAL READING

Note: For complete citations, see Bibliography, pp. 417–428.

BROWN, "By Gifts to Charity."

HANES, "*Going the Second Mile*,"—How a Foundation Has Helped its Community.

HEADLEY, "The Community Foundation."

——, "The Transforming Power of a Will."

MALLORY, "Charitable Gifts in Estate Planning."

PIERCE, "Has Your Town a Nest Egg?"

SMITH, "Philanthropy and Estate Planning."

YOUNG, "Planning and Management of Charitable Foundations."

11

Corporate Trusts

𝕿HE PURPOSE OF THIS CHAPTER is only to introduce the student to the corporate trust, not to treat the subject exhaustively. Since bonds and notes of corporations constitute a substantial portion of the property in estates and trusts, the student should, at least, know some of the fundamentals of corporate trusteeship. Besides, whether or not he ever has anything directly to do with estates or trusts or with corporate finance, he himself is likely to inherit or to acquire the bonds or notes of corporations.

Definition of Corporate Trust

The broadest possible definition of a corporate trust is that it is one created by a corporation. But this definition does not suffice. A corporation, the same as a natural person, can and does create living trusts, insurance trusts, employees trusts, charitable trusts, and, in fact, any and every kind of trust except one under will.

But this is not what one usually means when one speaks of *corporate trusts*. Rather, one means a trust created by a corporation to secure its outstanding bonds, notes, or other obligations. In this chapter this is the only sense in which the term is used.

Difference between Personal and Corporate Trusts

There are two main differences between personal trusts and corporate trusts. One relates to the possession of the property; the other, to the number of beneficiaries.

1. *Possession of property.* In a personal trust the property usually is turned over to the trustee to be retained by him throughout the duration of the trust. In a corporate trust, on the contrary, possession of the property (other than stocks, bonds, and other types of intangible personal property) is retained by the corporation. For example, an industrial corporation bor-

rows money for operating purposes by conveying its plant and equipment to a trustee as security for the loan. If it had to turn its plant and equipment over to the trustee, that would defeat completely the purpose of the corporation in obtaining the loan. Ordinarily, it would be only in case of default that the trustee would take over the property.

2. *Number of beneficiaries.* The beneficiaries of a personal trust usually are one person or a limited number of persons—a wife, child, parent, other kinsman, or friend—or a small number of individuals—the children of the same parents, or the brothers and sisters and nephews and nieces of the same family. The beneficiaries of a corporate trust, on the other hand, usually are a large number of bondholders or noteholders, mounting into the thousands. With respect to the indefinite number of beneficiaries, a corporate trust partakes of the nature of a charitable trust as described in the preceding chapter.

Difference between Trust and Mortgage

Technically and even in ordinary conversation, a *mortgage* is a conveyance, assignment, transfer, or delivery of property directly *to the lender* to secure a loan or other obligation, conditioned upon the reconveyance, reassignment, transfer, or delivery of the property of the borrower back to him upon the payment of the debt or satisfaction of the obligation. There are only two parties involved in the transaction—the borrower and the lender. In this technical sense a mortgage is not practicable in corporate financing, for there would be far too many lenders to be included in one instrument.

A *trust*, by contrast, is a conveyance, assignment, transfer, or delivery of property to a trustee for the benefit of bondholders or noteholders. There are three parties or groups of parties involved in the transaction: the borrowing corporation, the trustee, and the lending bondholders or noteholders. In view of the very large number of lenders involved, the trust is the only practicable device for securing corporate obligations.

The student should understand that the instrument of conveyance, assignment, transfer, or delivery to the trustee frequently is referred to as a *mortgage* although it is, in fact, an instrument of trust. Just as we called the instrument creating a living trust or insurance trust a *trust agreement,* so now let us call the instrument creating a corporate trust a *trust indenture.* However, the student should understand that the trust indenture still goes by several other names—mortgage, trust mortgage, deed of trust, trust agreement, debenture agreement, collateral trust agreement—with many modifying, descriptive adjectives.

Technically, *conveyance* refers to real property only, and the *instrument of conveyance* refers to a deed or, if a trust is involved, a deed of trust. *Assignment* or *transfer* refers to intangible personal property—shares of stock, bonds, and notes. *Delivery* refers to tangible personal property—automobiles and machinery and equipment detached from the building or grounds. In the interest of brevity, let us call the method of getting any kind of property into the hands of the trustee a *conveyance;* the instrument of conveyance, a *trust indenture;* and the obligation secured, a *bond* or *note.* At points it will be necessary to use more descriptive terms; but these will stand for most of the discussion.

Trust Distinguished from Other Forms of Corporate Financing

Although a corporate trust proper exists only when property is conveyed to a trustee by means of a trust indenture for the security of bondholders or noteholders, the student should be familiar also with other, equally common plans of corporate financing.

1. *Issue of stock.* First of all, a corporation issues shares of stock which are purchased for a price and thereby raises working capital. If, however, its sale of stock does not bring in adequate working capital, it turns to the other forms of financing.

2. *Line of credit.* Next, it might be able to establish with a bank or banks a line or lines of credit, on the strength of which and without pledge of assets it could obtain additional working capital. In the case of a close (family) corporation, the principal stockholders might be required to endorse the notes of the corporation.

3. *Individual lender.* The corporation might find one or more individuals, possibly its larger stockholders, who would make a loan or loans, secured or unsecured, to their corporation.

In the case of borrowing from banks or individuals, there would be no basic difference between corporate and individual financing.

4. *Income or revenue notes or bonds.* Without making any conveyance of its property as security for money borrowed for operating capital, the corporation might be able to raise money by issuing bonds or notes and pledging itself to pay them out of its income or revenue. These usually are known as *debentures* or as *income* or *revenue bonds* or *notes.*

5. *Unsecured notes.* If the corporation already is well established and has good credit rating, it may be able to raise the needed working capital by issuing and selling to the investing public its unsecured bonds or notes. In this case no specified property is conveyed to a trustee as security, and the lenders—the bondholders or noteholders—must depend upon the general solvency of the corporation and, in event of default, would come in as unsecured creditors.

6. *Secured bonds and notes.* Where the corporation needs more working capital than it can raise in any or all of the foregoing ways, it may put out a bond-issue or a note-issue, go to the public, and by sale of its bonds or notes, usually through a sales agency, borrow, here a little, there a little,

from literally hundreds of thousands of lenders. These lenders already have been referred to repeatedly as *bondholders* or *noteholders*. They hold the bonds or the notes of the corporation as evidence of its obligation and commitment to pay its debts to them. If the debt is secured by the conveyance of property or if duties are imposed upon a trustee, it is a corporate trust.

The main difference between the note and the bond of a corporation is one of duration of the obligation. A short-term obligation, that is, one that is to be satisfied in a comparatively short time, usually is known as a *note;* a long-term obligation, as a *bond*. This distinction obtains also in government financing.

When the student sees and examines the bonds or notes of a corporation, he should go far enough in his examination to learn what, if any, security for his loan the holder of such a bond or note has; that is, whether it is secured by the pledge of property or of income or is unsecured.

TRUST INDENTURE ACT OF 1939

As already indicated, a large proportion of corporate financing is done by the issue and sale of corporate bonds and notes. Many different corporations of all sorts, some good and some bad, would like to issue their bonds or notes and sell them to the investing public. Many of these obligations would be purchased by uninformed and, possibly, unsuspecting people. In the light of this possibility and with the development of corporate financing through bond- and note-issues, it has become essential to the economic welfare and stability of our country and its people that some measure of governmental protection be afforded the investing public. Consequently, in 1939, a major step in this direction was taken.

Qualification

In August, 1939, the Congress of the United States passed the Trust Indenture Act which became effective in February, 1940. The act was designed to protect investors in the bonds and notes of corporations by providing certain provisions to be included in the corporation's written obligations to the persons from whom it borrowed money by the sale of its bonds or notes, and by imposing certain duties and responsibilities upon a trustee.

Since the common name of the instrument containing these protective provisions is a trust indenture, the legislation is known as the Trust Indenture Act. It requires that the trust indenture grant the trustee adequate rights, powers, duties, and responsibilities to enable it to protect the bondholders or noteholders; that there be no conflict of interest between the corporation and the trustee or between either of them and the underwriters (the one who markets the bonds or notes); that the corporation furnish financial and other information to the trustee. Unless these and other prescribed conditions are satisfied, the Securities and Exchange Commission will not issue the registration regarding the security, without which the bonds or notes cannot be offered for sale to the public. As soon as the registration statement is issued by the Commission, the indenture is said to be "qualified," and thereupon the bonds or notes can be offered to the public.

Qualification not Required

However, not all corporate trust indentures are required to be "qualified" as a condition precedent to the offer of sale of the bonds or notes to the public. The following are relieved of this requirement:

a. Indentures under which the securities of railroad companies are to be issued, since railroad companies are subject to regulation by the Interstate Commerce Commission;

b. Indentures for securities that are not to be offered to the *general* public;

c. Indentures for security issues not exceeding $1 million; and

d. Indentures under which securities of charitable objects (as defined in the preceding chapter) are to be issued.

KINDS OF TRUST INDENTURES

Although, as already explained, a mortgage is a two-party—borrower and lender—arrangement that does not involve a third party—a trustee—many of the corporate trust indentures are called *mortgages,* and we may as well recognize and accept this terminology. In so doing, we may classify trust indentures into these three groups: mortgages, collateral trust agreements, and unsecured indentures.

Mortgages

Mortgages securing corporate obligations, in turn, are classified under many heads; the principal ones are listed below.

1. *First.* A first mortgage, as the name implies, is one that constitutes a first lien (nothing ahead of it) on the property securing the obligation.

There are second, third, and even fourth mortgages, indicating that there are one, two, or three liens ahead of them. But these mortgages, although qualified, probably would be offered to the public under some other name, since few investors would be interested in purchasing third- or fourth-mortgage securities.

2. *Refunding.* A refunding mortgage constitutes a lien under which securities may be sold to raise funds with which to pay off existing obligations. Naturally, the purchaser would wish to know the nature of the re-

funding; consequently, adjectives are attached to the name of these mortgages, and they are known, for instance, as *first and refunding* mortgages or *refunding and improvement* mortgages, indicating in the one case that it still will be a first mortgage and in the other that the money will be used for improvement.

3. *Prior lien.* The term *prior lien* simply indicates that the mortgage security is superior to some other lien on the property. It is a rather indefinite term which puts the purchaser on notice to inquire further into the nature of his security.

4. *Leasehold.* This term reveals that the underlying security is only a leasehold and not a fee-simple ownership of the property. The security depends upon the length and terms of the lease. If the term is long, say, ninety-nine years, and the possibility of forfeiture of the lease remote, the security may be attractive. Anyhow the term *leasehold*, puts the student or the investor on notice to inquire into the length and the terms of the lease.

5. *Chattel.* The term *chattel* applied to a mortgage means that the underlying security is tangible personal property, such as unattached machinery, tools, and equipment as distinguished from real property, on the one hand, and securities, on the other.

Other adjectives applied to mortgages securing bond- and note-issues are: *consolidated, general, adjustment, unifying, development*, and *extension*. These adjectives, in the main, indicate the purpose for which the issue was made.

Collateral Trust Agreements

The term *collateral trust agreement* applies to trust indentures in which the underlying security is stocks, bonds, notes, installment obligations, and property other than real property.

However, the same indenture may cover both real property and the other kinds of property. Therefore, the student or investor must not take for granted that the terms *mortgage* and *collateral trust agreement* are or need be mutually exclusive.

Unsecured Indentures

The term *unsecured indenture* applies to an indenture under which no property of any sort is put in trust as security for the obligation. The general, unpledged assets of the corporation, subject to the claims of all other creditors, are the only security.

Although this security, if it may be called a security, has an uninviting name, the obligations of a well-established corporation with high credit standing may be more attractive to the investor and, in fact, may be a better investment than the secured obligations of a corporation with less attractive status or credit standing.

KINDS OF CORPORATE OBLIGATIONS

The kind of trust indenture usually or frequently gives its name to the security. These securities may be classified under these ten heads: mortgage bonds, collateral-trust bonds, debentures, income bonds, revenue bonds, sinking-fund bonds, convertible bonds, serial bonds, bonds of a specified series, and joint bonds.

Mortgage Bonds

Already we have described the different names by which mortgage bonds are known—first, second, third, fourth; refunding; prior lien.

Collateral-Trust Bonds

These are secured, not by real property, but by stocks, bonds, and other securities. Ordinarily they are called *notes,* not bonds.

Debentures

These are the unsecured obligations of the issuing corporation under which the lender—the owner of the debenture—is dependent upon the general solvency of the corporation.

Income Bonds

The bondholder looks only to the income or earnings of the corporation. In some cases past-due interest is cumulative; in others, it is not.

Revenue Bonds

These are secured only by the revenues of the corporation and generally are not enforceable against the other assets of the corporation. Ordinarily, they are the bonds issued by an "authority," such as a town, school district, or a drainage district, which will be discussed later.

Sinking-Fund Bonds

In the case of these bonds the indenture contains provision and commitment for the retirement of the bonds periodically out of a sinking fund created by the corporation.

Convertible Bonds

The holder of these bonds has the right to convert them into other securities of the corporation.

Serial Bonds

A serial bond is one of a series of different but periodic maturities.

Bonds of Specified Series

Bonds of a specified series—usually called by letter or date—may be issued, each series differing in some way from all other series of the corporation; for example, the bonds may be of Series A or of 1975.

Joint Bonds

Two or more corporations may join in issuing joint bonds, thus making them the obligations, not of one, but of all of the participating corporations.

From the foregoing definitions or descriptions the student should be able at least to identify and distinguish the different kinds of corporate obligations which he is likely to encounter on the market, in estates and trusts, or in the hands of investors.

SPECIAL KINDS OF CORPORATE TRUSTS

There are two kinds of corporate trusts which deserve special mention because they have distinguishing features from each other and from all other kinds of corporate trusts. They are equipment trusts and revenue-bond trusts.

Equipment Trusts

The *equipment trust* is a kind of corporate trust which is confined largely to railroad companies and is related to their equipment, that is to their cars and locomotives.

The railroad company already may have trusteed its property to raise operating capital. In due course comes the time when the railroad needs more cars and locomotives. It prefers not to issue a second, third, or fourth mortgage or deed of trust on its property, and, if it did, it might have difficulty in selling its securities. So, it arranges with a manufacturer of cars and locomotives to make the new ones it needs and to pass title to them, not to the railroad company itself (for then the cars and locomotives might pass under the outstanding mortgages on the property) but to one or more of the representatives of the company—usually two, called *vendors*—who, in turn, would trustee the new cars and locomotives as security for equipment-trust certificates issued by the trustee. These certificates usually are sold to the public at par. But they represent only about three-fourths of the estimated value of the equipment, thus providing a normal margin of security. In this way, the railroad company is able to finance its equipment without becoming involved in its outstanding secured obligations. When the equipment trust certificates are paid off, the trust is terminated, and the railroad company thereupon becomes the outright owner of the equipment thus acquired.

Revenue-Bond Trusts

Municipalities and other statutory "authorities" finance the building and maintenance of bridges, tunnels, waterworks, sewage-disposal plants, and other public works by authorizing, issuing, and selling revenue bonds. In these cases the property itself is not, and perhaps under the law could not be, conveyed to a trustee as security, but the revenue realized from tolls is pledged and the trust property, therefore, consists of the pledge of the revenue. The trustee is under a duty to see that the tolls are collected, that they are accounted for, and that they are used for the payment of the interest and the ultimate liquidation of the bonds themselves.

This is only a bare outline of the creation and objectives—not the administration—of corporate trusts. At best, it merely introduces the student to the subject. Corporate trusteeship is but one branch of corporate financing, and corporate financing is in itself a broad field of economics that lies far beyond the boundaries of a textbook on estates and trusts. Some of the administrative aspects of corporate trusts will be discussed in Chapter 19.

COLLATERAL READING

Note: For complete citations, see Bibliography, pp. 417–428.

KIMBALL, "Administration of Corporate Trusts," 28.

POHL, "The Administration of Trust Indentures by Corporate Trustees," 247.

"Panels on Problems of Corporate Trust Departments," 35 *Trust Bulletin* (April, 1956), 26.

12

Powers of Appointment

𝔓owers of appointment recently have assumed so much importance as devices for the disposition of interests in property that a discussion of them has a place in a text on estates and trusts.

Definition of a Power of Appointment

A power of appointment is defined as a power created or reserved by a person having property subject to his disposition enabling the donee of the power to designate, within such limits as the donor may prescribe, the transferees of the property or the shares in which it shall be received.[1] It is understood more easily by illustration than by definition. For example, *A*, the owner of Warren Place, a plantation, prefers to have *B*, his son, instead of himself, dispose of the property. So *A* devises Warren Place to *B* for life, remainder as *B* by deed or will may appoint. In this way *A* shifts the ultimate disposition of Warren Place from himself to his son *B* and enables *B* ultimately to dispose of it as *B* thinks best.

The following would be an illustration of a person reserving to himself a power of appointment: *A* creates a living trust with *B* to pay the income for life to *A's* wife, *C*, and after *C's* death to pay over the principal to their son *D* with the provision that, if *D* should predecease *C*, the property would go as *A* directed in his (*A's*) will. Thus *A* reserves a power of appointment under his will, exercisable only if *D* should predecease *C*.

ELEMENTS OF POWERS OF APPOINTMENT

There are certain elements essential to a power of appointment; that is, elements the absence of any one of which would keep it from being a power

---

[1] *Restatement of Law of Property*, Ch. 26, Sec. 441.

of appointment. These elements are: a creator of the power, a person who receives the power, property to which the power relates, the power itself, and the beneficiary of the exercise of the power.

Creator of Power

The creator of a power of appointment usually is known as the *donor* (giver). If the power is created by will, he may be known simply as the *testator;* if, by deed or agreement, as the *grantor* or *settlor. Donor* is the term in common use and the one that is used in this chapter.

Recipient of Power

The person who receives the power is known as the *donee* (to whom it is given), which is the term used in this chapter.

Property

The property to which the power relates may be any kind of property—real or personal. This frequently is referred to as the *subject matter* of the power.

Power

There cannot be a power of appointment without terms of the power any more than there can be a trust without the terms of the trust. While the power may be unrestricted or, in varying degrees, restricted, it must exist.

Under recent federal tax legislation, particularly the Revenue Code of 1954, many powers—in the trustee or in the beneficiary—are treated for tax purposes as if they were powers of appointment but which are not powers of appointment in the sense in which the term is used in this chapter. This chapter will be confined to powers of appointment as the term is understood in the general, as distinct from the tax, law.

Object of Power

The persons, corporations, or charitable objects to or among which the donee *may* appoint the property are known as the *objects* of the power.

Appointee of Power

The persons, corporations, or charitable objects in whose favor the power actually *is* exercised—that is, the beneficiaries of the exercise of the power—are known as the *appointees* (the ones appointed).

KINDS OF POWERS OF APPOINTMENT

For practical purposes powers of appointment fall into two main groups —general and special. General powers and special powers each, in turn, are classified as *powers presently exercisable* or as *testamentary powers*—that is, powers exercisable only by the donee's will. In order, however, to understand legal literature on powers of appointment the student must be acquainted with all the usual classifications.

General

A power of appointment is general when the donee has the power to pass on an interest in the property to whomsoever he pleases, including himself or his estate. *A*, the donor, conveys or devises Warren Place to *B*, donee, for life, remainder as *B* shall appoint by will. *B* has a general power of appointment.

Special

A power of appointment is *special* (also called *limited* or *particular*) when the donee is authorized to appoint interests in the property only to specified objects or classes of objects. *A* devises Warren Place to *B* for life, remainder as *B* shall appoint among his (*B's*) children. Here *B* has a special power of appointment in that he can appoint the property only to his own children.

Another classification of powers is according to the method of exercising the power.

Testamentary

The donor may give the donee a power of appointment, either general or special, exercisable only by will. This is known as a *testamentary power of appointment*. The fact that it can be exercised only by will does not keep it from being a general power if it otherwise is unrestricted.

By Deed

The donor may give the donee a power of *appointment exercisable only by deed*—that is, by an instrument in writing during the donee's lifetime; and this, too, may be either a general or a special power.

Referring to special powers only, powers of appointment are classified into exclusive and nonexclusive powers.

Exclusive

A special power of appointment is exclusive when the donee may exercise it wholly for one or more of a class of objects to the exclusion of others of that class. For example, *A* gives *B* power to appoint property, either by will or deed, to one or more of *B's* children and in such shares and proportions as *B* may direct. This is an exclusive power in that *B* can appoint all the property to one or more of his children to the exclusion of the others.

Nonexclusive

A special power of appointment is, as the term implies, nonexclusive when the donee cannot exclude any members of the class of objects, although he may make the appointments in unequal shares.

1. *Illusory.* Under the heading *nonexclusive* power comes the term *illusory*. Suppose *A* gives *B* a special power of appointment over an estate of $1,000,000 to *B's* children so expressed as to be nonexclusive, but without indicating the proportions of the appointments to the several children. Should *B* appoint $1 to one child and the remaining $999,999 to the other children, the appointment to the one child would be known as an *illusory appointment* and under the law of most states would not be tolerated. That is to say, the courts of those states would require that a substantial portion, not a nominal portion only, of the property be appointed to each person in the class.

Still another classification of special powers of appointment is that of discretionary power and power in trust.

Discretionary

If the donee of the power is not placed under a duty by the donor to exercise it, but may exercise it or not as he chooses, it is a *discretionary power of appointment*. If he does not exercise the power, then, unless it is otherwise provided by deed or will, the unappointed property usually reverts to the donor's estate.

In Trust

If by the terms of the power it is the donee's duty to exercise it, it is known as a *power in trust*, or a *power coupled with a duty*, or an *imperative power*, and, if the donee dies without exercising it, the court itself will exercise it.

It is not always easy to judge, either from the wording of the deed or the will or from the circumstances, whether the donor intended it to be a discretionary power or a power in trust. The fact that he made a gift-over to someone else, on default of exercise of the power, would be strong, but not conclusive, evidence that he intended it to be a discretionary power. The fact that he did not make a gift-over is equally strong, but not conclusive, evidence that he meant to make it the duty of the donee to exercise the power and, therefore, a power in trust.

Still another classification of powers of appointment is based upon the interest or noninterest of the donee in the property to which the power relates.

Collateral

If the donee of the power has no interest in the property himself, the power is said to be *collateral* or *naked*. *A* gives property to *B* in trust for *C* for life, then to *C's* children as *B* shall appoint, *B* having no interest in the property. *B's* would be a collateral or a naked power of appointment.

In Gross

If the donee himself has an interest in the property but his power is limited to the appointment of an interest in the property which will arise only after his own interest has terminated, he has a power of appointment in gross. For example, *A* gives property to *B* for life, remainder as *B* shall appoint by will. *B* has a life estate in the property but his power of appointment applies to an estate in fee which will arise only after his own life estate has terminated.

Appendant or Appurtenant

If the donee himself has an estate in the property and if the exercise of the power would take effect wholly or partly out of his estate, he is said to have a power *appendant* or *appurtenant*.

While at the moment these definitions of the different kinds of powers of appointment may seem to be academic and of practical value only as an aid in understanding the legal literature of the subject, it will be found later in this chapter, particularly in the section on release of powers of appointment, that it makes a great deal of difference whether a power is collateral or a power in trust or a power coupled with an interest in the property.

CURRENT INTEREST IN POWERS OF APPOINTMENT

The current, widespread interest in powers of appointment is traceable largely to the federal Revenue Acts of 1942, 1948, and the Revenue Code of 1954. Moreover, interest in powers of appointment is likely to survive further changes in federal tax laws. We must introduce at this point a brief discussion of the taxability of property passing under powers of appointment in order to show how these Revenue Acts and the Code have, in fact, aroused interest in powers of appointment.

Revenue Act of 1942

Prior to October 21, 1942, which was the effective date of the Revenue Act of that year, property covered by a power of appointment was included in the gross estate of the donee of the power for estate-tax purposes only if the power was general—that is, exercisable in favor of the decedent, his estate, his creditors, or the creditors of his estate—and then only if it exercised.

Under the Revenue Act of 1942, all property covered by a power of appointment, whether exercised or not, was included for estate-tax purposes in the gross estate of the donee of the power unless it was a special power limited to specified objects.

The specified objects were: (a) the wife or husband of the donor, (b) the wife or husband of the donee, (c) descendants of the donor, (d) descendants of the donee, (e) wife or husband of any descendant of the donee. These were known as the *familial* (pertaining to the family) *exception.*

In addition to the members of the family, the donor might give the donee a power of appointment to a *charitable object* without making the property includable in the donee's estate.

In addition to the familial and the charitable-object exceptions, there was the *fiduciary exception.* The donor might give a donee, who did not receive any beneficial interest, vested or contingent, in the property or thereafter acquire any interest in it, a power of appointment over property without making the property includable in the donee's gross estate for federal estate-tax purposes. An illustration of the fiduciary exception would be the gift of property by *A* to *B* (a friend of *A*) in trust to appoint the property, whether general or special, and, if special, whether within or without the objects included in the familial exception. *B* himself would have no beneficial interest in the property and, if he were to die, the property would not be included in his estate for estate-tax purposes.

Illustrations may help to clarify the meaning of these rather abstruse and involved statements and at the same time will enable one to avoid the use of legalistic terms.

A, a husband-and-father, with a wife, *B*, two sons, *C* and *D*, *C's* wife, *E*, and three grandchildren *F*, *G*, and *H* (the children of *C* and *E*) could give property to his son *C* with power to appoint the property to or among *B*, *D*, *E*, *F*, *G*, and *H* (but not to *C* or *C's* estate or *C's* creditors), without making the property includable in *C's* estate for estate-tax purposes.

Or, *A*, a wife-and-mother, with a husband *B* and children and daughter-in-law as in the preceding paragraph, could give property to *C* with power to appoint to or among *B*, *D*, *E*, *F*, *G*, and *H* (but not to *C* or *C's* estate or *C's* creditors) without making the property estate-taxable to *C*.

Notice that *A* could not give *C* the power to appoint the property to himself or to *C's* estate or to *C's* creditors without making the property includable in *C's* estate for estate-tax purposes.

Thus, while the Revenue Act of 1942 discouraged the creation of general powers of appointment, it opened the door for and called special attention to special powers of appointment exercisable for members of the donor's family. As Professor Richard R. Powell of the Columbia University Law School, Reporter for the *Restatement of the Law of Property*, said soon after the passage of the Revenue Act of 1942,

Under this "familial" exception a power can be exercisable in favor of a group as inclusive as those in the past selected as their distributees by 90 per cent of testators and still be tax exempt.[2]

Revenue Act of 1948

The Revenue Act of 1948 gave still further impetus to the creation of powers of appointment—this time, of general powers—by making it possible for a husband to give or leave his wife up to one-half of his "adjusted gross estate" under a general power of appointment without subjecting that portion of his estate to his federal estate taxes. Likewise, it made it possible for a wife to give or leave her husband up to one-half of her "adjusted gross estate" under a general power of appointment without subjecting that portion of her estate to her estate taxes.

Under this Act a husband might give his wife, or a wife her husband, the property outright or might give it in trust with a general power of appointment in the wife or husband, as the case might be. In either case the donee of the power had to be entitled to all the income payable at least annually and had to have the power to appoint the principal, free of the trust, to himself or his estate or in favor of either himself or his estate, whether or not the power was exercisable in favor of others, and with no power in any other person to appoint the principal to any person other than the donee of the power. In a word, the donee of the power—the wife or the husband—must have complete dominion over the property, with this one exception: the donor might specify whether the power was exercisable by deed during the donee's lifetime or by will at the donee's death or by either deed or will. But to qualify for the marital deduction, the surviving wife or husband must be given a *general* power of appointment, whether exercisable by deed or will or either.

[2] 23, *Trust Business* (April, 1944), 13 at 15–16.

As will be brought out below in the material concerning the purposes served by powers of appointment, this provision of the Revenue Act of 1948 opened the door for, and invited the widespread use of, general powers of appointment to meet certain family situations, just as the Revenue Act of 1942 opened the door for, and invited the use of, special powers of appointment to meet other family situations.

This discussion of two federal Revenue Acts, now superseded by the Revenue Code of 1954, is justified by the conviction that the provisions of these Acts relating to powers of appointment were landmarks in the use of powers of appointment in the disposition of property. Even though all references to powers of appointment were stricken from the tax laws, unless the creation and exercise of such powers were prohibited or were made prohibitive taxwise, it is likely that property owners, estate planners, and draftsmen of wills and trust agreements, having been introduced to the advantages of such powers, would continue to employ them as devices of ever-increasing use and popularity in the disposition of property.

PURPOSES SERVED BY POWERS OF APPOINTMENT

For the student of estates and trusts who himself is not a lawyer or law student, the main interest in powers of appointment centers about their practical usefulness in the disposition of property.

In recent years, lawyers and estate planners seem to have vied with one another in their tributes to the usefulness of powers of appointment. For example, Professor W. Barton Leach, of the Harvard Law School, Reporter for the *Restatement of the Law of Powers of Appointment,* said of them:

> The power of appointment is the most efficient dispositive device that the ingenuity of Anglo-American lawyers has ever worked out. Its use is definitely on the increase . . . the power of appointment is the answer to more of the problems that face the draftsmen of wills and trusts than any other device.[3]

Professor Powell, in the article already referred to, says that powers of appointment have for centuries been the best device for postponing decisions to await wisdom based on later facts. René A. Wormser of the New York Bar, a specialist in both the theory and the practice of estate planning, speaks of powers of appointment as being extremely useful and, in fact, in many situations essential.[4]

What is the justification for such superlative appraisement of powers of appointment? Powers of appointment find their justification (1) in permitting the postponement of decisions as to the disposition of property awaiting wisdom based on later facts and (2) in providing for the delegation of the duty to make decisions based on later facts.

[3] *24 American Bar Association Journal* (October, 1938), 807.
[4] Wormser, *The Theory and Practice of Estate Planning,* 91–92.

The best way, perhaps, to show the usefulness of powers of appointment in both these respects is to take for illustration a family situation and follow it through in some detail. *A*, the husband-and-father, is 33 years of age; *B*, his wife, is 30. They now have three children—*C*, a son, 6; *D*, a daughter, 4; and *E*, another daughter, 1. They hope and expect to have several more children. *A*, a businessman, already has accumulated a sizable estate for a man of his age. He expects to inherit considerable property from his father and *B*, from hers; but neither of them is counting upon this. Nor does either of them know the contents of either father's will. *A*, with the aid of a competent estate planner, goes about planning his estate and preparing the necessary documents. What, if any, need will he find for powers of appointment?

Postpone Decision

When *A*, with the aid of his wife, *B*, as well as his estate planner, undertakes to make a present decision regarding their children, now existing or born later, he faces what is, perhaps, the estate planner's most baffling problem. This problem is aggravated still further when it comes to planning for or thinking in terms of *C's* or for another son's future wife or *D's* or *E's* or another daughter's future husband.

If *A* had any assurance that he would live out his life expectancy, he could wait until his children were grown and married before making his decisions regarding them and his daughters-in-law and sons-in-law, and he could make his decisions in the light of then existing facts. But he is reminded by the estate planner that, although he is only thirty-three and probably will live out his expectancy, nevertheless he must make his will "as if he were going to die tonight."

A does not know nor can he find out what the future needs of any of his children will be. He does not know how many children he will have to provide for. He does not know how any of his children will develop physically, mentally, socially, or morally. He does not know what their occupational abilities and aptitudes will be. He does not know what the economic conditions will be under which they will have to live out their lives. Realizing his own inability to project himself into the future, he asks his estate planner in utter perplexity, "What can I do?" The estate planner's ready answer is, "You can give someone a power of appointment in the exercise of which he or she can make decisions based on later facts."

1. *In-laws.* If *A* knew or could know now whether or not his son, *C*, after he grows up, will marry and, if so, what kind of woman, he could plan now for *C*. If he knew or could know whether or not his daughter, *D*, or his daughter, *E*, or any other daughter will marry and, if so, what kind of man, he could plan regarding her. *C* may not marry at all; he may marry his equal

or his superior in every respect; he may marry otherwise; he may have a happy married family life or just the opposite. *D* may not marry; she may marry the best type of husband or otherwise; she may have a happy or an unhappy family life. It has been said that the daughter-in-law is the forgotten person in estate planning; that parents plan for their sons and their sons' children without ever thinking that their sons may have a wife to be provided for. If the daughter-in-law is the forgotten person, the son-in-law is perhaps equally the unconsidered person in estate planning. In many cases what the son-in-law does or persuades his wife to do with her inheritance means more regarding the daughter's comfort and happiness than that which she herself, uninfluenced by her husband, would do. When the in-law prospect is called to *A's* attention, he asks, "What can I do about it?" The estate planner answers, "You can give someone a power of appointment in the exercise of which he or she can deal with the in-law situation in the light of facts as they will be at that time."

Delegate Decision

Having learned that he can postpone decisions about his children and his in-laws and having decided that that is the wise thing for him to do, *A's* next question is, "To whom shall I delegate the duty to make the decisions?" *B*, his wife, naturally is the first person to be considered. She is three years younger than he is; her life expectancy is about five years longer than his, making, in all, a difference of eight years; they are her children as well as his; the in-laws, if ever there are any, will be hers as well as his; she can be counted upon more than anyone else to do what she thinks is best for the children and the in-laws in the light of her knowledge of their needs based upon later facts. She is as much interested in their welfare as he is.

In giving her a power of appointment, *A* has a wide variety of choices. He can give her the power to appoint by deed only or by will only or by either deed or will. He can give her a general power of appointment under which she can appoint to whomsoever she pleases in any way she pleases. He can give her a special power of appointment under which she can appoint only to specified objects or within the specified classes of objects. He can make that power exclusive, in which case she can appoint all the property to one or more members of the class to the exclusion of others; or he can make it nonexclusive, in which case she must appoint a substantial portion of the property to each member. Under present tax laws he might be disposed to give her a special or, as it is now called, a *nongeneral* power of appointment as to one-half of the property and a general power as to substantially the other half so as to take advantage of the tax-saving under the Revenue Code of 1954. At the moment tax-saving is not the point of discussion. The point is selecting an interested, intelligent person who will be likely to be living and capable of making a wise appointment in the light of wisdom based on later facts.

If *A's* and *B's* children were adults, *A* might give his sons and daughters powers of appointment and thus postpone still further the time of decision as to the ultimate disposition of the property.

While the purposes served by powers of appointment may be illustrated most vividly and impressively in family situations such as the one just described, the needs for postponing decisions and for delegating the making of decisions may exist in many other situations. The need for postponing decisions may apply to parents, brothers, sisters, or friends. The person to whom the decision may be delegated may be some other member of the family or some other individual or the trustee, whether an individual or a bank or trust company. But whatever the situation, the two tests of the usefulness of powers of appointment are the need for postponing decisions and the availability of someone to whom the making of the decisions with reasonable assurance may be delegated.

Referring to the illustration, *A*, in giving his wife a power of appointment, must have in mind that she, too, may die or become incapacitated while their children are still young and before any of them has married. Facing this ever-present possibility, he should provide, as best he can in the light of his present inability to forecast the ultimate needs of his children, for the disposition of his property in the event *B* should fail to exercise her power of appointment.

CREATION OF POWERS OF APPOINTMENT

Just as there are no required words or phrases for making an outright gift by will or for creating a trust under will or by agreement, so there is none for creating a power of appointment. It is possible to create a power of appointment without using the word *appoint*. The test is whether the words used in the deed or will as a whole show a manifest intent to create a power of appointment and, if so, the terms of the power.

General

The following is, perhaps, a typical provision of a will giving the testator's wife a general power of appointment:

Upon the death of my said wife, or, if she shall not survive me, then upon my death, to pay over the principal to such persons (including, but not limited to, my said wife or her estate), and/or corporations, in such estates, interests, and proportions and in such manner, without any restriction or limitation whatsoever, as my said wife may, if she survive me, in and by her last will duly admitted to probate and not otherwise appoint; or, in default of such appointment, then to divide the principal of the trust, as it shall then exist, into as many equal shares as I shall have children then surviving and children of mine who shall then be deceased but shall have left issue surviving.

Applied to *A* in the illustration, this provision would give *B* a general power of appointment. If she predeceased *A* or died without effectively exercising her power of appointment, *A's* children would receive the property in equal shares at her death, the issue of a deceased child representing the parent.

Special

But suppose *A*, instead of giving *B* a general power of appointment, preferred to keep his estate in the family and, therefore, gave her only a special power. The following is the wording of a special power of appointment to *A's* children:

(Property in trust for *B* for life.) Upon *B's* death, to such of my issue and spouses of my issue as she shall appoint by will; and if she shall make no effective appointment, then in equal shares to my children, the issue of a deceased child representing and taking the share of a deceased parent.

While a well-drawn power of appointment, whether general or special, would, no doubt, contain a number of other provisions, particularly in the light of the Revenue Code of 1954, these two illustrations of powers of appointment—one general and the other special—will serve, at least, to introduce the student to the wording of powers of appointment as they appear in wills and trust agreements.

By Deed

Commonly it is said that a power of appointment may be created by *will* or by *deed*.

Will includes any instrument admissible to probate under the applicable law. *Deed* connotes an instrument under seal, acknowledged before a proper officer, and recordable in a public office, such as the office of the register of wills. However, applied to powers of appointment the term *deed* has a somewhat broader meaning. It is permissible to create a power of appointment by a trust agreement or other instrument not under seal, not acknowledged, and, therefore, not recordable, and yet this would be known as appointment by deed. If, however, there is any possibility that any of the property to be appointed may be real property, then, by all means, any instrument—whether trust agreement or declaration of trust—creating a power of appointment should be executed in full compliance with all the requirements for recording and thus make the instrument, in fact, a deed and, as such, a link in the chain of title to any real property involved in the exercise of the power.

RELEASE OF POWERS OF APPOINTMENT

The Revenue Act of 1942 for the first time made the donee's release of his power of appointment a matter of general concern to property owners. This Act, it will be recalled, made property under power of appointment includable in the donee's estate for estate-tax purposes unless the power came within one of the three exceptions previously mentioned—familial, charitable, or fiduciary. This meant that property under existing powers of appointment that did not come within any of these exceptions would be taxable to the donee unless he could release the power. The Act gave the donee a specified time within which to release his power, if he would escape either gift or estate taxation, and from time to time the Congress extended that period.

For each donee of an existing power in 1942 the question arose: Could he release his power of appointment? For the answer to his question he had to look to the common law, to the statutes of his state, and to the deed or will giving him the power.

At Common Law

At common law the donee of a general power of appointment was under no duty to exercise it; he could exercise it or not as he chose, and, therefore, could release it if he chose. The donee of a special power could release it if it was a discretionary power; he could not release it if it was a power coupled with a duty, commonly called a *power in trust*, or an *imperative power*. Whether it was a discretionary power or a power in trust depended upon all the facts of the case. Collateral powers—that is, powers to donees who themselves had no interest in the property, such as trustees—were not releasable.

By Statute

When the common law did not answer many of the questions relating to the releasability of powers of appointment, people who turned to the statutes of their respective states or of the states in which the property was located, found many statutory laws incomplete and uncertain. After the passage of the Act of 1942, a majority of the states adopted statutes on the release of powers of appointment. While the several statutes differ somewhat in their wording, they have a common purpose and the following Delaware statute may be accepted as typical:

(1) Any power which is exercisable by deed, by will, by deed or will, or otherwise, whether general or special, other than a power in trust which is imperative, is releasable, either with or without consideration, by written instrument signed by the grantee and delivered as hereinafter provided.

(2) A power which is releasable may be released with respect to the whole or any part of the property subject to such power and may also be released in such manner as to reduce or limit the persons or objects, or classes of persons or objects, in whose favor such power would otherwise be exercisable. No release of a power shall be deemed to make imperative a power which was not imperative prior to such release, unless the instrument of release expressly so provides.

(3) Such release may be delivered to any of the following:

(a) Any person specified for such purpose in the instrument creating the power.

(b) Any trustee of the property to which the power relates.

(c) Any person, other than the grantee, who could be adversely affected by an exercise of the power.

(d) The Recorder of Deeds in any county and, when so filed, the Recorder of Deeds shall record the same in a separate docket, provided, however, that any such release, recorded in any county record prior to the passage of this act shall be deemed to be sufficient delivery within the provisions of this Act.

(4) This section shall apply to releases heretofore and hereafter executed but nothing herein contained shall be deemed to affect the validity of any release heretofore executed.[5]

Under this statute, the donee may release his power as to part of the property but not as to the rest of it; he may reduce his power from a general power to a special power, thus bringing it within the excepted classes—familial, charitable, or fiduciary. He is instructed to whom he must deliver his release if it is to be effective.

For the purposes of determining whether the decedent had released a power created after 1942, it is provided that the lapse of the power shall be considered a release if the property over which the power existed exceeded the greater of $5,000 in value or 5 per cent of the value, at the time of such lapse, of the assets out of which the exercise could have been satisfied.

By Deed or Will

The deed or will itself may authorize the donee of the power to release it or it may, on the contrary, expressly prohibit the donee from releasing it.

Suppose in the illustrative case A had suspected that, if he gave B a special power of appointment to their issue and their issue's husbands or wives and gave her the right to release it, pressure might be brought to bear upon her to release the power so as to let the property go as a portion of the donor's unappointed property. In that case he might declare expressly that it could not be released by her and that any attempted release would be void. In any case, by giving the donee the right to release the power the donor makes it possible for the donee, by releasing the power, largely to upset his estate plan and frustrate his purposes.

[5] Code 1953, Title 25, Sec. 502; *Wills, Estates, and Trusts*, Sec. 1040.

On the other hand, *A* may be able to imagine developments in his family under which he would wish his wife to release her power of appointment and have the property go as it would go in default of her exercise of the power of appointment. In that case he should incorporate in the deed or will an express *right to release* the power. This provision sometimes is worded as follows:

All powers created by this will are releasable in whole or in part. In addition to any other method of release recognized by law, any such power may be released by an instrument in writing, filed with any court which has granted probate of this will, declaring the donee's intention to release.

EXERCISE OF POWERS OF APPOINTMENT

In the case just illustrated, *A* gives *B* a special power of appointment as to one-half of his estate and a general power as to the other half. In time *B* comes to the point of exercising her power. If the deed or will provides that she can exercise it by deed only, she cannot exercise it by will; if by will, she cannot exercise it by deed; if by deed or will, she can exercise it by either; if *A* specified the terms upon which she can exercise the power, she must observe and adhere to those terms.

There are three ways in which a donee can exercise a power of appointment, which may be called specific, general, and implied.

Specific

B, in her will or trust agreement, may spell out the provisions of *A's* will creating the power and then exercise it. For example:

Whereas, under the will of my deceased husband, *A*, I have as to certain property therein described a power of appointment by will; now I, therefore, in the exercise of that power, dispose of the property as follows:

Whenever a person knows that he is the donee of a power, he should make a direct reference to the source of the power and exercise it specifically. But it is possible, unfortunately, for a person to have a power without knowing it. This leads to a discussion of two other ways of exercising a power.

General

In some states it has been held that a general devise or bequest, outright or in trust, under a residuary clause covers property under a general power of appointment provided the intention to exercise the power or powers is manifest. For example:

I bequeath and devise all the residue of my property, real and personal, including any property over which I may have a power of appointment, to ———.

In these states such a general reference to powers of appointment is construed as being sufficient to include that property.

Implied

In still other states it is not necessary for the donee to make even a general reference to the power. In some of these states by statute a general residuary clause carries property under power of appointment. In other states, the same end is accomplished by judicial decision. If the will of the donee disposes of the subject matter of the power or if the provisions of the will of the donee would be inoperative if the power were not exercised, the intention to exercise the power ordinarily is considered to have been shown. In most states there seems to be a tendency toward relaxing the rule that an intention to exercise the power must be shown clearly. If the tenor and effect of the will, in the light of all the circumstances at the time of the execution of the donee's will, would be consistent with his exercise of the power, his will will be construed as though he had exercised it. There are judicial decisions to this general effect in several states. But if the donee's will contains no reference to the power or to the subject matter of the power, the power would not be construed as having been exercised.

LIMITATIONS UPON POWERS OF APPOINTMENT

Both in creating and in exercising powers of appointment, the donor or the donee, as the case may be, must have in mind two limitations. One is that the exercise of the power must not violate the applicable rule against perpetuities; the other, that it must not violate the rule against accumulations.

Rule against Perpetuities

The rule against perpetuities has a different running period for general powers and for special powers.

1. *General.* If the donee has a general power of appointment by deed or will, the period within which the appointee's interest must vest is measured from the date of the *exercise* of the power by the donee; if by will only, from the date of *creation* of the power—that is, from the date of the death of the testator—for the will does not become effective until then. In the case used for illustration in which *A* gives *B* a general power of appointment as to one-half of his estate, the period is measured from the time she exercised the power by deed or, if she exercised it by will, from the date of her death. Where the common-law rule still prevails, as it does in most

states, the interests of the appointees under *B's* deed of will must vest in a life in being at the time *B* exercised the power (the date of the deed if by deed, or the date of her death if by will) and twenty-one years and a few months thereafter. In states in which the common-law period has been reduced by statute, the shorter period would apply.

2. *Special.* If the power is special, then, except in the State of Delaware, the period begins to run from the time of the *creation* of the power. It frequently is said that *A* by giving *B* a special power of appointment, in effect, makes his will and leaves certain blanks as to the ultimate disposition of a portion or all of his estate so that *B*, the donee of the power, can fill in the blanks later, and that then, for the purposes of the running of the rule against perpetuities, *A's* will should be read as if *A* himself had filled in the blanks at the time he made his will.

The draftsman of a deed or will exercising a special power of appointment, if he is not to run the risk of violating the rule against perpetuities, must read and fit together the donor's deed or will creating the power and the donee's deed or will exercising it; otherwise he is likely to violate the rule and throw the property back into the donor's estate.

In Delaware by statute, in the exercise of a special power of appointment, the period permissible under the rule begins to run, not from the *creation* of the power by the donor, but from the *exercise* of the power by the donee. As to the running of the rule, it puts special powers on a parity with general powers.[6]

Rule against Accumulations

In most states the period permissible under the rule against accumulations during which the income may accumulate is the same as that under the rule against perpetuities—a life in being plus twenty-one years, plus a few months. But in a few states the period has been shortened and accumulation is permitted only for charitable purposes or during a person's infancy. Powers of appointment must be exercised in the light of the applicable rule against accumulations.

Governing Law

If the donor resides in one state and the donee in another, which law governs? The general rule is that, in the event of conflict of laws, the law of the donor's residence governs. The theory is that, after all, it is the donor's disposition of his property that is being made. The donee of the power is his representative in carrying out his plan of disposition. Therefore, the law of the donor's residence, not the donee's, should control. In estates in which real property is the subject matter of a power of appointment, the

6 Code 1953, Title 25, Sec. 501; *Wills, Estates, and Trusts,* Sec. 1019.

law of the situs of that property must be complied with, else there may be a cloud upon the title to the property.

Failure to Appoint

Suppose the donee of the power fails effectively to exercise it. If it is a general power or even a special power, other than an imperative power in trust, the unappointed property will pass to the person who under the terms of the deed or will are to take in default of appointment. But if the deed or will does not provide for a gift-over on default of appointment, the unappointed property usually will revert to the estate of the donor.

If it is an imperative power in trust—that is, where the donee is under a duty to exercise it—if he fails to do so, the court will exercise the power. For example, suppose *A* leaves one-half his estate in trust for *B* for life, and after her death to one or more of his children or issue of deceased children in such portions as she shall see fit to make (an *exclusive* power). Should *B* die without making the appointment, the court would divide the property equally among the children, the issue of a deceased child taking the parent's share. The court would not exclude any of them nor divide the property among them unequally as *B* herself might have done.

Throughout this chapter there have been repeated references to the federal Revenue Acts of 1942 and 1948, which were codified in the federal Revenue Code of 1954. In addition to these the student concerned with other tax aspects of powers of appointment should study the Powers of Appointment Act of 1951.

From the foregoing discussion it is apparent that the disposition of property by the grant and exercise of powers of appointment has assumed vastly increased importance and employment in estate planning since 1942.

COLLATERAL READING

Note: For complete citations, see Bibliography, pp. 417–428.

CASNER, *American Law of Property*, Vol. 5, Part 23.

DURAND, "Which State's Law Governs Exercise of Power of Appointment?" 424.

GRISWOLD, "Tax Problems Involved in the Exercise and Release of Powers of Appointment," 7.

STEPHENSON, *Drafting Wills and Trust Agreements*, Vol. II, Ch. IV.

Wills, Estates, and Trusts, Secs. 439–442, 445, 1019, and 1040.

PART II

ADMINISTRATION OF PROPERTY
IN ESTATES AND TRUSTS

In the passage of property in estates and trusts from owner to receiver, as discussed in Part I, there is an unavoidable period of time, of shorter or longer duration, during which the property must be in the hands of and under the administration of someone other than the owner or the receiver.

In case of the property of a deceased person and the settlement of his estate, that period may be only a year or, at most, only a few years; of a minor, only during the period of his minority; of an incompetent person, during his incompetence, which may mean his lifetime; of the beneficiary of a personal trust or the appointee under a power of appointment, during the period permitted by the applicable rule against perpetuities; of the beneficiaries of a charitable trust, during unnumbered generations.

The quality of the disposition of property, as discussed in Part I, depends partly upon the terms of the instrument of gift—the applicable law, the will, or the trust instrument—and partly upon the person or persons through whom it passes from owner to receiver.

Therefore, discussion of the administration of the property and of the persons, natural or corporate, who administer it as it passes from owner to receiver becomes an essential part of a text on estates and trusts.

13

Fiduciaries

$\mathcal{T}$HIS CHAPTER, WHICH IS introductory to the discussion of the administration of property in estates and trusts, is largely one of definition and description.

Kinds of Fiduciaries

A *fiduciary* has been defined as an individual or a trust institution charged with the duty of acting for the benefit of another party as to matters within the scope of the relationship between them. The definition goes on to say that the relationships between a guardian and his ward, an agent and his principal, an attorney and his client, one partner and another partner, a trustee and a beneficiary, are examples of fiduciary relationship.

The fiduciary who administers the property of a minor or incompetent person generally is called a *guardian*; one who settles and distributes the property of a deceased person, an *administrator* or *executor*; one who administers property in trust, a *trustee*; and one who acts for another by the latter's authority, an *agent*.

GUARDIANS

A guardian is known by several other names, such as *committee, curator, conservator, tutor*. In some states the person who administers the property of a minor is known as *guardian*, while the one who administers the property of an incompetent person is known as *committee* (with accent on the last syllable).

In most cases, a *minor* is a person under 21 years of age. In a few states the age is 21 for men and 18 for women; in some, 21 for unmarried, and 18 for married women (in these states marriage is said to "emancipate" the woman).

175

An *incompetent person* is one who has been declared by a court of competent jurisdiction to be legally incompetent to manage his own affairs on account of his mental (not physical) condition. Legally, he becomes an incompetent person only after he has been so declared by the court. His physical condition has no bearing upon his legal competence or incompetence to manage his own affairs.

The court that has jurisdiction over the affairs of minors and incompetent persons goes by many different names, such as *probate, surrogate's, ordinary, orphans', prefect's.*

Kinds of Guardians

Going back into the evolution of guardianship under the common law, one finds many kinds of guardians, such as *in socage, by nature, for nurture, by custom, in chancery.* The definitions of these terms are not pertinent here and would be of little interest or aid to the student who is not concerned with legal history.

The kinds of guardians the student will find in present-day literature are: *natural, testamentary, general, special, by judicial act, de son tort, ad litem, of property,* and *of person.* In Chapter 4 we discussed the different kinds of guardianships. Now, in discussing the different kinds of guardians, we shall find that the terminology is much the same.

Minors and incompetent persons alike are known as the *wards* of their guardians.

1. *Natural.* The parent of a minor is known as his *natural guardian.* Originally, the father had priority over the mother. At the present time in most states the court will appoint whichever parent seems better for the child.

2. *Testamentary.* The parent in his will may nominate a guardian for his minor child and, in the absence of substantial reason to the contrary, the court will appoint his nominee. It is important to note that the parent only nominates, that the court appoints the *testamentary guardian,* and that it can appoint a different guardian than the nominee should it think it best for the minor that it do so.

3. *General.* The *general guardian* is one who administers all of the ward's property. This is the most common kind of guardian.

4. *Special.* A *special guardian* is one appointed to administer specified property or to serve for a specified time or purpose.

5. *By judicial act.* In a broad sense every guardian is one by judicial act. But when one is appointed by the court for some specified purpose, he sometimes is known as a *guardian by judicial act.*

6. *De son tort.* A *guardian de son tort* (by his own wrong) is one who acts as if he were guardian when, in fact, he is not. Suppose he takes

over and administers the property of a minor or incompetent person without appointment or after his appointment has been revoked. He is responsible for his administration of the property as if he actually were the duly appointed guardian.

7. *Ad litem.* A *guardian ad litem* is one appointed by the court to represent and protect the interests of a ward in litigation. Sometimes he is known as a special guardian. If he is the general guardian, he will represent the ward and one *ad litem* need not be appointed.

8. *Of property.* Where the duties of the guardian are confined to the ward's property, he is known as the *guardian of the property*.

9. *Of person.* Where the duties of the guardian are confined to the person of the ward—his food, shelter, clothing, schooling, medical care, discipline—he is known as *guardian of the person.*

In some cases someone is appointed simply guardian of the ward without specifying whether of the property or the person; and in these cases he finds himself guardian of both the property and the person. If the guardian is a corporation, it probably will make payments for the ward to the person who stands in the place of a parent or to the institution in which the ward may be residing at the time.

Who May Be Guardian

Any resident individual twenty-one years of age, who can qualify by giving the required bond with surety, is eligible to appointment as guardian of the property or the person or both. At the time of his appointment he must be a resident of the county of the ward. If the guardian should leave the state and take the ward with him, it would raise administrative problems which will be discussed later.

1. *Parent.* The parent is the natural guardian of both the property and the person of the ward and, unless there should be some compelling reason to the contrary, would be appointed.

2. *Nominee of minor.* In some states a minor of fourteen years or over can nominate his own guardian and the court will appoint his nominee unless there should be sound reason for its not doing so. This, of course, would not apply to an incompetent person, for, in the eyes of the law, he would not be mentally competent to make such a nomination.

3. *Corporation.* In every state a corporation which is authorized to serve as a fiduciary may serve as guardian of the property of a minor or incompetent person. But it is not true that in every state it can serve as guardian of the person. In Connecticut, for example, a bank or trust company can serve as "guardian or conservator of the estate, but not of the person, of any person." [1]

[1] General Statutes 1949, Sec. 5781, as amended, Laws 1953; for restrictions in other states, see *Wills, Estates, and Trusts,* Sec. 17,001.

ADMINISTRATORS AND EXECUTORS

The estate of a deceased person is settled and the property distributed by either an executor or by some kind of administrator.

If the deceased person made a valid will and has named an acceptable executor, the court would appoint his nominee executor of his will. He would be executor of the will, not of the estate, as he so often is called.

Kinds of Administrators

Whereas, in the main, there is only one kind of executor, there are several kinds of administrators.

1. *With the will annexed.* The legal name for this kind of administrator is *cum testamento annexo* (usually abbreviated, *c. t. a.*). If the testator has failed to name an executor of his will, if the one he has named has failed to qualify, or if the court has refused to appoint his nominee, the court would appoint an administrator with the will annexed to take over, wind up, and distribute the property according to the terms of the will.

2. *Of undistributed assets.* The legal name for the administrator of undistributed assets is *de bonis non* (abbreviated, *d. b. n.*). Suppose the property owner has died without a valid will, that the court has appointed an administrator to settle his estate, and that the administrator has died or become incapacitated or had been removed before the settlement of the estate has been completed. In any such case the court would appoint an *administrator de bonis non* to take over and complete the settlement and distribution of the estate.

3. *Of undistributed assets under terms of will.* The legal name of an administrator of undistributed assets under terms of will is *cum testamento annexo de bonis non* (abbreviated: *c. t. a. d. b. n.*). Suppose the property owner has made a valid will and named an executor, that the court has appointed his nominee, that the executor has died or become incapacitated or been removed before the settlement of the estate has been completed and the property distributed. In this case the court would appoint an administrator to complete the settlement of the estate and to distribute the property under the terms of the will.

4. *Ancillary.* Suppose the deceased person has left real property or tangible personal property in a state or a country other than the one of which he was a resident. In this case the court would appoint an *ancillary administrator* to take over, administer, and account for the out-of-state property to the resident executor or administrator.

The property owner himself can name an executor under his will for each state in which he owns property, and the respective courts will be disposed to appoint his nominees.[2] Under similar conditions it might be necessary to appoint an ancillary guardian or guardians of the property.

[2] *Wills, Estates, and Trusts,* Secs. 2559–2562, 2690.

Who May Be Administrator or Executor?

1. *Administrator*. The court would not appoint a nonresident individual administrator, nor in many states could it appoint a nonresident corporation. Should it do so, it would not have jurisdiction over its own appointee.

a. Order of priority. In most states there is a statutory order of appointment of administrators. The order under the North Carolina statute is, perhaps, typical:

(i) The husband or wife; (ii) the next of kin in the order of their degree, where they are of different degrees; if of equal degree, to one or more of them, at the discretion of the court; (iii) the most competent creditor who resides within the state, and proves his debt on oath before the clerk of the court; and (iv) any other person legally competent.[3]

2. *Executor*. A property owner can nominate the individual executor of his choice, and, if otherwise competent, the court will appoint his nominee. It may require a nonresident to give bond with surety which it would not require of a resident executor, and possibly it might require him to have a local process agent; that is, one to represent him in the event of litigation.

But no such freedom of choice applies to a corporate executor. As to this, the states fall into three main groups. The largest group do not permit an out-of-state corporation to qualify as executor. The next, smaller group, known as *reciprocal states*, permit a corporation of State *A* to qualify in State *B* if State *A* permits a corporation of State *B* to qualify in State *A*; that is, if they reciprocate. There are a few states that permit an out-of-state corporation to qualify as coexecutor with a resident individual coexecutor.[4]

TRUSTEES

Trustees, who frequently are named after the kind of trusts they administer, go in pairs, either in contrast with each other or as complements to each other. The principal pairs of trustees are: under will or agreement, individual or corporate, private or court, managing and custodian, and responsible and advisory.

Kinds of Trustees

1. *Under will or agreement*. A *trustee under will*—one named in the decedent's will—also is known as *testamentary trustee* and in this way is distinguished from a trustee under agreement.

A *trustee under agreement* is one under a living trust, an insurance trust,

---

[3] General Statutes, Sec. 28–6; *Wills, Estates, and Trusts*, Sec. 2610.
[4] *Wills, Estates, and Trusts*, Secs. 17; 101–17, 102.

or any other kind of agreement made by the property owner during his lifetime and also made operative during his lifetime. Another name for this kind of trustee is *inter vivos* (among the living) trustee.

2. *Individual or corporate.* The distinction here is based, not upon the trustee but upon the purpose of the trust. As discussed in Chapter 11, a corporate trust is one created by a corporation to secure the payment of its outstanding bonds or notes or other obligations. The trustee may be either an individual or a corporation. Individual trustees of other types of trusts also may be individuals or corporations.

3. *Private or court.* A *private trust* is one created by will, deed, or other instrument; a *court trust*, one in which the trustee is appointed by the court.[5] Also, if the trustee of a trust under will or even of a living trust is required to account to the court, he is known as the *trustee of a court trust.*

4. *Managing and custodian.* Managing trustee and custodian trustee are statutory terms. In England, Wales, Australia, and New Zealand, it is not uncommon for a charitable or educational institution—say, a college— to place its endowment property in the safekeeping, custody, and book-keeping of a trust corporation as *custodian trustee* and leave the management and investment of the property in the hands of the governing board or a committee of the board known as the *managing trustees.*[6]

In this country the same objective may be accomplished by the trust instrument. The advantage of the statutes is that they unify and clarify the respective duties and responsibilities of the custodian trustee and of the managing trustees.

5. *Responsible and advisory.* In Australia and New Zealand there is still another pair of trustees that complement each other. They are the responsible trustee and the advisory trustee. The *responsible trustee* is responsible for the administration of the trust. The *advisory trustee* serves in an advisory capacity only. The responsible trustee is not bound to take his advice. But if the advisory trustee thinks that the responsible trustee is committing or threatening to commit a breach of duty, he can bring the latter into court.[7]

In this country the same end may be accomplished, not by naming two trustees—one responsible and the other advisory—but by naming one trustee and the other adviser to the trustee.

Who May Be Trustee?

Any resident individual twenty-one years of age and mentally competent can be trustee. In most states a nonresident individual can be named. The law of the state in which the property is located may make require-

[5] *Regulation F—Trust Powers of National Banks*, Secs. 10 (a) and (b), (Federal Reserve System).

[6] Stephenson, *Trust Business in Common-Law Countries*, 70, 117, 297, 414.

[7] *Ibid.*, 298, 414.

ments, such as bond with surety and process agent, that it would not make of a resident trustee.

Also, there are restrictions upon the right of an out-of-state corporation to serve as trustee of real property or tangible personal property. During his lifetime a property owner can take his intangible personal property across the state line and create a living trust that will continue after his death. But the right of an out-of-state corporation to serve as trustee under his will is governed by the laws of the state in which his will is probated.

One must not take for granted that the restrictions are the same for corporations serving as administrator or executor, on the one hand, and as trustee, on the other. A state may permit an out-of-state corporation to qualify and serve as trustee which would not permit it to do so as executor.[8]

Should a property owner name a trustee who could not serve, this alone would not nullify the trust itself. In such case, the court would appoint a trustee who could serve. One of the fundamental principles of the common law of trusts is that a trust shall not fail for want of a trustee.

CORPORATE FIDUCIARIES

In the United States there are about 3,000 corporations that are authorized to serve in various fiduciary capacities. Nearly all of them are either state banks or national banks, and the property held by them in fiduciary capacities is divided about half-and-half between the two kinds of banks. Of the 3,000 there are less than one hundred corporations which are neither banks with a trust department nor trust companies with a banking department, and the number of corporations engaged in the trust business which are not banks seems to be declining.

Trust Institutions and Trust Business

At this point it will be well to introduce the two terms *trust institutions* and *trust business* which recur time and again in any discussion of the administration of property in estates and trusts.

The American name for a corporation that is engaged in serving in fiduciary capacities is *trust institution*. It is not an ideal name, for it connotes a charitable or educational institution rather than a business enterprise. But it is far too embedded in our terminology to be changed. The British name for such a corporation is *trust corporation*. A trust corporation is to be distinguished from a trust company in that in England the latter is an investment-trust company; that is, one engaged in marketing investment-trust shares. In Australia and New Zealand the name is *executor, trustee,* and *agency company*.

[8] See *Wills, Estates, and Trusts*, Secs. 17, 101–17, 102; and Stephenson, *Studies in Trust Business*, 2d ser., Ch. XVI, 329.

In our country the rendering of all kinds of services as fiduciary is known as the *trust business*. A corporation that was engaged only in settling the estates of deceased persons would be engaged in the trust business and would be a trust institution.

Historical Background of Corporate Fiduciaries

The first trust institution in the United States was the Massachusetts Hospital Life Insurance Company of Boston which, still in existence, was chartered by the Massachusetts Legislature in 1818, and began forthwith to engage in a type of trust business. However, it did not receive express legislative authority to engage in the trust business until 1823. In the meantime, in 1822 the Farmers' Fire Insurance and Loan Company of New York City (later the Farmers' Loan and Trust Company; later still the City Bank Farmers Trust Company; now the First National City Trust Company) was chartered and by its charter was authorized to engage in the trust business.

It was not until about 1850 that banks began to go into the trust business in earnest and forty years later, by 1890, there were scarcely more than one hundred, if that many, corporations engaged in the trust business. It was not until 1913 that national banks were authorized to go into the trust business, and not until 1925 that the Supreme Court of the United States removed the last barrier to their doing so.

The facts that at the present time about one-half of the corporations engaged in the trust business are national banks and that they are handling about one-half of all the property in estates and trusts committed to the administration of banks speak well for their activity and success in this field.

Trust Powers

All powers of a trust institution, whether they relate to estates of deceased persons, guardianships, agencies, or trusts, are referred to as its *trust powers*. Perhaps it would have been better if in the beginning these powers were referred to as its *trust authority* to distinguish it from its dispositive and administrative powers as discussed in this text, but it is too late now to change the terminology. However, the student must keep in mind the distinction between the authority of a corporation to engage in the trust business and its powers to administer and distribute property.

The statutory right of a corporation to engage in the trust business is granted by some legislative body or by some administrative agency created by that body.

1. *State banks.* Originally, a corporation desiring to engage in the trust business obtained its charter directly from its state legislature. Some of the older trust institutions still operate under their legislative charter. But, at present, in most states the right to grant permission to a corporation to

engage in the trust business has been delegated by the legislature to some administrative agency, such as the state banking commission or department or banking commissioner.

In most states this administrative agency has the right either to grant the corporation authority to engage in all kinds of trust business or to limit it to certain specified kinds. In a few states the grant of authority to engage in banking includes the power to engage in the trust business also; that is, trust business is regarded as an integral part of banking. In most states, however, a bank must obtain from some administrative agency a special license to engage in the trust business.

2. *National banks.* The right of a national bank in a given state to engage in the trust business is circumscribed by the right of state banks in the same state to do so. A national bank may be granted authority to engage in the trust business to the extent, but only to the extent, that state banks in the given state can.

A national bank, desiring to enter the trust business, would make its application to the Board of Governors of the Federal Reserve System. The Board would refer the application to the Federal Reserve Bank of the district in which the bank would be located. The Bank would make an investigation of the need for a trust department or for another one and report its recommendation, favorable or unfavorable, to the Board. Whereupon, the Board would grant or decline to grant authority to the national bank to open a trust department. Furthermore, the Board might grant general or limited authority to the bank. Most national, as well as state, banks which are granted authority to engage in the trust business at all are granted general authority to engage in any and all kinds of trust business.

COFIDUCIARIES

When two or more individuals or corporations or one or more individuals and one or more corporations engage in the settlement of an estate or administration of a trust, they are known as cofiduciaries.

While these cofiduciaries may be two or more individuals, or one or more individuals and one or more corporations, the most common types of cofiduciaries are two or more individuals, or one or more individuals and one trust institution. One seldom encounters two trust institutions serving as cofiduciaries of the same estate or personal trust. It is quite common for a property owner to name his wife and his son or business associate coexecutors or cotrustees, or for him to name one or more of them and a trust institution coexecutors or cotrustees.

Most cofiduciaries are either coexecutors or cotrustees. One seldom hears of coguardianships. It is common, of course, for a trust institution to be guardian of the property, and the mother, of the person of the minor; but these are not coguardians in the usual meaning of the term.

As between coexecutors and cotrustees, there are three differences that should be noted. One relates to the duration of the relationship; another, to the respective responsibilities and liabilities; and the third, to the functions—one of liquidation, the other of administration.

Differences between Coexecutorships and Cotrusteeships

1. *Duration.* A coexecutorship continues only until the estate is settled and the property distributed, which, at most, will be only a year or two. A cotrusteeship, on the contrary, may continue throughout the first, and the second, and on into the third generation after the creation of the trust. It is far less likely, therefore, that an individual cotrustee will survive and serve throughout the duration of a long-term trust than throughout the comparatively short period of settlement of an estate.

2. *Responsibilities and liabilities.* It is stated as a general principle of law that the responsibilities and liabilities of coexecutors are several and those of cotrustees, joint. When, for example, a property owner names his wife and his bank coexecutors, each is responsible only for her or its acts or omissions. Whereas, when he names them cotrustees, he makes them jointly liable for the administration of the trust. The wife cannot turn over to the bank the full administration of the trust, while she looks after the home and the family. Nor can the bank relieve itself of liability by placing the blame for a breach of duty upon the wife, as its cotrustee.

3. *Liquidation and administration.* The function of an executor or of coexecutors is primarily one of liquidation of the property in the estate; that of a trustee or of cotrustees, one of administration of the property. The executor or coexecutors assemble the property of the estate, pay the debts, taxes, and other expenses, and then turn the property or what is left of it over to those who are to receive it under the terms of the will. The investment or management problems of an executor are of short duration. The major function of a trustee or of cotrustees, on the other hand, is to invest funds and manage property over a longer period of time. This will involve the solution of many, some of them unexpected and unpredictable, investment and management problems.

These three differences between executorship and trusteeship predispose some property owners to name coexecutors but not cotrustees.

SEPARATE FIDUCIARIES

In place of cotrustees, in England, businessmen frequently name two trustees: a *business trustee,* usually an individual, to administer their business; and a *general trustee,* usually a trust corporation, to administer the other property.

Business Trustee

In this country many businessmen would like to have a trust institution to administer the liquid assets of their estate, and an individual, a son or business associate, to administer their business or business interests. So, they name the trust institution and the individual cotrustees, expecting, if not so saying in the will or trust agreement, that the trust institution will administer the liquid assets and the individual, the business assets.

This arrangement unavoidably casts upon the two trustees joint responsibility with respect to all of the assets, liquid and business alike. The two cannot agree between themselves that one of them will administer the liquid and the other the business assets.

In England, the businessman facing a similar situation would name his son or business associate his business trustee and his trust corporation his general trustee, and provide that the business trustee shall account to the general trustee and the latter, in turn, shall account to the court, thus unifying the administration of the trust in accounting procedure and yet keeping the administrative functions of the two trustees separate and distinguishable.

In this country, it would be possible for the property owner to name the individual trustee of his business and the trust institution trustee of his other property, and to provide for the individual trustee to account to the trust institution and the latter to the court, should court accounting be required. This would require very careful draftsmanship. The advantage of the British plan is that the term *business trustee* has come to have a more or less standard meaning. British trust corporations are loath to accept a trust involving the carrying on of a business and they themselves advise the appointment of a business trustee.[9] In this country, somewhat to the contrary, trust institutions accept and, in some cases, welcome trusts involving the carrying on of a business.

ADVISERS AND DIRECTORS

Still other types of fiduciary are adviserships and directorships to other fiduciaries—usually to executors and trustees.

Advisers

A property owner, preferring not to name an individual coexecutor or cotrustee will name him *adviser* to the corporate executor or trustee. A businessman will name his son or business associate adviser. A husband-and-father will name his wife adviser to the trustee, expecting that she will

[9] Stephenson, *Trust Business in Common-Law Countries*, 83–85; "Cotrustees or Several Trustees?" 249.

confer with the trustee regarding the care, especially the schooling, of the children.[10]

Such adviserships serve good purposes. But there are certain possible pitfalls which must be guarded against. Suppose the adviser fails or refuses to advise? Suppose he is out of reach of the trustee. Suppose, in the considered judgment of the trustee, the advice is bad. Is the trustee protected in acting without advice or upon bad advice? The *adviser* provisions of the will or trust agreement should cover all such points. Where the individual named adviser is meant to be adviser and nothing more, the following provision is not an uncommon one:

> With respect to all matters concerning which my executor or my trustee shall deem consultation and advice requisite or desirable, it is my desire that my executor or my trustee, as the case may be, consult and advise freely with my wife, if she shall be available for such consultation and advice; but in expressing this desire I do not mean to impose any legal limitations upon my executor or my trustee, nor do I mean to relieve my executor or my trustee of any legal liabilities in connection with the settlement of my estate or the administration of the trusts created under the terms and provisions of this will. Nor do I mean to impose any legal responsibilities upon my wife. This provision shall not be construed as limiting any of the powers conferred upon my executor or my trustee by virtue of any of the foregoing terms and provisions of this will.

Directors

Sometimes a property owner creates a living trust and provides that the trustee shall not make nor change any investments except as directed by himself during his lifetime. Or he provides in his will that his trustee shall not make or change any investments without the consent or approval of the investment house with which he has had a long and satisfactory relationship. These are known commonly as *direction* or *consent trusts*.

Such directorships are fraught with as many or more baffling administrative problems than are adviserships. Suppose the director fails or refuses to direct or consent. Suppose he is out of reach of the trustee. Suppose his direction involves what the trustee considers would be a breach of its duty. Suppose the director in giving a direction is actuated by self-interest—a case of divided loyalty. The general rule of law is that, if the director is the sole beneficiary of the trust, the trustee can accept and act upon his direction with impunity. But if he is not the sole beneficiary of the trust, the director is, in effect, a cofiduciary with the trustee and the latter, blindly following direction, may commit a breach of trust for which it will be liable. As a consequence, many of the more experienced trust institutions are loath to accept direction or consent trusts.

[10] Stephenson, "Cofiduciaries or Consultants?", 741.

AGENTS

An *agent* is anyone who acts for another by the latter's authority. The world is full of agencies, but the vast majority of them have nothing whatever to do with estates and trusts. However, there are agencies that are in aid of the settlement of estates and administration of trusts and guardianships. These agencies fall into three main groups: (1) for individuals, (2) for corporations, and (3) for institutions.

For Individuals

The principal agencies for individuals are: for other fiduciaries, safekeeping, custody, management, and escrow.

1. *For individual fiduciaries.* Sometimes a property owner names his wife executrix and trustee with the expectation that his bank, serving as her agent, will, in fact, settle his estate and administer his trusts. Such an agency is an anomalous relationship and trust institutions, as a rule, do not welcome them.

However, trust institutions, as well as individual fiduciaries, do employ agents, such as rental agents, collection agents, and farm managers, to aid them in settling estates and administering trusts. A fiduciary may employ an agent to do for him whatever needs to be done that he himself reasonably cannot be expected to do himself.

2. *Safekeeping.* A property owner may create, usually with his bank, a safekeeping agency under which he turns over his securities and, perhaps, other valuables to his agent to keep for him. The safekeeper has no other duty than to keep them safely and in due time return them to the owner or deliver them upon his order.

3. *Custody.* The property owner, especially if he expects to be absent from home for some time, may create a custodianship under which the custodian, usually his bank, not only safekeeps the property but also performs ministerial, as distinguished from managerial, services with regard to it, such as collecting and crediting interest and dividends, and attending to calls, maturities, and conversions of securities. A *ministerial duty* is one that involves only carrying out instructions; a *managerial duty*, one that involves the exercise of judgment and discretion.

4. *Managing.* The property owner, going the next step in imposing responsibility upon his agent, may appoint a *managing agent* and impose upon him managerial as well as and in addition to ministerial duties. These managing agencies usually fall into two classes: (*a*) for securities and (*b*) for farms.

a. For securities. The agent may have the duties not only of safekeeping and custody of the securities but also of analyzing them as investments and from time to time recommending changes. Ultimate responsibility for the change remains in the property owner.

b. For farms or ranches. A farm owner or ranch owner may appoint a *manager* of his farm or ranch. This agency service appeals especially to absentee landowners, to aging people, and to women who desire to be relieved of the burdens of management.

5. *Escrow*. Escrow agency is a common and useful device in the sale and purchase of real property. For example, *A* agrees to sell and *B* agrees to buy a farm or residence at an agreed price. It may take days, weeks, or sometimes months even to attend to all of the preliminaries to the closing of the deal. In the meantime *A* or *B* might die or might change his mind. So *A* has prepared and delivers to *C* (called an *escrow agent*) a deed to the property, and *B* delivers to *C* a certified check for the purchase price. As soon as the preliminaries, such as title insurance and satisfaction of prior liens, have been attended to, *C* delivers the deed to *B* and the purchase price to *A*, and the agency is terminated. This is the simplest type of escrow agency. *C* might have to use part of the purchase price for paying off prior liens on the property, in which case he would have more active duties.

For Corporations

The principal agencies for corporations are: transfer, registrar, paying, and depositary.

1. *Transfer*. Practically all of the larger industrial corporations, especially if the stock is listed on a stock exchange, have a trust institution to serve as their agent to transfer their shares of stock and registered bonds and keep the transfer books.

2. *Registrar*. Similarly, they have a trust institution to register the issue or transfer of their stock to prevent overissue. The student will see on the face of one of these certificates of stock the name of one well-known bank or trust company as transfer agent and of another as *registrar*.

3. *Paying*. Any of these corporations may employ a trust institution to serve as its *interest-* or *dividend-paying agent* and its bookkeeper for these payments.

4. *Depositary*. In connection with reorganizations, refinancing, or any other major change in the corporation, the corporation may appoint a trust institution *depositary* to receive and hold its securities while the reorganization or other change is in process.

For Institutions

Public institutions, such as colleges, hospitals, and units of government (such as cities, counties, or school districts) create agencies—endowment, fiscal secretaryships, and treasuryships. Some religious bodies find it to their advantage to name a trust institution their financial secretary and treasurer to keep books for them. Endowment is perhaps the most common type of institutional agency.

1. *Endowment.* A college, for example, receives and holds property properly earmarked for its endowment. It cannot place the property in trust for it cannot re-trustee property that already has been trusteed to it. So, it names a trust institution its *endowment agent* to receive, safekeep, analyze, and review securities, manage farms and business houses, and make recommendations to the institution. As was brought out in Chapter 10, this type of agency is especially attractive to younger, struggling charitable and educational institutions.

The foregoing, it is hoped, gives the student a bird's-eye view of the number and variety of services being rendered by fiduciaries for many of which the fiduciary bears a special name. All told, there are over eighty named services being rendered by American fiduciaries.[11]

[11] 39 *Trust Bulletin* (October, 1959), 50.

COLLATERAL READING

Note: For complete citations, see Bibliography, pp. 417–428.
ATKINSON on *Wills and Administration.*
LORING's *Trustee's Handbook*, Shattuck rev.
WINDLE, "Principles and Policies Applicable to Direction Trusts."
American Institute of Banking, Vol. I, Ch. 1 (New York Trust Department Services).

14

Fiduciary Principles

𝕿HE PRECEDING CHAPTER PRESENTS all of the principal capacities in which persons serve in connection with estates and trusts: guardians, administrators and executors, trustees, corporate fiduciaries, cofiduciaries, separate fiduciaries, advisers and directors, and agents. It was pointed out that each of these capacities involves a relationship and that the relationship is fiduciary. We come now to a consideration of certain principles, or perhaps it would be more accurate to say, a principle, inherent in all fiduciary relationships. Upon this principle has been built all the duties and powers of guardians, administrators, executors, trustees, and agents and all the rights of heirs, distributees, devisees, legatees, wards, beneficiaries, and principals. It is the principle of loyalty to beneficiaries.

Principles and Policies Distinguished

It is necessary first to distinguish between principles and policies and to observe the distinction hereafter.

1. *Principles.* A *fiduciary principle* is a fundamental doctrine governing the conduct of a fiduciary. It is a general truth equally applicable to all fiduciaries and to all fiduciary relationships. It is a part of the common law which is applicable throughout the English-speaking world. A principle does not change except as the common law itself changes, and then only by slow, imperceptible evolution. A given principle governs a fiduciary whether he likes it or not. He cannot change it, no matter how much he might like to do so.

2. *Policies.* A *fiduciary policy*, on the contrary, is only an attitude or a course of action adopted by each fiduciary for the performance of requisite functions. A policy is changeable at the will of the fiduciary.

A fiduciary accepts principles; he creates and adopts policies. Whereas a principle is a *must* in the law, a policy is only a *should* in the mind of the fiduciary. It is appropriate, therefore, to speak of *governing* principles and of *guiding* policies.

Depositories of Statements of Principles

Gradually, over the centuries of development of the common law, fiduciary principles have evolved. Beginning as unwritten customs, they have been crystallized, one at a time, in judicial decisions. As time has gone on, some of them have been codified in statutes. They have been stated, restated, and clarified in legal treatises, textbooks, and articles on fiduciary subjects.

To send a student of fiduciary principles to the tens of thousands of judicial decisions, to the statutes, and to the treatises, textbooks, and articles to ferret these principles out for himself would be even more baffling than to send him hunting for a needle in a haystack. He must have aid and guidance.

1. *Treatises and texts.* Confining oneself, by way of illustration only, to trustee-beneficiary relationships, to one's own country, and to one's own time, one need be reminded of only a few of the treatises and texts which are depositories of statements of fiduciary principles.

a. Loring's *Trustee's Handbook.* In 1898, Augustus Peabody Loring published *A Trustee's Handbook*, which Mayo Adams Shattuck forty years later said has "played a significant part in the almost dramatic growth of trust administration." It has gone through five editions, the latest one being known as the "Shattuck Revision of 1940." This handbook contains 425 pages.

b. *Restatement of the Law of Trusts.* Work on a restatement of the law of trusts by a group of distinguished lawyers, headed by Professor Austin W. Scott of the Harvard Law School, began in 1927, and the *Restatement* was published in 1935. The first edition of the *Restatement* is nearly 1,500 pages long.

c. Bogert's *The Law of Trusts and Trustees.* In 1935, Professor George Gleason Bogert, then of the Faculty of the School of Law of the University of Chicago, began publication of *The Law of Trusts and Trustees*, which eventuated in eleven volumes (nearly 6,000 pages).

d. Scott's *The Law of Trusts.* In 1939, following the publication in 1935 of the *Restatement of the Law of Trusts*, Professor Scott published *The Law of Trusts*, the first edition of which consisted of four volumes (over 3,000 pages), exclusive of annual supplements. In 1956, Professor Scott published a second edition of his treatise, consisting of five volumes (4,056 pages).

These four treatises and texts, selected out of a much larger group, apply only to fiduciary principles involved in trustee-beneficiary relationships. In addition to these, there is a comparable amount of published material on fiduciary principles involved in executor-distributee, administrator-heir-and-next-of-kin, guardian-ward, and principal-agent relationships which govern fiduciaries in rendering these different kinds of fiduciary services.

The voluminousness of the published material on fiduciary principles has made it highly advisable, if not absolutely necessary, to summarize those principles in some practical way and present them in manageable length and form. This was accomplished, in part at any rate, in 1933, in the formulation and adoption of "A Statement of Principles of Trust Institutions," by the Trust Division of the American Bankers Association.

Principles Common to All Fiduciaries

Professor Scott has said that the following principles are common to all fiduciary relationships:

1. That the fiduciary is under a duty to act for the benefit of the other party to the relation as to matters within the scope of the relation;
2. That ordinarily he is under a duty not to delegate to a third person the performance of his own duties as fiduciary;
3. That as to matters within the scope of the relation he is under a duty not to profit at the expense of the other party to the relation;
4. That, if he enters into a transaction with the other party to the relation, he is under a duty to make a full disclosure of all the circumstances known to him affecting the transaction and, if the transaction is unfair to the other party to the relation, the latter can set it aside.[1]

The late Justice Cardozo of the Supreme Court of the United States, then speaking as Judge Cardozo of the New York Court of Appeals, made the following, now classic, statement:

Many forms of conduct permissible in a workaday world for those acting at arm's length, are forbidden to those bound by fiduciary ties. A trustee is held to something stricter than the morals of the market-place. Not honesty alone but the punctilio of an honor the most sensitive is then the standard of behavior. As to this there has developed a tradition that is unbending and inveterate. Uncompromising rigidity has been the attitude of courts of equity when petitioned to undermine the rule of undivided loyalty by the "disintegrating erosion" of particular exceptions. Only thus has the level of conduct for fiduciaries been kept at a level higher than that trodden by the crowd. It will not consciously be lowered by any judgment of this court.[2]

According to both Professor Scott and Justice Cardozo, undivided loyalty is the basic principle of every fiduciary relationship. In fact, Professor Scott says that the duty of loyalty is the most fundamental duty owed by the trustee to the beneficiaries. As truly he might have said that it is the most fundamental duty owed by the administrator or executor to the distributees

[1] Scott on *Trusts*, Sec. 2.5.
[2] *Meinhard* v. *Salmon*, 249, N.Y. 458, 464; 164 N. E. 545, 546; 62 A. L. R. 1 (1928).

of the estate, and by the guardian to his ward, and by the agent to his principal.

DISCHARGE OF FIDUCIARY OBLIGATIONS

One principle of the fiduciary relationship is that, once a person has accepted the relationship, he is under a duty to discharge all of its attendant obligations.

Freedom to Decline

A person is not bound to accept appointment as administrator when it is offered him by the court; however, once he has accepted it, he must discharge the obligations of the office and can be relieved of those obligations only by the court itself.

He is not bound to accept appointment as executor although he is named in the will and although the court offers him the appointment; but, once he has accepted the appointment, he must serve unless or until he is relieved by the court.

He is not bound to accept appointment as guardian of the property of a minor or incompetent person, and this is true even though he may be the parent; however, once he has accepted the appointment, he must serve unless or until he is relieved by the court.

He is not bound to accept appointment as trustee under will; but, once he has accepted, he must serve unless or until he is relieved by the court or unless the will itself permits him to resign.

Even in the case of a living trust, he is not bound to accept the trusteeship; but, once he has accepted it, he must serve unless he is relieved by the settlor or the court, or unless the trust agreement gives him the power to resign.

However, a person may enter voluntarily into a transaction which results in his becoming a trustee, as in the case where a guardian purchases real property with his ward's money but takes title in his own name. This is known as a *resulting trust*—that is, one resulting from the transaction in the light of the relationships between the parties. Furthermore, a person may engage in a fraudulent transaction as a consequence of which he will be treated as if he were trustee—a *constructive trustee*, which is in the same class as the guardian *de son tort* (by his own wrong). For example, *A* places money in *B's* hand for some specified purpose. Instead of using it for that purpose, *B* disobediently uses it to buy real property and dishonestly takes title in his own name. The law declares that *B* is constructive trustee of the property for *A* and, although it be against *B's* will, imposes upon him the same obligation as if he were trustee. Apart from these two exceptions, a person cannot be forced to accept a trust; but, once he has accepted it, he must administer it.

A person cannot be forced to accept an agency; but, once he has accepted it, he must perform all the duties inherent in the relationship.

So, the first fiduciary principle is that, while a person is not obliged to accept a fiduciary relationship, once he has accepted it, he must discharge the obligations of that relationship. This leads directly to a second principle implicit in the discharge of the fiduciary obligation—that of obedience.

Obedience to Terms of Relationship

In the "Statement of Principles," referred to above as a sort of summation of fiduciary principles, it is declared that the terms of the trust instrument must be carried out with scrupulous care and with particular attention to the duties imposed therein upon the trustee.[3] This principle applies equally to all other fiduciary relationships.

A person may include in his will, trust agreement, or agency agreement terms that are unwise, shortsighted, ill-tempered, whimsical, and ill-advised in every respect. But, once the fiduciary has accepted the relationship, he is under a duty to carry out the terms of that relationship unless or until it becomes illegal, impossible, or against public policy for him to do so. Obedience to those terms may impose upon him the duty to do what he thinks is not, and what, in fact, *is not* for the best interest of the beneficiary. But it will be for the court, not himself, to relieve him of the duty to obey those terms. Furthermore, where the terms of the relationship require the fiduciary to exercise his own discretion with respect either to the disposition or the administration of the property, the principle of obedience requires that he himself exercise that discretion and not go to the court to exercise it for him.

LOYALTY TO BENEFICIARIES

It is no wonder that Professor Scott speaks of the duty of loyalty as the most fundamental duty that a trustee owes his beneficiary, because it is the duty from which all other duties of a trustee stem. Similarly, it is the duty from which all the other duties of an administrator or executor, guardian, trustee, or agent stem.

Definition of Beneficiary

The term *beneficiary* as used in this section includes all persons, institutions, and objects for whose benefit the relationship exists—that is, distributees of estates, wards of guardianships, principals of agencies, as well as beneficiaries of trusts.

In this chapter, instead of discussing what loyalty requires a fiduciary

[3] Art. III, Sec. 1.

to do—that is, his positive obligations—perhaps it will be of more practical value to the student to call his attention to some of the things that the principle of loyalty to his beneficiary will not permit a fiduciary to do—things which, Justice Cardozo would have said, would lower the level of conduct of a fiduciary to that of the crowd.

Sale to Fiduciary Individually

The principle of loyalty makes it improper for a fiduciary to sell to himself individually property which is the subject matter of the relationship, unless the other parties to the relationship, all of them being of age and competent, consent to the sale after the fiduciary has made a complete disclosure to them of all the pertinent facts or unless the court orders or approves the sale.

Such a sale is improper whether it is made publicly or privately, directly or indirectly. For example, an executor should not buy for himself property belonging to the estate offered for sale at public auction even though he pays what then is a fair price for the property. If later he should sell it at a profit, he would have to account to the distributees for the profit. Nor can he arrange with a third person to buy the property in his, the third person's, name, with the understanding that after the sale he will turn it over to the executor for what he paid for it.

There are many instances in which it would be to the financial advantage of everyone concerned for the fiduciary to sell the property to himself. He might be willing to pay more for it than anyone else would. It is not, as Justice Cardozo would have said, a question of honesty alone but of the "punctilio of an honor the most sensitive" that keeps a fiduciary from selling the property to himself. That the courts are so uncompromising on this point is a credit to their conception of the fiduciary relationship as well as to the relationship itself.

However, as already pointed out, the beneficiaries, provided they all are of legal age and competent, may consent to the fiduciary's selling property to himself and their consent would be binding upon them. But it would not be binding upon others—that is, upon minors or incompetent persons, or other persons under legal disability, or even upon persons, although of age and competent, who had not consented to the sale. Furthermore, the court itself may authorize the sale beforehand or approve it afterwards if it finds as a fact after a full disclosure that the sale was or will be advantageous to the beneficiaries.

Sale to Member of Fiduciary's Family

Suppose A, executor, sells estate property to B, his wife, or she buys it at a public sale, in either case for a fair price and without any understanding between A and B that she really was buying it for him and with his money. Some courts have held that such a sale is voidable; that is, it may be set aside and declared void; others, that the husband-and-wife status of *A* and *B* is a circumstance to be taken into consideration but is not conclusive in deciding whether it is, to all intents and purposes, a sale by *A*, executor, to himself individually and, therefore, voidable.

Suppose *A*, executor, sells estate property to his son or daughter or to some other member of his family or to his business associate. While the mere fact that the sale to a member of the family or kinsman or business associate of the fiduciary does not of itself violate the principle of loyalty, it raises the issue and puts the fiduciary distinctly on the defensive in proving his loyalty.

Sale to Directors, Officers, or Employees of Trust Institution

Suppose *X* Bank is trustee under the will of *A*. In the trust estate there is a residence for sale. Can *X* sell it privately to one of its directors, officers, or employees? If the residence is put up for sale at auction, can one of them buy it for himself?

A private sale, without the consent of the beneficiaries, all of them being of age and competent, or without the approval of the court after full disclosure of all the pertinent facts, would be improper. A sale at auction would be subject to attack, in which both *X* and its director, officer, or employee who bought the property would be on the defensive and, in the language of the law, would have the laboring oar.

Suppose *X* should sell trust property to *Y* Company, a corporation with which it is affiliated or in which it is financially interested. This, too, would be improper, and the sale might be set aside.

National banks are prohibited by regulations of the Board of Governors of the Federal Reserve System from selling property held by them in fiduciary capacities to their directors, officers, employees, or affiliates, except under certain specified conditions which, in effect, do not weaken the restriction.[4]

Sale under Terms of Relationship

In the case of an executorship or a trust under will or a living trust, the will or the trust agreement itself may authorize or even may direct the executor or the trustee, as the case may be, to sell estate or trust property to the executor or to the trustee or to some member of his family or some business associate. In this case, the principle of loyalty requires that the fiduciary sell or offer to sell the property to himself or to other specified persons as authorized by the terms of the relationship. Loyalty here requires that the fiduciary carry out the terms of the authorization or direction, with-

[4] *Regulation F—Trust Powers of National Banks,* Sec. 11 (a), (Federal Reserve System).

out taking any advantage of his relationship to the possible disadvantage of the beneficiaries.

Sale of His Own Property to Himself as Fiduciary

The counterpart of the sale by the fiduciary to himself individually is that of the sale by the individual to himself as fiduciary. The principle and the application of the principle of loyalty apply in the one case as in the other.

For example, *A*, trustee under *B's* will, has securities of his own and the trust under *B's* will has funds to be invested. Can *A* properly sell his own securities to himself as trustee under *B's* will, granting that they are proper investments for the trust and that the price is the same as *B* would have to pay for them on the market? The answer is *no*, unless the terms of the trust otherwise provide. Although it may be an honest transaction in every respect and although the sale by *A*, individual, to *A*, trustee, might mean a saving to the beneficiaries of the trust of a broker's commission, the temptation to *A* to violate the principle of loyalty is too great for the courts to sanction the practice. Again, it is not honesty alone but the "punctilio of an honor the most sensitive" that should govern the fiduciary's conduct.

The beneficiaries can have the sale set aside or they can let it stand and make the fiduciary account for any and all profit he may have made on the sale by himself as an individual to himself as a fiduciary. Whenever a fiduciary sells his own property to himself as a fiduciary, he has everything to lose and nothing whatever to gain.

This principle applies to a bank or trust company and to an individual fiduciary in the same way. For example, *X* Bank has both an investment department, in which it has securities for sale, and a trust department, in which it has trust funds to be invested. Is it proper for *X*, through its investment department, to sell securities to *X* as trustee under *A's* will? Again, the answer is *no*, unless the terms of the relationship so provide. The answer is the same even though the investment department makes no profit out of the transaction. The reasoning is that to permit it would put too much of a temptation in the way of the bank or trust company to serve some selfish, which would mean disloyal, purpose in selling its own securities to its fiduciary accounts.

For another somewhat similar example, *X* Bank purchases mortgages for its own account and later transfers them to its fiduciary accounts as they need them. Or it purchases and pools mortgages and issues mortgage-participations to its fiduciary accounts. This, too, is regarded as improper unless authorized by statute or by the trust instrument. It involves a possible, if not probable, conflict of interest between the bank or trust company as seller and its fiduciary accounts as purchasers.

As for national banks, Regulation F of the Board of Governors of the

Federal Reserve System provides that they must not sell to their fiduciary accounts the bank's own property or that of its directors, officers, or employees or their interests in the stock, obligations, or property acquired from affiliates of the bank.[5]

Again, as in the case of sales by the fiduciary to himself personally, the terms of the will or trust agreement or, especially, of the agency agreement may provide for sales by the fiduciary of his own property to the fiduciary account. Where this is true, the principle of loyalty requires that the fiduciary take no selfish advantage whatever of this power and make no sales that would, in his judgment, not be for the best interest of the beneficiaries.

Investment in Fiduciary's Own Shares of Stock

In a later chapter on the investment of trust funds, the bank's own shares of stock as trust investments will be considered from the investment angle. In this chapter, however, it is considered only insofar as the principle of loyalty is involved.

X Bank takes over, as executor and trustee under the will of one of its directors, officers, or employees, shares of its own stock. Should it, in the absence of express authority by statute or in the will, retain those shares any longer than is reasonably needed to dispose of them at the fair market price? The answer is *no*. The reasoning is that a situation may arise in which it would be to the advantage of the bank itself to retain the shares while it would be to the advantage of the estate or trust for it to dispose of them. For example, suppose it were known by the general public that the bank was selling out the shares it held in its estates and trusts. That in itself not only might depress the market for its shares but also might raise some question as to the condition of the bank or might, in an extreme case, start a run on the bank.

Or, for another example, X Bank as trustee under A's will, has funds to invest. Its own shares are available on the open market at a price which, it knows, would make the shares a good investment for A's trust. Should it, in the absence of express authority by statute or in the will, invest in its own shares? Once more, the answer is *no*. The reasoning, as above, is that, while the bank shares may be a good investment at the moment, a situation may arise in which there would be a conflict of interest between the bank itself and its trust account.

On both these points—that of retaining investments and that of making new investments in the bank's own shares—Professor Scott has stated the law as follows:

The trustee ought not to put itself in a situation where its own interests may conflict with those of the beneficiaries. For this reason it seems clear that it

[5] *Ibid.,* Sec. 11 (*b*).

is improper for a corporate trustee to make an investment in the purchase of its own shares, even though the purchase is not made from itself, and that it is improper for the trustee to retain such shares although it received them as original investments, unless it is authorized to do so by the terms of the trust or by statute.[6]

National banks are prohibited by Regulation F of the Board of Governors of the Federal Reserve System from investing trust funds in their own shares unless authorized to do so.[7]

Competition for Investments

The principle of loyalty is applicable to competition for investments between an individual or a bank and trust company and himself or itself as a fiduciary.

First, take the case of the individual fiduciary. A is trustee under B's will. In the trust there are uninvested funds awaiting investment. A himself has funds of his own he would like to invest. C offers A a 5 per cent mortgage, to be amortized over fifteen years, on improved residential property—C's own home—at 50 per cent of its valuation conservatively appraised, and C is known to be a solvent and reliable person who meets his obligations promptly. This would be an ideal investment for either A himself or for the trust under B's will. Should A purchase the mortgage for himself or for the trust?

Before attempting to answer this question, take the case of a bank. It is trustee under A's will. It has funds of its own it would like to invest to yield 5 per cent. The trust under A's will also has funds awaiting investment. The bank or trust company is offered the same mortgage as that described in the preceding paragraph—an ideal and desirable investment for either the bank or the trust. Again, should the bank purchase the mortgage for itself or for the trust?

In answering this question, A, the individual trustee, has only himself to consider. He is under a duty to beneficiaries to keep the property on a productive basis. If he kept trust funds uninvested longer than was reasonably necessary, he would be guilty of a breach of trust and would make himself liable, at least, for the current rate of income on trust investments. If it came to light that he had bought a good 5 per cent mortgage for himself when he needed it for his trust, he would have difficulty convincing the beneficiaries and other persons as well that he had been absolutely loyal to the beneficiaries, much less that he had lived up to Justice Cardozo's standard, the "punctilio of an honor the most sensitive."

In answering this question, X Bank may have more difficulty than the

[6] Scott on *Trusts*, Sec. 170.15.
[7] Sec. 11 (*a*).

individual in that it has to consider both its duty to its own stockholders and its duty to all its fiduciary accounts with funds to invest.

Since there are no statutes or court decisions on the point, so far as found, the author, as well as the student, has no other recourse than to resolve the matter for himself. The author reasons this way: when the stockholders of a bank open a trust department and accept trusts, they understand or they should understand that the bank will be under a duty to be absolutely loyal to the beneficiaries of its trust accounts. This will be the bank's most fundamental duty. The bank's duty to earn dividends for its stockholders always must be secondary to its duty of loyalty to its trusts. Stockholders should understand that their bank would not be absolutely loyal to its trusts if it took for itself investments, the income from which its trust beneficiaries needed for their support and comfort. Some banks have already met this issue squarely by adopting a fixed policy of offering every mortgage that qualifies for a trust investment to the trust department before offering it to the banking department. Although this reasoning may lean over backwards in favor of the beneficiaries to the disadvantage of the stockholders, such banks never will have to apologize either to their beneficiaries or to the general public for such favoritism.

Competition between Fiduciary Accounts

With regard to competition between fiduciary accounts over investments, the principle of loyalty comes into play in two ways—one of which was discussed in the preceding section.

The trustee under will decides to buy the mortgage described above for his fiduciary accounts and not for himself. The trustee has several accounts, each of which has uninvested funds and is in need of good investments. So, the question arises: which account shall take the mortgage? Again, so far as known, there is no direct authority on the point. It would seem that, among the several accounts, the mortgage should be sold to the account the funds of which had been uninvested the longest, or the one in which there was the greatest immediate need for income. Having favored one trust by selling it this mortgage, the trustee should favor another trust when another good investment became available, so that in the long run all the accounts would be treated impartially. In such a case the standard to apply would be that of the prudent man acting in good conscience under similar circumstances and acting so that over a reasonable period of time no fair-minded beneficiary of any account would have any occasion to say or to feel that the trustee had favored one account at the expense of another or of other accounts.

We come now to purchases and sales between fiduciary accounts. One trust has a good investment which for some good reason it needs to cash in. Another trust has cash on hand which it needs to invest. The same individual or bank is trustee of both trusts. Is it proper for the trustee to sell the investment out of one trust and buy it into the other? The answer is *yes*, provided the transaction is fair to both trusts. Here is where the principle of loyalty comes into play again. Suppose the trustee of the selling trust would like to get rid of the investment before he distributes the trust principal because it is not an investment that the beneficiaries would be willing to accept. He is tempted to transfer the investment to another trust which would continue for years. To yield to such a temptation would be a flagrant violation of the duty of loyalty. Or the trustee might be tempted to favor the purchasing trust at the expense of the selling trust, and this would be equally a violation of the principle of loyalty. In order to avoid being tempted, much less yielding to such temptation, the trustee should treat the investment in the selling trust as if it were an investment being offered by an outside owner or broker and should purchase it for the other account if, but only if, it were an investment it would purchase from an outside owner for the particular account. Applied to mortgage investments, a mortgage should not be transferred from one trust to another without a new appraisement and a recheck of everything that might affect the desirability of the mortgage as a new investment for the purchasing account. In a word, the investment, although transferred from another account with the same trustee, should be regarded as a new investment for the purchasing account.[8]

Fiduciary's Use of Property for His Own Purposes

Loyalty does not permit a fiduciary to use for his own purposes the property he is holding as a fiduciary. For example, an administrator or executor should not use for his own purposes property—an automobile, say—belonging to the estate. A trustee should not occupy a residence belonging to the trust estate, although he pays a fair rental and takes good care of the property, unless the beneficiaries, all of them being of age and competent, consent for him to do so, or unless the will or trust agreement authorizes him to do so. He should not rent or lease business or farm property to himself. In none of these cases does it need to be a question of honesty. Nor does it need to be a question of a fair return on the property. The fiduciary may be the soul of honesty and he may pay as much or more rent than anyone else would pay. It is a question of loyalty—"of the punctilio of an honor the most sensitive." There is too much temptation for a fiduciary to use the property to his own advantage and to the corresponding disadvantage of the beneficiaries for the courts to sanction any such dealing by the fiduciary with the property.

Nor does loyalty permit a fiduciary to lend to himself funds belonging to the fiduciary account. More than that, it does not sanction a bank's lending the funds of its fiduciary accounts to its own directors, officers, or

[8] *Ibid.*, Sec. 11 (*c*).

employees or to the directors, officers, or employees of its affiliates. Here again it is not a question of honesty. Nor is it a question of security. It is wholly a question of loyalty. Take a mortgage, for example. The fiduciary should not be under any temptation—because the mortgagor is one of its directors, officers, or employees—to indulge him in his payments of interest or principal when, if he were not connected with the bank, it would push the collection while the property still was good for the debt and the mortgagor, solvent.

Deposit of Fiduciary Funds in Fiduciary Bank

A bank deposit is, in the eye of the law, an unsecured loan to the bank. It is a general principle of law that a fiduciary should not invest fiduciary funds in unsecured loans. When a bank as trustee, for example, deposits trust funds awaiting investment or distribution in its own banking department, it is, in effect, not only making an unsecured loan but also making a loan to itself. When it deposits trust funds in another bank, it is, in effect, making an unsecured loan to that bank.

As a matter of law, there is a sharp conflict of authority as to a bank's depositing fiduciary funds in its own banking department. In some states the point is covered by statute; in others, by court decisions. In some states the bank can deposit such funds in its own banking department; in others, it cannot do so. In the *Restatement of the Law of Trusts* it finally was declared, after much debate, that a bank which deposits trust funds in its own banking department commits a breach of trust unless by the terms of the trust it is authorized to do so. In view of this conflict of authority, the student should ascertain what the law of a given state is on the point.[9]

Under Regulation F, Section 9 (b), a national bank cannot deposit fiduciary funds in its own banking department unless it delivers to its trust department specified collateral securities equal at all times to the amount of the deposit.

When it comes to the principle of loyalty, a bank as fiduciary is not disloyal to its beneficiaries in depositing fiduciary funds in its own banking department if, under all the circumstances, it is reasonable and prudent for it to make the deposit; that is, if the bank itself is safe and if in making the deposit the bank is not thinking of its own interest but only that of its beneficiaries. But if the bank in making the deposit is actuated in the least by a selfish motive, for instance, to bolster its reserves in a time of economic stress, it commits a breach of trust—an act of disloyalty to its beneficiaries. If the bank remains solvent, there would be no loss to the beneficiaries. But if the bank should close and be unable to pay off its depositors, including its trust department, in full, the directors and officers of the bank—whoever was responsible for making the deposit, knowing the unsafe condition of the bank—would be personally liable for any loss to the beneficiaries. The

[9] Scott on *Trusts*, Sec. 170.18.

fact that at the present time each deposit in each insured bank is insured through the Federal Deposit Insurance Corporation up to $10,000 keeps this from being, in practice, a point of as much importance as otherwise it might be.

The principle of loyalty would be involved no less if the fiduciary, whether an individual or a bank, deposited fiduciary funds in a bank for the good of the bank and not in the interest of the beneficiaries. Suppose, for example, the executor was also president of the bank and he deposited estate funds in his bank to bolster its reserves. Or suppose one bank as executor knew that another bank in the community was in a shaky condition and, in order to keep that bank open and possibly prevent a run on all the banks, it kept its fiduciary funds deposited in the other bank. These would be violations of the duty of loyalty, and the executor-bank would be personally liable for any loss sustained by the beneficiaries on account of the deposit.

Fiduciary Purchasing Property

The principle of loyalty requires not only that a fiduciary shall not purchase property from his fiduciary account, as already discussed, but also that he shall not purchase property from a third person in which his fiduciary account has an interest. The following are illustrations of some of the situations in which the principle of loyalty comes into play.

A, as trustee, holds in the trust estate a valuable ten-year lease on property. Before the expiration of the lease, he renews the lease, not for the trust, but for himself.

A, as trustee, holds in the trust estate a business building on which there is a mortgage of $25,000. *A* takes over the mortgage himself and thus makes himself as trustee debtor to himself as an individual. While the transaction itself may not be an act of disloyalty—it may, in fact, be an act of loyalty to the beneficiaries—nonetheless the transaction is too closely connected with the administration of the trust for the trustee to profit by it. Instead, he must account to the trust for any profit he makes out of the transaction.

A, as trustee, purchases for himself property which, in good conscience, he should purchase for the trust. He commits an act of disloyalty to his trust. This already has been illustrated and discussed in connection with the purchase of mortgages by the fiduciary for himself which he should have purchased for his trust. Nor is the offense of the fiduciary's disloyalty lessened in any degree—it may, in fact, be aggravated by underhandedness—by his purchasing the property through or in the name of some other person with an understanding that the purchase really is for himself.

Profits out of Dealings with Fiduciary Property

The principle of loyalty perhaps comes into its sharpest focus when applied to profits made by the fiduciary out of dealings with the fiduciary property. The following are illustrations of some of the ways in which the principle comes into play on this point.

A is in the mortgage-loan business. He is also trustee under the will of *B*. As trustee he holds funds awaiting investment. He is offered a highly desirable mortgage. In line with his regular business he is entitled to a bonus or commission for making mortgage loans. If he takes the mortgages for one of his outside customers, he is entitled to compensation for his services. But suppose he takes it for the trust. He must account to the trust for any and all compensation he receives for negotiating the loan.

Or *A* is an investment broker. Also he is trustee under *B's* will. The trust has funds to invest or investments to sell. If *A* buys or sells for his customers, he is entitled to his broker's commission. But if he buys or sells for his trust, he must account to it for any and all profit he makes on the transaction.

Or *A* is in the fire insurance business. Also he is trustee under *B's* will. He is under a duty to keep the trust property properly insured. The insurance companies he represents are as strong as any in the country. Their rates are as low. His commissions are the same as those of other insurance agents. Why should he not insure the trust property in his own companies? It will cost the trust the same in premiums whether he himself writes the insurance or places it with some other insurance agency. The trust itself stands to lose nothing by the transaction; in fact, it even may stand to obtain better coverage at no additional expense. Nevertheless, the law has decreed that *A* must account to his trust for any and all profit he makes by writing insurance on the trust property.

Or *A* and *B* are fellow officers and fellow stockholders of *X* Company. *B* names *A* executor and trustee under his will and later dies. *A* qualifies and serves first as executor and then as trustee. As executor and trustee *A* properly and with due authority retains *B's* large, perhaps controlling, holdings in *X* Company. He continues to receive a salary from the company, and he is entitled also to compensation as executor and as trustee under *B's* will. So far, it is clear that *A* would not be expected to account to *A's* estate for any part of his salary as an officer of the company in which *B's* estate was a stockholder.

But suppose *A*, prior to *B's* death and his appointment as executor and trustee under *B's* will, had not been a stockholder of *X* Company; that after *B's* death, *A* used the stock in the estate to have himself elected an officer of the company; and that he drew a salary from the company in addition to receiving the usual allowance or commissions for serving as executor and trustee. Must he account to the estate for his salary as officer of the company?

At this point the principle of loyalty comes into play. If he used the shares he held in trust to have himself elected an officer of the company solely in the interest of the beneficiaries, which usually would be the case, his receiving salary as an officer and compensation as fiduciary would not be an act of disloyalty. If, on the other hand, he abused his power as trustee to have himself elected an officer of the company, thinking of what would be profitable to himself rather than of what would be for the interest of his beneficiaries, he would have to account to the trust for his salary.

Competition with Beneficiaries

The duty of loyalty requires that a fiduciary shall not compete with his beneficiaries. Competition over investments has been discussed already. There are many borderline cases, not involving investments, which make the application of the principle difficult.

For example, A and B during their lifetime were engaged in competitive businesses and yet were friends. B desired that his business be held intact and carried on until his son C would be old enough to take it over and carry it on. So, he named A executor and trustee under his will not only because A was his friend but also because he thought A, being in the same business, would know how to hold it intact and carry it on. Here A as a businessman finds himself in competition with himself as a fiduciary. However, the competition was not of his making, and he would not violate the principle of loyalty by continuing to carry on his own business even though it involved competition with the beneficiaries of B's estate and trust.

But suppose A and B had been friends but had not been engaged in competing businesses. Here, as in the preceding paragraph, B desired that his business be held intact, carried on, and eventually turned over to his son C. Because of the friendship between A and B and because of B's confidence in A's integrity and good business judgment, B named A executor and trustee under his will and authorized or directed him to carry on the business until C was ready to take it over. After A took over B's estate, he found that B's had been a profitable business far beyond A's expectations and he decided that he himself would like to go into the same kind of business, so, he proceeded to open a competing business. This would be a clear case of disloyalty to the beneficiaries of A's estate. The least that B could do would be to resign both the executorship and the trusteeship. But, more than that, if he had used his offices as executor and trustee to obtain information about A's business which he used to the disadvantage of the beneficiaries in the competing business, he would have committed a breach of duty for which he would be liable to the beneficiaries.

Different Standards of Conduct

From all the foregoing illustrations of applications of the principle of loyalty inherent in the fiduciary relationships, it must have become crystal-clear that a different standard of conduct is applied to a fiduciary's dealings with his beneficiaries and to his dealings with other persons.

1. *Dealings with other persons and with beneficiaries*. In his dealings with other persons the fiduciary is held to the standard of the man of ordinary prudence, care, and skill. He must be honest. As the owner of the property he has the usual powers, duties, and rights of property owners— no more, no less—except as those powers, duties, or rights are modified by the terms of the particular fiduciary relationship.

But in his dealings with his beneficiaries he is held to a level of conduct that is "higher than that trodden by the crowd." His own interests must, in every case, yield to those of his beneficiaries. Because this is so, if he deals with his beneficiaries he must make a full disclosure of all the pertinent facts and take no advantage of his position as fiduciary, else the transaction may, at the pleasure of the beneficiaries, be set aside, or he may be held to it and made to account for all the profits and stand all the losses of the transaction himself. If he purchases fiduciary property for himself or sells fiduciary property to himself, the purchase or sale can be set aside by the beneficiaries, no matter how fair the transaction might have been, or they may hold him to the transaction and make him stand the loss or account for the profit. If he uses the fiduciary property for his own purposes, he must account for the profits and stand the losses. If he enters into competition with his beneficiaries he can be made to account for the profits. If he makes a side profit, such as a bonus or commission, by virtue of his fiduciary relationship, he must account for it and turn it over to the fiduciary account and not keep it for himself.

The one basic, fundamental principle of all fiduciary relationships is that the fiduciary must be *absolutely* loyal to his beneficiaries at all times, in every way, in big things as well as in little ones, in spirit as well as in letter. A fiduciary must be honest; but he must be more than honest. Within the scope of his relationship he must act for his beneficiaries toward what he regards as being their best interests. Unless he is willing to accept and to have applied to himself this high, exacting standard of conduct, he should not accept the fiduciary relationship.

2. *Lay and professional fiduciary*. A pertinent inquiry would be: as regards the observance of fiduciary principles, what, if any, is the difference between the standard of conduct required of a lay fiduciary, on the one hand, and of a professional fiduciary or a trust institution, on the other?

For example, a property owner names his son executor and trustee under his will. This is the first time the son ever has been or, perhaps, the only time he ever will be called upon to settle an estate or administer a trust. He is as unfamiliar with fiduciary principles as any other member of the general public would be.

Or, the property owner names his bank executor and trustee under his will. His bank has been engaged in the trust business many years; it has settled thousands of estates and administered thousands of trusts; it has advertised for and solicited appointments as executor and trustee under will,

What, if any, is the difference between the standard required of the son and that of the bank?

The standard required of the son is that he exercise such care and skill as a man of ordinary prudence would exercise in dealing with his own property. This is the minimum. Is the standard required of the professional fiduciary or the trust institution higher than that?

On this point Professor Scott says:

> The general rule is the same in both cases, namely that the trustee must exercise such care and skill as a man of ordinary prudence would exercise. . . . If the trustee has greater skill and more facilities than others have, he is under a duty to employ such skill and facilities. Moreover, . . . if a trustee has held himself out as having a higher degree of skill or greater facilities than others have, he may incur a liability by failing to come up to the standard which he has set. These principles are applicable to trust institutions. . . .[10]

In recognition of the fact that the professional individual fiduciary or the corporation that makes a business of rendering fiduciary services may be held to a higher standard of care and skill than a lay fiduciary would be, trust institutions in their "Statement of Principles" have declared that "a trust institution should devote to its trust investments all the care and skill that it has or *can reasonably acquire.*" [11]

The principle of loyalty requires that an individual who makes a profession of rendering fiduciary services or a corporation that is engaged in fiduciary business should, in good conscience, employ all of the skill and exercise all of the care that he or it has already or reasonably, by due diligence, can acquire.

This entire chapter has been an attempt to express and illustrate the pervasive *spirit of loyalty* that should prevail in all fiduciary relationships.

COLLATERAL READING

Note: For complete citations, see Bibliography, pp. 417–428.

Bogert on *Trusts and Trustees,* Secs. 598 and 612.

Loring's *Trustee's Handbook,* Shattuck Rev., Secs. 18–19, 62–71.

Scott on *Trusts,* Secs. 170–175. 25.

Stephenson, "Fiduciary Principles and Policies."

Federal Reserve System, *Regulation F—Trust Powers of National Banks,* "A Statement of Principles of Trust Institutions," (appendix).

[10] Scott on *Trusts,* Sec. 174.1.
[11] Art. IV, Sec. 2.

15

Settlement of Estates

𝕿HE TERM *settlement* applied to an estate, as used in this chapter, is employed in the American, as distinct from the British, sense. In this country to settle an estate is to wind it up and distribute the property to the persons entitled to receive it. In Great Britain to settle an estate is to dispose of property for someone's benefit, usually but not always through the medium of a trust. In Great Britain one hears of a father's *settling* property *upon* his daughter or of marriage *settlements* either before or after the marriage.

At this point in the development of our subject the hitherto separate channels, intestate distribution and testate distribution of property, as presented in Chapters 2 and 3, come together for a discussion of the settlement of both testate and intestate estates. This is proper in that (1) there are few, if any, basic differences in procedure for settling testate estates and intestate estates and (2) about half in number of the estates being settled in this country are testate and the other half, intestate. However, in monetary volume a much larger proportion of the estates are testate.

Steps in Settlement of Estate

The settlement of an estate may involve these eight steps: (1) procedure prior to appointment of administrator or executor, (2) appointment of administrator or executor, (3) assembling property belonging to estate, (4) safekeeping or safeguarding that property, (5) interim management of that property, (6) assembling, passing upon, and paying debts, taxes, and expenses of settlement of estate, (7) accounting for settlement of estate, and (8) distributing net estate.

PROCEDURE PRIOR TO APPOINTMENT

In the settlement of most estates there is no procedure prior to the one leading up to the appointment of the administrator or the executor. But as regards not a few estates there is an unavoidable interval between the death and burial of the deceased person and the appointment of the administrator or executor and during this period something must be done with or about property in the estate.

In some states a will cannot be offered for probate until after a specified number of days—ten, for example—from the death of the testator.

The member of the family entitled to apply for appointment as administrator of the estate may be absent or unable to take over the settlement of the estate. This is especially true in wartime. Likewise the executor named in the will may be absent or unable to assume his duties. It may be known that the deceased person left a will, but it may have been impossible for the time being to locate or to get possession of it. There may be a contest brewing over the will itself, or over the appointment of the executor or of an administrator. Still other things may happen to delay or to prevent the probate of the will or the appointment of an executor or an administrator.

Meanwhile, many things about the property in the estate may exist which, if not attended to promptly, may mean irreparable loss to the heirs, next of kin, devisees, legatees, creditors, and other persons financially interested in the estate. For example, the deceased person may have been a merchant and at his death there may have been perishable goods on a railroad siding. He may have been a farmer who died in the midst of his growing season when cultivation must be carried on without delay or in the midst of harvest season when harvesting and marketing could not be delayed. He might have been engaged in a business which could not be closed down even for a day without loss to everyone concerned. The deceased person may have left livestock which would have to be fed and cared for.

Every state makes and, in the nature of things, must make provision for meeting such situations. It is done by the appointment of someone—an individual, a bank or trust company—to take over at once, to do what has to be done to protect and preserve the property, and to carry on until an executor or administrator is appointed to settle the estate. This temporary appointee of the court is known as *temporary administrator, receiver, collector,* or *curator.*

Sometimes a person, knowing that he has been named executor or thinking that he will be appointed administrator, may take over prior to his or to any appointment and do what he thinks has to be done. While he would be responsible for his acts, he would not be penalized if he had acted in good faith for what he thought was in the best interest of the estate.

Personal representative is a common term for both administrator and executor.

APPOINTMENT OF ADMINISTRATOR OR EXECUTOR

The procedures for the appointment of an administrator and that of an executor naturally are somewhat different.

Administrator

The appointment of the administrator is the function of the probate court. The procedure is prescribed by statute and varies from state to state and, in some states, from county to county.

1. *Person entitled to appointment.* The first thing the probate court must decide is who, provided he is qualified and is willing to serve, is entitled to the appointment. The laws of each state prescribe the order of the persons entitled to be offered the appointment, of which the following is typical: if the deceased were an unmarried man or woman, the appointment would be offered (1) to one of the parents, (2) to one of the grandparents, brothers or sisters, (3) to one of the uncles, aunts, nephews, or nieces, (4) to one of the great-uncles, great-aunts, first cousins, grandnephews or grandnieces, (5) to one of the creditors of the estate, (6) to any other person legally competent, and (7) to the public administrator. If the deceased were a married man or married woman, the appointment would be offered first to the surviving widow or widower and next to one of the children or grandchildren. The court would not appoint a person under legal age and, in many states, would not appoint a nonresident, or, in some states, one who had been convicted of a felony. The court may appoint two or more coadministrators. It may appoint a bank or trust company sole administrator or co-administrator. Persons with prior right to be considered for the appointment may renounce in favor of persons below them in the order of preference or in favor of an outsider. The court will be influenced by the wishes of the family and usually will make the appointment either in the order named or according to the preferences of the more responsible members of the family. However, the court has the power to disregard the specified order or even, in a very extreme case, to disregard the request of the family and appoint the individual, the bank, or the trust company best suited, in the judgment of the court, considering all the circumstances, to settle the estate properly.[1]

2. *Administrator's bond.* The next step is the execution of the administrator's bond. If the administrator to be appointed is an individual, in most states he will be required to enter a bond with surety and the surety or sureties may be either individuals who can justify—that is, swear that they own property in the amount of the bond over and above their debts and exemptions—or a surety company. Before the court can know the amount of the bond to be required, it must be informed as to the estimated gross value of the personal property. At this stage it usually cannot be more than an estimate, and additional bond may be required later, should the size of the estate prove to be greater than estimated. The amount of the bond usually is twice the estimated value of the personal property. But this varies somewhat from state to state. In North Carolina, for example, if a duly authorized surety company is surety, the bond need be only 125 per cent of the assets

[1] For a state-by-state list of those who may claim appointment as administrator, see *Wills, Estates, and Trusts,* Secs. 2009–2015.

and, if the estate exceeds $100,000, it need be only 110 per cent of the assets. If the administrator to be appointed is a bank or trust company, in most states it will not be required to offer surety on its bond, although it may be required to execute a bond without surety.

Fixing the bond is not, by any means, a formality. Beneficiaries and creditors alike may look to the surety or sureties for their protection. And if the judge or the officer of the court that makes the appointment should be negligent with respect to the bond and loss should result to the beneficiaries or creditors of the estate, he might be liable for the loss on his own official bond in those states in which he is a bonded officer of the court.

3. *Letters of administration.* The third and last step is the issue of letters of administration to the administrator. These are the administrator's evidence of authority to settle the estate, in the course of which he may have occasion to use many certified copies of the letters.

Executor

If the deceased left a will, it is probated prior to the appointment of the executor.

1. *Probate of will.* Probate of the will means proof to the probate court in the manner required by the law of the state that the paper-writing is the will of the deceased person. Even a nuncupative will must have been reduced to writing before it is offered for probate. In some states there are two forms of probate of a will. One is known as probate in *common form;* the other, as probate in *solemn form.*

a. Probate in common form. A will is said to be probated in *common form* when (1) the paper-writing is presented to the court, (2) the subscribing or attesting witnesses prove the signature of the testator, and (3) the witnesses, if they are subscribing as distinct from attesting, swear or affirm that the testator signed the will in their presence and, in some states, in one another's presence, and that at the time of his signing he was of sound mind and not subjected to undue influence. Thereupon, without further formality, the court admits the will to probate and in due course appoints the executor.

b. Probate in solemn form. Probate in *solemn form,* as the term implies, is a formal procedure. The will and a petition for probate are filed in court. A day is set for a formal hearing on the petition. All the beneficiaries are notified of the hearing. The hearing itself is a formal court proceeding. Arguments for and arguments, if any, against the admission of the will to probate are heard. A jury finds the facts; the judge enters the judgment for or against the probate.

The practical difference between probate in common form and probate in solemn form is: it is much easier to contest a will probated in common form successfully than it is to contest one probated in solemn form.

This is so, naturally, because, when the will is offered for probate in solemn form, the objections, if any, to its admission to probate would be brought out and the issues of fact and of law determined at that time.

In those states which have both forms, it is customary to offer a will for probate in common form when there is not likely to be any contest over it but to offer it in solemn form, as a precautionary measure, when a contest seems at all probable.

2. *Executor's willingness to serve.* In most cases the executor named in the will is willing and ready to serve and the appointment follows in due course, but this is not always the case. The court may decide that the person named is not fit to serve and may refuse to appoint him. Or the person named may renounce; that is, decline to serve. The person so renouncing may express no preference as to the one who should be named or he may renounce in favor of someone else, in which latter case the court would be disposed but not bound to name the one in whose favor he had renounced.

3. *Executor's bond.* Whether the executor will be required to give a bond with surety will depend, first, upon the laws of the state and, second, upon the provisions, if any, of the will about bond. In some states a testator can relieve his executor of giving bond or, at any rate, of giving surety on his bond; in other states, he can do so with respect to legacies but not with respect to debts of the estate.

4. *Letters testamentary.* *Letters testamentary* are evidence of the authority of the executor to settle the estate under the will. As in the case of letters of administration there will be many calls for certified copies of the letters or of what in some states are called "short certificates."

Administrator with the Will Annexed

The appointment of an administrator with the will annexed partakes of the naure of the appointment of both an administrator and an executor. It is like the appointment of an executor in that it is predicated upon the probate of a will, and like that of an administrator in that the court must make its own appointment without the benefit or guidance of a nomination by the testator. The testator's provision about relieving the executor of giving bond would not be applicable to the administrator with the will annexed.

ASSEMBLING PROPERTY

In point of time, the next step after the appointment of the administrator or executor is assembling the property belonging to the estate. This involves, first, letting creditors, debtors, and other interested persons know who has been appointed administrator or executor to settle the deceased person's estate and, second, taking the appropriate steps to get possession of the property.

Notice to Creditors and Debtors

Although the term in common use is *notice to creditors*, in fact, it is a notice also to debtors, as the following actual notice shows:

Having qualified as administrator of the estate of ———, deceased, late of ——— County, ———, this is to notify all persons having claims against said estate to present them, duly verified, to the undersigned administrator at his home at ———, ———, within one year from the date hereof, or this notice will be pleaded in bar of recovery. All persons indebted to said estate will make prompt payment.

This the ——— day of ———, ———.

Administrator of the Estate
of_____

The time, place, and method of publishing this notice are governed by the law of the state of which the deceased person was a resident. Since this notice to creditors has so much effect upon the length of time it will take to settle the estate, more about it will be said in the section on paying debts, taxes, and expenses.

Cash

Cash belonging to the deceased person would be deposited in a bank in a separate account to the credit of the administrator or executor—that is, separate from the administrator's or executor's own bank account.

Bank Balances

The deceased person's own bank balances would be transferred to the administrator's or executor's official, not personal, bank account.

Whether funds would be permitted to remain in a savings account would depend upon the law of the given state. In some states such funds would be permitted to remain in a savings account on interest unless or until needed in connection with the settlement of the estate; in other states they would have to be withdrawn by not later than the next interest period.

Joint bank accounts may offer some problems. According to the law of the state or according to the terms and conditions of the deposit, one part of the account may belong to the estate of the deceased person and the other part to the survivor, or all of it may belong to the survivor and none to the estate.

Brokerage Accounts

Brokerage accounts require the immediate attention of the administrator or executor. Unless there is a will and unless the will expressly authorizes or directs the continuance of the account for not over a specified length of time, the administrator or executor should close the account and take over the cash or securities belonging to the estate. Not to do this promptly may make the administrator or executor personally liable for losses to the estate sustained by keeping the account open longer than was reasonably necessary.

Contents of Safe Deposit Box

The administrator's or executor's right of immediate or sole entry of the safe deposit box of the deceased person may be restricted by the state law. In some states the box must be sealed by the bank or safe deposit company and not opened by the administrator or executor except in the presence of a representative of the state tax department.

The box, when opened, may contain property labelled as belonging to some person other than the deceased person. The administrator or executor should not surrender possession of this property, even so labelled, if he has any doubt as to the true ownership and not even then without making a record and taking a receipt from the person to whom the property is delivered.

The fact that one safe deposit box is located is not conclusive evidence that there is not another one. The administrator or executor should make diligent inquiry of every reasonable source as to the existence of other boxes.

Life Insurance Contracts

The administrator or executor has legal responsibility only with respect to insurance policies payable to the estate of the deceased person. But even as to policies payable to a named beneficiary, other than the estate, or under which the proceeds are left with the insurance company under an option of settlement, the administrator or executor ordinarily will use his good offices and, in many cases, his greater experience to aid the named beneficiaries in collecting the proceeds promptly.

Jointly Owned Property

During recent years there has been a substantial increase in the volume of co-owned or jointly owned stocks and registered bonds. As explained in Chapter 1, if these stocks and bonds are owned by the deceased person and someone else—usually, but not always, the surviving widow or widower—

as joint owners with right of survivorship, then the estate has no property interest in them and the surviving joint owner becomes the sole owner. If, however, they are owned in common and not jointly, the estate is part owner and the administrator or executor is under an obligation to take appropriate steps to take over the estate's interest in them. The taking over of co-owned or jointly owned stocks or bonds may raise legal problems which should be referred to the attorney of the administrator or executor.

Personal Effects

In intestate estates, the personal effects of the deceased usually are included in the family allowances. In some states in testate estates as well, personal effects, up to a specified value or of a specified kind, are set over to the family as allowances and not included in the inventory of the estate. In either case, the taking over of the personal effects calls for the exercise of the utmost tact and diplomacy, otherwise good relations with the members of the family may be marred at the beginning of the settlement of the estate.

Book Accounts

The book accounts of a professional man or of the sole proprietor of a business—a merchant, for example—are property of his estate which must be taken over by the administrator or executor who must use every reasonable effort to collect them. To what extent he may accept compromise settlements of accounts depends upon the law of the state and, for an executor, upon his powers under the will. In any case, unless the account is forgiven by the testator in his will, it is the administrator's or executor's duty to use every reasonable effort to collect the account in full.

Rights

The deceased person may have rights, such as patent rights, book royalties, and oil royalties, each type of which must be collected by the administrator or executor and put into shape to be realized upon.

Real Property

At common law, the ownership of real property passed directly and at once to the heirs or devisees, and the personal property, to the administrator or executor, and this is still so in some states. But in other states the distinction between real property and personal property has been abolished and all the property has to pass through the hands of the administrator or executor. However, even though the real property passed directly to the heirs or devisees, the administrator or executor still would have responsibility with respect to current rents and growing crops. In the event the personal property should be insufficient to pay the claims against the estate, the administrator or executor might have to sell real property to raise the necessary cash. So, it would not be accurate to say that the administrator or executor has responsibility for the personal property only.

Property in Other States

In assembling the property the administrator or executor must look for and attend to property located in other states. This property may be real property, tangible personal property, or evidence of intangible personal property (certificates of stocks and bonds, for example). The administrator or executor may be able to take over some of this property without qualifying in the other state or states; he may be required to qualify in the other state or states; or he may not be permitted to qualify. In the last case an ancillary administrator would have to be appointed in the other state. The handling of property by an ancillary administrator is known as ancillary administration, that is, in aid of or subordinate to the principal administration.

Businesses and Business Interests

The administrator or executor may find a business (sole proprietorship) or business interest (partnership) belonging to the deceased person. He would have to take over the sole proprietorship; but the surviving partner would liquidate and account for the partnership interest. The administrator's or executor's duties regarding a business will be discussed later with interim management, and with the handling of estate and trust business.

SAFEKEEPING AND SAFEGUARDING PROPERTY

An administrator or executor is responsible for safekeeping, safeguarding, and insuring the property during the period of settlement of the estate.

Inventory

Safekeeping and safeguarding involve, first, making, keeping, and filing with the court a complete inventory of the property belonging to the estate. In most states the law specifies the time within which the inventory must be filed, with provision for a supplementary inventory to cover after-discovered property.

Appraisement

The law and practice of the states vary widely as to appraisement, that is, putting a money-value on the property covered by the inventory. In some states, the administrator or executor makes his own appraisement; in other states, the court appoints appraisers. The appraisement, no matter how or by whom made, is subject to review by the court and, for tax purposes, by representatives of the tax department.

Appraisement is the work of specialists—specialists, for example, in the appraisement of farm property, of urban property, of interest in close corporations, of jewelry, of works of art, and of books.

Perishable Goods

Perishable goods which have not been disposed of already by a temporary administrator must be disposed of, each in the appropriate way, by the regular administrator or executor. Thus, safekeeping and safeguarding the value of property may, in fact, mean consumption and disposition rather than the preservation of the property in its original form.

Safekeeping Valuables

The administrator or executor is under a duty to safekeep the valuables —furniture and furnishings, heirlooms, furs, works of art, and the like—belonging to the estate as a prudent man would safekeep valuables of the same kind. This means that certain of these valuables would be kept in safe deposit boxes; others in storage vaults; and still others in the places and in the ways prudent men safekeep such property.

Safeguarding Other Property

Other types of property, which is not of the kind that can be kept in safe deposit boxes or vaults, must be safeguarded in the ways appropriate for safeguarding that kind of property. An unoccupied residence or unused business building, for example, so long as it remains in the hands of the executor, might require the services of a watchman or periodic opening up and inspection to guard against escaping gas and water or against depredations on the unoccupied or unused property.

Property Insurance

In addition to the physical safekeeping and safeguarding of the property in appropriate ways, the administrator or executor is under a duty to keep the property insured in the ways and in the amounts a prudent man would keep his own property of that kind insured. Under the present laws in Great Britain an administrator or executor *may* insure the property against loss from fire at the expense of the estate; in this country he *must* do so or be personally liable for the loss resulting from his failure properly to insure. The fact that the deceased person himself had not insured the property will not relieve the administrator or executor of his duty to do so. The test is not what the deceased person did but what a prudent man would do.

INTERIM MANAGEMENT OF PROPERTY

Interim management of property is listed here as a separate step in the settlement of an estate mainly in order to emphasize its importance. The adjective *interim* is used to indicate that the management is limited to the period during which the administrator or executor is settling the estate.

Ordinarily, it is said that the function of an administrator or executor is to liquidate; whereas, that of a trustee or guardian is to manage. But the fact needs to be emphasized that an administrator or executor also has important managerial functions.

Raising Cash

From the day the administrator or executor makes an inventory and appraisement of the property and arrives at an estimate of the amount of claims against the estate, he must be preparing to have the cash on hand with which to pay the debts, taxes, and administration expenses of the estate. Although it is not the normal function of an administrator or executor to invest funds, it is distinctly his function to sell investments, if need be, to raise the necessary cash. It takes fully as much investment acumen, which is one phase of management, to sell wisely as to buy wisely. The fate of the estate may be determined in no small degree by the managerial ability or lack of ability displayed by the administrator or executor in raising the money to meet the cash requirements of the estate.

Carrying on Business

If the deceased person's business was a close corporation, then, theoretically, it will be carried on by the surviving stockholders, but, actually, the administrator or executor may have to take an active part in the management. If it was a partnership, then the surviving partner will liquidate the deceased partner's interest; but even then the administrator or executor may have to give a guiding, steadying hand. If it was a sole proprietorship, the full responsibility for the interim management of the business falls upon the administrator or executor. In every state, by common law or by statute, he is authorized to carry on the business pending sale, liquidation, or distribution. The ultimate value of the business or business interest may be affected vitally for good or ill by the way he carries on the business or manages the business interest during the relatively short period he is in charge.

In a later chapter the continued management of businesses and business interests, including farms, mines, and the like, by a trustee after the estate has been settled will be discussed. At this point we are concerned only with the unavoidable management during the period that the estate is in process of settlement.

PAYMENT OF DEBTS, TAXES, AND EXPENSES

Let us suppose that the administrator or executor has reduced to possession all the property belonging to the estate; has kept it properly safeguarded and insured; has given to each kind of property the type of interim management it required; and, having done all this, is ready now to give attention to paying the debts, taxes, and expenses, preparatory to winding up and distributing the estate.

Debts

Regarding the payment of debts owed by the deceased person, the administrator or executor has, first, to pass upon the validity of the claims, and, then, the order of payment.

1. *Proof of claims.* One of the primary duties of an administrator or executor is to pass upon and accept or reject a claim filed against the estate. Not only must he require that the claim be verified—sworn to—but, if he has any doubt about the validity of the claim, he must go behind the verification and, if he feels justified, reject or reduce the claim even at the risk of having to stand suit on the claim as presented. Whether he has the right to compromise the claim depends upon the law of his state or, in the case of a will, upon the powers of the executor under the will.

The length of time within which a claimant can file his claim against the estate to a large degree determines the time it takes to settle and distribute the estate. At common law and by statute in many states the period is twelve months from the date of qualification or the date of the publication of the first notice to creditors. This, perhaps, is the origin of the term *executor's year*—meaning that creditors have a year within which to present their claims. But in many states this period has been shortened by statute to nine months, to six, and recently it has been suggested that it be shortened still further to four or even to three months.

2. *Order of payment.* After passing upon the validity of claims comes the order of payment of claims that have been presented, proved, and accepted. If the estate is solvent, this is not so important because all the accepted claims will be paid in full. But suppose the estate is not solvent or suppose the administrator or executor, thinking it is solvent, pays claims out of order.

Every state prescribes the order of preference of payment in case there is not enough to pay all of the claims in full. The following order is, perhaps, typical: (*a*) debts which by law have a special lien on property to an amount not exceeding the value of the property; (*b*) funeral expenses; (*c*) taxes; (*d*) debts due to the United States and to the state; (*e*) judgments of any court of competent jurisdiction, within the state, docketed and in force, to the extent to which they are a lien on the property of the deceased person at his death; (*f*) wages due to any domestic servant or mechanical or agricultural laborer for a period of not more than one year immediately preceding the death; (*g*) claims for medical services within twelve months preceding the decease; and (*h*) all other debts and demands. Every debt must be paid *pro rata* in its class.[2]

Taxes

This section relates, not to the taxation of estates, but only to the administrator's or executor's duty as regards the payment of taxes owing by the estate.

1. *Taxes due.* The taxes due by the estate may include the usual ad valorem taxes on real property, tangible personal property, and, in some states, upon intangible property evidence of which is located in the state; federal and state income taxes both during the tax period before and the period after the death of the decedent; state inheritance taxes; federal and state estate taxes. They may include taxes not only on property in the hands of the administrator or executor but also on that in the hands of a trustee or of someone to whom the property was given outright during the lifetime of the deceased person under such circumstances (in contemplation of death, for example) as to render it taxable as a part of the estate.

2. *Taxpayer.* Next, after the determination of the amount of each kind of taxes due, comes the determination of the taxpayer of each kind. Under the law the taxpayer may be the administrator or executor, or he may be a trustee, or the taxes may be apportioned. The terms of the will may dictate who shall pay the taxes or how the taxes shall be apportioned.

At the present time there is perhaps no duty of an administrator or executor more important or more exacting than that of determining the amount of each kind of taxes due, determining the taxpayer in each case, and raising the cash for taxes without sacrificing the assets of the estate.

Expenses

Expenses generally include all out-of-pocket expenses incurred by the administrator or executor in settling the estate and specifically the compensation of appraisers of the property, the attorney of the administrator or executor, the administrator or executor, and the court costs.

1. *Out-of-pocket expenses.* Even in the early days, when an adminis-

2 For the state-by-state order of payment, see *Wills, Estates, and Trusts*, Sec. 2652.

trator or executor was not compensated for his services, it being considered a position of honor and not an occupation, he was entitled to reimbursement for all his actual out-of-pocket expenses properly incurred in the settlement of the estate.

2. *Appraisers' compensation or allowance.* The appraisers in some states receive a statutory per diem for their services; in others, a commission on the value of the property appraised; in other states, an allowance by the probate court of what is customary or what it regards as reasonable compensation for the service rendered; and, in still others, appraisement is regarded as a part of the administrator's or executor's work. In some states the appraisement by outside appraisers is a formality and the appraisers' compensation or allowance, nominal; in other states, it is a serious undertaking and the appraisers' allowance or compensation, substantial.

3. *Attorney's compensation or allowance.* The attorney indicated is the attorney of the administrator or executor and not of the estate. At common law his compensation was a lump-sum allowance by the court for services rendered the administrator or executor. At the present time in some states the attorney's compensation is a commission fixed by statute; in other states the common-law rule still prevails.

4. *Court costs.* In every state there are certain court costs of settlement of an estate. They are figured by the court itself according to the law and, as a rule, do not constitute a very substantial item compared with the total value of the estate. However, they are an item which the administrator or executor must have in mind and for which he must provide.

ACCOUNTING

The last two steps in the settlement of an estate, which sometimes are treated as one, are accounting to the court and making the distribution. They are treated here as separate steps because they involve different activities.

Form of Accounting

At the beginning of the settlement of an estate, the administrator or executor "charges himself"—this is a term in common use—with the property he finds then or later in the estate. At the end of the period, he files with the court an accounting showing what he has received, what he has paid out and for what purposes, and what he has left over—that is, the net estate—for distribution according to the laws of intestate distribution in a case of an intestate estate or according to the terms of the will in case of an estate left under will.

The form of the accounting is determined by the law or practice of the state or, perhaps it might be more accurate to say, according to the practice of the county in which the accounting is being filed. In some states the accounting is an informal proceeding; the administrator or executor presents and files his account and, unless objected to by the court, that is all there is to it. In other states it is a formal proceeding with notice to all interested parties, representation of the administrator or executor by legal counsel, and a formal hearing. Whether the accounting is a formal or informal proceeding, interested parties have a right to object to the accounting and to have a hearing on it—that is to say, they are entitled to their "day in court."

Discharge of Administrator or Executor

In some states, after the administrator or executor has made his accounting and made the distribution according to the order of distribution set forth in the account, he is entitled to discharge. In other states there is no formal discharge; he remains administrator or executor for an indefinite period.

Naturally, on the one hand, the surety on the bond desires that the administrator or executor receive from the court a formal discharge or from the distributees a formal release, and the administrator or executor himself would prefer to feel that his duties had been performed in full.

But, on the other hand, not infrequently property belonging to an estate is discovered long after the usual period for settling the estate has elapsed. If the administrator or executor has been discharged, it may be necessary to make a new appointment to complete the settlement of the estate. Whereas, if the administrator or executor has not received a formal discharge, in the event of discovery of property after the first accounting and the distribution have been made, the estate is reopened and the original administrator or executor takes over the after-discovered property and proceeds with the final settlement of the estate.

DISTRIBUTION

The distribution of the net estate usually involves at least three steps—namely, making the schedule of distribution, making the distribution, and obtaining releases and receipts.

Schedule of Distribution

The *schedule of distribution* is a statement of who is to receive what property.

In the case of a will and an estate ample for all the gifts, the schedule can be made up directly from the will. If it is an insolvent estate, then, of course, there is no distribution. If the estate, although solvent, is not sufficient to satisfy all the gifts, then, according to the law of the state or the terms of the will, certain gifts may have to be eliminated or abated (reduced); and for an administrator or executor this may be both a difficult and an unpleasant duty.

In making up the schedule of distribution, the executor must take into account also *lapsed gifts*, that is, gifts that cannot be made because of the death of the devisee or legatee prior to the death of the testator. In some cases the gift lapses, and the property becomes a part of the residuary estate. In other cases the property passes, by right of representation, to the child or children of the deceased devisee or legatee. In making up the schedule of distribution, determination of which gifts lapse and which do not may become a rather vexatious legal problem.

In the case of an intestate estate and particularly when no surviving widow or widower or children survive, the making of the schedule of distribution may be extremely difficult. The chart of consanguinity applicable to that estate must be followed; some of the next of kin may be absent, unknown, or unheard of for years; there may be disputes over who is entitled to take; and the preparation of the schedule may be, in effect, a difficult exercise in genealogy.

Distribution

Once the schedule has been prepared at whatever cost of time and labor, and, as a rule, filed with and as a part of the accounting, the next step is the actual distribution. This means the conveyance, transfer, or delivery of the property to the person entitled to receive it either under the will or under the applicable laws of intestate distribution.

Receipt or Release

As a matter of self-protection as well as a usual legal requirement, an administrator or executor making a distribution would take from the distributee an appropriate receipt for the property, or a release of the administrator or executor from further liability to the distributee on account of the property. In practice, where the settlement of the estate has proceeded in due course, no contests or disagreements have developed, and the relations between the administrator or executor and the distributees are good, the administrator or executor sometimes sends a form of receipt *and* release to the distributee accompanied by informal instructions as to executing it and by a statement to the effect that, as soon as the receipt and release, duly executed, have been returned, the distribution will be made.

What is done with the receipt or release or the receipt *and* release, after it has been returned, duly executed, to the administrator or executor is a matter of local law or practice. In some states it is retained by the administrator or executor; in others, it is filed in court along with the other papers of the estate. In any case it is or should be retained as evidence of the actual distribution.

1. *Refunding bond.* At the time for making the distribution the administrator or executor of a large or complicated estate still may not be sure that additional taxes will not be assessed against the estate or against the distributees. After he has determined and paid all the taxes he finds are due, instead of postponing further the distribution of the net estate, he makes the distribution but receives from the distributee a refunding bond—that is, an obligation to return the distribution or the necessary part of it in case that should be necessary to meet additional taxes. Or, instead of making a complete distribution and taking a refunding bond, he may make a partial distribution, holding back enough for undetermined taxes and distribute later, after all taxes have been paid, any balance of the estate so retained.

PERSONAL SERVICES

This chapter on the settlement of estates should not be closed without some mention of the personal, as distinct from the financial, business, or property services an administrator or executor renders the family or the next of kin of the deceased person.

In this connection, one naturally thinks of funeral arrangements and collection of insurance. Personal services in connection with these are important, but, important as they are, they are rendered, if at all, within a few days after the death. As for the funeral arrangements, in many cases the members of the family themselves take charge and would resent the executor, unless he was a member of the family, having anything to do with them. Since an administrator hardly would be appointed until after the funeral, seldom would he have occasion to attend to funeral arrangements.

The personal services that continue and that count most are those rendered the members of the family and the next of kin of the deceased person throughout the entire period of settlement of the estate. This is a period of major adjustments in personal affairs, as well as in business affairs. The widow, if bereft of her husband, must adjust herself to becoming head of the family. The widower, if bereft of his wife, must adjust himself to paying more attention to household and domestic affairs. Surviving parents and surviving children have their adjustments to make. In the making of all such adjustments they naturally look to the administrator or executor for advice and, possibly, a sympathetic hearing. He may, in fact, be the only one to whom they can turn.

Men and women, in making wills and naming executors, should have in mind these personal services which their executors can and will render the members of their family as well as the business services they will render their estate. Probate courts, in appointing administrators, after consulting with the family, should have in mind the type of administrator who would serve the family needs acceptably as well as settle the estate properly.

COLLATERAL READING

Note: For complete citations, see Bibliography, pp. 417–428.

ATKINSON on *Wills and Administration.*

DODGE and SULLIVAN on *Estate Administration and Accounting.*

SIMES and BAYSE, *Problems in Probate Law: Model Probate Code.*

American Jurisprudence, Vol. 21, *Executors and Administrators.*

Corpus Juris Secundum, Vol. 34.

Ruling Case Law, Vol. 11.

Estate Law Reporter, Secs. 6001–6351.

Wills, Estates, and Trusts, Secs. 2001–2668.

16

Administration of Guardianships and Personal Trusts

THIS AND THE NEXT two chapters will be devoted to the administration of guardianships and personal trusts. While there are some differences, as will be brought out, between the administration of guardianships and that of personal trusts, they are not enough to require or to justify a separate chapter on each. However, there are enough differences between the administration of guardianships and personal trusts, on the one hand, and of employees, charitable, and corporate trusts, on the other, to justify separate treatment of the two groups. Furthermore, the investment of funds and the handling of businesses, which are integral parts of the administration of guardianships and trusts, are such important activities as to justify treatment separate from other phases of administration and separate also from each other.

Differences between Guardianships and Personal Trusts

Two basic differences between the administration of a guardianship and of a personal trust relate (1) to the source of the fiduciary's authority and (2) to the duration of the relationship.

1. *Source of authority*. The sole source of the guardian's authority is the statutory and judicial law of the state in which he serves. The dual sources of the trustee's authority are the law and the trust instrument under which he serves.

2. *Duration of relationship*. The guardianship of a minor can last only during the minority of the ward and of an incompetent person only during the period of mental incompetence which, however, may be the lifetime of the ward. Personal trusteeship may last not only during the lifetime of one beneficiary but also during that of one or more successive beneficiaries.

GUARDIANSHIPS

The first step in the administration of a guardianship is the selection and appointment of the guardian.

Appointment

As previously stated, every guardian is either appointed by the court or, if he has been nominated by a parent or elected by the minor himself, his appointment is confirmed by the court. In every state and in every county or probate jurisdiction of every state, there is a court that has jurisdiction over matters of guardianship. In some states—Connecticut, for example— the probate jurisdiction is a town instead of a county and in some—as in Virginia—both county and city. This court goes by many different names, as does the probate court, and in many states is the same as the probate court. There is historical significance in the fact that in Delaware, Maryland, New Jersey, Pennsylvania, and perhaps in some other states, the court which has jurisdiction over guardianships is known as the "orphans' " court; but with the passage of time this court has been given jurisdiction over many other matters than those connected with orphans.

Seldom would the court itself take the initiative in appointing a guardian of either a minor or an incompetent person. In fact, it seldom would know of the need for such an appointment unless or until the matter was brought to its attention.

In practice, the first step toward the appointment of a guardian would be taken only when the actual need for a guardian arose. That need might arise out of the transfer of securities that had been registered in the name of a minor or of a person then mentally incompetent, or out of the collection of insurance payable to a person who is a minor or an incompetent person, or out of the distribution to a minor or incompetent person of a share of an intestate estate or of an outright gift under will. When any such situation develops and nothing further can be done unless or until a guardian has been appointed, the members of the family or other interested parties—possibly creditors—formally or informally, according to the law or practice of the jurisdiction, would bring the need for the appointment of a guardian to the attention of the proper court.

Upon the presentation of facts showing the need for a guardian and, in the case of an incompetent person, after a commission or jury had declared the person incompetent, the court would take steps to make the appointment. In any case the court would comply, as nearly as its duty would permit it to do so, with the wishes of the responsible members of the family. Or, in some states, if the minor were fourteen years of age and had elected his guardian, the court would confirm his election by making the appointment. Or, in those states in which a parent may name a testamentary guardian, the court, in the absence of a strong reason to the contrary, would make that appointment. The court would go as far as it could go in good conscience in appointing the person most agreeable to the minor himself, if he had reached the age of decision, and to the responsible members of the family or the most interested parties. There is no other point perhaps at which the law and human kindness and considerateness come into closer relationship with each other than in connection with the appointment of a guardian for a minor or incompetent person.

It is comparatively rare, even in those states in which it is provided for, that the court is called upon to appoint, or appoints, separate guardians of the property and of the person. Ordinarily, as previously stated, the court appoints a single guardian who takes over and administers the property and deals with the person who stands in the place of a parent as though he were a formally appointed guardian of the person.

Qualification

Each state provides its own statutory procedure for the qualification, as well as the appointment, of the guardian. It would be profitless to detail this procedure for any given state. For our purpose, the main point regarding the qualification is the guardian's bond. A guardian, the same as an administrator, is required to execute a bond for the faithful execution of his office and, also like an administrator, there is no one to relieve him of the duty to execute the bond or to relieve the court of its duty to require him to execute it. A trust institution would be required to give bond, but in most states it would not be required to give a surety on its bond.

Following the qualification and appointment, the court would issue to the guardian his letters of guardianship. These, like letters of administration for an administrator and letters testamentary for an executor, are evidence of his authority to take over and proceed with the administration of his ward's estate.

Duties

The duties of a guardian of the person are almost as unrestricted and indefinable as those of a parent. Within the limits of the available funds, they are to do everything for the welfare of the ward that a parent under similar circumstances would do.

The duties of a guardian of the property are a combination of the duties of an administrator or executor and those of a trustee. In general, these duties are: (1) to assemble the property belonging to the ward; (2) to safekeep and safeguard the property; (3) to manage the property; (4) to use the income and, if needed, principal for the benefit of the ward; (5) to make an accounting for the administration of the guardianship; and (6) at the termination of the guardianship to deliver the property to the ward or to his legal representative. The duties numbered (1), (2), and (5) partake of the nature of the duties of an administrator or executor; those numbered (3), (4), and (6), of a trustee. The duties which are similar to those of a trustee of a personal trust will be discussed later under the administration of trusts.

Ward's Domicile

In the administration of guardianships of both minors and incompetent persons, but more often of minors, this practical problem not infrequently arises: the surviving parent or person standing in the place of a parent, with whom the minor resides and makes his home, changes his or her domicile (permanent home as distinct from temporary residence) to another county or state and thereby changes the domicile of the ward. What becomes of the guardianship?

For an extreme but not impossible illustration, a father, dying intestate in Portland, Maine, leaves property to a minor, and the court appoints the child's mother guardian of the child's property. In the course of a few years the mother moves her home across the continent to Portland, Oregon, takes her child with her, and severs all her ties with her former home in Portland, Maine. What becomes of the guardianship? Does the Maine court retain its jurisdiction over the guardian and over the ward's property, or is the guardianship transferred to Oregon and the mother reappointed guardian? Or is a new guardian appointed in Oregon?

The laws of the several states provide for the removal of both the person and the property of a ward from one county to another in the same state and from one state to another. While the statutes vary in detail, in general they require the guardian to make an accounting to the court that made the appointment and to obtain an order of removal. Whereupon the court will send a transcript of the record to the county, whether within or without the state, to which the ward or his property has been or is to be removed. In one way or another statutory provision is made for the protection of both the person and the property of a ward in the event of removal from county to county or from state to state.

If the guardian is a bank or trust company, the removal of the ward or his property from county to county within the same state does not offer much of a problem because ordinarily it may serve in any county in the state and, according to the laws of the state, make its accountings either to the court that made the appointment or to the court of the county in which the ward has made his home. But in the case of removal from state to state, the individual and the bank or trust company are in practically the same position; for, according to a comparatively recent study, there are only about fifteen states in which an out-of-state bank or trust company can serve as guardian of either the property or the person of a minor or incompetent person.[1]

[1] Stephenson's *Studies*, 2nd Ser., p. 329; *Wills, Estates, and Trusts*, Secs. 13.571–13.573.

PERSONAL TRUSTS

The administration of a personal trust—whether it is a trust under will, a living trust, an insurance trust, or any other kind of trust—means carrying out its terms.

Terms of Trust

The terms of a trust are to be found (1) in the applicable law of trusts and (2) in the provisions of the trust instrument. The terms to be found in the law of trusts prevail unless the creator of the trust otherwise provides in his trust instrument.

The administration of trusts does not yield to definitive treatment so easily as does the settlement of estates or the administration of guardianships. Whereas the duties of an administrator or guardian and mainly those of an executor are fixed by law, the duties of a trustee are fixed largely by the trust instrument. There is almost no limit to the variations in the terms of trusts set forth in wills and trust agreements. It has been said that the purposes for which trusts can be created are as unlimited as the imagination of lawyers.

The following cases are illustrative of the endless variations in the terms of trusts: At one extreme, *A* can put in trust with *B* an item of tangible personal property—say, a portrait or a piece of jewelry—to be safekept and delivered to *C* when *C* reaches the age of twenty-one years or, if he dies before reaching that age, delivered to *D* at *C's* death. *B's* duties are to keep the property safely in a vault or safe deposit box, to keep it insured, and to deliver it to *C* or *D*, as the case may be, upon the happening of the specified event. Or, *A* can insure his partner's or fellow stockholder's life and put the policy in trust with *B* to collect the proceeds at the death of the insured and use the proceeds for the liquidation of his interest in the business. *B's* duties are to collect the insurance and pay over the proceeds as directed in the instrument. In each of these illustrations active trust administration is reduced to the minimum.

At the other extreme, *A* can put in trust with *B* a going business for *B* to carry on for the benefit of *A's* family, involving, as it would, all the burdens and responsibilities incident to the carrying on of such a business. Or, *A* can put in trust with *B* a miscellany of property—real and personal; tangible and intangible; productive and unproductive; local and foreign—and charge *B* with the duty of administering that property or the property into which it may be converted over a period of seventy-five or one hundred years for a succession of beneficiaries of every type and character. In each of these illustrations active trust administration is expanded to the maximum.

Duties of a Trustee

The duties of a trustee as listed in the *Restatement of the Law of Trusts* are: (1) to administer the trust; (2) to be loyal; (3) not to delegate; (4) to keep and render accounts; (5) to furnish information; (6) to exercise reasonable care and skill; (7) to take and keep control; (8) to preserve the trust property; (9) to enforce claims; (10) to defend actions; (11) to keep trust property separate; (12) duties with respect to bank deposits; (13) to make the trust property productive; (14) to pay income to beneficiary; (15) to deal impartially with beneficiaries; (16) duties with respect to co-trustees; and, (17) duties with respect to persons holding power of control.[2]

Of these seventeen stated duties of a trustee, the following relate to the preservation of the trust property: to take and keep control, to preserve the trust property, to enforce claims, to defend actions, to keep trust property separate, and those with respect to bank deposits.

Of the seventeen duties, the following relate to the management of the trust property: not to delegate, to exercise reasonable care and skill, to make the trust property productive, duties with respect to cotrustees, and duties with respect to persons holding power of control.

The following relate to the distribution of the trust property: to pay income to beneficiaries and to deal impartially with beneficiaries.

The following relate to accounting for the trust property: to keep and render accounts and to furnish information.

Of the seventeen, this leaves only the duty to administer the trust and the duty of loyalty, which are basic duties of every trustee and which already have been discussed in Chapter 14.

Whatever the degree or kind of administration required, the duties of the trustee may be grouped under these four heads: (1) preservation, (2) management, (3) distribution, and (4) accounting. In one trust, preservation may be the main responsibility of the trustee; in another, management; and in still another, distribution.

PRESERVATION OF PROPERTY

In the administration of a trust the trustee is under a duty to take and keep control of the trust property, to preserve it, to enforce claims, to defend actions, to keep the trust property separate, and to handle bank deposits in the manner required by the applicable law.

[2] Secs. 169–185; Scott on *Trusts*, Secs. 169–189.

Control

In administering the trust, the trustee must both *take* and *keep* control of the trust property.

1. *Taking.* If he is trustee under will, he should not leave the property in the hands of the executor; nor should he leave it in the hands of a third person unless the latter is his duly authorized agent or representative; nor should he leave it in the hands of a beneficiary unless under the terms of the trust the beneficiary is entitled to keep it in his possession.

In taking control of the trust property, the trustee may be under a duty to have it designated as trust property—for example, to take title to real property in his name as trustee or to have securities transferred to him as trustee.

2. *Keeping.* Having taken control, he should keep control of the trust property throughout the duration of the trust. He may and, in the course of administration, must, temporarily, yield possession of the property—as to a broker, agent, or lessee. Or, under the terms of the trust, the beneficiary himself may be entitled to the possession and use of the trust property. But in any case he must keep ultimate control of the property.

Protection

While the trustee is neither an insurer nor a guarantor of the protection of the trust property or of its money-value, he is under a duty in protecting it to exercise the care and skill of a person of ordinary prudence. For example, he should use trust funds to keep buildings in repair; to prevent theft of, or damage to, or trespass upon, the property; to keep the property insured; to prevent mortgaged property, so far as possible, from being sold under foreclosure; to keep the taxes paid; and to make other expenditures of trust funds on hand or available to preserve the trust property.

Enforcement of Claims

If the trustee finds claims owing the trust estate, he is under a duty to take every reasonable step to enforce those claims. This may mean suing on claims; or extending the time for payment; or taking additional security; or compromising; or appealing a decision from a lower to a higher court. Unless the instrument otherwise provides, it means in all cases doing what a man of ordinary prudence would do to realize on the claim for the benefit of the trust estate.

Defense of Actions

The trustee is under a corresponding duty to defend actions against the trust estate. In defending actions, as in enforcing claims, he must, in the absence of a provision to the contrary in the instrument, act as a man of ordinary prudence under similar circumstances would act. If it would cost more to fight a small, even though unjust, claim in court than to pay the claim, he should pay it. If it would be less expensive to the estate to compromise than to litigate, he should compromise.

Separation of Property

This means three things: (*a*) keeping the trust property separate from the trustee's own property, (*b*) keeping the property of each trust separate, and (*c*) identifying it as trust property.

1. *From trustee's own property*. A trustee should not deposit trust funds in his own bank account, no matter how innocent or even praiseworthy his motive may be. He should not mingle crops—grain, for example—from a farm he holds in trust with similar crops from his own farm. The courts in some states have gone so far as to hold that he should not keep trust securities in a safe deposit box with his own securities.

2. *From property of other trusts*. The trustee should not only keep the property of each trust separate from that of any other trust, but also separate from that of any other property he may have in his possession, for example, the property of an executorship, administratorship, guardianship, or agency. Ordinarily, an individual trustee should not deposit the funds of two or more trusts in the same bank account; the duty of a bank or trust company in this regard is discussed later.

3. *Earmarked as trust property*. A trustee is under a duty to keep the trust property at all times identifiable as such. Trust cash would lose its identity if it were deposited in the trustee's own bank account. He should not take real property or certificates of stock or registered bonds in his own name, unless he is authorized to do so by statute or by express provision in the trust instrument.

This principle of separation and of earmarking of trust property is based upon one of the essential elements of a trust, already discussed—namely, that there must be specific trust property—a trust *res*—of which the beneficiary is the beneficial owner. He must be able to say, "*This* property is being held and administered in trust for *my* benefit." He cannot say this unless the property is separate and the property itself is in evidence and identifiable as his property. However, this does not mean that a trustee cannot have an undivided interest with other co-owners in property, provided the percentage of his interest is definite. This is true of bank deposits, to be discussed next.

Bank Deposits

Although a trustee should not lend money without security and a bank deposit is, in law, such a loan, nevertheless, a trustee may make such a deposit if (1) he exercises reasonable care in the selection of the bank, (2) earmarks the deposit as a trust deposit, (3) does not leave the money on deposit an unreasonable length of time, and (4) is free to withdraw the deposit at any time. If he fails in any of these respects and a loss results, he may be guilty of a breach of trust.

A trustee's duty regarding bank deposits offers a bank or trust company more of a problem than it does an individual. An individual, who is administering one or, at most, only a few trusts, easily can open a separate bank account for each trust. But a bank or trust company, which is administering hundreds or thousands of trusts, estates, guardianships, and agencies, faces two problems: (1) Is it proper to deposit trust funds in its own banking department? and (2) Is it proper to deposit all its trust, estate, guardianship, and agency funds in one bank account?

While the law on the first point still is somewhat unsettled, the prevailing opinion seems to be that, in the absence of authority by statute or the trust instrument, a bank or trust company should not deposit trust funds in its own banking department; and in some states it is forbidden to do so by statute.

A bank or trust company can carry all its trust funds in one bank account whether or not it can carry the deposit in its own banking department. This is not regarded as a violation of a trustee's duty to earmark its trust property because, although the funds of each trust are not earmarked as separate deposits on the books of the banking department, they are so earmarked on the books of the trust department.

MANAGEMENT OF PROPERTY

At this point the difference between the settlement of estates and the administration of guardianships and trusts becomes the most impressive. Whereas the primary responsibility of an administrator or executor is to preserve and distribute the property, that of an active guardian or trustee is to manage, as well as preserve, the property. Throughout this section the term *trustee* may be understood to include *guardian* unless otherwise specified.

Delegation

A trustee is under a duty himself to do and not to delegate to others the doing of things which he ought personally to do.

This does not mean that he cannot employ persons to do things in connection with the administration of the trust which he reasonably could not be expected personally to do. He can, for example, employ bookkeepers, accountants, rental agents, farm managers, and other types of servants, agents, or representatives that a man of ordinary prudence would employ in the management of property of similar character.

It does mean that he cannot turn over to anyone else the administration of the trust. He is the trustee; he has accepted the trust; with his acceptance he has undertaken to carry out the terms of the trust; he is responsible, subject to the exception mentioned below, for the acts or omissions of the person he employs.

Making the trustee responsible for the acts of his agents in all cases may, in some cases, work what would seem to be an undue hardship upon him. For example, the trustee exercises due care in the selection of an agent to do things that a man of ordinary prudence under similar circumstances would employ an agent to do. Thereafter, the trustee properly supervises the conduct of his agent. But, despite the trustee's care in selecting and in supervising his agent, the latter acts dishonestly or negligently and a loss to the trust results. Should the trustee be held responsible for what his agent has done or failed to do? If the trustee was not negligent in any way with respect to the employment or supervision of the agent, he might not be responsible for the loss. But there still is so much uncertainty about the matter that many modern trust instruments contain provisions expressly authorizing the trustee to employ agents, and some states have statutes to that effect. The English Trustee Act of 1925 authorizes a trustee to employ agents—such as lawyers, bankers, and brokers—and provides that the trustee shall not be liable for the default of such agents if employed in good faith.[3]

Care and Skill

As was brought out in Chapter 14, a trustee or a guardian is under a duty to exercise such care and skill as a man of ordinary prudence would exercise in dealing with his own property. If he has greater skill and has better facilities than the man of ordinary prudence has, he is under a duty to exercise all the skill and all the facilities that he has. Whether he should be held to the standard of skill he *claims* to have (whether or not his claim is justified) still is an unsettled question of law. Suppose, for example, a person claims to be a specialist or an expert in administering trusts and on the strength of such claims he is appointed trustee. Then it turns out that he has no more skill than that of a person of ordinary prudence, if that much, and the beneficiary of the trust does not receive the specialized or expert service that the trustee claimed he would render. The difficulty about holding the "expert" trustee to the higher standard of skill would be in measuring the damage the beneficiary suffered. How much would the loss have amounted to if the trustee had lived up to the standard of skill he claimed to have instead of living only up to that of the man of ordinary prudence?

[3] Stephenson, *Trust Business in Common-Law Countries*, p. 715.

Productivity

In most cases, but not in all, a trustee is under a duty to make the trust property reasonably productive. Productivity, frequently, is one of the main purposes of the trust.

But there are cases in which preservation, conservation, and distribution, not productivity, constitute the main purposes of the trust; and, in these cases, productivity may not be one of the duties of the trustee.

In those cases, which are in the vast majority, where productivity is one of the major purposes, the trustee is under a duty to make the property as productive as due consideration to the safety of the principal will permit.

The following are some of the applications of this duty. A trustee ordinarily must not let trust funds, which are available for investment, remain uninvested an unreasonable length of time. This does not mean that he must invest them simply in order to be able to say he has invested them. There may be circumstances under which he would be justified in retaining investable funds uninvested for a considerable length of time. Ordinarily, he would not be justified in keeping funds invested in low-yield securities, merely because they are safe investments, when a man of ordinary prudence would invest his funds in higher-yield securities without sacrificing the safety of principal. If property is unproductive when it comes into the trustee's hands—unoccupied or uncultivated real property, for example—he may be under a duty to sell it and convert the proceeds into productive property. If the property is unproductive because of its condition, the trustee may be under a duty to repair, remodel, or recondition the property so as to make it productive.

Cotrustees

Earlier in this chapter we discussed the duty of a trustee not to delegate to another person the duties that the trustee himself personally should perform. This applies to a cotrustee as much as it does to anyone else. Unless otherwise provided by the terms of the trust, one trustee cannot turn over to his cotrustee the administration of the trust. Should he do so, he would commit a breach of trust. More than that, he might be liable for permitting breaches of trust committed by the cotrustee.

In the administration of a trust, cotrustees share the work and the responsibility. Although each trustee is liable only for his own breaches of trust and not for those of his cotrustee, he may be liable for his own breach of duty to his beneficiary as a result of doing any of the five things specified below.

The creator of a trust has the choice of naming a sole trustee, cotrustees with or without segregating their duties, or separate trustees, charging each with the duty of administering a different part of the estate. If each of the cotrustees has his own specified duties, he is not responsible for the other trustee's failure to perform his duties. If each trustee is sole trustee for a specified portion of the estate, he is not responsible for what the other trustee does or does not do, with respect to his position. Each trustee is responsible only for the administration of his own trust. But if two or more cotrustees are named without any segregation or specification of the duties of each, all of them are responsible for participating in the administration of the trust.

And if one of the trustees himself commits a breach of trust, each other trustee is liable if (1) he participated in the breach of trust, (2) he improperly delegated the administration of the trust to the trustee who committed the breach, (3) by his failure to exercise reasonable care he enabled the other trustee to commit the breach, (4) he approved or acquiesced in or concealed the breach, or (5) he neglected to take proper steps to compel the other trustee to make good the loss to the trust estate resulting from his breach.[4]

Power of Control

Under some wills and trust agreements the power of control of the trust administration is placed, to a greater or lesser extent, in some person other than the trustee himself. For example, A puts cash or securities in trust with B and C (cotrustees) for the benefit of D and provides in the trust agreement that B and C shall not make or change trust investments without the approval, consent, or instruction of A (the settlor) or C (one of the cotrustees) or D (the beneficiary) or E (a broker or banker or business associate or member of A's family or some other person who is not a beneficiary of the trust). In the course of administration of the trust B (one of the trustees) decides that certain funds should be invested, that certain investments should be converted, or that some other change should be made in the investments. He calls the matter to A's or C's or D's or E's attention, according to the terms of the trust, asking his approval of or consent to the investment or to the change in the investment, and A, C, D, or E, as the case may be, does not respond. Is B safe in letting the funds remain invested or the investments remain unchanged? Or, B has on hand funds which he thinks should be invested or investments which he thinks should be changed. But under the terms of the trust he is not to make or change any investment except upon the instruction of A, C, D, or E. Is he under a duty to call A's or C's or D's or E's attention to the need for the investment or for the change? If he receives instructions which in his judgment, if followed, will not be for the best interests of D (the beneficiary), is he safe in carrying out the instructions? Is he safe in disregarding the instructions and making or changing the investment in the way he thinks and, in fact, the way that is for the best interest of D? To what extent is a trustee protected

[4] Scott on *Trusts*, Sec. 224.

in replying unquestioningly upon the terms of the trust in seeking, obtaining, and acting upon the exercise of a power of control lodged in someone other than the trustee himself?

The general rule is that, if the power of control exists for the benefit of the person who has the power, the trustee is protected in following the terms of the trust as to approval, consent, or instruction. But if the power of control exists for the benefit of someone other than the person who has the power, then the trustee will not be protected in taking and following instructions of the holder of the power if to do so would be a violation of the duty of the holder of the power to the beneficiary. Illustrations will help to clarify these two rather abstruse statements of law. If *A* creates a trust with *B* for *A's* own benefit and provides that *B* shall not make or change any investment except upon *A's* own approval, consent, or instruction, *B* is safe in awaiting and acting upon *A's* approval, consent, or instruction, for *A* is the only person interested in the matter. But if *A* creates a trust with *B* for *C's* benefit and provides that *B* shall not make or change any investment without *D's* (*A's* broker's or banker's) approval, consent, or instruction, then *B* would not be safe in acting upon *D's* approval, consent, or instruction if *D*, in giving such approval, consent, or instruction, would be violating his duty to *C*. *D* himself, as the holder of the power, has a fiduciary relationship to *C* in the violation of which *B* should not participate.

The practical effect of all this is that a trustee cannot, with safety to himself, blindly and unquestioningly act upon approvals, consents, or even instructions, where the holder of such power is acting or is supposed to be acting for the benefit, not of himself, but of some other person. Trusts in which the trustee can act only upon the instruction of someone else frequently are known as *direction trusts*. The point of this section is that a direction trust, instead of relieving the trustee of responsibility, may increase his responsibility by making him responsible not only for his own conduct but also for the supervision of the conduct of the director himself. As brought out in Chapter 14, this possibility is a feature that disinclines many experienced trustees to accept direction or consent trusts.

DISTRIBUTION OF PROPERTY

In the distribution of the property the trustee is under a duty to pay the income to the beneficiary and to be impartial in his dealings with the beneficiaries.

Payment of Income

The duty of a trustee as to the payment of income to the beneficiary may be and usually is determined by the terms of the trust as set forth in the instrument rather than by the general law of trusts. The will or trust agreement may specify the frequency of the payments, whether they are to be paid to or applied for the beneficiary, or whether income is to be accumulated.

Unless the trust instrument otherwise provides, the trustee may make the payments to or for the beneficiary at reasonable intervals—say, monthly or quarterly or semiannually, according to the needs of the beneficiary. Furthermore, he may equalize the payments by holding back income to meet present or anticipated expenses. For example, if the trustee knows that there will be a big tax installment due later in the year, he may begin early in the year holding back part of the gross income and building up a reserve for that year's taxes.

As regards the payment of income, the trustee's problems frequently relate to payments to or for beneficiaries under legal disability. Suppose the beneficiary, though a minor, is a college or university student. Can the trustee make payments direct to the beneficiary, or should he pay the student's bills, or should he make payments only to a guardian? If the will or trust agreement does not authorize the trustee to make payments direct to the beneficiary, the only absolutely safe course for the trustee to follow is either to pay the bills himself or await the appointment of a guardian. Many modern wills and trust agreements give the trustee the option of making payments to or for minor beneficiaries in any one of four ways according to the circumstances: (1) to the guardian (if there is one) of the person; (2) to the person who stands in the place of a parent; (3) to the minor himself if he is mature enough to use it wisely; (4) make or apply payments *for* the beneficiary. The guardian has no trust instrument to guide him and is governed by the applicable law.

Impartiality

1. *Immediate beneficiaries.* A trustee is under a duty to deal impartially as between or among several beneficiaries. This is not so difficult when the dealings are with present, immediate beneficiaries. Unless the instrument otherwise provides, the trustee must pay over or apply the income, share and share alike, between or among them. In the absence of authority, he cannot pay over or apply the income according to the respective needs of the beneficiaries.

2. *Intermediate and ultimate beneficiaries.* The real problem of impartiality comes in the trustee's dealings as between immediate beneficiaries and ultimate beneficiaries. For example, A creates a trust with B for the benefit of C (A's wife), designating that after her death the principal is to go to D (A's son), with no provision for the use of principal by or for C. This means that she is entitled to the net income only. C is wholly dependent upon her income from the trust, and D is disposed to insist upon the letter of the trust. To what extent, if any, is B justified in investing even at some

risk of the safety of the principal in order to increase the income for *C*?
Much as *B* would like to favor *C*, it is his duty to hold the scales absolutely
in balance as between *C* and *D*. If any preference is to be shown, it must be
authorized by the creator of the trust. Because this is so, in an increasing
number of wills and trust agreements, under which property is left in trust
for life beneficiaries and then for ultimate beneficiaries, provision is made
for favoring the life beneficiary, even to the extent of using principal,
should that be necessary or needed for the comfort or requirements of the
life beneficiary.[5]

ACCOUNTING FOR ADMINISTRATION

A trustee is under a duty to keep and render accounts and to furnish
information to the beneficiaries. Again, a guardian's duty to account is not
basically dissimilar to that of a trustee.

Accounts

A trustee must both keep and render accounts.

1. *Keeping.* A trustee's accounts should show what he has received,
what he has expended, what gains have accrued, and what losses, if any, have
been incurred on changes in investments. Subject to statutory requirements,
a trustee may use his own judgment as to the form of his accounts. Whereas
an individual trustee, being trustee of one or only a few accounts, may keep
his accounts by hand, a bank or trust company with hundreds or thousands
of accounts would keep its accounts by machine. It is the substance and not
the form of the account that counts.

2. *Rendering.* A trustee must render an accounting when called upon
to do so at reasonable times. In every case he owes his beneficiary a duty to
make accountings to him. In trusts under will in most states he must account
also to the court which has jurisdiction over the account. In living trusts
and insurance trusts he usually does not account to the court unless the
trustee or the beneficiary desires a court accounting. In a few states a
trustee under a living trust or insurance trust may be required to account
to the court, as well as to the beneficiary, unless the trust instrument relieves
him of that duty.

A trustee's duty as to rendering accounts may be and frequently is expressed in the trust instrument. The provision about accounting in the will
or trust agreement either may go further than the statute does in requiring
the trustee to render accounts or it may relieve him of some duty to account
which would be required by statute if it were not for a provision in the
instrument.[6]

[5] Stephenson's *Studies*, 2nd Ser., p. 289.
[6] Stephenson, *Drafting Wills and Trust Agreements*, Vol. I, Ch. X, p. 196.

Information

Akin to the trustee's duty to render accounts is his duty to furnish the beneficiary all pertinent information about the trust.

1. *Third persons.* A trustee's duty to furnish information is a duty he owes the beneficiary and him alone. In fact, the trustee is under a duty to decline to furnish information about a trust to anyone who is not a beneficiary unless he is authorized by the beneficiary to do so. This is what is meant by the confidentiality of the trust relationship. Frequently a person with the best of motives will ask the trustee for information about a trust; and, when the trustee declines to give it, that person should understand that the trustee, reluctantly perhaps, is acting in the line of duty.

2. *Beneficiaries.* But when it is the beneficiary or one of several beneficiaries who is seeking the information, it is the trustee's duty to furnish him any and all information that is pertinent to the trust property or to the trust administration. A beneficiary is entitled, for example, to know what the trust estate consists of and how the trustee has handled it. He is entitled to inspect the property, the books, the accounts, the papers, and anything and everything that relates to the trust. Furthermore, where there are several beneficiaries—present and future, whose interests are vested or contingent— each of the beneficiaries is entitled to information about the trust. For example, suppose A creates with B a trust for C for life, remainder to D after C's death. D is as much entitled to information about the trust as C is and is also as much entitled to information during C's lifetime as after C's death.

As between the trustee and the outside world, the keynote of trusteeship is confidentiality. As between the trustee and any and all beneficiaries, it is complete openness.

PERSONAL SERVICES

In Chapter 15 only brief mention was made of the personal services an administrator or executor renders the distributees of an estate. This brevity of treatment was not due to the fact that these services are relatively unimportant but that the time is so short within which they can be rendered. It is only during the "executor's year" which may, in fact, be only a few months, that the administrator or executor has an opportunity to render personal services to the distributees.

In this chapter on the administration of guardianships and trusts, personal services deserve comparable space with business, financial, and property services. Courts appoint guardians and people create trusts under will, living trusts, and insurance trusts because they think the guardian or the trustee will render personal services to their wards or beneficiaries equally as beneficial as business and financial services to the property. Whereas the distributee of an estate sustains a personal relationship with the administrator or executor only during the brief period that the estate is in process of settlement, the beneficiary of a trust may sustain that relationship throughout his entire lifetime. In fact, there are some older banks and trust companies which have been serving as trustee a century or more that are now rendering personal services to the third generation of successive beneficiaries in the same family.

Personal Trusts

The personal services expected of and actually rendered by the trustee in personal trusts are different both in degree and in kind from those expected and rendered in other trusts. In trusts under will, living trusts, and insurance trusts, on the one hand, the beneficiaries are few in number and the trustee has, and is expected to have, direct dealings with them. In employees trusts, charitable trusts, and corporate trusts, on the other hand, the trustee is not expected to have nor does he, in fact, have many direct dealings with noteholders, bondholders, or the beneficiaries of these other trusts. Consequently, most of what is said below about personal services relates to services to the beneficiaries of trusts under will, living trusts, and insurance trusts.

Guardianships

Where there are two guardians of a minor—one of his property and the other of his person—the guardian of the property is under a duty to concentrate his attention upon the property of his ward, and the guardian of the person, upon the personal needs of his ward. But where there is only one guardian—a guardian of the estate without specification that he is guardian also of the person—the personal services rendered by the guardian are essentially similar to those rendered by a trustee. The personal services of a guardian or trustee fall into two general classes: (1) those of a general nature which are dissociated from the estate and (2) those associated with the estate.

Dissociated from Estate

In theory, a guardian's or trustee's duty to render personal services to beneficiaries relates only to services associated in some way with the estate. In practice, it frequently does not work out that way at all. For example, a husband creates a trust under will for his wife. After his death, she has no one else to turn to for advice on any matter. Her children are young. She has no brother, sister, parent, or friend in whom she is willing to confide. Naturally, she turns to the trustee—the person in whom her husband had enough confidence to leave the estate he had provided for her support and comfort. While the trustees might, in theory, draw the line between matters connected with and those not connected with the estate, in practice, if he is worthy of the confidence reposed in him, he will not do so. Instead, he will advise her as best he can on any and all matters she presents to him.

Or, for another example, a father creates a trust for his minor children. After their father's and their mother's death, the children may have no one except the trustee to turn to for advice on any matter. They, or the persons who take the place, so far as possible, of their parents, may seek the trustee's advice on all kinds of personal problems, without stopping to ask or to think whether they are related in any way to the trust estate. Again, no trustee, who is worthy of the confidence reposed in him by the creator of the trust, will draw the line between matters associated with and those dissociated from the trust estate.

Associated with Estate

Personal services associated with the trust estate lend themselves to some degree of classification, as follows:

1. *Living expenses.* In the case of a family trust or of a trust for the wife as surviving head of the family, advice as to living expenses is the kind of advice which perhaps most frequently is sought by the widow-and-mother. First, she wishes to know how much she can count on for family living expenses during each month, quarter, or the customary period, whatever that may be, and how regular and dependable, from period to period, that amount will be. If it is less than she has been accustomed to, she desires advice as to how and where she can reduce expenses with the least discomfort to herself and her children. At this point she may have her first lesson in family budgeting, and the trustee may be called upon to be her teacher.

In advising with regard to living expenses, one of the trustee's practical problems is that of putting himself into the position of the beneficiary and understanding the standard of living to which she and her family have been accustomed. Suppose, for example, the individual trustee or the trust officer has been accustomed to $15,000 a year for his own family living expenses, while the beneficiary and her family have been accustomed to only $5,000. Or, the other way round, suppose she and her family have been accustomed to $15,000, and the trustee to $5,000. It may not be easy for them to adjust their respective ideas of living-expense requirements to each other's standards.

2. *School and school expenses.* In the case both of a family trust and of a trust for children of school age, two of the points on which the trustee's advice frequently is sought relate to schools and school expenses.

Shall the child be kept in public school or sent to a private school? After graduation from high school or private school, shall it be college; if so, what college? If college, in what subjects shall he major? In what extracurricular activities shall he participate?

Advice as to which school to select is tied up with school expenses. Can the trust estate stand the expense of a private school or college or university? If so, what school or college or university comes within the price range? If the trustee is authorized to use principal for school expenses, which will be for the best interest of the schoolboy or schoolgirl—to consume most of the trust estate on his or her schooling or to hold most of it in reserve for him or her in later life?

3. *Vocation.* One of the recently developed services to young people is known as *vocational guidance*—that is, guiding and advising them in the selection of a lifework—whether business or professional, and which business or which profession. Shall the son continue in his father's business? What professional training—in law or medicine or education, for example—shall he seek? How much can the trust estate afford to spend on his professional training? If he decides to enter a business other than his family business, what business? With whom? And in what capacity? If he decides to enter a given profession, where shall he locate? Shall he, for example, open his own law office or shall he seek a law clerkship in the office of some well-established lawyer or firm of lawyers?

While all such advice is, in one way, dissociated from the trust estate, it is, in another way, closely associated with it in that the beneficiary's choice of a vocation may be influenced greatly or even determinatively by the ability of the trust estate to provide for the expense of professional training or for the opening of the business career.

It has been said that in estate planning it is more important to leave, or to give a beneficiary, earning power than it is to leave or give him property. With earning power, he will be able to build up his own estate; without it, he may not be able even to keep the property given or left him. So, advice on the choice of a vocation and on the ways and means of obtaining the essential training for that vocation may, in the long run, be the most useful personal service a trustee ever renders a beneficiary.

4. *Hospitalization or institutionalization.* In Chapter 4 mention was made of the frequent need for hospitalizing or institutionalizing an incompetent ward. A trustee's, as well as a guardian's, personal services frequently are needed in this respect. For example, in a family trust or in a trust for the widow-and-mother, one of the children in the family may be mentally retarded—not imbecilic or feeble-minded, but simply mentally retarded and unable to keep up with his classes in a regular school. Is this a case for special tutoring and keeping him in a regular school with other children, or is it a case for a special school for mentally retarded children?

Or, in the case of an adult beneficiary, he may not be legally incompetent but, to all intents and purposes, he may be actually incompetent. It may not be practicable or desirable to talk with him about his own condition. It may be a case for advising with the normal, responsible members of the family as to what will be the best thing to do with or for the unfortunate beneficiary. Or, where there is no member of the family who can assume responsibility, the trustee himself may have to take the initiative and, according to the circumstances of the particular case, either persuade the beneficiary voluntarily to enter a hospital or other institution or else have him committed to one.

5. *Financial problems.* Financial problems connected with living expenses of the family and school expenses of the children already have been mentioned. But they are not, by any means, all of the kinds of financial problems on which the beneficiary seeks or needs the advice of his trustee. The trustee, having under his administration a trust estate which may constitute all the property the beneficiary has, is the person to whom the beneficiary naturally turns for advice on all manner of financial problems. These include the whole gamut of problems growing out of personal, family, business, and professional transactions.

The person, then, who accepts a guardianship or a trust should understand that in administering it he will be called upon, not only to preserve and manage the property and make it productive, but also that he may be called upon to render almost every type of personal service that human beings require for their comfort and welfare. In number and variety, the personal services guardians and trustees actually render are very nearly coextensive with human needs.[7]

[7] For a more detailed discussion and illustration of the personal services rendered by trustees, see Stephenson's, *Reflections of a Trustman*, Ch. XI; "The Trustman in Perspective—as a Social Man," 13.

COLLATERAL READING

Note: For complete citations, see Bibliography, pp. 417–428.

Guardianships

American Jurisprudence, Vol. 25, *Guardian and Ward*.
Corpus Juris Secundum, Vol. 33.
Ruling Case Law, Vol. 12.
Wills, Estates, and Trusts, Secs. 13,001–13,072.

Personal Trusts

Bogert's *Handbook*, Chs. 9–16.
Loring's *Trustee's Handbook*, Shattuck rev., Ch. 5.
Scott on *Trusts*, Secs. 169–185.
Shattuck and Farr, *An Estate Planner's Handbook*, Ch. 7, 140.

17

Investment of Trust Funds

𝕿HE PRINCIPLES, duties, and powers incident to the fiduciary relationships are brought into play more often and more impressively in connection with investments than with any other phase of administration.

Investment Functions of Fiduciaries

An administrator or executor usually is not under a duty to *make* investments. Yet, as pointed out in Chapter 15, he frequently is under a duty to convert existing investments into cash to pay debts, taxes, and expenses. It takes quite as much investment knowledge and judgment to sell wisely as it does to buy investments. So in this respect investments are a matter of major concern to administrators and executors as well as to guardians and trustees.

A managing agent usually goes no further than to recommend investments, leaving it to his principal to make the decision. Nevertheless, it takes as much investment knowledge and experience to make sound investment recommendations as it does to select sound investments themselves. When, as sometimes is the case, the agent himself is under a duty to make investments, there is little or no basic difference between his investment duties and those of a trustee.

Most of the discussion of investments, however, centers about guardians and trustees and, more about trustees than guardians.

During the decade since the publication of the first edition of this textbook in 1949 there has been such a marked change of attitude on the part of both businessmen and trustees towards businesses and business interests as trust investments that it is deemed advisable in this edition to include a chapter on investment in businesses. In the present chapter most of the statements regarding investment powers and duties apply equally to all kinds of trust investments—stocks and bonds, as well as businesses and business interests.

246

However, the chapter that follows will be confined to powers and duties peculiar to businesses and business interests.

SOURCES OF INVESTMENT POWERS

The sources of investment powers are the common law, the statutes, the instruments, and the courts.

Common Law

Since both a guardian and a trustee are under a duty to make and keep the property productive, they both, in the nature of their relationship to the ward or beneficiary, must have the power to invest funds.

Statutes

The statutes of every state contain more or less specific authority or direction to guardians and trustees as to the investments they *must* or *may* make.[1]

Instruments

Wills, trust agreements, declarations of trust, and agency agreements usually or frequently contain investment authorizations, instructions, or directions.

Courts

In many states the court will approve or disapprove proposed investments by a trustee or guardian. In some states the court will not approve beforehand but will approve or disapprove an investment already made. In a few states, unless the instrument otherwise provides, the court must approve all investments made by trustees under will as well as by guardians.

INVESTMENT POWERS

As regards the investment powers of guardians and trustees, the states fall into three main groups. These groups are the prudent-man-rule states, the legal-list states, and a few states that are partly prudent-man and partly legal-list states.

In Prudent-Man-Rule States

In most states the legislature does not tell a guardian or trustee in what he shall or may or shall not or may not invest, nor does it authorize anyone

[1] *Wills, Estates, and Trusts*, Secs. 15.301–15.303.

else to tell him. Instead, the legislature is silent or else by statute leaves it for the guardian or trustee himself to select his investments according to his own judgment as a prudent man in obedience to the terms of the relationship. These are known as the *prudent-man-rule* states. Some of them are prudent-man-rule states by judicial decision; others, by statute.

1. *By judicial decision.* In the *Restatement of the Law of Trusts*, the prudent-man rule is stated as follows:

> In making investments of trust funds the trustee is under a duty to the beneficiary (*a*) in the absence of provisions in the terms of the trust or a statute otherwise providing, to make such investments and only such investments as a prudent man would make of his own property having primarily in view the preservation of the estate and the amount and regularity of the income to be derived; (*b*) in the absence of provisions in the terms of the trust, to conform to statute, if any, governing investments by trustees; (*c*) to conform to the terms of the trust (except under certain specified conditions).[2]

The heart of this statement of the rule is: "to make such investments and only such investments as a prudent man would make of his own property having primarily in view the preservation of the estate and the amount and regularity of the income to be derived."

The classic statement of the prudent-man rule by judicial decision, made in 1830 by the Supreme Judicial Court of Massachusetts in the case of Harvard College v. Amory, is as follows:

> All that can be required of a trustee to invest is that he shall conduct himself faithfully and exercise a sound discretion. He is to observe how men of prudence, discretion, and intelligence manage their own affairs, not in regard to speculation, but in regard to the permanent disposition of their funds, considering the probable income as well as the probable safety of the capital to be invested.[3]

Since the Massachusetts court was the first to declare the rule, over the past century and more it has come to be known as the "Massachusetts rule." In recent years, however, as the rule has spread from state to state, it has come more generally to be known as the "prudent-man rule."

2. *By statute.* Prior to 1942, only a small number of states had adopted the prudent-man rule by statute. In 1942, a group of lawyers drafted a Model Prudent-Man Investment Statute which since then has served as the pattern for most of the prudent-man-rule statutes. The statement of the rule in the model statute is as follows:

> In acquiring, investing, reinvesting, exchanging, retaining, selling, and managing property for the benefit of another, a fiduciary shall exercise the judgment and care under the circumstances then prevailing, which men of prudence,

2 Sec. 227; Scott on *Trusts*, Sec. 227.
3 9 Pick, 446, 461.

discretion and intelligence exercise in the management of their own affairs, not in regard to speculation but in regard to the permanent disposition of their funds, considering the probable income as well as the probable safety of their capital.[4]

Note the similarity between the rule as stated by the Massachusetts court in 1830 and as stated in the Model Statute in 1942. In the Massachusetts decision the standard is: "how men of prudence, discretion, and intelligence manage their own affairs, not in regard to speculation, but in regard to the permanent disposition of their funds, considering the probable income as well as the probable safety of the capital to be invested." In the Model Statute it is: "the judgment and care under the circumstances then prevailing, which men of prudence, discretion and intelligence exercise in the management of their own affairs, not in regard to speculation but in regard to the permanent disposition of their funds, considering the probable income as well as the probable safety of their capital."

Two states—Michigan and Minnesota—have adopted the prudent-*trustee* rule and one state—Connecticut—the prudent-*investor* rule. It is doubtful that there is any fundamental difference in the power or in the duty of the guardian or trustee whether he is operating under the prudent-*man*, the prudent-*trustee*, or the prudent-*investor* rule. The practical disadvantage of a change in terminology, if not in substance, is that it necessitates judicial determination which may, in turn, lead to confusion as to the full scope of the rule when stated in other words.[5]

In Legal-List States

In the legal-list states, the legislatures tell guardians, trustees, and any other fiduciaries who are under a duty to invest funds, in what they *must* or in what they *may* invest funds unless the terms of the relationship otherwise provide.

In some states, the legislatures specify the investments or the classes of investments in which the fiduciary must or may invest. In other states, it prescribes certain statistical standards as to earnings and dividends which the property must meet in order to qualify as an investment. In other states, the legislatures authorize some administrative agency—such as the state banking department—to make and from time to time to issue lists of legal investments. In still other states, the legislatures prescribe a list of investments for savings banks and declares that they shall be legal also for the investment of guardians' funds or trust funds. In at least one state—Illinois—the legislature has put trustees under the prudent-man rule, but has kept guardians under

---

[4] "The Prudent-Man Rule for Trust Investment."

[5] See *Wills, Estates, and Trusts*, Secs. 15,301 and 15,302 for the different wordings, state by state, of the prudent-man rule.

the legal-list rule. In the legal-list states, there is not a great deal of uniformity as to the investments in which trustees, guardians, and other fiduciaries must or may invest, except that it would be true to say that in nearly every state government bonds, bonds of the state, and mortgages on improved real property within that state would be included in the legal list.

1. *Mandatory*. In one group of the legal-list states, the list of authorized investments is said to be mandatory. This means that, unless otherwise provided by the terms of the relationship, the fiduciary *must* invest his funds within the perscribed list. If he invests outside the list, that in itself is a breach of trust and, no matter how much prudence, discretion, and intelligence he may have exercised, he will be liable for any loss to the beneficiaries which may result from his making a nonlegal investment.

2. *Permissive*. In another group of legal-list states, the list of authorized investments is said to be permissive. That is to say, the legislature tells the fiduciary in what property or classes of property he *may* invest. If he invests within the list, he will be presumed to have invested properly, and any beneficiary who thinks otherwise has the burden of proving that the fiduciary committed a breach of trust by the way he invested the funds. If he invests outside the list, while he will not be presumed to have invested improperly, he will take upon himself, in case any beneficiary objects to the investment, the burden of proving that it was a proper investment. In these states, were the fiduciary to go outside the permissive list, the prudent-man rule would apply to investments outside the list, and for this reason some of these states sometimes are classified as prudent-man-rule states.

In States Partly Prudent-Man and Partly Legal-List

In recent years two of the most populous states—New York and Pennsylvania—have begun, apparently, to move towards the prudent-man rule by authorizing trustees to invest a stated percentage of the trust property in prudent-man investments while retaining the remainder in legal-list investments. In New York it is "thirty-five per cent of the aggregate market value at that time of all the property of the fund held by such fiduciary." [6] A recent Pennsylvania statute provides that "no investment in common stock shall be made which at that time would cause the market value of the investments in common stocks to exceed one third of the market value of the estate, not including in such market value the value of any participation in a common trust fund." [7]

Finally, there is a small and diminishing group of states which cannot be classified as prudent-man, legal-list, or partly each because, as yet, investment statutes and decisions have not been developed or clarified.

[6] *Ibid.*
[7] *Ibid.*

Under Trust Instruments

Many wills and trust agreements set forth the investment powers of the trustee. The variety of those powers is limited only by the desires or even by the whims of settlors and testators. All that this text can do is present a few illustrations of the investment powers that may be found in wills and trust agreements.

1. *Instrument silent.* A settlor or testator has the right to keep silent as well as to speak up about the investment of the funds in his trust. If he keeps silent, the state laws as to investments will come into play. If it is a prudent-man-rule state either by judicial decision or by statute, the prudent-man rule of that state will apply. If it is a legal-list state, he must or may, according to whether it is a mandatory or permissive statute, invest within the list.

2. *Expression as to original, silent as to new investments.* The will or trust agreement may contain specific authorizations or directions as to original investments—that is, investments taken over from the settlor or the executor—and yet be silent as to new investments. In later sections much more will be said about original investments. The point here is that the settlor has the right to express his authorization or direction as to original investments and yet keep silent as to new investments. So long as the original investments are retained the authorization or direction regarding them remains in force. But when an original investment is converted into cash and the proceeds are to be invested, the same rule applies as though the instrument were silent throughout as to investments. That is to say, in a prudent-man-rule state the proceeds would be invested under that rule; in a legal-list state, under the rule, whether mandatory or permissive, of that state.

3. *Investment directions.* The settlor or testator may direct his trustee either as to the retention of original investments, as to new investments, or both. The trustee must comply with those instructions unless to do so would defeat the purposes of the trust. Whether it would defeat the purposes of the trust would be for the court and not for the trustee himself to decide. If the trustee believes that to obey the directions would defeat the purposes of the trust in whole or in part, he is under a duty to bring the matter to the attention of the court and obtain its instructions. Only in an emergency would he act without the prior approval of the court, and even then he should request the court to approve after the fact what he already had done under the emergency.

4. *Investment authorizations.* The settlor or testator may give his trustee, not directions, but authorizations as to specified types of investments. For example, he may authorize, but not direct, his corporate trustee to invest in its common trust funds. He may authorize his trustee to invest in life insurance policies or in annuity contracts. Such authorizations are illustrated in Part IV.

5. *Investment restrictions.* The settlor or testator may tell his trustee in

what he shall not invest. For example, he may say that his trustee shall not invest in mortgages. In that case, the trustee would commit a breach of trust if he invested in mortgages. If, under any conceivable state of facts, mortgages were the only kind of investments available to the trustee, rather than keep funds uninvested during a long period of vain search for other investments, the trustee would be under a duty to ask the court to change the terms of the trust so as to permit the trustee to invest in mortgages.

6. *Employment of investment counsel.* The testator or settlor may authorize his trustee to employ investment counsel. If he does so, it is highly important that the will or trust agreement specify the respective duties of the trustee and of the investment counselor and say whose word shall be final and what the trustee shall do if the counselor fails to act. Unless this is done, confusion of authority is bound to ensue.

7. *Capitalization of income.* Within the limits of the applicable rule against accumulations, the testator or settlor may authorize or direct the trustee to add income to principal and thus capitalize income.

The important points as regards both investment directions and investment restrictions are (*a*) that the trustee cannot follow blindly the directions or restrictions to the defeat of the purposes of the trust and (*b*) that he cannot take it upon himself, except in an emergency, to disregard those directions or restrictions even to prevent what he regards as a defeat of the purposes of the trust. Where defeat of the purposes of the trust is, in the judgment of the trustee, threatened by instrument directions or restrictions, it is the duty of the trustee to bring the matter to the attention of the court, with notice to all interested persons. Thereupon it becomes the duty of the court to change those instructions or restrictions if but only if not to do so would, in the judgment of the court, defeat, wholly or partially, the purposes of the trust.

8. *Prudent-man rule as to original, legal-list as to new investments.* A settlor or testator may, by his trust agreement or will, put his original investments under the prudent-man rule and yet put all new investments under the legal-list rule of his state. He may do this without saying anything about new investments. Suppose he says that his trustee shall use his own judgment at to retaining or disposing of original investments but says nothing about new investments or even about the investments of the proceeds of the sale of original investments. In that case, in a legal-list state new investments would have to be within the legal list and in a prudent-man-rule state the rule would apply.

9. *Prudent-man rule as to new, legal list as to original investments.* The settlor or testator may direct his trustee to retain all his legal-list investments and invest the proceeds of original investments only in legal-list investments. At the same time, he may authorize his trustee to make all investments of new funds, except those arising from the sale of original investments, under the prudent-man rule.

10. *Prudent-man rule as to all investments.* If the settlor or testator desires to give his trustee broad discretion as to investments, he is likely to authorize him to make all investments under the prudent-man rule. In this case, as the trustee sold original investments, he would invest the proceeds under the prudent-man rule. He would invest all new funds in the same way. Thus, as soon as the original investments that did not stand the test of the prudent-man rule were sold and the funds invested, the entire trust would be under the prudent-man rule.

One practical difficulty in looking to the will or trust agreement for authority to invest under the prudent-man rule is the different ways in which the rule is worded in instruments. Suppose in a legal-list state the instrument states simply that the trustee shall use his own judgment and discretion in making and changing investments. Some courts have held that this does not broaden the investment powers of the trustee, that it means only that he must use his own judgment and discretion *within* the legal list. Suppose the instrument says that the trustee shall use his own judgment and discretion and that he shall not be confined to the legal list but fails to specify certain types of securities in which the trustee may invest. In some states, until recently at any rate, there has been such a disinclination to invest trust funds in common stocks that trustees have been fearful that the court would not approve their investment in common stocks unless authority to do so was expressed in unmistakable terms in the instrument itself. Cognizant of this fact, the draftsmen of the Model Prudent-Man Investment Statute added the following clause to their statement of the rule:

Within the limitations of the foregoing standard, a fiduciary is authorized to acquire and retain every kind of property, real, personal or mixed, and every kind of investment, specifically including but not by way of limitation, bonds, debentures and other corporate obligations, and stocks, preferred and common, which men of prudence, discretion, and intelligence acquire or retain for their own account.

This problem of draftsmanship, which, as the court decisions attest, has been a serious one in many states, is met completely when the will or trust agreement specifies, as does the Model Statute, the general types of property which may be construed as coming within the prudent-man rule.

A few states have extended their prudent-man investment statute to include as permissible investments shares in investment trusts.

11. *Investments subject to consent, approval, or directions of settlor or of third person.* The settlor can provide in his trust agreement that the trustee shall not make or change any investment without his own or without some third person's consent, approval, or direction. The testator can provide for the consent, approval, or direction of some third person. These conditions must be met by the trustee unless to do so, in the judgment of the trustee, would be a violation by the person whose consent, approval, or

direction is required in his duty to the beneficiaries of the trust. It is not for the trustee himself to be judge of the violation but, if he thinks there is a violation, it is his duty to bring it to the attention of the court.

One of the practical difficulties about trusts requiring some third person's consent, approval, or direction, is that, if he fails or refuses to act, the trustee is left with uninvested funds on his hands. He is aware that he is not complying with his duty to make and keep the property productive, and yet he hesitates to bring the dereliction of the third person to the attention of the court. This is particularly so when the settlor himself is the person whose consent, approval, or direction is required. If the trust should be for his sole benefit, then the trustee would not be liable for keeping funds uninvested. But if someone other than the settlor is beneficiary, which usually is the case, the trustee must consider his duty to the beneficiary and not be lulled into inactivity or a sense of safety by the inaction of the settlor.

INVESTMENT DUTIES

In general trust administration, a fiduciary probably considers his duties first and then his powers with respect to those duties. In the investment of trust funds, the probable order is to consider his powers first and then his duties. If a fiduciary has a duty to do or to refrain from doing a thing, he has or he can obtain the power to do or to refrain from doing that thing. Likewise, with regard to investments, if a trustee has a duty, he has or he can obtain the requisite power to perform it. The converse is true also: if he has the power, he is under a duty to exercise that power in the administration of his trust.

The duties of a trustee to invest should be treated under three heads—first, his duties regarding original investments; second, his duties regarding new investments; and third, his duties regarding both original and new investments.

Original Investments

When a trustee takes over a trust containing original investments and investigates, first, his investment powers and, then, his investment duties according to the terms of the trust, he may find one or more of the following situations regarding the original investments: (1) the original investments may have been proper for the trust and they still may be proper; (2) they may have been proper at the time they were received but they may have become improper since then; (3) they may have been nonlegal investments (in a legal-list state in which the trustee was restricted to the legal-list as to new investments) but the trust instrument may have authorized the trustee to retain original investments whether or not they were legal-list investments when received; (4) they may have been nonlegal investments in a legal-list trust but the instrument was silent about the retention of original investments; and (5) they may have been nonlegal investments when received under a trust instrument which authorized the receipt but was silent about the retention of original investments.

In ascertaining his duty regarding original investments the trustee is under a duty to determine, first, in which of the five categories the original investment belongs and, then, the extent of his power to deal with that situation. His ultimate duty is to exercise his investment powers regarding original investments in the way that will serve the best interests of the beneficiaries.

For his duty and power regarding the original investments, the trustee looks first to his instrument and then to the statute and, if he fails to find guidance in either of these sources, he may have to go to court for instructions.

1. *Provision in instrument regarding original investments.* The following is, in substance, a common provision in wills and trust agreements regarding the retention of original investments:

> To retain, without liability except for his own negligence for loss or depreciation resulting from such retention, original property, real or personal, at any time received by him, the trustee, from the settlor, for such time as to him shall seem best, although such property may not be of the character expressly approved by law or authorized by the terms of this trust instrument for other funds of this trust and although it represents a large percentage of the total property of the trust; to dispose of such original property by sale, exchange, or otherwise as and when he shall deem it advisable and to receive and administer the proceeds thereof as part of the trust estate; and, if unproductive property is retained, then upon the sale, exchange, or other disposition thereof, to make a reasonable apportionment (in the judgment of the trustee) of the proceeds between the income and the principal of the trust estate.

This provision covers several points of practical value in the administration of the trust. It relieves the trustee of liability for losses or depreciation resulting from the retention of otherwise unauthorized or nonlegal original investments; but it does not, and it should not, relieve the trustee of liability for losses or depreciation resulting from his own negligence. It permits the trustee, in retaining the original investments, to disregard the principle of diversification which otherwise would come into play. It permits the retention of unproductive property and, in order to be fair as between the income beneficiaries and principal beneficiaries of the trust, it permits apportionment of the proceeds of the sale of such property between income and principal.

2. *Statutes on retention of original investments.* Many states have adopted statutes regarding the retention of original investments by trustees. The substance of the usual statute is that the fiduciary may retain original investments, even though they would not qualify for investments under

the terms of that trust, so long as in the discretion of the trustee it is prudent to retain such investments. Differences in the wording of the statutes on the retention of originals seem in some states to put upon the trustee the burden of proof that the retention was prudent and in other states to put the burden upon the beneficiary to prove that the retention was imprudent. But, whatever the differences in wording, the effect of the statute is to permit a trustee to retain original investments in property when he could not make new investments.

A typical statute is that of New York:

No fiduciary holding funds for investment shall be liable for any loss incurred with respect to any investment not eligible by law for the investment of trust funds if such ineligible investment was received by such fiduciary pursuant to the terms of the will, deed, decree of court, or other instrument creating the fiduciary relationship or if such ineligible investment was eligible when received, or when the investment was made by the fiduciary; provided such fiduciary exercises due care and prudence in the disposition or retention of any such ineligible investment.[8]

The Model Prudent-Man Investment Statute contains the following reference to the retention of original investments:

And within the limitations of the foregoing standard (that of the man of prudence, discretion, and intelligence) a fiduciary may retain property properly acquired, without limitation as to time and without regard to its suitability for original purchase.

The point of this provision of the Model Statute is that, if the original investment should not be one which the prudent man himself would make, the trustee may, nevertheless, retain it without limitation as to time—that is, he need not dispose of it as soon as he reasonably can do so—provided it is such an investment as the prudent man, being the owner, would retain. It is, in effect, the application of the prudent-man rule to original investments the same as to new investments.

New Investments

After a trustee has taken over a trust for administration and invested the funds, he may come face to face with any one of six situations with regard to the investments he himself has made: (1) his new investments may be legal under a trust instrument that is silent about investments; (2) they may be legal under a trust instrument that expressly authorizes investment in nonlegal investments; (3) they may be nonlegal under a trust instrument that is silent about trust investments; (4) they may be nonlegal under a trust instrument the investment provisions of which are expressed in general terms only—as that the trustee shall use his own judgment or discretion in

[8] *Wills, Estates, and Trusts*, Sec. 15,301.

making or changing investments, or that the trustee shall invest in good income-producing, interest-bearing, or dividend-paying securities; (5) they may be nonlegal under a trust instrument that expressly authorizes the trustee to invest in nonlegal securities; and (6) they may be new investments under an instrument in which the settlor has given express directions which are impossible of fulfilment.

With regard to new investments, the trustee's first duty is to make the investments according to the terms of the trust; second, to keep the investments to compliance with terms of the trust; and, third, to select investments that will serve the best interests of the beneficiary.

Duties Applicable to Both Original and New Investments

A fiduciary, except as otherwise provided by the terms of the relationship, is under a duty to live up to the standard of the prudent man, whether he is dealing with original investments or new investments, and whether he is investing according to a legal list or under the prudent-man rule. The latter is a point that especially needs emphasizing.

It is well understood that, although a trustee is given full discretion as to investments, he nonetheless is under a duty to invest the funds as and only as a man of prudence, discretion, and intelligence would invest his own funds, not in regard to speculation, but in regard to the permanent disposition of his funds, considering the probable income as well as the probable safety of his capital.

What apparently is not so well understood by the public is that a trustee must live up to the standard of the prudent man although he is investing under a mandatory or a permissive legal list. Within the circumscription of the legal list, he must invest as a prudent man would invest within that list. Similarly, a permissive legal list does not permit a trustee to shut his eyes to the needs of his beneficiaries and invest in anything or everything that happens to be on the permissive list.

The basic difference in this respect is that under the prudent-man rule, the trustee has all available investments from which to make his selection; whereas, under a legal list, he has a prescribed list within which he must or may make his selection. But whether under the rule or the legal list, in making his selection he must live up to the standard of the prudent man under similar circumstances, unless the terms of the trust itself lower that standard.

1. *Limitations upon investment under prudent-man rule.* Stating that a trustee under the prudent-man rule has all available investments from which to make his selection does not mean that he can select *any* investment. The courts are in general agreement that there are at least ten types of investments in which a trustee, although operating under a prudent-man rule, should not invest trust funds because, by common consent, they are not the

type of investment a prudent man would make for regularity of income or safety of principal. They are as follows: (1) speculative investments, including those purchased on margin at a substantial discount because of a common doubt as to their eventual worth; (2) those lacking in seasoned performance as to safety or yield; (3) those in enterprises in which the trustee himself has a personal interset; (4) those in a business being carried on as a proprietorship or partnership; (5) those on a temporary basis for quick turnover or sale at a profit; (6) junior mortgages; (7) real property located outside the state in which the trust is being administered; (8) unproductive property; (9) personal loans without security; and (10) wasting property.

Retention of investment in a business being carried on as a proprietorship or partnership will be discussed in the next chapter.

2. *Diversification.* Ordinarily it is the duty of a trustee to diversify the investments, considering the original investments and the new investments as together constituting the trust estate, so as to distribute the risk of loss. This means diversification not only as among stocks, bonds, mortgages, and real property but also diversification of investments in any one security, in any one industry, in any one class of securities, or in any one locality.

Although diversification is important, it should not be made a fetish. A trustee should not feel that he must diversify simply in order to be able to say he has diversified. As indicated above, the provisions of instruments relating to the retention of original investments takes cognizance of the fact that such retention may upset the normal ratios in diversification. There may be circumstances in which a trustee, as a prudent man managing his own investments, would invest entirely in one or in a very few securities—in government bonds in wartime or for a short period, for example—or even for the time being would keep his funds uninvested.

No attempt is made here to suggest ratios between government bonds, industrial bonds, common stocks, preferred stocks, mortgages, and other types of investments. These ratios vary from year to year or even from month to month according to economic or political conditions. More than that, the ratios vary widely according to the investment policies of different trustees.

The main point of this section is to call attention to the trustee's duty, except under extraordinary circumstances or except under the express terms of the trust, to adopt a sound policy of diversification so as to distribute the risk of loss.

3. *Analysis.* Whether it is an original investment or a new investment, a trustee is under a duty to make periodic analyses of every investment in the account. The factors involved in the analysis would depend upon the type of the investment. If it were a mortgage, analysis might mean inspecting the premises to see what condition they are in, having the property reappraised, investigating the financial condition and the dependability of the mortgagor, and investigating the trend of the neighborhood in which

the property is located. Such an analysis is needed to find out whether the property is good security and the debtor, a good personal risk. If it is a stock or a bond, analysis means a statistical study of the corporation—its financial condition, its earnings record, its dividend-paying record. It means a study of the place of the security under analysis in the general financial structure of the corporation. It means a study of the whole industry in which the corporation is engaged, whether it has a future—as, for example, the aircraft industry—or has, at best, a doubtful future—as the buggy manufacturing industry in this motor-age as compared with the horse-and-buggy age.

Without such an analysis, informal though it be, the trustee cannot know whether to retain or to dispose of that particular investment. Further, analyses of individual investments must be made, not once only but often enough to enable the trustee to keep up with the changes in the security itself, in the company, in the industry.

4. *Review*. A trustee is under a duty not only to analyze the individual investments in the account but also to review the investments in the account as a whole. This means, as it were, laying out all the investments in the account on a table, studying them in their relation to one another and to the purposes of the trust. A stock, bond, or mortgage, considered by itself, may be a good investment. But, considered as one item in the group of investments constituting the account, it may be out of place. How often the investments in a trust account should be reviewed depends upon the circumstances. If the investments are likely to change in value with a considerable degree of frequency and unexpectedness on account of the nature of the business or on account of general conditions, then frequent reviews are needed. In a trust composed largely of mortgages or of government bonds or of other bonds that change little in value or in character from year to year, the need for review may be less frequent. A safe rule for a trustee to apply is to review at least once a year.

5. *Impartiality*. The trustee's duty to be impartial as regards beneficiaries of the same class—income beneficiaries, for example—and impartial also as regards beneficiaries of different classes—income beneficiaries and principal beneficiaries—has been discussed in the preceding chapter. The point is brought up again because it is in the investment of funds that a trustee encounters his strongest temptation to be partial. For example, *A* creates a trust under his will to pay income to his wife for life, then to pay over the principal to his children; he puts his trustee under the prudent-man rule; he fails to give his trustee any power to use principal for his wife. It is a net-income trust. On account of the drop in the yield of investments or the decreased purchasing power of the income, the income from the trust is not enough to meet the living expenses of the wife. Shall the trustee invest for income-yield even at the possible expense of the safety of the principal? The answer is *no*. Between two investments equally safe as to principal, the trustee naturally would and should select the one with the higher yield. But

for the trustee deliberately to invest for yield at the expense of safety of principal would be a violation not only of the prudent-man rule itself but also of two of the fundamental principles of trusteeship—namely, that of impartiality between or among beneficiaries and that of absolute loyalty to all the beneficiaries.

6. *Conflicts of interest.* In the investment of trust funds a trustee is under a duty not to permit the intrusion of any conflicts of interest between himself and his beneficiaries. This is the duty, as discussed in Chapter 14 that keeps a trustee from selling trust property to himself, from selling his own property to the trust, from using trust property for his own purposes, from making any side profits—such as bonuses, commissions, and the like— resulting from his administration of the trust.

7. *Undivided loyalty.* We come back now to a discussion, begun in Chapter 14, of a bank's retaining its own shares of stock in an account of which it is trustee, or investing trust funds in its own shares. This is not a case of actual conflict of interest but rather of a possible divided loyalty. A trustee owes his beneficiary, above all things else, undivided loyalty.

8. *Bank's own shares of stock.* The issue about the bank's own shares of stock in its estate and trust accounts arises more often in connection with retention of original investments than with the making of new investments. A substantial stockholder of a bank makes his will and names his bank executor and trustee. He and his family prize his bank stock highly, not only because he and they regard it as a good investment, but also for senti-mental reasons. Neither he nor they desire the bank shares sold. Yet his own bank, as the executor and trustee under his will, may find itself under a duty to sell the shares unless he himself has provided against such sale. Consider the following possible situations.

He is silent about his bank stock. If his trust must be invested within the legal list, his bank stock would have to be sold within a reasonable time because in a legal-list state it might not qualify as a legal investment.

He is silent as to his original investments, including his bank stock, but the statutes of his state authorize a trustee, unless otherwise provided by the terms of the trust, to retain original investments. The weight of authority is that the trustee would have to sell the bank stock within a reasonable time. The reasoning is that statutory authority to retain original investments would not include the retention of investments that might involve a divided loyalty.

He authorizes his trustee to retain original investments but says nothing about his bank stock. The weight of authority is that this would include his bank stock. The reasoning is that, when he authorized his trustee to retain his original investments, he had in mind his bank stock as well as his other investments and meant that his trustee should retain this stock as well as his other investments.

He authorizes his trustee to retain his original investments and specifies his bank stock. Here the case is clear, and the trustee could retain the bank stock according to the terms of the trust.

When banks are trustees, it is important that a stockholder naming his bank executor and trustee under his will state in his will what he wishes done with his bank stock. If he wishes it retained he should say so definitely. If he wishes it distributed in kind, he should say so. If he wishes to leave its retention, sale, or distribution to the discretion of the trustee, he should say so. In a word, if a stockholder of a bank names it his executor and trustee, he should specify what he wishes done with his bank shares. The following are illustrative (not model) provisions in the will of a bank stockholder about his bank stock:

Retention. In its discretion, to retain as long as it shall deem wise to do so, any shares of stock I shall own at the time of my death in the ———— Bank; and such retention shall not be deemed a violation of its duty of undivided loyalty or of its duty with respect to diversification of investments.

Acquisition as stock dividends or in exercise of rights. To receive and retain, so long as it deems wise to do so, shares of stock in the ———— Bank issued as stock dividends; to subscribe for, receive, and retain, so long at it deems wise to do so, the proportion to which my estate or any trust under my will may be entitled of any additional shares of stock hereafter lawfully authorized by the stockholders of the said ———— Bank; and to assent to any amendment of the charter, reorganization, merger, or consolidation of the said ———— Bank and to receive and retain so long as it deems wise to do so, shares of stock in any bank or trust company resulting from such reorganization, merger, or consolidation.

As to new investments. To acquire by purchase, exchange, or otherwise additional shares of stock in the ———— Bank or of any bank or trust company resulting from a reorganization, merger, or consolidation of the said ———— Bank.

Exercising powers. To exercise the same discretions, rights, powers, and authority with respect to my shares of stock in ———— Bank as is conferred upon it by this instrument with respect to other property in my estate.

9. *Investment requirements of particular trust.* Even though the same individual or the same bank may be trustee of numerous trusts, the investment requirements of each trust must be considered. Trusteeship is not a wholesale business. The *Restatement of the Law of Trusts* lists the following eight points that a trustee should consider in selecting the investments of each trust: (*a*) the length of the term of the investment—for example, the maturity date, if any, and the power to call or redeem, if any; (b) the probable duration of the trust; (*c*) the probable condition of the market with respect to the value of the particular investment at the termination of the trust, particularly if at the termination of the trust the investments must be converted into cash for distribution; (*d*) the probable condition of the market with respect to reinvestment at the time a particular investment

matures; (e) the aggregate value of the trust estate and the nature of the other investments; (f) the requirements of the beneficiary or beneficiaries, particularly with respect to the amount of income; (g) the other assets of the beneficiary or beneficiaries, including earning capacity; and (h) the effect of the investment on increasing or diminishing taxes.[9]

COLLECTIVE INVESTMENT

One of the distinctive features of trust business as carried on by trust institutions is that in most states it is permissible for them to provide for the collective investment of trust funds. This is accomplished by means of a common trust fund or a bank fiduciary fund. Only a bank or trust company is authorized to establish and operate a common trust fund or a fiduciary fund, and even then only for the use of its own fiduciary accounts.

Collective investment means the pooling of the investable funds of two or more—usually a large number of—trusts and guardianships, investing the pool as a single fund, and letting each trust or guardianship own the share of the whole fund represented by its fractional participation.

The need for the collective investment of funds arises from the difficulty in finding suitable investments for small trusts and guardianships and in providing suitable diversification. The smallness of the fund to be invested puts the beneficiaries of the trust or guardianship at a disadvantage. The beneficiaries who most need productive and sound investments have the greatest difficulty in obtaining them. The common trust fund has been developed to meet this situation.

Commingled Funds

About 1928, several of the trust institutions of the country—notably, the City Bank Farmers Trust Company of New York, (now, First National City Trust Company), the Brooklyn Trust Company of Brooklyn, New York, and the Equitable Trust Company (now Bank of Delaware) of Wilmington, Delaware—began to pioneer in the field of collective investment by establishing what later came to be known variously as *uniform, composite,* and *commingled funds.*

Common Trust Funds

Shortly after these early funds were established, the federal income tax authorities and, later, the courts held that the funds themselves were taxable entities. This meant double taxation of the group of beneficiaries who most needed all the income it might be possible for them to have—one, an income tax on the fund itself and the other, a tax on the income from the fund

[9] Scott on *Trusts,* Sec. 227. 12.

received by the participating account. So, in 1936, the Congress of the United States, by an amendment to the Revenue Act of that year, provided that a bank or trust company might establish a common trust fund that would not be subject to income taxes itself, provided (*a*) the fund was operated by a bank or trust company within the meaning of the federal Revenue Act; (*b*) the establishment of such a fund was permissible under the laws of the state in which the bank was located; and (*c*) the fund was operated in accordance with regulations promulgated by the Board of Governors of the Federal Reserve System. This meant, first, the adoption of enabling legislation—either statutory or judicial—in the several states to permit banks in those states to establish and operate common trust funds. Next, it meant the promulgation by the Board of Governors of the Federal Reserve System of regulations governing common trust funds.

The Board acted promptly. As of December 31, 1937, it promulgated regulations. These are Section 17 of Regulation F. They provide for the establishment of three kinds of common trust funds. The first is a fund made up of funds not exceeding $1,200 from any one account. This fund is not subject to such strict regulations as the two other funds. The second, known as the *common trust fund for general investment*, is made up of contributions of not over $100,000 (originally, it was $25,000) from any one account; and this fund is subject to detailed regulations. The third fund is known as the *mortgage investment fund* and is composed of mortgages; and this, too, is subject to detailed and strict regulations.

Since 1937, one state after another has adopted enabling acts for the establishment and operation of common trust funds until most states have such acts. The State of Missouri permits the establishment of common trust funds by a judicial decision rather than by a statute.

Experience has demonstrated that common trust funds not only make it possible for a trust institution to provide sound and productive investment service for very small trusts and guardianships but also materially to reduce the trustee's or guardian's expense in administering these small accounts. Many of the trust institutions which have common trust funds now are advertising for and soliciting small trusts provided they are authorized to invest them through their common trust fund.

Bank Fiduciary Fund

The authorization and establishment of common trust funds did not go all the way in solving the investment problems of small guardianships and trusts. There were many banks and trust companies whose volume of trust business did not seem to them enough to justify their establishing and operating an individual common trust fund.

In 1954, the State of New York came to the aid of its smaller trust institutions by authorizing the establishment of the Bank Fiduciary Fund, whereunder they might purchase for their guardianship and trust accounts participations in this fund, called *shares*. These shares may be purchased and held only by banks serving in a fiduciary capacity as trustee, executor, guardian, or committee; the investments in this fund are restricted to legal investments in New York State, which means that 35 per cent of them may be in common stocks; and the fund is examined and regulated by the State Banking Department.

The Bank Fiduciary Fund seems to have met a real need of smaller trust institutions and the beneficiaries of their trusts and wards of their guardianships. Other states are considering like programs, and, no doubt, sooner or later will establish similar funds.

In this chapter no attempt has been made to discuss trust investment policies, much less trust investments themselves. Instead, the discussion has been confined to the principles, powers, and duties of fiduciaries (particularly, guardians and trustees) regarding general investments.

COLLATERAL READING

Note: For complete citations, see Bibliography, pp. 417–428.

General

BOGERT's *Handbook*, Secs. 105–112, 345–373.
BOGERT on *Trusts and Trustees*, Secs. 611–708, 158–455.
LORING's *Trustee's Handbook*, Shattuck rev., Ch. VIII, 141–173.
SCOTT on *Trusts*, Secs. 227–231, 1197–1256.
STEPHENSON, *Drafting Wills and Trust Agreements*, Vol. I, Ch. 6.
Wills, Estates and Trusts, Secs. 15,001–15,101, 15,301–15,304.

Common Trust Funds

American Bankers Association, New York, Trust Division, *Common Funds —A Handbook on Their Purposes, Establishment, and Operation.*

Bank Fiduciary Funds

BUEK, "New York's Bank Fiduciary Fund."
———, "Recent Developments in New York Bank Fiduciary Fund."
TIERNEY, "New York's Bank Fiduciary Fund—Advantages, Objections, and Pitfalls."
TREMAN, "A Bank Fiduciary Fund for Multiple Bank Participations."

18

Investment in Businesses

𝕿o INTRODUCE this chapter, the term *investment in businesses* requires some explanation.

Businesses and Businessmen

The term *business*, frequently employed in contradistinction to *profession*, is a human enterprise that is conducted for profit at the risk of loss. It is easy to classify a store or a factory as a business and a merchant or a manufacturer as a businessman. If the store or factory is owned and operated by one person, by two or more partners, or by a small number of stockholders in a closely held corporation, it is easy to classify the proprietor and each of the partners or stockholders as being engaged in a business.

Difficulty in classification arises when one comes to consider the status of any one of the thousands of stockholders of a big corporation which itself is engaged in a mercantile or manufacturing business. Each shareholder is a part-owner of the business, but does that alone make him a businessman engaged in that business? It would be utterly unrealistic to classify the owner of a few shares of stock of General Motors Corporation, for example, as being a businessman engaged in the business or businesses of that corporation.

It is a great deal more realistic to say that a person is engaged in business only when he, himself, has some direct responsibility for the conduct of that business. It is in this restricted sense that the term *investment in businesses* is employed in this chapter.

Traditional Attitude toward Trustees' Investment in Business

The traditional attitude, in both law and practice, is one of hostility toward a trustee's investment in a business. In the *Restatement of the Law of Trusts*, "employment of trust property in the carrying on of trade or

business" is listed as one of the improper forms of investment for a trustee.[1]
Professor Scott elaborates this principle by saying:

> A trustee cannot properly use trust property in the carrying on of a trade
> or business, even though it is not an untried enterprise. Not only is it improper
> for him to invest trust funds in the carrying on of such a trade or business, but
> where a testator leaves his estate in trust and the estate includes his interest in a
> business, whether conducted by him alone or by a firm of which he is a mem-
> ber, it is the duty of the trustee to withdraw the testator's property from the
> business, unless it is otherwise provided by the terms of the trust.[2]

Furthermore, even though the owner of a few shares of stock out of a
large number of shares of a corporation in the management of which he has
no part is not himself engaged in the business of that corporation, nonetheless the traditional attitude of the courts is one of hostility toward a
trustee's investment in shares of stock. In 1869, in the now famous case of
King v. *Talbot* [3] the Court of Appeals of New York State held that to invest
in shares of stock was to employ the trust fund as capital in trade and that it
was improper for a trustee to use the trust fund in trade. In the same case
the court said that "the just and true rule is that the trustee is bound to
employ such diligence and such prudence in the care and management as, in
general, prudent men of discretion and intelligence in such matters employ
in their own like affairs." Thus far, this sounded very much like the prudent-
man rule which had been the law in Massachusetts since 1830; but the New
York court went on to say that its statement of the rule did not permit a
trustee to employ trust funds in trade or business by the purchase of shares
of stock.

Despite the fact that at the present time a large percentage of trust
funds is invested in shares of stock, either under an applicable prudent-man
rule or under the terms of the trust, the traditional attitude persists and prevails that a trustee must not invest trust funds in a business unless it is so
provided by the terms of the trust. This principle of law places upon a
trustee engaged in carrying on a business the burden of proving that in
doing so he is acting under authority of statute, order of court, or terms of
trust. He cannot assume that he has some inherent or implied power to
carry on the testator's or settlor's business.

REASONS FOR INVESTMENT IN BUSINESSES

Upon inquiry it would be found that, almost without exception, a
trustee or a guardian carrying on a business would be doing so as an
original and not as a new investment.

[1] Sec. 227 (f).
[2] Scott on *Trusts*, Sec. 227.6.
[3] 40 N. Y. 76.

New Investment

It is almost inconceivable that a trustee, of his own motion, would start a business. He would hesitate even though the will or trust agreement *authorized* him to do so. He even might hesitate to accept a trust in which he was *directed* to start and carry on a business. Unless the settlor or testator himself already had laid the basis of the business, he need not expect his trustee both to lay the basis and then to develop the business from the start.

The same general statement would apply to a guardian. For a minor he scarcely could obtain an order of court to start a business and for an incompetent person he could not obtain such an order unless the basis already had been laid by someone else.

Wherein, then, is investment in businesses a worthwhile topic for discussion in this text? Because, sooner or later, every executor or administrator will find himself with a business on his hands to handle and every trustee or guardian one on his hands to administer.

Original Investment

The estate of every businessman contains a business or interests in one or more businesses. If the executor or administrator accepts the appointment, he accepts it with the business attached. He cannot say, "I accept all but the business; someone else will have to take over the business." He must accept all or none of the assets of the estate that are under the jurisdiction of the court that makes the appointment.

However, in the hands of an executor or administrator, a business should be regarded as an asset to be disposed of rather than as an investment to be retained. The business will remain in his hands and under his management only during the "executor's year," by the end of which it must have liquidated, sold, turned over to the distributees, or turned over to a trustee or guardian. This chapter deals with business as an investment, not merely as an asset. Thus, business as an investment may become a long-range reponsibility.

A guardian is appointed by the court to take over, take care of, and manage the business inherited by his ward. His ward may be an infant. The guardianship may run for almost twenty years. Conceivably, there may be sound reason for continuing the business as an investment until the ward reaches his majority.

Or a guardian may be appointed to take over, take care of, and run the business of a man who has been declared mentally incompetent. If the incompetency is likely to be temporary, the function of the guardian may be to carry on the business only during his ward's incompetency and then turn it back to him. If the prospect is that the ward will be incompetent the rest of his life, the court might give the guardian an extended period within which to liquidate or sell the business and possibly might authorize the guardian to carry it on until the incompetent person's son was old enough to take it over.

However, it is in trusts—and of these, trusts under will—that one finds most investments in businesses. Only rarely and only under special circumstances would a businessman put his business in trust during his lifetime. But with increasing frequency one finds businessmen who for one reason or another want their business retained after their death and carried on for years as an investment.

The businessman's estate may consist largely of his business and his life insurance. His business may have been profitable. He may have a sentimental attachment to it. He may want it carried on, possibly in the family name, as a sort of memorial to his family. It is businesses carried on for sentimental reasons that give trustees the most trouble because sentiment and economics frequently conflict with each other.

Or the businessman may have a son, who is a minor or still in school, for whom he wishes the business retained and the son already may have manifested a desire and intention to step into his father's shoes. Naturally, the father wants his business retained as an investment for his son.

Then again, the businessman may have loyal and faithful younger associates in his business to whom he desires that it be turned over. But at the time and even at his death they are not able to finance the purchase of the business. So, under his will he puts his business in trust, arranges for his trustee to incorporate it, and, by a buy-and-sell agreement, arranges for these younger associates of his gradually to purchase the stock of the corporation and, eventually, to own the business.

Why businessmen so often do desire that their business be retained, kept intact, and carried on as a going concern is not the point at issue at the moment; the fact is, they do. Why they do is a matter of speculation. In recent years, many small businesses have been, comparatively, more profitable than fixed-income securities and even some common stocks. As more and more businessmen plan their estates and, under their plan, leave their estates in trust, they are, increasingly, inclined to include their business, along with their other assets, in trust. Whatever the reason, the fact is that investment in businesses is increasingly the practice of businessmen and, correspondingly, an increasing problem and responsibility of trustees.

KINDS OF BUSINESSES IN TRUST

Just as it is true that, given time, every kind of property that people can own will find its way into a trust, so every kind of business will, sooner or later, come up for consideration as a trust investment. It would be futile to attempt to classify businesses and then discuss each one separately as an investment. Most of what needs to be said about any business would be equally applicable to every business. It may be helpful to discuss businesses under three heads: business in general; farming; and mineral, oil, and gas activities.

Business in General

Most businesses in trust as an investment are a type of manufacturing goods or of selling goods. Most of the discussion that follows, therefore, relates to businesses in general and most of what is said applies to every kind of business.

Farming

Although farming varies widely from state to state and even from section to section in the same state, from soil to soil, from crop to crop, and from climate to climate, there are certain characteristics of farming everywhere and of every kind that distinguish it from other businesses and are more or less common to all kinds of farming. Much of the discussion that follows applies to these common characteristics of farming.

Mineral, Oil, and Gas Activities

Mineral-, oil-, and gas-producing activities are confined to a comparatively few sections of our country. Therefore, instead of generalizing about these special fields, it has been decided to eliminate discussion of the subject in this chapter and, in place thereof, to include in the collateral reading at the end of this chapter citations to material composed by men who have had experience with mineral-, oil-, and gas-producing property. In 1959, the Trust Division of the American Bankers Association published a handbook, *Handling Businesses in Trust*, a substantial portion of which is devoted to discussion, with appropriate forms, of handling oil, gas, and mineral property in trust. From this handbook, the student will be able to obtain information he requires about this kind of property.

ESTATE PLANNING RELATED TO INVESTMENT IN BUSINESSES

If a business is to be held in trust and carried on successfully beyond the period required for orderly liquidation, sale, or delivery to ultimate owners, a great deal of estate planning therefor is essential. In the absence of such planning recorded in the will, no other course will be open to the executor or administrator than to liquidate, sell, or deliver the business to its ultimate owners within a reasonable time after the death of the business-man-owner.

In planning the estate as far as it relates to the business the questions to be answered are: Should the business be retained in trust? If so, why?

Reasons for Retaining

Does the owner want it retained only or mainly because of his sentimental attachment to it? Because under his control and management it has been outstandingly successful? Because he wants to keep it in the family and in course of time have it turned over to his son or sons? Because he wants to make it possible for his associates or employees to take it over as soon as they can finance it? Because he thinks that his business, properly handled, will be a valuable asset in his trust estate? Unless his prospective trustee is convinced that the businessman's reason for wanting his business retained and carried on after his death is sound and his prospective plan practicable and workable, he should advise against retention and, if driven to it, decline to accept the appointment even though it meant losing the trusteeship of the general estate.

Management of Business

If the businessman desires that his business be retained and carried on, and if the trustee is willing to accept the business in trust, in planning his estate, the businessman himself should, so far as he can, provide for the succession. He may incorporate his business. He may indicate how he thinks his business should be carried on after his death. He may suggest who he thinks would be the best person to carry it on and in what way. He should avoid leaving directions, as distinct from suggestions or recommendations, lest they cripple the trustee in the administration of the trust. He may make his suggestions and recommendations in a memorandum accompanying his will rather than in the will itself. In one way or another the businessman should give his trustee the benefit of his best judgment as to the carrying on of his business after his death.

If the business should be retained and carried on, and if the businessman himself has not provided for the succession, who should manage it? While the trustee would give the business general supervision, he would not be expected to be an active, everyday manager of the business. Unless there is a real likelihood that a manager of the business already is in its employment or could be found, there should be no commitment by a prospective trustee to take over and carry on the business.

Capitalization of Business

Before a businessman decides to leave his business in trust, and before anyone agrees to accept it in trust, there should be an understanding between them as to how the business is to be financed. Does the business itself have ample operating capital? Or does it have ample bank credit for operating purposes? If not, should the trustee employ for financing only the property in the business even though it meant partial liquidation? Or should the trustee be authorized to go into the general assets or credit of the estate for operating capital for the business? These are vital questions to be faced, considered, and answered before a decision as to investment in the business is reached.

Incorporation of Business

If it already is an incorporated business, the trustee, upon taking over the business, would become a stockholder and the liability of the general estate for the obligations of the business would be limited to its investment in the business as represented by its stock ownership. But if the business were a proprietorship or a partnership, all of the assets of the estate, business and nonbusiness alike, might be liable for the obligations of the business. In the light of this possibility, the prospective trustee should insist upon having power to incorporate the business so as to limit its obligations to the assets of the business itself.

Closing the Business

As with the owner during his lifetime, so with the trustee after the owner's death, plans with regard to the business may go awry. A new process or product may render a business in trust obsolete and unprofitable. The son for whom the business is being held in trust, pending the time when it would be turned over to him, may die, become incapacitated, or decide that, after all, he does not want to go into the business for his lifework. Even though there be every reasonable prospect that the business will prosper and that the purpose of the trust will be served, the trustee, nonetheless, should have the power to close the business by liquidation, sale, or otherwise, should that, in course of time and under the circumstances, seem to be the advisable thing to do.

Powers of Trustee

If a trustee is to carry on the business successfully for a period beyond that necessary for orderly liquidation, sale, or delivery to the ultimate outright owner, he must, in justice to himself, have ample powers of administration. In many cases these powers should be more expansive than those granted by statute. It is not enough for the businessman simply to authorize his executor, and then his trustee, "to retain and carry on any business in which I shall be engaged or financially interested at the time of my death for such time and in such way as to him shall seem to be for the best interests of my estate." Experience has taught trustees charged with the duty of carrying on a business that they are likely to need powers spelled out with a great deal more particularity than the general power described in the foregoing statement.

Furthermore, a trustee in carrying on a business is likely to need powers under the will or trust agreement, even in addition to ample powers under the statutes of his state, because he may be called upon to administer property located in a state or states other than the one in which he is appointed.

Limit upon Liability

Since, according to the definition we have adopted, a business is an enterprise carried on for profit but at the risk of loss, there always has been and always will be risk of loss in carrying on a business whether by owner or by trustee. Who is to stand the loss—the trustee or the beneficiaries of the trust?

If the loss is attributable to the trustee's negligence or wrongdoing, he should stand the loss. There is no place for an exculpatory or immunity clause—that is, a provision relieving the trustee from liability for his own negligence—in a will providing for carrying on the testator's business.

POWERS OF TRUSTEE REGARDING BUSINESS

As stated above, if the trustee is to carry on the business successfully, he must have ample powers, either under the statute or the trust instrument, to do so. The next question, then, is: What are these powers?

The following is a composite list of powers related to businesses in trust composed of the author's own list [4] and that in the *Handbook on Handling Businesses in Trust* of the Trust Division of the American Bankers Association.[5] Some of the powers in this list already have been commented upon, and the comments need not be repeated; others of these powers may need brief explanatory comment.

Introductory statement. With respect to any business which I may own, or in which I may be financially interested, at the time of my death, I grant my executor and trustee, in whichever capacity he may be serving as to a particular transaction, the following powers which I authorize him to exercise in his absolute, uncontrolled discretion:

Since the business, if carried on at all, must be carried on throughout the executorship and on into the trusteeship, it is advisable to give the executor and the trustee corresponding powers regarding the business. Otherwise, someone may raise a question about the power of the executor to carry on, as distinct from sell or liquidate, the business. Besides, it may

[4] *Drafting Wills and Trust Agreements*, Vol. I, Sec. 7.31, pp. 135–136.
[5] Pp. 87, 88.

not be easy always to tell in which capacity the executor-trustee is acting.

1. *Retain and continue.* To continue any business which I may own, or in which I may be financially interested, at the time of my death, whether as sole proprietor, partner, or stockholder, for such time as he may deem to be for the best interest of my estate;

2. *Delegate duties.* To delegate such duties, with the requisite powers, to any employee, manager, or partner as he may deem proper, without liability for such delegation except for his own negligence;

It is for the good of the business even more than for the relief of the trustee that he not only have many and varied duties regarding the carrying on of the business but that he actually delegate some of them to other persons. The trustee himself is not likely to be a specialist in any phase of the business, and every business requires specialists of one sort or another.

While this provision is for the relief of the trustee in certain respects, it does not relieve him from liability for losses to the business or to the estate traceable to his own negligence. The trustee might be negligent in the selection and then in the supervision of his agent, in which case he should be liable for losses traceable to such negligence.

3. *Raise capital.* To employ in the conduct of any such business not only my capital investment therein at the time of my death but also such additional capital out of my general estate as he may deem proper;

The businessman may not want to give his trustee power to employ the assets of his general estate for additional capital for the business. If the business is incorporated, he probably would want the business to finance itself. This matter should be discussed carefully with the businessman, with all the pros and cons presented and considered, and his definite decision should be recorded in the instrument.

4. *Borrow money.* To borrow money for any such business, either alone or along with other persons financially interested in the business, and to secure such loan or loans by a pledge or mortgage not only of my property or interest in the business but also of any part of my property outside the business as my executor or trustee may deem proper;

If the executor-trustee is a bank, it might be given power to borrow from its own banking department at the prevailing interest rates and with the normal margin of security.

As in the preceding section, on raising capital, so here, the businessman may, upon sound advice and judgment, prefer not to empower the executor-trustee to encumber and, thereby, jeopardize the general estate by borrowing against it for the sake of the business. Yet, if he has full confidence in his executor-trustee, he may be willing to take this calculated risk. Anyhow, it is a matter that should be explained to him, discussed with him, and resolved, and the decision should be recorded in the instrument.

5. *Incorporate business.* To organize, either by himself or jointly with others, a corporation to carry on the business; to contribute all or any part

of my business as capital to such corporation; to accept stock in the corporation in lieu thereof; and, if he deems it advisable, to provide for different classes of stock;

If at the time the testator makes his will or at the time of his death, the business is a proprietorship or partnership, the above is a power that very well may be exercised by the executor-trustee. After incorporation, the trustee's interest will be represented by shares of stock, and, if advisable, there may be both preferred and common stock and, in fact, any other kind or class of stock that is common in business corporations.

6. *Deposit with voting trustees.* To deposit securities with voting trustees;

After the businessman's death, a situation very well may arise in which it would be advisable, in the judgment of the executor-trustee as in that of any other prudent businessman, to create a voting trust and have all of the shareholders, including the executor-trustee, deposit their shares with voting trustees. This provision simply empowers the executor-trustee to do what any other prudent businessman under similar circumstances would do.

7. *Sell business.* To sell any business, any interest in any business, or any stock or other securities representing my interest in any business as and when and upon such terms as shall seem to him to be for the best interest of my estate;

8. *Liquidate business.* To liquidate, either by himself or jointly with others, any business or any interest in any business at such times and upon such terms as shall seem to be for the best interests of my estate;

These two powers—the power to sell and the power to liquidate—should be incorporated in practically every will providing for carrying on a business as an investment. Unless the businessman is willing to give his trustee these powers, he should not leave his business in trust but, instead, himself should provide for it to be turned over, free of any trust, to the ultimate owner or owners whom he wants to have it.

It may be hard for a successful businessman to realize that, after his death, his cherished business, which has been the joy of his life and the main source of his estate, should be sold or liquidated for the good not only of his general estate but also, and often more importantly, for the good of the persons for whom he would provide.

Should it come to closing the business, sale as a going concern rather than liquidation would, ordinarily, be the better course for the trustee to take.

9. *Change nature of business.* To enlarge, diminish, or change the scope or nature of the activities of the business;

If the business is to be continued for an extended period of time, it very well may be that in course of time it will be advisable for the trustee to enlarge, diminish, or change the scope or nature of the activities of the business. The original business—wagonmaking, for instance—may have lost out.

Another business—truck and trailer manufacturing, for example—may have come into brisk demand. The trustee already has the plant, much of the equipment, and well-trained personnel to change over from wagonmaking to truck and trailer manufacturing, and, thereby, convert a dead or dying business into an alive, active, and profitable business.

10. *Financial statements.* To accept as correct financial or other statements of the corporation from time to time as to its condition and operation unless he has actual notice of the inaccuracy or incompleteness of any such statement or has been negligent regarding obtaining or examining any such statement;

Here again, the rule of the prudent businessman should apply. If he would accept such statements as being, on their face, accurate and if he has no reason to suspect otherwise, the executor-trustee should have the same privilege. But, if the latter has had his suspicions aroused in any measure or any way, he should not have any exculpatory or immunity provision to fall back and rely upon.

11. *Seek orders of court.* In all appropriate cases, in the exercise of the trustee's own judgment, to seek orders of court for guidance and instruction in carrying on, liquidating, or selling the business;

The trustee would have the inherent power to go to court for its guidance and instruction on all appropriate issues related to the carrying on, liquidation, or sale of the business. But the trustee might feel fortified in having this power expressed in the instrument, showing that both the businessman and his draftsman had this possibility in mind.

12. *General provision.* Generally, to exercise with respect to the continuance, management, sale, or liquidation of any business or business interest I own at the time of my death all the powers which I myself could have exercised during my lifetime. I intend hereby to grant to my executor and trustee every power which can be delegated; therefore, the naming of any power and failure to name any other shall not be construed to be the exclusion of any such other unnamed power which my executor or trustee may desire to exercise; as I intend hereby to give my executor and trustee every conceivable power to do every conceivable act that in his judgment will assist him in carrying out to the fullest extent his duties as set forth in this instrument. I specifically absolve and exonerate my executor and trustee from any individual liability, except for his own negligence and wrongdoing, for any loss which may result to my estate or to others in connection with the exercise of the power and authority that I have hereby given my executor and trustee.

This omnibus grant of power, the substance of which is taken from a will, no doubt was designed by the draftsman to inspire in the executor and trustee activity and courage with respect to the business. But it does not—it could not—absolve the executor or trustee of his fiduciary obligations. It relieves him of liability for errors of judgment but not for losses resulting from his own negligence or wrongdoing.

SELECTION OF TRUSTEE

Not as an afterthought but as an original and integral part of the planning for the continuance of his business and in many cases determinative of his ultimate decision as to having his business retained and carried on is his selection of the trustee or trustees who would have responsibility for carrying it on. These are questions that he must face and, with the help of his advisers, answer: Shall I name an individual or a bank sole trustee? Shall I name an individual and my bank cotrustees? Shall I name separate trustees—my bank as trustee of my general estate and an individual trustee of my business?

Individual Trustee

If the businessman decides to name an individual trustee of his general estate, he may be predisposed to name the same individual trustee of his business. If he decides to name his bank, he may be disposed to name it trustee of his entire estate, including his business. There would be no point here in discussing the comparative merits of the individual and of the corporate trustee, except to say that, if the business is to be carried on for an extended period of time, the corporate trustee offers the advantages of continuity of existence and capacity.

Cotrustees

Businessmen sometimes are disposed to name their bank and a member of the family or a business associate cotrustees, taking for granted that the bank will administer the general assets and the individual, the business. The disadvantage of this arrangement is that, unless the respective duties of the bank and of the individual are separated and stated in the instrument, the bank and the individual each will be jointly liable for the administration of the entire estate. As a matter of self-protection, neither the bank nor the individual can afford to leave the entire administration of any portion of the estate to the other.

Separate Trustees

As was brought out in some detail in Chapter 13, the British have a plan regarding businesses that deserves further study and more widespread adoption in the United States. Instead of having cotrustees and expecting one of them, usually the trust corporation, to administer the general assets and the other, an individual, to administer the business assets, the businessman names his trust corporation his general trustee, the individual of his choice his business trustee, and provides for each of them to administer the portion of the estate assigned to one or the other. Then, according to the arrangement, the individual as business trustee accounts to the trust corporation as general trustee and the latter, in turn, accounts to the beneficiaries and, in appropriate cases, to the court. This casts upon the individual, who may be the son or associate of the businessman, responsibility for carrying on the business in which he, in case of the son, has a personal interest or in which he, in case of the associate, has both a personal and a financial interest. Then associated with the individual trustee is the corporate trustee which, although not a specialist in the business, is a specialist in trust administration.

FARMS IN TRUST

Not all farming is a *business* in the sense in which the term is employed in this text—that is, an enterprise carried on for profit and at the risk of loss. All farming is carried on at the risk of loss, to be sure, but it may not be carried on primarily for profit. The family-sized farm, resided on and operated by the owner and his family, scarcely would be classified as a business. It is primarily the home of the farmer and his family and is operated primarily as their home and means of livelihood. It is only when the farming operation gets beyond the family, when it is operated, partly if not entirely, as a profit-making, loss-risking enterprise that it properly can be classified as a business.

In the light of the recent phenomenal increase in the acreage of the profitable farming unit, due to mechanization and capital requirements, the family-sized farm is diminishing and the farm operated as a business is increasing. That farming as a business is on the increase is revealed by the fact that demand for farm management has reached the point where many trust institutions have organized farm-management divisions of their trust department to operate farms in estates and trusts.

When a farmer-businessman desires that his farm or farms be retained in trust and operated by a trustee, he should consider, reach, and record in his will his decision on points applicable to all businesses which have already been discussed. But, in addition to these points, he should cover many other points that are especially or exclusively applicable to farming.

Powers of Trustee

The following is a composite list of powers related especially or exclusively to farming:

The trustee is authorized to:

1. *Continue and carry on.* To continue and carry on any farming operation in which I shall be financially interested at the time of my death and to operate alone or as partner or stockholder any other farm or farms which may be acquired by the trust or trusts and, in doing so, by way of illustration and not limitation of its powers;

This gives the trustee power, not only to carry on the farming operations of the deceased farmer but also to acquire and carry on other, additional farming operations. By lease or even by purchase it may be necessary for the trustee to acquire additional acreage in order to enlarge the farming operation as a whole to the point where mechanization will be practicable and profitable.

2. *Operate.* To operate the farm or farms with hired labor, tenants, or sharecroppers;

The trustee should be free to employ the method of operation that is likely to be the most profitable and that is in common usage in the community. In the case of a large acreage or of several farms, he may have to operate some with hired labor, others with tenants, and still others with sharecroppers.

3. *Lease and rent.* To lease or rent the farm or farms for cash or for a share of the crop or crops;

In some cases it may be desirable to enter a long-term lease with a substantial farmer; in others, to rent the land from year to year; in some, to rent for cash; and in others, for a share of the crop or crops. The trustee should not be strait-jacketed as to his method of operation.

4. *Apportion receipts and expenses.* To determine whether cash received shall be allocated to income or to principal or apportioned between them, and, if apportioned, in what proportions; and to determine whether cash paid out shall be charged to income or to principal or apportioned, and, if apportioned, in what proportions;

As any farmer knows, it sometimes is impossible to tell whether a given receipt should be credited all to income or all to principal or apportioned between them and whether a given expense should be allocated all to one or the other or apportioned. The trustee simply must be given leeway in handling these items.

5. *Machinery and equipment.* To purchase or otherwise acquire farm machinery and equipment;

This may be the largest expense item in the operation; yet the trustee must have this power if he is to operate successfully.

6. *Construct, repair, improve.* To construct, repair, and improve buildings of all kinds needed, in his judgment, for the operation of the farm or farms;

Unless the trustee has this power, he cannot carry on successfully for an extended period of time

7. *Borrow money*. To make or obtain loans or advances at the prevailing rates of interest for farm purposes, such as for production, harvesting, or marketing, or for the construction, repair, or improvement of farm buildings, or for the purchase of farm machinery or equipment or livestock;

Elsewhere in the will the trustee's power to borrow may be set forth. But it may be reassuring to the trustee of the farm or farms to be given express power to borrow for the stated farm purposes.

8. *Soil conservation*. To employ approved soil conservation practices in order to conserve, improve, and maintain the productivity and fertility of the soil;

The trustee, the same as any other good farmer or farm manager, should have the unquestioned power, as well as the duty, to employ approved soil-conservation practices.

9. *Natural resources*. To protect, manage, and improve the timber and forest on the farm or farms and sell the timber and forest products as and when, in his judgment, it will be for the best interest of my estate;

In a mineral-, oil-, or gas-producing area, there would, naturally, be some specific reference to the handling of these special kinds of natural resources.

10. *Drainage*. To ditch and drain damp or wet lands when and where needed and to install irrigation systems;

The trustee, the same as any other good farmer, must ditch, drain, and irrigate land to make and keep it productive.

11. *Livestock*. To engage in livestock raising or in dairying, if he shall deem it advisable, and to construct such fences, buildings, and plant and cultivate such pastures and crops as shall be deemed necessary or advisable in carrying on such a livestock or dairying program;

The will from which the foregoing power was taken was designed for farmers who are switching over from row-crops to stock raising and dairying; and the lawyer who drafted this provision intended that there never should be any question of the trustee's power to make the switch.

12. *Farm practices*. In general, to employ the method or methods of carrying on the farming operations and to engage in the farm practices that are, in his judgment, in common use by other progressive landowners and farmers in the community or communities in which the farm or farms are located;

13. *Farm management service*. To employ overseers, farm managers, and farm-management services for the operation or management or supervision of the farm or farms.

If it should be a large farming operation or if there should be several farms or ranches widely scattered over a county or state or even in another state, the best interest of the operation may require the employment of overseers or managers or farm-management services. In the agricultural areas of the country such services are developing and serve a good purpose in retaining and carrying on farms.

Just as the businessman may have property in more than one state, so the farmer may have farmlands in different sections or even in different states with varying farm methods and practices. The trustee should have power to do whatever good farmers in those areas do with respect to their own farming operations.

Armed with these powers, a trustee scarcely could say that he did not succeed as trustee of a farm or farms because he did not have ample powers.

The conclusion of the whole matter of investment in business, whatever the kind of business, seems to be that, if the business is to be carried on, the executor and then the trustee should have ample power to do whatever a prudent businessman would do with respect to that business.

COLLATERAL READING

Note: For complete citations, see Bibliography, pp. 417–428.
As was done in connection with Chapter 9 on employees trusts, it has seemed advisable to give the student a list of citations from which he can make a choice of collateral reading on phases of businesses, farming, and oil, gas, or mining property in which he may be particularly interested.

Businesses in General

American Bankers Association, New York, Trust Division, *Handbook on Handling Businesses in Trust.*

BURFORD, "Basis of Business Assets—Effect of Death on Partnership Interest and Close Corporation Stock."

CHAPMAN, R. P., "Widening Horizons for Management of Property in Trust."

———, "Handling Businesses in Trust."

COWDERY, "Basis of Compensation for Handling Businesses in Trust."

———, "When a Trustee Has a Business to Handle."

———, "Making the Most of a Business Interest."

———, "Business Interests in Trust."

EGGER, "Liquidation and Valuation of Business Interests in Estates."

ELLISON, "Continuous Review Service for Business Interests."

McKENNEY, "Some Estate Planning Considerations Involving Business Interests."

MADURO, "Stock Perpetuation—An Approach to Continuing Closely Held Business Interests."

PFLEIDERER, "Value of Estate Planning when Handling Businesses in Trust."

STRATFORD, "Handling Businesses in Trust."

WILLCOX, "Valuation of Close Held Business Interest."

WOLF, "Twenty Pointers on Liquidation of Business Interests."

"Management and Retention of Small Business," a committees report.

Farms

ANDREWS, "Farm Management Service."
BORLAND, "How a City Bank Handles Farms in Trust."
BURY, "Ranch Management as a Trust Service in the Southwest."
McLEAN and DRAPER, "Handling Farms in Trust in the Southeast."
ROBINSON, "Handling Farms in Trust in the Midwest."
SAVIDGE, "Farm and Ranch Operations in Trust."
TROWBRIDGE, "Farm Property Problems in the Pacific Northwest."
"Farm Management by Banks." A manual.

Oil, Gas, and Mineral Property

COOK, "Disposition of Oil and Gas Interests."
EARLY and KIRKPATRICK, "Oil and Gas Interests—Avoiding Estate Problems by Adequate Drafting."
REED, "Supervision of Oil and Gas Interests by Corporate Trustees."

19

Administration of Employees, Charitable, and Corporate Trusts

𝕿 HE SAME FIDUCIARY principles and many of the administrative activities as already discussed apply alike to personal trusts and to employees, charitable, and corporate trusts. But there are certain administrative aspects which are restricted to these three types of trusts as a group, some of which, in turn, are distinctive to each of the three types in the group. The purpose of this chapter is to introduce the student to these restricted or distinctive features.

EMPLOYEES TRUSTS

Let us make these six assumptions: (1) that the employer-corporation has decided, upon the advice of a specialist, that it will adopt an employee-benefit plan and that a trust is the plan best suited to its requirements; (2) that it has selected the trustee to administer its employees trust; (3) that the trust instrument has been drawn by competent and experienced counsel; (4) that the plan has been "qualified" under the Internal Revenue Code so as to take advantage of the income-tax saving; (5) that, if it is a contributory or negotiated plan, it has been accepted by the employees or by the appropriate union of employees; and (6) that the plan has been adopted by the board of directors of the employer-corporation and the trustee or the board of trustees or, if the trustee is to be a trust institution, by its board of directors or its acceptance committee. In a word, let us assume that all of the preliminaries have been attended to properly and adequately and that the administration of the trust is ready to begin.

Features Common to all Employees Trusts

There are three features that are common to practically all employees trusts.

1. *Separation of assets.* The assets of the trust and those of the employer-corporation are kept separate from each other. This is one of the requirements of "qualification." The accomplishment of this gives the trusteed plan an advantage over the self-administered plan.

2. *Employees' accounts.* In a contributory or a profit-sharing plan, someone—either the corporation or the trustee—must keep account of employees' contributions to the plan and of employees' benefits received under the plan. Whether this should be done by the corporation or the trustee will be discussed later in this topic.

3. *Selection of eligible employees.* Someone must select the eligible employees and prescribe the terms of eligibility. This, of course, is the function of the employer-corporation and not the trustee. An employer scarcely would delegate to a trustee the duty of selecting its eligible employees. An experienced trustee would hesitate to accept responsibility for doing so. In fact, to transfer that duty from the employer to the trustee could, largely, defeat the purpose of the trust.

Duties of Trustee

The duties of the trustee are determined by the nature of the trust and range all the way from custodianship to trusteeship as active as those under any personal trust.

1. *Purchase of annuity contracts.* If, under the terms of the trust, the trustee is to purchase either immediate or deferred annuity contracts and if the employer-corporation has supplied the funds with which to purchase them, the duties of the trustee may be summarized as follows: (*a*) To receive and keep possession of the contracts; (*b*) to pay the premiums on the contracts out of funds supplied by the corporation; (*c*) to set up an account for surplus funds or funds awaiting the payment of premiums; (*d*) to keep and periodically render accounts to the corporation; (*e*) to elect the options under policy contracts on order of the corporation or its duly authorized committee; (*f*) to issue notices to the insurance companies; (*g*) to compromise and adjust claims with the insurance companies; and (*h*) generally to carry out the instructions of the corporation or its committee.

In this type of employees trust the duties of the trustee are largely ministerial, that is, to carry out the instructions of the corporation or its committee. This committee goes by several different names: *pension committee, advisory committee, retirement committee.* The trustee has no managerial duties whatever.

2. *Administration of noninsured plan.* But, suppose under the plan

the trustee itself is to receive the funds, make the investments, and make the payments to the employee-beneficiaries. In that case the duties of the trustee may be as active and as exacting as they are in any personal trust. The following are some of administrative responsibilities and possible problems:

a. Actuarial calculations. In Chapter 8, we emphasized the importance of accurate actuarial calculations at the beginning. But, after the trust has been established, continued accuracy of those calculations becomes, in part at least, an administrative responsibility of the trustee. The payments into the hands of the trustee must be sufficient to meet both the current-service and the past-service commitments to the employees. The trustee may be under a duty to call the employer's attention to deficiencies in these payments.

b. Investments. According to the plan, the trustee may be under the duty, in one case, to make and change investments within a list prescribed by the employer; in another case, on order of the employer or its committee; and in still another, in the exercise of the trustee's own discretion.

> *i.* Prescribed list. In the first case, the trustee is under a duty to make and change investments only within the list prescribed by the employer. If the latter specifies "government bonds," then it must be government bonds only. Should the trustee invest outside the list, it would commit a breach of trust and make itself liable for any loss sustained thereby.

> *ii.* On order. In the second case, where the trustee is to invest on order of the employer or its committee, the trustee may find itself in a precarious position. Suppose the committee orders the trustee to invest employee-trust funds in highly speculative investments or in a disproportionate volume of the stock of the employer itself, and the trustee's considered judgment is that they are not proper investments for that trust, and that it will not be for the best interest of the employees for it to make those investments. In that case, the committee itself would be in a fiduciary relationship to the employees. The trustee could not stand idly by and see the committee commit a breach of duty and excuse itself by saying that it was only carrying out the order of the committee. As in the case of a direction trust discussed in Chapter 16, the trustee must not let the director, even though it be a committee of the employer-corporation, commit a breach of duty and do nothing about it. To do so would be, in effect, to participate in a breach of trust.

> *iii.* Trustee's discretion. In the third case, where the trustee itself has full responsibility for making and changing investments, it will be governed by the investment statutes and decisions that control the administration of the trust. In a prudent-man state it would make

prudent-man investments; in a legal-list state, investments within the legal list.

c. Collective investment. A comparatively recent and significant development in the investment of employee-trust funds is the collective investment of those funds. In some cases a trust institution, as trustee, will purchase for its employees trusts units of participation in its common trust fund. One of difficulties with this is that, under present regulations, not over $100,000 in any one account can be invested in the common trust fund or funds of the same trust institution.

The growing practice of larger trust institutions with a large volume of investable funds in employees trusts is to establish separate commingled funds especially adapted to the needs of these trusts. Some of them are establishing two types of commingled funds, called *balanced funds*, one of which is an all-stock fund and the other, and all-bond fund. This gives the trustee more leeway in adapting the investments to the requirements of the different trusts.

Some of these institutions make a difference in the investments in pension trusts and in profit-sharing trusts. In a pension trust the tendency seems to be to invest more for capital gains, that is, in common stocks, than for immediate income; whereas in a profit-sharing trust, more thought may be given to current income and, therefore, a smaller percentage is invested in "growth" stocks.

d. Employer's own securities. If the trustee has absolute discretion as to the selection of investments for its employees trusts, it probably would be disinclined to invest funds in the stocks or bonds of the employer-corporation even though for other trusts they would qualify as prudent-man investments, and even then it would not permit the corporation's own stocks or bonds to constitute anything approaching a majority of the investments in the trust. The policy of some of the larger corporations is not to have any of their securities in their employees trust. Furthermore, the Treasury Department would not permit the trustee to invest a large per cent of the fund in the corporation's own stocks and bonds under penalty of "disqualifying" the plan for the income-tax saving.

Employees' Accounts

A recurring question about the administration of employees trusts is: Should the employer-corporation or should the trustee keep the individual employee's account? Some one must, in the nature of things, keep an account of each employee's eligibility for benefits and of the benefits received by him. The prevailing opinion is that these accounts should be kept by the corporation and not by the trustee. If the trustee, rather than the corporation, keeps them, it would not only entail a vast amount of detailed bookkeeping for which it would be entitled to additional compensation, but also tend to dissociate the employer and employee in their relationships with each other.

CHARITABLE TRUSTS

The general fiduciary principles outlined in Chapter 13 apply alike and equally to charitable trusts and to personal trusts.

Let us assume now, as we did with respect to employees trusts, that all of the preliminaries have been attended to, that there is property in the trust to administer and income or principal or both to be distributed according to the terms of the trust. What, then, are some of the administrative duties, responsibilities, and problems of the trustee that are, more or less, peculiar to charitable trusts?

These distinctive duties, responsibilities, and problems apply to foundations rather than to trusts created by individual property owners for specified charitable objects. The administration of the latter is not basically different from that of any other personal trust. Consequently, the discussion that follows applies to foundations.

Separation of Administrative and Dispositive Functions

In a personal trust the dispositive functions of the trustee are fully as active and exacting as the administrative functions. In a foundation, on the contrary, the dispositive functions are reduced to the minimum and the administrative functions remain the same as in personal trusts.

The primary dispositive function of the trustee of a foundation is to see that the distributions are to *charitable objects* within the legal meaning of that term. The trustee makes its distributions, not direct to individual beneficiaries, but to charitable objects designed for service to individuals. In foundations, the trustee invests and manages the property and, according to the terms of the trust, turns the income or the principal or both over to or as ordered by the distribution committee. In an institutional foundation, as described in Chapter 10, the trustee invests and manages the property and makes the distributions to or on the order of the governing board of the institution. In a corporation foundation, the trustee invests and manages the property and makes the distributions as ordered by the corporation or its appropriate agency or committee.

It is highly essential, therefore, that the trustee keep separate its own administrative functions and someone else's dispositive functions.

Selection of Trustee

As discussed in Chapter 10, in the case of a multiple-trustee community foundation, each donor selects his own trustee and channels his gift through that one. The trustee of his choice, normally, would be the bank or trust company with which he did his own banking or trust business. But, conceivably, he might select one of the other eligible trustees.

The trustee so selected by the donor would receive and administer the property given to it in trust for the foundation. It would not seek gifts for the sake of administering them. It would encourage gifts for the foundation but leave the trusteeship to the donor's own selection.

Administrative Problems Peculiar to Community Foundations

Specialists in the administration of community foundations report the following problems in the administration of this type of charitable trust.

1. *Responsibility for distribution.* As pointed out in a preceding paragraph, normally, the responsibilities for administration are committed to the trustee and for distribution to the distribution committee. But in some cases, these specialists say, the trust instrument does not make it clear whether or not the trustee has any responsibility for following the proceeds and seeing that the distribution committee is making distributions according to the terms of the trust.

2. *Remittance dates.* In personal trusts, payments to beneficiaries can be and usually are paid on fixed dates. In a community foundation, on the contrary, they are made as ordered by the distribution committee and vary from account to account. The New York Community Trust, for example, in 1959, was administering over 1300 different accounts, each with its own remittance dates.

3. *Income payable annually.* Specialists in community-foundation administration say that one of their minor problems is that of meeting the requirement under the terms of the trust that all of the income of a given account be paid over annually. It would seem simple enough for the trustee to pay over to the distribution committee the income or the balance of the income by the end of the fiscal year of that account. But if there is delay in the reorganization of the committee or in its order of distribution, the trustee may not be able to make the distributions on the annual basis as required.

4. *Active distribution committee.* The last sentence suggests still another problem. In a large community foundation there is little difficulty in keeping an active distribution committee. But in a small or family foundation with a self-perpetuating distribution committee, the original members of which were members of the family, in course of time, as the original members die or become incapacitated, it may become increasingly difficult to have at all times an active and interested distribution committee.

5. *Problems of distribution committee.* Although this chapter is, theoretically, confined to the administrative duties, responsibilities, and

problems of the trustee, passing mention should be made of the dispositive problems of the distribution committee to which the trustee, in good conscience if not in law, should not close its eyes.

If the designated charitable object fails, the committee is under a duty to divert the income to some other charitable object within the purview of the foundation. But the committee faces these questions: (*a*) Has the original object failed? (*b*) If so, what other object will come nearest carrying out the desires and intentions of the donor of the designated gift?

Suppose the income from the trust far exceeds the needs of the specified object. Then these questions arise: (*a*) What are the present needs of the specified object? (*b*) To or for what objects shall the excess income be used? Although the finding of answers to such questions as these is the primary responsibility of the distribution committee, the trustee, serving in an advisory capacity only, will help the committee to find the answers.

CORPORATE TRUSTS

Once more, let us assume that all of the preliminaries have been attended to properly, that the trust indenture and all the other essential papers have been executed and delivered, and that the trustee is ready to begin the administration of the corporate trust.

The administrative activities and responsibilities of the trustee covers one period in all cases and, in some cases, unfortunately, a second period. The first period is the one before default, when the corporation is meeting all of its obligations under the indenture promptly and to the letter. The second period is the one at and after default, when the corporation has failed to meet one or more of its material obligations under the indenture. The activities, responsibilities, and problems of the trustee before default and those at and after default are quite different.

Duties of Trustee

In addition to the specified duties of the trustee itself as set forth in the indenture, the trustee is under a duty also to see that the corporation performs certain duties imposed upon it by the indenture. The following is a bare outline of these duties:

1. *Opinion of counsel.* To verify the receipt of the prescribed opinion of counsel for the corporation with respect to the recordation of the trust indenture;

2. *Insurance statement.* To see that the trustee receives the required annual insurance statement and that it complies with the insurance covenants of the corporation;

3. *Maintenance statement.* To see that the corporation furnishes the

required maintenance statement, that it is in the prescribed form, and that it denotes compliance with the maintenance covenant; and

4. *Financial statement.* To see that it receives the required financial statements from the corporation.

Before Default

The following are the main duties of the trustee before default in which the student will be interested: authentication of bonds, registration of bonds, temporary and definitive bonds, exchange of bonds, conversion of bonds, replacement of bonds, redemption, sinking funds, release of property, pledged securities, equipment trusts, revenue-bond trusts, and termination of trust.

1. *Authentication of bonds.* After all of the preliminaries have been attended to, the first duty of the trustee is to authenticate the bonds. This means to sign a certificate on the bond itself identifying it as being issued under a specified trust indenture. This validates the bond. It is a declaration to the world that the bond has been issued pursuant to the terms of the specified indenture. One readily sees that the trustee must exercise extreme care to make sure that all of the conditions have been met.

2. *Registration of bonds.* As will be discussed in the next chapter, registration of bonds is primarily an agency function. The same trust institution may and sometimes does serve as both trustee and registrar of the same bond issue. When it does so, it must keep its duties as trustee and as registrar separate. The duties of the registrar will be discussed in the next chapter.

3. *Temporary and definitive bonds.* Even after all of the preliminaries have been attended to, there usually is a lapse of time before engraved bonds are ready for delivery, in which case, the corporation issues temporary, usually printed, bonds and the trustee delivers them to the bondholders. Then, when the definitive bonds are in hand and ready for delivery, the trustee has the responsibility of making the exchange and of seeing that the surrendered, temporary bonds and the delivered, definitive bonds match each other in amount.

4. *Exchange of bonds.* For the convenience of bondholders, the trust indenture usually provides for the exchange of bonds—that is, for the exchange of registered bonds for coupon bonds and vice versa, for the exchange of bonds of different denominations, and, as stated above, for the exchange of temporary bonds for definitive bonds. Under the terms of the trust indenture the trustee usually is charged with the duty of making these exchanges under the terms of the trust indenture.

5. *Conversion of bonds.* This means something entirely different from the exchange of bonds as just described. Under the terms of the trust in-

denture the bondholder may have the privilege of converting his bonds into the stock of the company. The terms of convertibility are set forth in the indenture. Although conversion is primarily an agency function, it usually is committed to the trustee. In which case the trustee has the responsibility of supervising adjustments should the conversion result in fractional shares of stock, of seeing that the transfer taxes, if any, resulting from the conversion are paid, and of seeing that the conversion is accomplished promptly so as not to inconvenience the bondholders.

6. *Replacement of bonds.* Given time, the trustee under a large bond issue will come face to face with the problem of a lost, stolen, destroyed, or mutilated bond. Whose responsibility is it to solve this problem—that of the corporation or of the trustee? The responsibility is that of the corporation. But this does not mean at all that the trustee will not have or should not have an active part in the replacement process. The indenture, properly drawn, will set forth that the corporation may issue duplicate bonds and that the trustee must authenticate and deliver them on order of the corporation. As a condition precedent to issuing the order of replacement the corporation will require satisfactory evidence of the loss, theft, destruction, or mutilation of the bond and an indemnity bond with surety to protect the corporation in ordering the authentication and delivery of a duplicate bond.

Up to this point we have been outlining the duties and responsibilities of the trustee while the total bond issue still is outstanding, before the corporation has paid off or provided a sinking fund for paying off the bonds. We turn now to some of its activities related to the reduction and ultimately to the full satisfaction of the corporation's obligations under the indenture.

7. *Redemption.* Most trust indentures give the corporation the privilege of paying off its indebtedness in whole or in part prior to the maturity date set out in the bond, that is, of redeeming its bonds. The bondholders must be notified of the call for redemption. In the case of registered bonds the corporation or its registrar, which latter may be the trustee, has a list of the registered bondholders. Not so with coupon-bondholders whose bonds pass by delivery, notice to whom is usually given by publication a stated number of times in one or more newspapers in one or more stated cities. The corporation usually has to pay a premium for redeeming its bonds before maturity. In case of partial redemption, the trustee draws by lot the numbers of bonds to be redeemed, and these numbers are published in the notice in the newspapers. The corporation and the trustee have to work together in attending to the details, as set forth in the indenture, of redemptions.

8. *Sinking funds.* By periodic payments to the trustee the corporation may build up a sinking fund with which to retire the bonds as they mature. The details of the sinking fund are set out in the indenture, and the trustee

is under a duty to see that they are observed. The sinking fund may be either cumulative or noncumulative. If it is cumulative, the corporation will pay over to the trustee not only the amount necessary to pay the principal and interest on maturing bonds but also an amount equivalent to the interest on bonds already retired through operation of the sinking fund. From the corporation's point of view the practical difference is that, if the fund is cumulative, the corporation will pay the same amount each year, although part of its bonds already will have been paid off, and thereby accelerate the discharge of its obligation under the issue; whereas, if the fund is noncumulative, the corporation will pay each year a diminishing amount as its obligations become less and less.

9. *Release of property*. In the case of a long-term bond issue it is likely that, as the outstanding bonds diminish, the corporation will desire that certain items of its property covered by the indenture be released. In fact, the best interests of the bondholders themselves, as well as of the corporation, may require that certain property be released and, if additional security should be needed, that it be substituted for the property released. This process of releasing and, possibly, of substituting other property casts grave responsibilities upon the trustee. The property released and the property, if any, substituted for it must be appraised to determine the effect of the release and substitution upon the bonds. The details of this procedure are set forth in the indenture, and the trustee, for its own protection as well as that of the bondholders, is under a duty to see that these details are observed in every respect.

10. *Pledged securities*. As was brought out in Chapter 11, the indenture may cover stocks, bonds, mortgages, and other intangible personal property along with or instead of real property, plant, and equipment. The trustee will find in its possession these securities of the corporation. This impresses upon the trustee such special duties as these: (*a*) to see that pledged bonds are registered in its name unless the indenture provides for them to remain in the name of a corporation; (*b*) to see that interest and dividends on these securities be turned back to the corporation; (*c*) to see that the trustee gives the corporation its proxy to vote the stock; and (*d*) in case of merger, consolidation, or reorganization of the corporation whose stocks or bonds are in the trust, to give the trustee the right to receive under the trust stocks and bonds resulting from any such change in the setup of the corporation whose securities have been pledged.

11. *Equipment trusts*. Equipment trusts, whereby railroad companies finance the purchase of additional rolling stock, as discussed in Chapter 11, cast upon the trustee special duties among which are the following: (*a*) to receive a bill of sale of the running equipment directly from the manufacturer to the trustee, with warranty of title; (*b*) to obtain a statement from the vendors, as agents of the trustee and usually employees of the railroad

company, that they have received the equipment for which payment is requested and that the equipment is marked or plated as required by the lease; (c) to obtain opinion of counsel that the trustee has acquired good title to the equipment free and clear of all liens or other encumbrances; (d) to obtain from the railroad company a receipt for the equipment delivered to it; and (e) to obtain a certificate of cost of the equipment. Thus, an equipment trust is anything but a passive trust so far as the trustee's duties are concerned.

12. *Revenue-bond trusts.* As was brought out in Chapter 11, in a revenue-bond trust created by an "authority" for the financing of its bridges, tunnels, highways, waterworks, and sewage-disposal plant, the trustee has not and, perhaps, could not have title to the property itself but only to the tolls from the property. The principal duties of the trustee are: (a) to receive these pledged tolls; (b) to utilize them for the purpose specified in the indenture; and (c) to see that the "authority" files with the trustee the required financial statements and certificates of insurance as called for in the indenture.

13. *Termination of trust.* We come now to the termination of the trust. Every obligation of the corporation has been met and satisfied in full. The corporation has paid off, or is ready to pay off, every penny of its indebtedness under the bond issue. The trust indenture makes provision for this happy eventuality by providing that, once the corporation has paid off everything that it had promised to pay off in the indenture and has performed all of its convenants under the indenture, the trustee must execute an instrument acknowledging that the indenture has been satisfied in full and reconvey to the corporation any property then subject to the indenture. This instrument, executed by the trustee, may be issued in many counterparts to enable the corporation to have it recorded wherever—in whatever county or state—the trust indenture itself had been recorded.

Upon and After Default

But, suppose the bond issue does not have such a happy ending; suppose that the corporation does not meet its obligations as set forth in the indenture, that it defaults. This casts upon the trustee an entirely different set of duties and responsibilities. Whereas, as long as the corporation was meeting its obligations, the trustee was under a duty only to carry out to the letter its own commitments under the indenture; in the event of default, it will be under a duty not only to carry out the terms of the trust but also to apply the prudent-man rule in protecting the bondholders, which means giving the trustee some discretion in dealing with the situation.

1. *Events of default.* Events of default, to be found in the trust indenture, are substantially as follows: (a) failure by the corporation to pay principal at maturity or within a specified period of grace; (b) failure by the

corporation to make a sinking fund payment when due or within the specified period of grace; (c) failure by the corporation to pay interest as it becomes due or within the specified period of grace; (d) failure by the corporation to perform any other covenant within the specified period following the giving of notice by the trustee or by holders of a specified percentage of the bonds, with demand that such failure be remedied; (e) the filing by the corporation of a voluntary petition in bankruptcy, making an assignment for the benefit of creditors, or consenting to the appointment of a receiver; and (f) entry of a court order finding the corporation to be bankrupt or insolvent, approving petition for reorganization under federal bankruptcy laws, or appointing a trustee or receiver for the corporation provided it is not vacated within a specified number of days.

Any one of the foregoing events of default is likely to have fatal consequences to the corporation as a going concern, as well as entail substantial losses to the bondholders. Consequently, for the sake of all interested parties—the corporation, the bondholders, the trustee itself—the trustee should and, no doubt, would, go the limit of law and good conscience to prevent any such event of default. If, for example, the corporation failed to comply with a covenant or to supply certain documents, or failed to make principal, income, or sinking-fund payments on the due date, the trustee would call this failure to the attention of the corporation. It would use its good offices to enable the corporation to meet these obligations. If, however, the corporation could not or would not meet them, the trustee would be under a duty to give notice of failure of the corporation to comply with its obligations, and this might precipitate the beginning of the end of the corporation.

2. *Duties of trustee.* The trust indenture would set forth the duties of the trustee in event of default and the trustee would have to follow these to the letter. Whereas, as already started, before default, the duties of the trustee were limited to those set forth in the indenture, after default the trustee would be under a duty to do what a prudent man would do under the circumstances to protect the interests of the bondholders. To revert to terms used heretofore, before default, the duties of the trustees are largely *ministerial*—carrying out orders—after default, they would be both *ministerial* and *managerial*—exercising its best judgment for the protection of the interests of the bondholders.

The foregoing discussion of the administration of employees, charitable, and corporate trusts must have impressed upon the student the fact that the proper administration of these kinds of trusts has fully as great an impact upon society at large as does that of personal trusts. Whereas personal trusts serve individuals as individuals, employees, charitable, and corporate trusts serve groups of individuals and, together, both kinds of trusts serve society in general.

COLLATERAL READING

Note: For complete citations, see Bibliography, pp. 417–428.

Employees Trusts

McGill, *Fundamentals of Private Pensions.*

Charitable Trusts

Young, "Planning and Management of Charitable Foundations."

Corporate Trusts

Kimball, "Administration of Corporate Trusts."
Pohl, "The Administration of Trust Indentures by Corporate Trustees."

20

Performance of Agencies
Related to Estates and Trusts

I N CHAPTER 13, there were listed five types of agencies for individuals, four for industrial corporations, and one for institutions, which were, in one way or another, directly associated with or related to estates and trusts and, therefore, should, at least, be introduced to the student.

In this chapter we shall discuss the principal or distinctive duties and responsibilities of the fiduciary that performs each of these types of agencies. The procedure of the fiduciary for performing them is beyond the scope of this text.

AGENCIES FOR INDIVIDUALS

The five types of agencies for individuals listed in Chapter 13 were: for individual fiduciaries, for safekeeping, for custody, for managing securities and farms, ranches, or businesses, and escrow agencies.

For Individual Fiduciaries

This type of agency is confined almost exclusively to trust institutions. As illustrated in Chapter 13, a property owner will name his wife or his son executor and trustee under his will, expecting, if not recording, that his bank will serve as agent for the individual executor and trustee, take over the property, and, in all but name, settle the estate and administer the trusts. This is, perhaps, the most anomalous relationship known to the trust business and to experienced trust institutions the least desirable. While the individual executor or trustee can appoint an agent to do for him specified things that he cannot, reasonably, be expected to do himself, he cannot delegate to anyone else generally the settlement of the estate or administration of the

295

trust. If he undertakes to do so, he may make himself liable for breach of duty and, if the trust institution accepts such an agency, it may make itself liable for participating in a breach of duty. So, while the trust institution may accept an agency for rendering specified services in settling the estate or administering the trusts, such as safekeeping, custody, managing farms, escrow, it should not take over the general settlement of the estate or administration of the trust; it should confine its services to certain, specified capacities.

Safekeeping

The performance of a usual safekeeping agency is one of the simplest services rendered by a fiduciary. The property to be safekept usually consists of securities, documents, jewelry, and other highly valued or cherished property of comparatively small dimension.

1. *Duties.* The usual duties of the safekeeping agent are: (1) to receive the property, (2) to receipt for it, (3) to keep it safely in an appropriate safe deposit vault or box, and (4) to deliver it on demand to the principal or on his order.

2. *Responsibilities.* The principal responsibilities of the safekeeping agent are: (1) to protect and preserve the property and keep it safely as a prudent man would safekeep similar property and (2) to exercise due care in delivering the property back to the owner or on his order.

As to the first responsibility, the bank or trust company, being engaged in the business of safekeeping, may be held to a higher standard of care than a lay individual would be. It probably would be held to the standard of the reasonably prudent bank or trust company serving in that capacity.

As to the second responsibility, the safekeeping agent would be under a duty to exercise extreme care in delivering the property on the order of, instead of directly to, the owner. It could not afford to take chances by delivering the property on oral or telephone orders or to unidentified persons unknown to the safekeeping agent.

Custodian

After safekeeping, custody is the next step in the activity and responsibility of the agent. Custodianship usually applies to securities only.

1. *Duties.* The principal duties of the custodian are: (1) to receive, receipt for, and safekeep the securities (the same as in a safekeeping agency); (2) to collect the income and pay it to or on the order of the principal; (3) to execute the necessary ownership certificates required for income-tax purposes; (4) to notify the principal regarding all collections; (5) to collect the principal of matured or called bonds and matured mortgage notes and report all such collections to the principal and dispose of them as ordered by him; (6) to exchange temporary for definitive securities; (7) to notify

the principal of calls, subscription rights, defaults in principal or interest, and the adoption of protective measures regarding the security; (8) to buy, sell, receive, or deliver securities on specific instructions from the principal; and (9) to render periodic statements of the securities held in the account.

2. *Responsibilities.* The distinctive characteristic of a custodianship is that every duty of the custodian is ministerial, that is, to receive and follow instructions as set forth either in the agency agreement or as ordered by the principal. If the agent agrees to exercise and does exercise his own judgment or discretion about any phase of performance, it passes beyond custodianship into managing agency. Consequently, the primary, inescapable responsibility of the custodian is to obey instructions. And, if he fails to obey instructions and a loss to the principal results therefrom, he is liable for the amount of the loss.

The experience of those who make a business of serving as custodian (they are mostly trust institutions) has been that often, in the name of custodianship, managerial, in addition to ministerial, duties are imposed upon and accepted by the agent, and yet the agency is performed for the same compensation as though it were a custodianship and nothing more.

Managing

We come now to managing agencies, and, as set out in Chapter 13, they should be divided into managing agencies for securities and managing agencies for businesses, including farms, ranches, and real property; for the duties and responsibilities of each of the two types of managing agencies are quite different.

1. *For securities.* The duties and responsibilities of the managing agent for securities are far in advance of those of the safekeeping agent or custodian.

a. Duties. In addition to all of the duties and responsibilities of both a safekeeping agent and a custodian, a managing agent for securities has one or more or, in many cases, all of these other duties, many of which, as will be seen, are managerial: (*i*) to give the principal advance notice of pending maturities of bonds, notes, and mortgages; (*ii*) to prepare for the principal an annual statement of income for income-tax purposes; (*iii*) to pay taxes, such as ad valorem, intangibles, income, for the principal out of funds in the agent's hands; (*iv*) to see that insurance is kept in force and taxes paid on mortgaged property in the account; (*v*) to receive income from outside sources, such as rents, royalties, rights; (*vi*) to pay bills or make other remittances for the principal as ordered by him; (*vii*) to take advantage of opportunities to exchange convertible bonds and to purchase bonds for sinking funds; and (*viii*) to make analyses and reviews of securities in the account, and, on the basis thereof, to recommend retention, sale, exchange, conversion, or purchase. The last of all eight duties entails the most exacting responsibilities.

b. Responsibilities. Under the agency agreement the principal and the agent should have a definite understanding and commitment as to the analysis and review of investments and the recommendations regarding them. The agent may accept the duty to analyze and review them quarterly, semiannually, annually, or otherwise periodically, or, which is much more common, to analyze and review them and make recommendations as often as needed in the judgment of the agent for the good of the account. In the latter case, the analysis and review procedure in the agency account would not differ materially from that in a trust account.

In some cases, the principal and the agent may agree that the agent will not stop with making recommendations only but will, itself, make or change investments as its own judgment dictates. This would make the agency, to all intents and purposes, a living trust except that the title to the securities would remain in the principal. The principal would give the agent a power of attorney to assign and transfer securities.

If the agent makes a business of serving as managing agent—if, for example, it is a trust institution—it may be under a duty to make a different sort of analysis and review from that expected or required of a lay individual agent. The trust institution, in accepting the managing agency, would place itself under a duty to exercise the same procedure in analysis and review as it would exercise as trustee. It could not leave it to any individual in the trust department—not even to the head of the investment division—to analyze, review, and recommend investments himself, alone, unaided by other persons. Instead, the analysis would be made by investment analysts, the reviews by officers, and the recommendations by the investment committee of the trust institution.

2. For businesses, including farms, ranches, and real property. Managing agencies for businesses, including farms, ranches, and real property, appear to be a growing fiduciary service. Banks and trust companies are establishing farm-management divisions of their trust departments to manage farms and ranches in their estates and trusts. In these cases they are not managing agencies at all but are part of the settlement of the estate or administration of the trust. But in recent years these farm-management divisions have been branching out and offering much needed service in a managing-agency capacity to widows and women who have no one to look after their affairs, to aging people, and to absentee or otherwise occupied landlords. Already, in some of the agricultural areas of the country, farm-management agencies have become a substantial part of the business of trust institutions. Furthermore, farm-management has become an independent enterprise. Trust institutions, as well as individuals, employ farm-management concerns as agents to manage farms and ranches in estates and trusts. This tends to confirm the point made in Chapter 18 that the handling of businesses in estates, trusts, and in agencies as well, already has become a substantial part of the fiduciary services being rendered in this country. It is interesting to note also that it is a substantial part of the business of Australian trust institutions.

a. Duties. There is no way of making a definitive record of the duties of the managing agent of a business or of a farm or ranch or of real property. The agent's duties must be adjusted to the nature and requirements and the location of the business or the farm, ranch, or the real property to be managed. In Chapter 18, we outlined first the powers and duties of the trustee of a business—of any business—and then those of the trustee of a farm. We referred to the recently published handbook of the Trust Division of the American Bankers Association, *Handling Businesses in Trust*, in which the handling of businesses, including farms, oil and gas interests, and businesses in general is discussed in detail. According to the terms of the agency agreement, the duties of the managing agent of a business or of a farm may be as active, as extensive, and as exacting as those of the trustee of that business or farm would be.

b. Responsibilities. Having in mind at all times that the owner and the managing agent of a business or farm are in a fiduciary relationship with each other, and that disloyalty or infidelity to this relationship on the part of the agent would be fully as serious and consequential as they would be in the trustee-beneficiary relationship, one readily understands that the agent's failure to carry out loyally the terms of the agency agreement would entail quite as serious consequences as his failure to carry out the terms of a trust. The fact that the agency relationship may be terminated at will by either principal or agent, unless the terms of the agreement otherwise provide, may mislead one into thinking that the duties and responsibilities of an agent are not so exacting as those of a trustee. As long as the relationship of principal and agent exists, the fiduciary principles presented and discussed in Chapter 14 apply to agents no less than to trustees.

Escrow

An *escrow* is the type of agency wherein money, securities, documents, or other property or evidences of property are deposited by two or more persons with a third person, to be delivered on a certain contingency or the occurrence of a specified event. For example, *A* delivers a deed, and *B*, a certified check to *C*, the deed to be delivered to *B* and the check to *A* upon the happening of certain specified events. The deed and the check are the *escrow;* the terms of the agreement of deposit, the *escrow agreement;* and the third person, *C*, the *escrow agent*.

1. *Duties*. The duties of an escrow agent are purely ministerial; he is a servant, not an agent, in legal contemplation. He is to do what he is instructed to do, that, and nothing more. Once he does more or less than that

he becomes more or less than an escrow agent. Many so-called escrow agencies are, really, managing agencies of one sort or another with certain escrow features, and the performance of these nonescrow duties raises problems and involves responsibilities unknown to escrow agencies proper.

The features characteristic of an escrow agency are: (*a*) an agreement among the three parties—that is, to use the illustration of the purchase and sale of real property, the seller, the purchaser, and the holder of the purchase price and the deed—covering every essential point of the arrangement, with nothing left for later negotiation or arrangement; (*b*) the deposit of the money, securities, documents, or property or evidences of property with the escrow agent; (*c*) an intentional surrender by the parties—that is, the seller and the purchaser, in the illustration—of dominion over the property and the documents; and (*d*) definite instructions to the escrow agent as to what he is to do in performing the agency, leaving nothing to his discretion and nothing for later arrangement between the other two parties. It is a closed arrangement with nothing left for later negotiation.

2. *Responsibilities.* The responsibility of the escrow agent is to carry out instructions—that and nothing more. But the performance of the agency may and sometimes does tempt the agent, with the best of intentions and motives, to violate the letter of his instructions. For example, the seller of the property may assure the agent that all of the liens on the property have been satisfied and that he, the seller, now is entitled to the purchase price. The agent, taking his word for it, delivers the purchase price to him only to find out later that there still is a cloud on the title. Or, the agency agreement calls for the purchase price to be paid in cash or with a certified check, and the agent accepts an uncertified check of the purchaser which, upon deposit, is returned unpaid. The escrow agent makes himself liable to the one or the other party for any and all loss resulting from his failure to follow instructions to the letter.

Experienced escrow agents protect themselves by insisting upon a formal agency agreement setting forth their duties and containing certain reasonable provisions protecting the agent except for his own negligence.

CORPORATE AGENCIES

If one were to go into the corporate agency division or department of a metropolitan trust institution and inquire as to the different kinds of agencies for corporations being performed by it, one would be told that it was performing many other kinds of corporate agencies than the ones that will be discussed in this text, such as, fiscal, tax-withholding, for stock splits, for stock combinations, for stock conversions, and for distribution of securities in connection with corporate reorganizations. The student, who does not anticipate ever being engaged in corporate agency work, may need to know of the existence and the conventional names of these agencies but at this point in his education he will not need to know the duties and responsibilities of such agents. So, we shall confine our discussion to the conventional corporate agencies: transfer agencies, registrarships, paying agencies, and depositaryships.

Transfer

The *transfer agent* of a corporation is its agent to effect the transfer of its stock from one owner to another. The agent to transfer registered bonds is known as a *registrar* and this will be discussed in the next section.

1. *Evolution of stock transfer.* In the beginning of corporate organization, there were no certificates of stock. The stockholder selling his stock simply had the corporation register on its own books the change of ownership. Next, came the issue of certificates of stock to the stockholder as evidence of his ownership. The stockholder desiring to sell or to give his stock surrendered his certificate to the corporation and it issued a new certificate to the new owner. Then, as corporate organization developed and industrial corporations came to have thousands of stockholders and changes of ownership of stock became numerous and voluminous, the larger corporations employed agents to do their stock-transfer work for them. And this was the beginning of the *stock-transfer agency* which has developed into one of the principal fiduciary services of metropolitan trust institutions. The *stock certificate* has become, in effect, a negotiable instrument passing title by assignment even prior to transfer on the books of the corporation or its transfer agent.

2. *Duties.* The two main duties of a transfer agent are: (*a*) to issue stock certificates and (*b*) to report the change of ownership. Incidental to the discharge of these two basic duties are the following:

a. Verification of signatures of officers of corporation. The agent is supplied by the corporation a list of authorized signatures and is under a duty to see that the certificate carries one of these authorized signatures, whether handwritten or duplicated in some authorized way.

b. Issue of certificate for original shares. One of the functions of the agent may be, not to transfer existing shares, but to issue original shares. This casts upon the agent the duty to see that the corporation has the right to issue the original shares. The agent must see that no overissue of stock is involved, that all government regulations have been complied with, and that all taxes connected with the issue have been paid. It must make certain that the requisite resolutions and documents incident to the issue are forthcoming from the corporation.

c. Transfer of shares. The transfer of existing shares from one owner to another is more of a dealing between the agent and owner than between agent and corporation. The agent must see that the transferring stockholder establishes his identity and proves his right to have the transfer made.

i. Identity of transferor. In practice, the identity of the individual stockholder may be established by the guaranty of his signature by some bank or trust company. The identity of a partnership or corporation may be established by the guaranty of the authorized signature of the partner or the officer of the corporation.

ii. Right to transfer. It is the right of the transferor to have the transfer made that imposes upon the agent the most exacting, sometimes vexatious responsibility.

If it is a transfer desired by an adult individual stockholder, the agent normally is protected by acting on his guaranteed signature.

But suppose the agent is put on notice or has reason to believe that the person seeking the transfer or for whom the transfer is sought is a minor. A minor, of course, cannot authorize nor direct a transfer of stock standing in his name. The agent will be under a duty to decline to make the transfer except upon the order of a duly appointed and authorized guardian. In recent years a number of states by statute have authorized the issue or transfer of shares to a custodian for a minor which legislation is designed to obviate the necessity of the appointment of a guardian to effect the transfer.

Still other problems arise in connection with the transfer of shares by a fiduciary. It is not enough for the executor or administrator or guardian or trustee to sign the stock power on the back of the certificate or sign a separate stock power, have his signature guaranteed, and send the certificate in to the transfer agent to make the transfer as directed. The agent has the responsibility of seeing that the fiduciary has the right to have the stock transferred as directed. This may involve its requiring the fiduciary to furnish various documents, such as, certified copies of wills and trust agreements, of letters testamentary or of administration, and letters of guardianship, showing the fiduciary's right to have the transfer made as requested.

The simplification of the transfer of securities in estates and trusts, with due protection to the agent making the transfer, has been a long and uphill struggle.[1] In recent years there has been promise of progress towards such simplification.[2] In its 1959 session, the Legislature of the State of New York adopted the Uniform Act for Simplification of Fiduciary Transfer.[3] In this Act, the discharge of the agent's duties related to the transfer of stock by fiduciaries involves (x) its interpretation of wills, trust agreements, and powers of attorney; (y) its familiarity with the powers of fiduciaries of different types to have stock transferred under the laws of the fiduciary's state or of any other state involved in the transfer; and (z) knowledge of the laws of taxation of transfers of stock.

d. Transfer of bonds. Furthermore, transfer agency applies to the

[1] Stephenson, *Studies;* "Transfer of Securities Held in Trust Accounts," 79.
[2] Mudge, "The Simplification of Corporate Fiduciary Transfer," 20; Christy, "The Model Fiduciaries' Securities Transfer Act," 10.
[3] Laws, 1959, Ch. 150.

transfer of registered bonds as well as shares of stock. Confusion has come about from the fact that the transfer agent of registered bonds usually is known as a *registrar*. Also known as *registrar* is the agent to transfer certificates of deposit, voting trust certificates, and registered stock-purchase warrants.

Referring now to the transfer agent or *registrar* (the common name) of bonds, we find that the agent has these distinctive duties: to register and to record transfers from bearer to specified owner, from specified owner to bearer, and from one specified owner to another. Bonds may be registered as to both principal and interest, or as to principal only in which latter case the interest coupons are payable to bearer. Keeping a record of all these different kinds of registration and seeing that the differences are observed in the transfers put heavy responsibilities upon the transfer agent of bonds.

3. *Responsibilities.* The transfer agent, whether of stocks or bonds, is the agent of the corporation whose shares or bonds are being issued or transferred. It is liable to the corporation for any loss sustained by it on account of a wrongful issue or transfer. In addition to responsibility for the proper issue or transfer as outlined above, the agent is responsible to the corporation for the custody of unissued certificates, for the disposition of cancelled certificates, for the handling of the replacement of lost, stolen, destroyed, or mutilated certificates, and, withal, for the bookkeeping and accounting incident to its transfer work. In addition to all this, the corporation may appoint the transfer agent to serve also as its dividend- or interest-paying agent. But this is a separate agency which will be discussed later and which should not be confused with the transfer agency itself.

Registrar

Let us come now to registrarships proper, eliminating further reference to so-called registrarships which are actually transfer agencies.

1. *Background of registrarship.* The origin of registrarship was an unhappy event in the business world. In 1847, the New York and New Haven Railroad Company, which had been incorporated in 1846 with an authorized capital of $3 million appointed its president, Robert Schuyler, its stock-transfer agent. Soon after his appointment he began to issue unauthorized shares of the company's stock and within the next six years issued nearly 20,000 such shares. This resulted in litigation extending over a ten-year period. The courts severely criticized the directors of the railroad company for leaving the president in supreme command and control of the transfer of its shares and made the company liable for the losses sustained by the holders of these unauthorized shares.

Out of this tragic experience of the corporation and its president developed the vigilance of this and other corporations to prevent any similar occurrence. The result was that registration of shares of stock became the established practice of corporations whose shares were offered to the public. At the present time, the New York Stock Exchange requires that all stock admitted to trading be registered, that the registrar be one approved by the exchange, that it be independent alike of the corporation and the transfer agent, and that the registrar enter an agreement with the exchange whereunder it will not register any additional shares of listed stock until so authorized by the exchange itself.

2. *Duties*. Since the primary duty of the registrar is to prevent overissue of the stock, it must keep some check upon the transfer agent as well as the corporation. It must, for example, examine the charter and by-laws of the corporation; have an authenticated specimen of the stock certificate which it must identify and register; have assurance that all regulatory requirements have been met; have a record of the outstanding stock, the amount of the new issue, and a statement of the conditions underlying the issue of the new stock.

3. *Responsibilities*. In the discharge of these duties, in the case of an original issue instead of a transfer of existing shares, the registrar must see that only the authorized number of shares is issued. In the case of the transfer of existing shares, it must see that the old shares and the new shares to take their place are equal in number.

Should there be an overissue traceable to the negligence or wrongdoing of the registrar, the losing stockholder would go back to the corporation to recover his loss and the corporation, in turn, would go back to its registrar to recover the loss traceable to its breach of duty.

Paying

The two principal types of paying agencies are dividend-paying and bond-paying.

1. *Dividend*. As mentioned in the discussion of transfer agencies, the corporation may employ the trust institution that serves as its transfer agent to serve also as its dividend-paying agent. The advantage of this arrangement is that the transfer agent has at all times an up-to-date list of stockholders and of their respective shares and can make up and mail out the dividend checks at less expense than the corporation itself could do.

2. *Bond*. Although the corporation itself may pay the interest on its outstanding bonds and notes and pay off the principal when due, the more common practice is for it to appoint the same trust institution that is trustee under its bond issue to serve as its paying-agent for its bond maturities, interest, and principal. Here again, as in the case of transfer agencies, the trustee of the bond issue and the bond-paying agent must keep its trust functions and its agency functions separate and distinct from each other.

3. *Duties*. If the paying agent, whether of dividends or of bond inter-

est or principal, is to perform its agency functions, it must have on hand the funds with which to make the payments when and as they fall due. While it is the duty of the corporation, not its paying agent, to supply these funds, the agent may feel that it is under a moral, if not legal, duty to notify the corporation of approaching maturities. In the case of dividend-paying, the agent must be on the alert for foreign stockholders liable for taxes to be withheld by the dividend-paying agent and, having withheld the amount of the tax due, remit it to the proper government agency.

In the case of a bond-paying agency, if it is a fully registered bond, that is, registered as to interest as well as principal, the agent would mail out to the registered bondholder an interest check just as it would mail out a dividend check on stock. If it was a coupon bond, whether wholly unregistered or registered as to principal only, the agent would pay the interest due on the bonds only upon receipt of the coupons. The number of these coupons and the large amount of money involved on each interest date make interest-paying on coupon bonds a tedious, although highly responsible, function of the agent.

The agent to pay the interest on bonds has duties not only to the corporation and its bondholders but also to the government. It must be familiar with and comply with all the government regulations regarding ownership certificates, tax withholding, and tax remittance to the government. In fact, tax-withholding duties give their name to certain agencies in some trust institutions; they are called tax-withholding agencies.

In the case of fully registered bonds, as to both principal and interest, the paying agent is under a duty to keep in touch with the registrar to see that the bonds paid off are released from the registrar's records, and, should the question arise, the agent must be in position to certify that the payment was made to the registered owner.

Depositary

A *depositary* is the person who receives a deposit of money, securities, documents, or other evidences of property. It is to be distinguished from the depository which is the *place* where these items are deposited. One is a person; the other, a place.

Among corporate agencies there are many kinds of depositaryships, the principal ones of which are: (1) for protective committees, (2) for voting trustees, and (3) for foreign securities.

1. *For protective committees.* If a corporation gets into financial trouble and goes or is thrown into bankruptcy or receivership, or if the stockholders or bondholders learn that it is about to get into such trouble, they may come together, pool their holdings, appoint a trust institution depositary to hold their securities, and appoint a protective committee to handle the situation as best it can for the best interest of all of the securityholders.

This may involve a complete reorganization of the corporation and the issue of a new type of stock or bond or both. The working out of this reorganization may take months or even years. Meanwhile the depositary holds the securities deposited with it and handles them in accordance with the terms of the agency agreement. The agent may issue certificates of deposit which may be either in bearer form or registered. Whereupon the depositary becomes, in effect, a transfer agent or registrar of those certificates.

2. *For voting trustees.* The numerous and widely scattered stockholders of a corporation may decide to commit the voting of their shares and, thereby, the control of the corporation to voting trustees, whereupon they enter a voting trust agreement and deposit their certificates of stock with the committee. For the shares so deposited the committee issues voting trust certificates.

The principal duties of the depositary of these voting trust certificates are (*a*) to receive the shares of stock, (*b*) to issue voting trust certificates, (*c*) to hold the stock in safekeeping, (*d*) to receive dividends on the deposited stock, (*e*) to distribute the dividends received as provided for in the depositary agreement, and (*f*), upon the termination of the voting trust agreement, to deliver the stock upon the surrender of the outstanding voting trust certificates.

3. *For foreign securities.* As a means of facilitating the investment of American funds in the stock of well-known and well-established foreign corporations, an American trust institution sometimes is appointed depositary of the stock of a foreign corporation. The stock is deposited with the agent. The agent, in turn, issues American depositary receipts which are negotiable and pass from hand to hand very much the same as the certificates of stock of domestic corporations. These certificates are in registered form and the registered holders receive dividends on the stock in the foreign corporation.

INSTITUTIONAL AGENCIES

Charitable and educational institutions and objects—using the term *objects* in its tax sense as explained in Chapter 10—create agencies. A distinctive type is the endowment agency.

Endowment

A charitable object—a college, a hospital, a church, for instance—may, in course of time, be in need for practically every type of agency service that is performed for individuals or for business corporations: safekeeping, custody, managing, escrow, transfer, registrar, paying, and depositary. However, there is not enough difference between these types of agencies performed for individuals and business corporations, on the one hand, and those performed for charitable and educational institutions and objects, on the other, to justify separate treatment of them. But there is one type of institutional agency, the performance of which does warrant some special treatment; this is an endowment agency. In Chapter 13, we already have defined and illustrated an institutional agency. Now, what are the duties and responsibilities of such an agency?

1. *Duties.* A hospital, for instance, finds itself the owner of endowment property—part of it general, and part, special. Its governing board and executive staff are thoroughly proficient in running the hospital, but they have had little experience in investing funds. So, the board, by proper resolution, creates an *endowment agency* with one or more trust institutions of its choice. It may create with one institution an agency for its general endowment property and with one or more others, for its special endowment property. In any case, the hospital board would have spelled out in the agency agreement the duties and responsibilities of the agent.

The agent would render the normal safekeeping and custody services. Going further, it would render such managerial services as the governing board of the hospital prescribed. If there were farms or business houses or mining, oil, or gas property in any of the endowments, the agent might be employed to manage all these kinds of property. If, as would be more likely, the property consisted of cash, stocks, and bonds, the agent would be employed to recommend the investment of cash and to analyze and review the securities and recommend changes.

In most cases the agent's function would be restricted to recommending changes in the endowment securities. However, the hospital board might authorize the agent itself to make changes, subject, of course, to the approval after the fact of the board.

In a word, the functions of the agent would be as limited or as extensive as the judgment of the governing board of the hospital desired. Perhaps there may be a tendency to give the endowment agents of charitable and educational institutions and objects more extensive managerial duties than the managing agent for an individual would have; this only because the governing board might not be as closely associated with the agent as the individual.

2. *Responsibilities.* The endowment agent, in accepting the agency, would be responsible: (*a*) for seeing that its duties were stated clearly and definitely in the agency agreement; (*b*) for exercising the same care and skill in managing endowment property as it would exercise in managing the property of an individual or of a business corporation; (*c*) for obeying the instructions of the governing board or the executive staff of the institution in all matters related to the agency; and (*d*) for making regular accountings to the institution. At all times the endowment agent must keep in mind that

it is performing an agency according to instructions and not administering a trust in the exercise of its own judgment.

It is hoped that this chapter on the performance of agencies will serve to introduce the student to the duties and responsibilities that an agent, whether an individual or a trust institution, undertakes in accepting an agency. After all, it never should be forgotten that an agent, no less than a executor, a guardian, or a trustee, is a fiduciary and is governed by fiduciary principles.

COLLATERAL READING

Note: For complete citations, see Bibliography, pp. 417–428.
ARTHUR, "Renegotiation of Agency and Custody Fees."
BECKWITH, "The Registrar—To Be or Not to Be."
CHRISTY, "The Transfer of Stock."
———, "Why Fiduciaries Should Support Model Securities Transfer Act."
CONRAD, "Simplification of Security Transfers by Fiduciaries."
STEPHENSON, "Transfer of Securities Held in Trust Accounts."
WILLIAMS, "Easing Problems of Stock Transfer."

PART III

PLANNING DISPOSITION

AND

ADMINISTRATION OF PROPERTY

In Part I we discussed the different ways by which property may be disposed of either by operation of law, as in administratorships and guardianships, or by act of the owner, as in executorships, trusteeships, and powers of appointment.

In Part II we have discussed the different persons, individual or corporate, who officiate in the disposition and administration of property as it passes from owner to receiver. As we have seen, persons who wind up and distribute the estates of deceased persons are known as *executors* or *administrators;* those who administer the property of minors and incompetent persons, as *guardians;* those who administer the property of individuals, corporations, institutions, and units of government, as *trustees;* and those who perform other services of great variety for all kinds of owners and for all kinds of property, as *agents.*

None of these dispositive devices is self-operative. None of these persons—known to us under the general name, *fiduciaries*—is a volunteer. The property owner has the privilege of selecting his own dispositive device; but, if he does not do so, the law will select one for him. He has the privilege also of selecting his own fiduciary; but, again, if he does not do so, the law, if need be, will select one for him.

The selection of his dispositive device and his fiduciary is, essentially, planning the disposition and administration of property, and commonly is called *estate planning.* No text on estates and trusts would be adequate without some discussion of estate planning.

This, then, is the relationship between Part III and the first two parts of the book.

21

Estate Planning

ALTHOUGH PLANNING the disposition and planning the administration of property are treated in this text as though they were separate activities, they are not so in fact. The two go, and ever must go, hand in hand. The property owner cannot plan the disposition of his property with one hand and the administration of that property with the other as though they were unrelated activities.

The joint and simultaneous planning of both disposition and administration of property is known as *estate planning*. It is advisable, therefore, to introduce discussion of planning the disposition and administration of property with a brief discussion of estate planning in general.

Meaning of Estate Planning

Estate planning is determining and expressing the method or methods of arranging or rearranging a person's property in order to accomplish the purpose or purposes he has in mind with respect to his property.

Estate Planning and Tax Planning Distinguished

Estate planning in general should be distinguished at once from tax planning in particular. *Tax planning* means planning the disposition and administration of property in such a way as to keep taxes at the minimum. Estate planning includes all phases of disposition and administration of property, including taxes. Tax planning, then, as will be brought out in more detail in the next chapter, is only one aspect of estate planning in general.

KINDS OF ESTATE PLANNING

There are two kinds of estate planning. One relates to an estate in process of being built; the other, to an estate already built. One involves construction; the other, reconstruction.

Future Estate

Planning a future estate may be illustrated as follows: *A* is 33 years of age; his wife, *B*, is 30; they have three children—*C*, 6; *D*, 4; *E*, 1; they expect to have several more children. *A* is a young businessman. *A* and *B* have bought and paid for their home and have taken the title to it in their joint names, so that in the event of the death of either the survivor would become the immediate and sole owner. *A* is beginning to get ahead in his business. He already has purchased some life insurance, and he is ready to purchase more. He has purchased some securities and is thinking of purchasing more. He realizes that he should make a will. Since he is in a business which is not associated in any way with investment and since his own interests do not lie in that field, he wonders whether he should not put the life insurance he already has and any additional insurance he may purchase into an insurance trust and also put into the trust the securities he already has or purchases and charge his trustee with the duty of paying the premiums. He and *B* discuss how much they should carry in a savings account to meet emergencies calling for ready cash. They discuss how much and what kinds of health or accident, as well as life, insurance he should purchase.

Most of these questions relate to property still to be acquired—that is, to a future estate. In the past, this type of estate planning has been neglected. Young husbands and wives with small children, without plan or guidance, have stumbled along during their most productive years accumulating a miscellany of property and have come to middle life with an unbalanced estate. Failure in the past to plan a future estate makes the planning of a present estate all the more difficult. In fact, the latter type of estate planning may not be able completely to undo the early mistakes that are made in not planning or in planning a future estate incorrectly.

Present Estate

1. *At middle age.* Take *A* and *B* and their family twenty years later. *A* then is 53; *B*, 50; *C*, 26; *D*, 24; *E*, 21; and *F*, *G*, and *H*, the three younger children, 18, 15, and 12 respectively. *A*, unfortunately, had not planned his estate twenty years earlier when he was just beginning to get ahead in his business. But he has succeeded in a financial and business way. At 53 he is recognized as one of the successful businessmen of the community. During the twenty-year interval he and *B* have purchased and moved into a more expensive home but one strictly in keeping with his means and increased family. He has purchased a considerable volume of life insurance represented by several policies of different amounts and under varying policy contracts—some payable in lump-sum and some left with the company under one of the options of settlement. He has acquired a considerable volume of securities—bonds and stocks in different corporations. He has purchased a summer cottage at a beach. All in all, he has accumulated what

would be regarded as a rather large estate, but it is composed of a mass of unorganized and unrelated property.

At this stage of their life, in planning their estate A and B are thinking mainly of the provisions they should make for their children. C, the oldest son, already is through school and has entered upon his own business or profession and is doing well. D, the oldest daughter, married well. E, the next daughter, is married, too, but not so well; her husband is extravagant and inclined to be a spendthrift. The future of the other three children is undetermined; they are still in school. The estate of A at 53 will be the basis of the illustrative will in Part IV of this text.

2. *At old age.* Now let another twenty years pass. A is 73; B, 70; C, 46; D, 44; E, 41; F, 38; G, 35; and H, 32. All the children are married, some well, others not so well. Grandchildren have been born and there will be more. The parents of most of $A's$ and $B's$ grandchildren will provide for them amply. $E's$ children, because of their spendthrift father, will need to be provided for specially. Estate planning now has become planning not only for A and B themselves in their own old age but also for their children and grandchildren for some of whom they wish to make special provision.

Thus, estate planning at each of the three stages of $A's$ family life and business life is a different kind of planning, although the main objective remains the same—namely, to provide for the wise and prudent disposition of the property for the accomplishment of the purposes A and B have in mind with respect to their property at each period.

PARTIES TO ESTATE PLANNING

There are, normally, six parties to estate planning, namely, the property owner, his chief beneficiary, a life insurance man, a tax man, a lawyer, and the fiduciary-to-be. Two other parties that may be included are an investment man and an accountant.

Property Owner

The property owner himself is, of course, an essential party to the estate planning process. It is his estate that is being planned. It is his family that is being provided for. His desires and purposes are the ones to be considered. The other parties should not be expected to plan his estate *for* him but only to plan his estate *with* him. This point needs to be emphasized because some property owners think that estate planning is some highly technical process to which they themselves can make only a very minor contribution.

Chief Beneficiary

The chief beneficiary for whom the estate is being planned should be a party to the planning. If the property owner is a husband-and-father, his wife, normally, should be made a party to the planning from the beginning to the end. This is so, not necessarily because she can make any substantial contribution to the property or business, legal, tax, or any other technical phase of the plan, but because she can make an invaluable and distinctive contribution to the personal side. This is a contribution which none of the other parties can make so effectively. She has, or she should have, her own ideas about her own or their children's position if her husband should die and she become the head of the family. She knows, perhaps better than he does, the characteristics of their children. If she is a party to the estate planning, she will be able to carry out the plan in spirit as well as in letter, much more so than if the plan, ready-made without her knowledge or approval, were handed to her in a sealed package—his will—after his death.

This point also is emphasized because many a husband still is disposed to plan his estate without even the knowledge, much less the assistance, of his wife. Since, under the present tax laws, the wife's property bears such a direct relation to the husband's, it has become almost a necessity for her to be called into the planning of her husband's estate. For example, he hardly would give or leave one-half of his estate to her with general power of appointment unless he was reasonably assured that she was sympathetic toward his general estate plan.

Life Insurance Man

Life insurance constitutes a substantial portion of most estates—small as well as large. None of the other parties to estate planning is, as a general rule, a specialist in life insurance. Yet the terms of life insurance policy contracts are highly technical. The estate plan as a whole may be helped or harmed materially if one rather than another mode of settlement is selected. The life insurance proceeds are to be considered not only as so much available cash, but also as to what they may mean to the general estate—in paying taxes, debts, and expenses; in providing for the immediate needs of the family; in protecting or liquidating the insured's business or business interests; and in providing income for the beneficiaries.

Tax Man

At the present time no estate large enough to be subject to gift, estate, or inheritance taxes can be planned safely or soundly without the assistance of a person who has made a study of and has up-to-date information on taxes. The next chapter is devoted to tax considerations. The only point here is that no sizable estate should be planned or replanned without the assistance of a tax specialist. Any step in planning the disposition of the property may raise the question: What will be the tax effect of this step? And there must be a party to the estate planning who is prepared to answer or to find the answer to this question.

Lawyer

A lawyer is an essential party to the effectuation of every estate plan. He is essential not only in the drafting of the will, trust agreements, and other instruments to put the plan into effect but also in advising as to the legal effect of every phase of the plan. The property owner, with the advice of the other parties to his estate plan, may decide that he would like to do things regarding his property or his beneficiaries that he cannot do lawfully. He may, for example, desire that the income from property in trust accumulate or that the trusts for his family continue longer than the law of his state permits. He may wish to do things which, although lawful in themselves, would have legal consequences which he or his other advisers had not anticipated and which he himself would not desire.

In estate planning the lawyer should be made a party not at the end but at the beginning of the process, so that he may guide the process in its development as well as help select and draw the instruments to put the plan into effect.

Fiduciary-to-be

The fiduciary-to-be, either the individual or a representative of the trust institution, is another essential party to the estate planning. So far as living trusts, insurance trusts, or agencies are concerned, he must be a party to the planning because he is a party to the agreement and has the privilege of accepting or declining the trust or agency. It is equally important that he should be a party to the planning leading up to the preparation of the will under which he or his institution is to be executor or trustee.

His distinctive contribution to the estate plan relates to the workability of the proposed provisions of the instruments that put the plan into effect. But, more than that, out of his experience he may make invaluable contributions to the plan itself. He, considering the plan as one that he will have to operate under, pays special attention to the workability of the various general-administration, investment, or distribution provisions. He pays special attention to the powers he or his institution will or may need to carry out the terms of the will or the trust. He may see pitfalls in practice, not in law, that may have escaped the other advisers. He should have an opportunity to say whether he or his institution would be willing to serve under the plan as worked out. An individual or a trust institution seldom, if ever, should be named executor or trustee under a will the contents of which he or it has not been consulted about beforehand. To name him or the institution executor or trustee without such consultation is to deprive the property owner of what may be a valuable contribution to the workability of the plan and to leave open and undecided his or the institution's willingness to serve under the plan.

Investment Counselor

The property owner's investment counselor, if he has a regular one, might not be a party to the estate planning itself, but he might have a major part in making the plan operative. The other parties to the planning might decide that his investments should be changed; but it would be an investment counselor who naturally would guide him in the making of these changes. If the counselor is called into the conference while the estate planning is in process, he may be able to make a substantial contribution, from the investment angle, to the estate plan as a whole.

Accountant

The professional accountant is coming more and more to be a recognized party in estate planning, and the other parties are coming more and more to rely upon him for guidance as to the mathematics of estate planning. The property owner's regularly employed accountant may know more about his affairs than anyone else does. He may have made the income tax returns for years. He may have made annual audits of the business. He may have been his confidential business or financial advisor. If so, his assistance may be invaluable and irreplaceable in planning the estate.

This presentation of the parties to estate planning makes estate planning appear to the property owner or any lay adviser of his to be a very formal and formidable procedure which only a courageous or desperate person would resort to. It envisions a conference table around which are seated the property owner, his wife, his life insurance adviser, his tax adviser, his lawyer, his fiduciary-to-be, and, possibly, his investment counselor, and his accountant. It would seem to contemplate not a single conference but a series of conferences during which the person's estate and the needs of his beneficiaries would be analyzed, his property fitted into a plan which best serves the needs of his beneficiaries, the necessary changes in his property provided for, and the instruments to make the plans operative drafted, gone over, put into final form, and executed.

But, in practice, estate planning is not so formal or so formidable a procedure. The process may start with any one of those advisers. He may talk first with his wife, and they decide that he should put his affairs into shape. Then he may talk with his life insurance man, his tax man, his lawyer, his investment counselor, or his accountant. Gradually and informally, each of the other parties will be brought into the process and given opportunity to make his distinctive contribution to the plan as a whole. Furthermore, the eight parties to estate planning are presented as though they, always and of necessity, were separate individuals. This is not so in practice. The lawyer, the accountant, or the life insurance man may be the tax man also. The eight are presented separately only to emphasize the number and variety of functions and talents that are requisite to sound planning of an estate.

STEPS IN ESTATE PLANNING

There are three essential steps in estate planning. One is analysis; the second is synthesis; and the third is the selection of mediums. *Analysis* means breaking a thing down into its component parts so that each part can be studied both separately and in its relation to other parts. *Synthesis* means putting these parts back together. *Selection* of mediums means choosing the means whereby the plan may be carried out.

Analysis

In estate planning analysis means two things. First, it means studying the individual and distinctive needs of each beneficiary of the estate. Second, it means studying each item of property in the estate to determine its fitness for a place in the estate plan.

1. *Beneficiaries.* In the illustration of *A's* estate planning at 33, then at 53, and finally at 73, the beneficiaries of *A's* estate would be *A, B,* their children, and their grandchildren. But there might be other individuals or there might be institutions *A* would wish to include in his estate plan. At 33. or even at 53, he might have a parent, a brother, sister, or friend for whom he would wish to provide. Or he probably would have one or more charitable institutions or objects for which he would wish to make some provision. His or *B's* personal needs would be different in their 30's, their 50's, and their 70's.

For none of these individuals, including *A* and *B* themselves, would any blanket and uniform provision serve the purpose. The situation of each individual beneficiary would have to be analyzed separately. For each of them the analyst should try to find the answer to such questions as: How much provision should be made? What kind of property? Upon what terms and conditions? When—now or at *A's* or at *B's* death?

Nor is a blanket provision likely to be the most appropriate for any of the charitable institutions or objects. Here also one analysis should be made to determine the amount and the kind of property and another to determine the amount and the kind of property and another to determine the terms and conditions that should be imposed to make the provision the most effective.

2. *Property.* Logically, analysis of the beneficiaries' needs precedes analysis of the property to determine its adequacy and its adaptability to meet those needs.

a. In the estate. It has been said that the average person's estate, unless or until it has been planned, is like piles of unrelated building material on the lot awaiting the hand of the architect and the builder to convert it into a house. Before the coming of the architect and builder, the average person's house-to-be consists of piles of lime or cement; sand; brick, stone, or timber; plumbing material; roofing material; hardware; finishing material; and wallpaper and paints. Likewise, before the coming of the estate planner and the fiduciary, the average man's estate-to-be consists of unrelated or, at any rate, unintegrated masses of real property (residential, business, agricultural; productive, unproductive); insurance (contracts with different companies with varying modes of settlement); tangible personal property (representing the accumulations of a lifetime and possibly of generations before); and stocks and bonds (in different companies; some good, some bad; some needing special and immediate attention).

b. Obligations. Analysis of the property must include also a study of the obligations that A may have—his debts, their nature, their maturity, the provision the property owner has made for paying them. Should he die, what would be the estimated shrinkage of his estate from taxes, debts, and expenses, and what provision has he made for paying them?

c. Earning power. Such analysis must include a study of his earning power, for during his lifetime this may be the most valuable asset in his estate. If he were to die and his earning power were cut off, where would that leave his estate and the provisions for his family?

d. Property outside the estate. Analysis of the property should include not only that in the estate at the time of the analysis but also outside property that may bear some relation to the estate. For example, the property owner, before he comes to have his estate planned or replanned, already may have made outright gifts or gifts in trust which might have to be taken into account in analyzing his present estate. He or his wife may be beneficiary, outright or in trust, of someone else's estate—of his or her father's, for example. They each may have a separate estate. If so, the property in his estate would have to be analyzed in the light of the property in her estate, and vice versa. He may have a power of appointment as to certain property. It may be a special power or it may be a general power. He already may have made transfers of portions of his estate for tax purposes which may have to be brought back into and made a part of his estate.

Thus, analysis of the property, as the first step in planning or replanning a person's estate, includes not only the property that he owns at the present time but also the property that his wife owns and the property that he or she may have given away in the past and the property over which either of them has a power of appointment.

Synthesis

The chemical term—*synthesis*—is used for want of a better term and as a companion term to *analysis*. It means, as already indicated, putting the property, after it has been analyzed, back together and fitting it into an estate plan that will serve the purpose the owner has in mind. As with analysis, both the beneficiaries and the property must be taken into account.

1. *Beneficiaries.* The special needs of each beneficiary must be considered. The needs of A or B at 30, at 50, or at 70 are not the same. The needs of C, the young and successful business or professional man, are not the same as the needs of D, the successfully married daughter, or of E, the unfortunately married daughter, or of F, G, or H, the younger children of the family, or of A's or B's mother or brother or sister who may be dependent upon them. Considering and providing for the special needs of each beneficiary of A's estate, including A himself, is the heart of estate planning. Failure at this point means the ultimate failure of the estate plan.

2. *Property.* Synthesis of the property may mean major changes in its composition. It may mean the sale or conversion of real property—the selling, for example, of a residence, a business house, or a farm that no longer is needed in carrying out A's estate purposes. It may mean drastic changes in his life insurance—possibly the purchase of more insurance, or the surrender of some, or the changing of the modes of settlement. It may mean the sale of some securities and the purchase of others. It may mean the conversion of A's business organization from a proprietorship or a partnership into a corporation. It may mean the purchase of insurance either by A on his own life for the benefit of his business or by A's business on the life of some key-man in the business and for the benefit of the business. It may mean a major change in A's policy regarding investments outside his business.

Synthesis takes more time than analysis. The estate planner may analyze A's estate in a comparatively short time; but it may take months or even several years to synthesize the property and fit it into the estate plan. Meanwhile, changes in A's family and in A's property will be taking place which may modify still further certain details of the estate plan.

Selection of Mediums

There are five principal mediums for disposing of property: (1) outright gifts during the owner's lifetime, (2) gifts in trust during his lifetime, (3) outright gifts by will, (4) gifts in trust by will, and (5) grant of powers of appointment either during his lifetime or at his death. The estate planner must select the mediums—there usually will be more than one medium—to accomplish the property owner's purpose or purposes.

At every stage of the property owner's life one of the mediums will be a will. The terms of his will, however, at 33 will be quite different from what those terms will be at 53 or 73. At 33, any provision he made for his children, all of whom would be minors, would be by means of a trust or a gift to his wife with a power of appointment. At 53, he might make outright gifts to some of his children, gifts in trust to others, and gifts with power of appointment to still others.

1. *Outright gifts during owner's lifetime.* At 33, the property owner hardly would consider outright gifts as an appropriate medium for disposing of his property. In the first place, he would not have enough property that early in his business life to begin to divide it. In the second place, his children would not be old enough to receive it outright. At 53, he might be disposed to make some outright gifts to his older children of whose fitness to receive property outright he was assured. For example, he might wish to make a substantial gift to *C* to help start him upon his business or profession. Or he might wish to make a substantial gift to *D* for the purchase of a home. At 73, *A* may be disposed to divide up most of his estate among his children, reserving only enough for his and *B's* requirements during their later years.

2. *Gifts in trust during owner's lifetime.* A living trust may be one of the property owner's chosen mediums for the disposition and administration of his property.

Even at 33 he might decide that it would be better to create a living trust for himself and *B* and let his trustee take over his investment responsibilities while he went on with his business. He might decide to put his life insurance in trust and let his trustee pay the premiums. At 53, he might decide that he should begin making gifts to or for his children and that as to some of them he had better make gifts in trust rather than outright. In the case of *E*, who is married to a near-spendthrift playboy, he perhaps would decide to protect any gift to her by means of a trust. At 73, having decided to dispose of most of his estate during his lifetime, *A* would make gifts in trust for those of his beneficiaries who, for some reason, *A* decided should not receive property outright.

Whether the trust should be revocable or irrevocable will depend upon the facts of each case. At 33, *A* scarcely would desire to make any living trust or insurance trust he created irrevocable; at 53, he might; at 73; he probably would. At 53, the need for flexibility would be likely to outweigh the value of tax-saving by making the trust irrevocable; at 73, the need for flexibility might have been reduced to the point where tax-saving outweighed it in importance.

3. *Outright gifts by will.* A person's will should be made, whenever it is made, as if he knew that he would die the day he made it. It would be hard for *A* at 33, at 53, or even at 73 to realize this. Planning for his beneficiaries as though he were to die the day he made his will, *A* would make outright gifts to those of his beneficiaries whom he decided should receive the property outright. He would be more likely to make outright gifts at 73 than at 53, and somewhat more likely to do so at 53 than at 33. But whether at 33, 53, or 73, the presumption should be that the gift should be outright. Or, to state it the other way, *A* should leave property outright unless there is, according to his best judgment on the best available advice, some positive reason for his not doing so.

4. *Gifts in trust by will.* If *A*'s best judgment so dictates, he should leave property in trust for those and only for those of his beneficiaries who, for some sound reason, should receive the benefits of property without being responsible for its care, and management. At 33, *A* probably would decide to leave all of his estate in trust under will—that is, to create a family trust for *B* and the children. At 53, he probably would decide to make outright gifts to some of his children and leave the bulk of his estate in trust either in a single family trust or in a separate trust for his wife and each of several of his children. At 73, *A* probably would decide to leave in trust only that portion of his estate going to beneficiaries who for some reason needed to have their share of his estate protected by a trust.

5. *Gifts with power of appointment. A* at 33, and even at 53, instead of trying to anticipate the future needs of their children himself, might decide to give or to leave property to *B* or to someone else with a special power of appointment to their children, grandchildren, sons-in-law, and daughters-in-law. Or he might decide to give one-half of his adjusted gross estate (as defined in the tax laws) to *B* with a general power of appointment. In either case, he might be influenced by tax considerations. But, aside from these considerations, there are many situations in which a gift with power of appointment is the best medium for the disposition of one's property.

Modes of Settlement of Insurance Proceeds

In none of the foregoing mediums that may be employed in putting an estate plan into effect is any emphasis placed on the kind of property involved. Still another medium may be considered: life insurance policy contracts. A large portion of the property in the estate being planned may consist of life insurance policies. So far as life insurance is concerned, a wide variety of modes of settlement offered by insurance companies offers still another medium. But it is outside the scope of this text to go further into this medium.

All of these mediums are available to the property owner at every stage of his life. One or another of them is adaptable to every amount or condition of his property or to every special need of each beneficiary. It is the function of his advisers to help him to select the mediums that will accomplish his purposes.

With this background of estate planning in general the student should be prepared to go into more detail about specific aspects of the subject.

COLLATERAL READING

Note: For complete citations, see Bibliography, pp. 417–428.
CASNER, *Estate Planning.*
MacNEILL, *Making the Most of Your Estate.*
SHATTUCK and Farr, *An Estate Planner's Handbook.*

22

Tax Considerations

$\mathfrak{A}$LTHOUGH A TEXTBOOK on estates and trusts designed for continuing use session after session cannot go into detail in discussion of federal, state, and local taxes related to estates and trusts, it must, nevertheless, include some general discussion of tax considerations in planning the disposition and administration of property.

It cannot go into detail because taxes and tax consequences are ever-changing. Any statement of tax detail might be out of date, inaccurate, and, therefore, confusing and misleading to the student by the time he came to the use of the text.

Yet it must include some general discussion of tax considerations because taxes do bear such vital relationship to the disposition and administration of property.

PLACE OF TAX CONSIDERATIONS IN PLANNING

It is the duty, as well as the privilege, of a property owner to save every dollar of taxes that he can save under the law and in good conscience. Only by each property owner's taking full advantage in good faith of every allowable tax-saving can the tax burden on all property owners ever be equalized. But this is not the kind of tax-saving that gives the most concern to property owners and their advisers in planning the disposition and administration of property. What does give these advisers concern is that some property owners make a fetish of tax-saving for its own sake.

Tax-Saving for Its Own Sake

Some property owners seem to make tax-saving their primary dispositive objective. They appear to be willing to make provisions less than the best for the needs of their beneficiaries if by doing so they can save some taxes. They seem to regard this country not as their own country but as someone else's. They approach their adviser with some such comment as this: "I want you to help me plan and arrange the disposition and administration of my property so the government (meaning the United States government) will not take all I leave." Contrast this approach with the attitude of Justice Oliver Wendell Holmes who said, "I always say that I pay my tax bills more readily than any others—for whether the money is well- or ill-spent I get civilized society for it." [1]

Saving taxes, on the one hand, and serving beneficiaries and supporting our government, on the other, are and always must be a matter of balancing. A property owner may be justified in making a different plan for the disposition and administration of his property than he otherwise would make if, by so doing, he can save taxes and yet not disserve his beneficiaries or his government. So far, so good. But when he goes further and tries to save taxes in disregard of the best interests of his beneficaries and the rightful claims of his government, he does a disservice to his beneficiaries at the expense of his government. In the words of Professor Barton Leach of the Harvard Law School, "Tax savings may prove a Pyrrhic victory if they are produced by dispositions which are unwise from the family point of view." [2]

Realizing the inadvisability as well as the impropriety of tax-saving for its own sake only, we proceed now to discuss tax considerations which should, in fact must, go into planning the disposition and administration of property.

KINDS OF TAXES TO BE CONSIDERED

There are five principal kinds of taxes which an administrator, executor, guardian, or trustee must consider. Since title to property in an agency remains in, and the tax liability rests upon, the principal, there would be little point in discussing taxes as they relate to agencies.

These five kinds of taxes to be considered are: (1) property taxes or, as commonly known, ad valorem, taxes. (2) income taxes, (3) gift taxes, (4) estate taxes, and (5) inheritance taxes.

Ad Valorem Taxes

Ad valorem taxes are the well known and almost universally imposed taxes on property based on its assessed value. They are imposed by states, by counties, by cities, by towns, by school districts, and by other taxing units. The are imposed upon real property, upon tangible personal prop-

[1] Howe, ed., *The Letters of Oliver Wendell Holmes and Harold J. Laski*, 1247.
[2] Leach, *Cases and Text on the Law of Wills*, 311.

erty, and upon cash on hand or in bank, and on other intangible personal property. The last sometimes is known as the *intangibles tax* or the *tax on intangibles* and frequently is at a different rate than that on real property and tangible personal property.

As regards these taxes, the fiduciary is under the duties to see: (1) that the property is properly and equably appraised for tax purposes; (2) that funds are available for the payment of the taxes; and (3) that they are paid and not overpaid when and as due, with advantage taken of every permissible discount.

Income Taxes

These are taxes not only upon income in the conventional sense of that term but also upon what, for tax purposes, is construed as income. There is quite a difference between the two interpretations of income. Income taxes are imposed by the federal government, by most state governments, and by some smaller taxing units.

The executor or administrator must give due consideration to at least three income-tax matters: (1) he must make the return and pay the taxes on the income for the portion of the tax year prior to the death of the deceased person; (2) he must do the same for the portion of the year after his death; and (3) he must attend to unsettled income-tax problems for prior years—these may be the most vexatious problems of all.

The guardian's income-tax considerations are substantially similar to those of any other property owner. The tax liability is that of the ward and the tax is payable out of the ward's property.

The trustee's income-tax considerations relate not only to the making of the tax returns and the paying of the taxes due, but also to the source or sources upon which to draw for funds with which to pay the taxes due.

Gift Taxes

Since 1932, the federal government has been imposing a tax on gifts made by property owners during their lifetime. It has been, and at the present time is, allowing an exemption of $30,000 worth of property and, in case of the joint gift by husband and wife, of $60,000 before the gift tax applies. In addition to this exemption, the property owner has been allowed an annual exclusion of $3,000 or, in case of a gift by both husband and wife, of $6,000, to each of as many persons to whom he or they make the gift.

Although the $30,000 or the $60,000 exemption may be spread out over any number of beneficiaries or years, once it has been consumed, it is gone forever. But the property owner can take advantage of the annual exclusion year after year and make his annual gifts to each of as many different persons as he pleases.

Thus, by taking advantage of the one exemption and the annual exclusions, the property owner alone, or the husband and wife together, can dispose of a considerable portion of his or their estate during their lifetime free of federal gift and estate taxes. Furthermore, if he or they go beyond the exemption and exclusions, the gift-tax rate has been only three-fourths that of the estate tax.

However, the gift may have been made in contemplation of death or through a trust that did not satisfy the law as to gift-tax-free gifts. In either case the property would not be subject to gift tax but would remain in the property owner's estate for estate-tax purposes. At the present time, a gift made within three years of the donor's death is presumed to have been made in contemplation of death; if earlier than that, it is presumed not to have been in contemplation of death. If the property owner, dying after September 23, 1950, had made a gift more than three years before his death, the property in that gift would not be included in his gross estate.

For state gift-tax laws the student must go to the laws of the individual states; it is impossible to generalize about them.

Estate Taxes

Estate taxes are taxes on property the passage of which is related to the death of the owner. They apply not only to property that passes on the death of the owner but also to certain property that he may have disposed of during his lifetime in a way that was related to his death; for example, a gift in contemplation of death.

The estate tax is a tax upon the property itself and not, as is an inheritance tax, on the privilege of receiving the property, that is, a privilege tax.

If an administrator's or an executor's only duties regarding estate taxes were to appraise or have the estate appraised, make the returns, and pay the taxes assessed, his work would be comparatively simple. But his task is complicated to an extraordinary degree by inclusion for estate-tax purposes of property that never passes through his hands or under his administration.

There are at least six such contingencies to which the administrator or executor must give consideration: (1) gifts or transfers in trust in contemplation of death; (2) property rights surrendered in contemplation of death; (3) property in joint ownership with right of survivorship or held as tenants by the entirety; (4) property under power of appointment; (5) life insurance; (6) gifts with a life estate reserved by the donor.

During his lifetime, a person may have made a gift which, after his death, the tax authorities decide had been made in contemplation of death. The property in that gift would be added to and become, for estate-tax purposes, a part of the deceased person's general estate. Or, what amounts to the same thing, he may have created an irrevocable living trust which, the tax authorities decide, was made in contemplation of death. That, too, would become estate-taxable as a part of his general estate. That the estate tax would be reduced by the amount paid in gift tax would lighten the tax burden on the general estate.

During his lifetime, the property owner may have transferred property in trust but reserved the right to revoke the trust. Here, again, the property in the trust would be added, for estate-tax purposes, to the general estate.

The property owner and his wife may have owned property as tenants by the entirety or as joint tenants with the right of survivorship. In either case, at his death the property would become hers outright. But if he had contributed money for the acquisition of the property, the appraised value of his contribution would be added to his estate for estate-tax purposes.

The property owner during his lifetime may have given property to his son for life with a power to appoint the property by will to his estate, his creditors, or creditors of his estate—a general power of appointment as discussed in Chapter 12. If the gift was not made in contemplation of death, the property under the power of appointment would be liable for estate tax in the son's estate.

A husband, by his will, may have left one-half of his adjusted gross estate to his wife with general power of appointment by her will, intending to take advantage of the marital deduction under the then prevailing Federal Revenue Code. But, unfortunately, the property so given consisted of terminable interests. The marital deduction would be disallowed as to these interests and the property removed from the marital deduction would become a part of his taxable estate.

The property owner may have insured his life and made the policy payable to his son. The proceeds would be a part of the father's taxable estate although it never would pass through the administrator's or executor's hands.

Thus, when an administrator or executor takes over an estate and begins to prepare the estate-tax return, he may find that he must include not only the property that he himself has taken over but also property with which he will have nothing to do except in connection with taxes.

Inheritance Taxes

Inheritance taxes are taxes imposed by the state, not the federal government, upon the distributive shares of the estate of the deceased person. In some states, they are known as *succession taxes*. Since, as already pointed out, inheritance taxes, in contrast to the estate tax, are taxes on the privilege of receiving property, unless otherwise provided by the terms of the will, the legatee receives his legacy less the inheritance tax on it and the devisee, the devise charged with the amount of the inheritance tax.

INFLUENCE OF TAX CONSEQUENCES UPON PLANNING

Apprised by his adviser of the various kinds of taxes to which his estate or the distributive shares of his estate will or may be subject and of the legitimate ways by which he can, in good conscience, avoid or reduce some or all of them, the property owner comes next to the point of balancing the advantages and the disadvantages of one or another kind of tax-avoidance or tax-reduction. As to each item of possible tax-saving he must set his adviser and himself the question: Will the adjustment of my estate plan so as to obtain these tax-savings be at the great sacrifice on the part of my beneficiaries?

Ad Valorem Taxes

Ad valorem taxes will have little influence one way or the other upon planning the disposition and administration of the property. If the owner gives property outright during his lifetime, the person to whom he gives it will become liable for all future ad valorem taxes on it. If he gives it outright by will, his general estate will be liable for the tax only during the executor's year, and thereafter the devisee or legatee will become liable. If he leaves it in trust under agreement or will, the income of the trust property will be liable primarily for the taxes. So these taxes will not influence the planning of the estate one way or the other.

Income Taxes

Income-tax avoidance or reduction frequently has a major influence upon an estate plan. Take a few examples from the income-tax law as it stands at the present time and has stood for some years.

The property owner by making outright gifts during his lifetime forthwith shifts the income-tax liability from himself to the person to whom he makes the gift.

If he makes an irrevocable gift in trust, he may, according to the terms of the trust, shift the income-tax liability to the trust or to the beneficiary. If the income is not distributed or is not distributable, it is taxable to the trust. If it is distributed or is distributable, ordinarily it is taxable to the beneficiary. But, although the trust is irrevocable, the property owner may have reserved such rights as to leave him substantially the owner of the property, in which case the income would be taxable to him.

Under the law in effect at the present time, a property owner can shift the income-tax liability from himself to the beneficiary or to the trust by making the trust irrevocable, not for all time, but for a stated period of time—not over ten years in some cases and not over fifteen in others.

These general statements about federal income-tax liability are subject to many limitations and refinements. The student must not accept them as complete statements of income-tax law prevailing at any future time or as prevailing at all except as modified or refined. They are given only to illustrate the fact that a property owner can, at the present time at any rate, reduce his own federal income taxes by making outright gifts or by creating irrevocable trusts for his lifetime or for not over the ten or fifteen years. By splitting the income in two, he may put each part into a lower tax-bracket and thereby reduce the over-all income-tax liability.

Gift Taxes

As already pointed out, at the present time a property owner alone can give $30,000, or a husband and wife $60,000, worth of property all in one year and all to one person or spread out over any number of years and among any number of persons without the property so given being subject to either federal gift tax or, after his death, to federal estate tax. In addition to this exemption, the owner alone can give $3,000, or a husband and wife together $6,000, a year to as many different persons as he or they please without the gifts being subject to gift or estate taxes. Take, for example, a husband, wife, and six children. The first tax year they can give to their children a total of $96,000; that is, the whole $60,000 exemption and the six $6,000 exclusions. Thereafter, so long as the law remains as it is now, they can give $36,000 a year—$6,000 to each of the six children—as long as they live. Furthermore, recent legislation permitting the transfer of stock to or by a custodian for a minor makes it easy to make gifts to children without the appointment of a guardian to transfer the stock.

So much for the tax-saving privilege. The following questions will arise in the mind of the property owner: Is the tax-saving worth the cost to my children and myself? In making these gifts and saving these taxes, may I be disfurnishing myself? Will I be running the risk of disserving my children by making these gifts to them during this stage of their life? May I not serve myself and my children better by keeping this property in my estate and paying the estate tax at my death?

Gift-tax saving has its disadvantages as well as its advantages, and the two must be balanced against each other.

Estate Taxes

As just stated, property given during the owner's lifetime may be freed of federal estate taxes. More than that, under the law in effect since 1948, a husband by his will can give up to one-half of his *adjusted gross estate* (a highly technical tax term which, at the present time, means substantially the gross estate less debts and expenses, but before taxes), and this one-half or part thereof will be removed from his estate for federal estate-tax purposes. Likewise, a wife can give her husband up to one-half of her adjusted gross estate with similar tax consequences.

But this apparent and alluring tax-saving may turn out to be what Professor Leach would call a Pyrrhic victory. While the property so left to the wife would be removed from his estate for estate-tax purposes, it would be added to hers. If they were near the same age, and if she had a substantial estate of her own, adding his one-half to her whole estate might result in an increase of the over-all estate-tax liability of the husband and wife.

Considered from another angle, the property owner may doubt the wisdom of giving his wife complete dominion over one-half of his estate. Yet he must do so if he is to experience this estate-tax saving. If he leaves her one-half in trust, as he may do, he must provide for her to receive all of the income annually to do with as she pleases. He can give the trustee power to consume principal, in addition to income, to meet her needs. He can give her the right to call for principal, in addition to income. He can give her the right to dispose of her one-half or any part of it during her lifetime. Or he can postpone her right to dispose of the principal until her death. But, if the marital-deduction tax-saving in his estate is to be effective, he must give her the right by deed during her lifetime or by will at her death to dispose of the property just as she pleases. Only in case she should fail effectively to dispose of it would he have any right to do so.

Since, in order for him to obtain the estate-tax saving by taking advantage of the marital deduction, he must give his wife complete dominion over what he gives her up to one-half of his adjusted gross estate, he may not be willing to go that far. He may decide that it might cost him more than it would be worth in tax-saving. He may reason that, if she should remarry, she might pass on what he had left her to a second husband or to her children by a second marriage and thereby disinherit his and her children.

As soon as the marital-deduction privilege became available after 1948, property owners and their advisers proceeded eagerly to take advantage of the estate-tax saving under the new law. But, as the years have passed, they have come to realize that there are disadvantages as well as advantges and that in many cases it will be better for all concerned for the property owner to assume the full estate-tax burden than to divide it with his wife—or she with him—and thereby run the risk of disserving the persons for whom he, or she, was planning the disposition and administration of the property.

Inheritance Taxes

By making gifts during his lifetime the property owner can save inheritance taxes on gifts under his will. By the terms of his will, as will be discussed later, he can shift the inheritance-tax burden from the respective gifts to his residuary estate and, thus, provide for his legatees and devisees to receive their gifts free of inheritance taxes.

But throwing the entire inheritance-tax load onto the residuary estate may be putting too great a burden on the part of his estate designed to take care of his family.

Although in large estates the inheritance taxes are, as a rule, considerably less than the federal estate tax, they, too, may influence the planning of the estate. The property owner may find it to the advantage or the disadvantage of his beneficiaries to place the inheritance-tax burden on the respective gifts or on the residuary estate.

It is apparent that tax consequences must be considered in planning an estate and that the property owner will be influenced one way or another by them.

PLACING THE TAX BURDEN

The tax consideration next in importance after tax-avoidance and tax-reduction, and in some cases even more important, is that of placing the tax burden. Who is to pay which taxes? The estate plan may be put awry by placing or misplacing the tax burden. This applies particularly to estate and inheritance taxes. The ad valorem tax burden goes with the property. The gift-tax burden rests primarily on the giver, with the property given or the one receiving it secondarily liable. But the estate-tax and the inheritance-tax burdens may be shifted from one to another part of the estate in a way that will affect the estate plan as a whole.

Estate Taxes

According to the terms of the will, the federal estate tax may be imposed upon the residuary estate, where it normally rests any way unless otherwise provided; it may be apportioned among all the gifts under the will, including the residuary estate; or it may be apportioned among the general or specific legacies and devises, the residuary estate, and the estate-taxable property disposed of during the owner's lifetime by outright gift or gift in trust.

1. *Imposed upon residuary estate.* The property owner can provide that all federal estate taxes shall be paid out of the residuary estate. This would mean that not only the estate tax imposed upon property in the general estate but also the estate tax on property that had passed during the owner's lifetime would be paid out of the residuary estate. Suppose, for example, he had made large gifts, over and above his one exemption and his annual exclusions, and that later they were held to have been made in contemplation of death and the property in the gifts taxable as a part of his general estate. Or suppose he had created one or more living trusts, the prop-

erty in which was held to be estate-taxable. Or suppose he had failed to qualify what he had left his wife for the marital deduction. Then, suppose he had intended that his residuary estate be the main source of support of his family and schooling of his children. To impose the entire tax burden—both that on the estate and that on property disposed of during his lifetime— might prove to be such a load as practically to disinherit his family. Thus, to impose the entire estate-tax burden upon the residuary estate may be more of a disservice to the beneficiaries than his failure to take advantage of the permissible tax-saving would be.

2. *Apportioned among gifts under will.* As already stated, the inheritance-tax burden naturally falls upon the respective gifts under the will. But it is possible for the property owner to provide by his will that the estate tax be apportioned among the respective gifts. This would mean that his general and specific legacies and devises and his residuary legacy and devise each would bear its proportionate part of the over-all estate tax. If, however, he failed to provide in his will and in his trust agreement that each gift made during his lifetime found later to be estate-taxable should bear its proportionate part of the estate tax, he might impose upon his general and specific legacies and devises an estate-tax burden that might defeat his desires with respect to those gifts.

Under recent statutes of several states, the federal estate tax is apportioned among the gifts under the will unless the will itself otherwise provides. This implies that in most cases apportionment is thought to be advisable. But without such a statute, the property owner must decide for himself whether he will or will not apportion the estate tax among the gifts under his will.

3. *Apportioned among general estate and taxable gifts during lifetime.* The property owner, let us say, during his lifetime makes several substantial outright gifts or gifts in trust which after his death are held to be estate-taxable. Should the entire estate-tax burden be imposed upon the residuary estate, it might prove to be such a tax burden as practically to wipe out the part of the estate designed for the support of the family and schooling of the children.

Inheritance Taxes

Since an inheritance tax is a tax, not upon the property, but upon the privilege of receiving the property, the tax burden naturally falls upon the person who receives it. But the property owner may want him to take the property free of inheritance tax. Accordingly, he may impose the tax upon the residuary estate or upon specified property. If he imposes it upon the residuary estate, he may do a disservice to the residuary beneficiaries who most likely would be members of his family.

Thus, whatever the kind of taxes, the placing of the tax burden becomes one of the major considerations in planning the estate.

TAX PROVISIONS

Most of the provisions of wills and trust agreements which really are designed to save taxes make no mention whatever of taxes. The provision itself has the tax consequence without any tax reference.

There are other provisions which do mention taxes that are designed to place the tax burden or to specify the source of funds for the payment of taxes.

This latter group of provisions of wills and trust agreements ranks in importance with other dispositive and administrative provisions. Without trespassing upon the field of the draftsman by suggesting the wording of these tax provisions, we may suggest some of the points about taxes that should be considered in drafting the will or trust agreement. The student will find suggested wording of these tax provisions in the author's *Drafting Wills and Trust Agreements—Administrative Provisions*, Chapter 8.

Some of these tax provisions relate principally to executors; others, to trustees; and still others, to the tax relationships between executors and trustees.

Applicable to Executor

1. *Paying inheritance taxes out of residuary estate.* The will should state whether inheritance taxes should be paid out of the respective legacies and devises or out of the residuary estate. We already have discussed the possible consequences of placing the tax burden one way or the other.

2. *Paying inheritance taxes on remainder interests.* The property owner may leave real property to *A* for life, remainder to *B*. *A's* life estate and *B's* remainder each will be liable for inheritance tax. *B* may not have an independent estate out of which to pay his tax. The will very well may provide for the payment of the tax on his remainder interest.

3. *Apportioning estate taxes.* If the point is not covered by the will, in most states the federal tax would be paid out of the residuary estate; in some states, as already pointed out, by recent legislation it would be apportioned unless otherwise provided. The will should, by all means, say whether it should be apportioned or paid out of the residuary estate.

4. *Designating property for tax funds.* The property owner may want certain, specified property to bear the tax burden to the relief of other property. If so, he should specify the property, being aware, of course, that if it could not bear the entire tax burden, the rest of the property in the estate would be liable for the deficiency.

5. *Relieving certain gifts of taxes.* The property owner may want to

relieve certain property of taxes, for example, a legacy to an indigent person. If so, he should provide for the relief of that property from taxes.

6. *Postponing settlement of estate.* In a large and complicated estate it may take more than the conventional executor's year to adjust and settle all of the tax claims and problems. It may be advisable, therefore, to give the executor some specified extension of time to attend to these tax matters.

7. *Withholding funds from distribution.* While the estate is being settled and distributed, there still may be unsettled tax problems. Instead of withholding all distribution until these problems are solved, it may be advisable for the executor to make a partial distribution, retaining enough funds to settle the tax claims. If so, the executor should have express power to make partial distribution and withhold sufficient funds for taxes.

Applicable to Trustee

The following are tax provisions especially applicable to trustees.

1. *Paying taxes out of income.* The general rule is that regularly recurring taxes, such as ad valorem and income, should be paid out of income. To put to rest any question about the matter, it may be advisable to provide in the will that they shall be paid out of income.

2. *Paying estate and inheritance taxes out of principal.* The general rule is that estate and inheritance taxes are payable out of principal. Again, it may put to rest any question about the matter by saying that the current income shall be freed of any obligation to contribute to these taxes.

3. *Apportioning taxes between income and principal.* In some cases, there may be doubt as to whether a given tax should be paid all out of income or all out of principal or apportioned between them. It may be helpful to the trustee and to the beneficiaries, as well, for the will or trust agreement to give the trustee the power to apportion.

4. *Advancing funds for taxes.* The beneficiary may not have the funds with which to pay the inheritance tax or the part of the estate tax imposed upon his legacy or devise. It may be advisable to give the trustee power to advance funds for such purpose without its interfering with the regular payments to the beneficiary.

5. *Contributing to beneficiary's estate tax.* Suppose the death of a beneficiary gives rise to taxes which the property owner desires the trustee, rather than the beneficiary's estate, to pay. If so, the trustee should be authorized to pay over to the beneficiary's estate the amount of the tax imposed by reason of his death.

6. *Designating how taxes on certain property be paid.* Suppose the property owner desires that the taxes on certain property should be paid out of other property, for example, that household goods and personal effects be received tax-free. He may say that taxes on all such property shall be paid out of the residuary estate or out of other specified property.

7. *Directing how certain property shall be treated for tax purposes.* Income for tax purposes may be quite different from income as commonly understood. The property owner has the privilege of saying in his will or trust agreement whether certain property—such as stock dividends—shall be treated as income or as principal for tax purposes.

8. *Relieving certain property of taxes.* The property owner may desire that certain property—the family home and its contents, for example,—shall be relieved of all taxes. Or, on the contrary, he may want the devisee of a life estate in real property to take subject to inheritance tax and possibly to its share of the estate tax.

9. *Setting up reserves for taxes.* The trustee should have specific, not merely implied or incidental, power to set up reserves for taxes chargeable to income. Else, importunate beneficiaries may insist upon receiving all of the income as soon as received by the trustee and question its power to withhold funds for regular, anticipated tax payments.

Tax Relationships between Executor and Trustee

Among the most important tax provisions of wills and trust agreements are those related to the relationships between the executor and the trustee. There are six such provisions that merit special consideration.

1. *Purchases and loans for tax purposes.* Where the property owner creates a living trust or an insurance trust, it usually is advisable for him to give the trustee power to make purchases from or loans to the executor under his will and to give the executor power to make sales to and obtain loans from the trustee as a means of raising funds for tax purposes without the sacrifice sale of securities in the estate. Since the beneficiaries of the trust and those under the will usually are the same persons—members of the property owner's family—it makes little difference to them whether given property is in the trust under agreement or the one under will.

2. *General estate bearing all estate and inheritance taxes including those of trust estate.* If the living-trust estate should turn out to be estate-taxable, and if the property owner wishes his general estate to bear the entire tax burden including that on his trust estate, he should say so in clear and unmistakable terms.

3. *Trust estate bearing all estate and inheritance taxes including those on general estate.* The property owner may decide to create a living trust or insurance trust and have it pay all of the estate and inheritance taxes, whether imposed on the trust estate or the general estate. This arrangement may be advisable where the general estate consists largely of nonliquid assets, for example, a large farming or manufacturing operation.

4. *Trust estate reimbursing general estate for amount paid out in taxes on trust estate.* Suppose the living-trust estate is held to be estate-taxable. The property owner may provide for his executor to pay out of the general

estate all taxes, including those on the living-trust estate, and then say that the trust estate shall reimburse the general estate for all taxes attributable to the trust estate.

5. *Trust estate making up deficiency.* The property owner may wish that the living-trust estate be called upon for any estate or inheritance taxes only after all of the assets in the general estate have been exhausted and then only for the deficiency.

6. *Apportioning taxes between trust estate and general estate.* The property owner may *direct* that his living-trust estate and his general estate each shall bear its proportionate part of the taxes, in which case it would have to be done. Or he may *authorize* apportionment and leave it to the trustee and the executor—who usually would be the same individual or trust institution—to apportion or not as seemed best for the beneficiaries.

An unusual and unexpected problem of apportionment may arise in connection with powers of appointment. A property owner, by releasing his power of appointment, may shift the tax burden; or he may give his wife one-half of his estate, expecting to take full advantage of the marital deduction and give her a general power of appointment over her half. She may fail to exercise the power and thereby leave the property to pass as he had directed in the event of her failure effectively to exercise the power. This conceivably might throw the estate-tax burden arising from the unappointed property back into his estate. This, however, seems not to be the law at the present time. Having such a possibility in mind, the property owner may be advised to provide for the apportionment of the taxes including those on the unappointed property.

This chapter probably has convinced the student as the writing of it has convinced the author anew that in planning an estate tax considerations involve infinitely more than the drafting of wills and trust agreements that will result in tax-saving. Of equal importance is including in those instruments provisions that will place the tax burden so as to render the least disservice to the beneficiaries.

COLLATERAL READING

Note: For complete citations, see Bibliography, pp. 417–428.
CASNER, *Estate Planning.*
SHATTUCK and Farr, *An Estate Planner's Handbook,* Ch. 8.
STEPHENSON, *Drafting Wills and Trust Agreements,* Vol. I, Ch. 8.

23

Planning Disposition
of Property

LET US ASSUME that the property owner, upon the advice of a tax specialist, desires to take full advantage of every legitimate tax-saving short of
letting it result in any real disservice to his beneficiaries and that, as between
saving taxes and serving his beneficiaries, serving his beneficiaries comes first.
He is ready now to settle down to planning the disposition of his property.
This he must do step by step. A "package" disposition of property—as "all
to my wife" or "all to my husband"—usually is evidence of an unplanned
estate. In what order, then, should the property owner consider the disposition of his estate?

PROVISION FOR FAMILY OR DEPENDENTS

One of the first questions that the estate-planning adviser should put to
the property owner is: What provision have you made or do you wish now
to make for the living expenses of the members of your family or other dependents during the period your estate will be in process of settlement and
distribution, which may be a year or more? If the property owner is a family man, and he has already made ample provision for his family during this
period, if his wife has an independent estate ample for this purpose, or if he
already has made ample provision for his dependents—parents, brother, sister, other relative or friend—this matter need not be pursued any further.
But if he has not done so, then provision for their living expenses during the
period his estate will be in process of settlement becomes an important step
in planning his estate. The following are some of the ways that may be suggested to him.

Deposit in Bank

The property owner may carry a joint bank account, checking or savings, with his wife having the right to draw immediately upon the account. But before he commits himself to this plan, he should be assured that this bank balance will, in fact, be immediately available to the survivor. Is there any real likelihood that the availability of this fund may be delayed for any reason, for taxes or some other thing? If so, some other source of funds for immediate needs of the family should be provided.

Transfer of Securities

The property owner can have enough securities issued or transferred to his wife for the income from them to meet the immediate needs of herself and their children. It is not uncommon for property owners to have stock issued or transferred to husband and wife "as joint owners with right of survivorship," with the understanding that whoever dies first the survivor will become the sole owner of the securities. Again, as in the case of joint bank accounts, tax problems may cause delay in the availability of the income or principal of these securities for immediate family needs.

Life Insurance

The property owner can have enough of his life insurance proceeds made payable to his wife in lump sum or left with the company under one of its options of settlement to supply the immediate needs of herself and their children or other dependents. If he already has adequate insurance for this purpose or still is insurable, this is a sure way of providing for his family during this period.

Living Trust

Another sure way is to create a living trust or an insurance trust and direct the trustee to begin making payments to his wife or his named dependents, his mother, for example, immediately following his death. If it is an insurance trust, then, upon the collection of the proceeds, funds will be available for these immediate needs.

These are only a few of the ways by which a property owner can provide for the immediate needs of his family or other dependents. Once the matter is called pointedly to his attention and its importance emphasized, he and his adviser can find a way to provide for immediate needs. The student himself may think of other ways. The only point here is that it is a matter that should be attended to in working out the estate plan.

HOUSEHOLD GOODS AND PERSONAL EFFECTS

Every property owner has a smaller or larger amount and variety of household goods and personal effects. The importance of disposing of them in the proper way may be out of proportion to their money value. The husband may be disposed to give these items to his wife; or she, to give them to him. But suppose they were killed in a common accident. The disposition may be to leave them to their children.

There are three things about the disposition of household goods and personal effects that deserve special consideration. One is to prevent a public sale of them; another, to prevent any disagreement over them; and last, to keep them out of trust.

Public Sale

In the settlement of an estate there is nothing more harrowing to the feelings of the surviving members of the family and other kinspeople and friends or more embarrassing to the administrator or executor than a public sale by auction of the household goods and personal effects of the deceased person. Yet this may have to be unless it is provided against in a will covering that point.

Disagreement

Where both parents are dead and the household goods and personal effects pass to their children, there always is the possibility that disagreements may develop among them over certain items. A single item of little monetary value—a piece of antique furniture, a portrait, a family album—may give rise to more disagreement among the members of the family than all the rest of the estate.

Trust

Household goods and personal effects are not adapted to trust administration and, if it is possible, they should be kept out of trust. As a trust asset, unless they are antiques, they may have little monetary value. The trustee may be scarcely more than a safekeeper over a number of years. Meanwhile, the property may deteriorate in substance.

In Form I in Part IV (the illustrative will) the author has endeavored to design a provision for the disposition of household goods and personal effects that will prevent a public sale, provide for settlement of disagreements, and keep the property out of trust.

FAMILY HOME

Next after disposition of household goods and personal effects comes consideration of provision of a home for the family. This matter is dealt with in any one of several ways, most of which have disadvantages as well as advantages.

Title in Wife

Sometimes a husband will put the title to their residence in his wife's name. This may be meant as a compliment to her, or it may mean an attempt to protect it against the claims of creditors in the event he should get into financial straits. One disadvantage of this arrangement is that, if she should die first, and without a will, he might find himself only a life tenant of the family residence. If she should outlive him, the residence might not be well adapted to their family needs after his death.

Title in Joint Names

A much more common arrangement is to have the title to their residence in their joint names with right of survivorship. In those states which still have tenancy by the entirety, a conveyance to a husband and wife, without more, makes them tenants by the entirety and upon the death of either the title passes to the survivor. In those states which do not have tenancy by the entirety, a husband and wife may take title to their residence, or any other real property, "as joint tenants with right of survivorship," under which, as in the case of tenancy by the entirety, upon the death of either the title passes to the survivor.

Among the possible disadvantages of tenancy by the entirety or joint tenancy with right of survivorship as regards the family residence, is the one that the house, the grounds, the location, the cost of upkeep, and many other things may make it ill adapted to the needs of the family. In fact, it may constitute a substantial portion of the deceased person's entire estate, and the cost of upkeep may be out of proportion to the family income.

Life Estate and Remainder

If the property owner dies without a will, in all likelihood his widow, by reason of her right of dower or substitute for dower, may find herself a life tenant of the residence with remainder to her children at her death. And not a few husbands-and-fathers who do leave a valid will wish to make sure that after the wife-and-mother's death, their children will receive the residence; so they leave her as a life tenant, remainder to their children.

The disadvantage of this arrangement is that in course of time this residence may become ill adapted to the family needs and an advantageous sale difficult to accomplish. Suppose disagreement over the sale should develop among the children. Suppose one or more of the children should have died with issue surviving who would have their deceased parent's interest in the property. The wife-and-mother, even though she had the funds, might hesitate to spend money for the upkeep of the property, for, she would reason, she had only a life estate in the property. The children, even though there was no disagreement among them, might hesitate, even if they had the funds, to make the improvements, for none of them would know how long their mother might live or which of the children would want and be willing to pay a reasonable price for the other children's interest in the residence at her death.

In most cases, the disposition of the family home through a life estate in the widow, remainder to the children, is an inadvisable arrangement.

In Trust

Although the wife-and-mother may be reluctant, when this step is reached in planning the disposition of the estate, to have the residence left her in trust, instead of outright, she may come to understand that a flexible trust with broad rights in her and powers in the trustee may, in fact, give her far more freedom of action with respect to the family home than an outright devise to her for life or even in fee simple would give her.

Again, in the illustrative will in Part IV, in the case of the disposition of household goods and personal effects, the author has endeavored to suggest a family-home provision that will enable the trustee to serve ever-changing needs of the widow-and-mother and her children.

GENERAL LEGACIES

After the property owner, if he is a family man, has provided for the needs of his family while his estate will be in process of settlement, for the disposition of his household goods and personal effects, and for a home for his widow and children, he probably will give attention to certain specific or general legacies he wishes to make to collateral kinspeople, to employees, to friends, and to charitable objects.

As to specific legacies or devises, the main point for him to decide and record in his will is: if the legatee or devisee should predecease him, would he want his gift to lapse or would he want it to go to some other named individual, to some charitable object, or would he want it to fall back into his residuary estate? Under the laws of most states a specific legacy or devise to the property owner's own child would not lapse but would go to the child's issue. Although the draftsman would know about this, the property owner himself should decide about the lapsing or nonlapsing of the gift.

Fractional Gifts

The general legacies, particularly the pecuniary legacies, require special attention in planning the estate. If the estate is comparatively large and the general legacies comparatively small—a few hundred or thousand dollars out of an estate amounting to hundreds of thousands or millions—these gifts need give no trouble. But suppose the gifts are comparatively large and the estate comparatively small, and that the property owner plans to provide for his family through his residuary estate. Suppose, for example, the estimated present value of his estate is $500,000 and that he proposes to distribute one-half of it in general and specific legacies and devises and to retain the other half in his residuary estate for his family, figuring that $250,000 will be ample for his widow and children. Then suppose that he dies during a period of economic depression when his $500,000 estate has depreciated to half that amount. In that case, while his specific and general legacies would be paid in full, his residuary estate would be exhausted and his own family disinherited. His wife might dissent from his will and take her share under the law. Even then the children would be left unprovided for. This is not, by any means, a farfetched illustration. During the depression of the early 1930's, some of the best of the stocks listed on the stock exchanges depreciated to one-tenth of their predepression market value resulting in this sort of situation.

The possibility of disinheriting or disfurnishing one's own family by disposing of too large a proportion of the estate in legacies and devises can be obviated by making the gifts in fractions or percentages of the net estate instead of in stated amounts. The man with the $500,000 estate, by present market values, wishing to distribute one-half in gifts to collateral kinspeople, employees, friends, and charitable objects, can leave one-half of his net estate, whatever that may amount to at his death, to these persons and objects and keep the other half in his residuary estate for his family. Then, if his estate should depreciate to $250,000, he still would have $125,000 left for his family.

If the property owner desires to provide for his family through his residuary estate and, if, at the same time, he wishes to make substantial legacies and devises to other persons or objects, it is highly important that his legacies be stated in fractions or percentages and not in dollar amounts.

PROVISION FOR MEMBERS OF FAMILY

After he has made these gifts to other persons than members of his immediate family, the property owner will turn his attention to provision for members of his immediate family—his wife, his children, and, possibly, his grandchildren.

Already we have discussed his provision for his family's living expenses during the executor's year, for the disposition of his household goods and personal effects, and for a home for them. They have the family home and its contents and funds for living expenses all the while the estate is being settled. So far, so good. But how should he provide for the members of his family after his estate has been settled and his property distributed? It may be well to discuss his provisions for the widow, the children, and the grandchildren separately.

Widow

The property owner can provide for his widow in one or more of the following ways: (1) by creating for her an independent estate, (2) by creating for her a marital trust, or (3) by making her a beneficiary of a family trust.

1. *Independent estate.* During their lifetime together, he can have property—stocks, bonds, real property—passed directly to her so that she becomes the absolute, outright owner of the property. Or, what may be more likely, he may have stock registered in their joint names with right of survivorship so that, upon his death, she will become the absolute owner. In the community-property states of the West and Southwest one-half of the property they accumulated during their married life which is still in their ownership at the time of his death would become hers by operation of law and thus she would be provided for.

2. *Marital trust.* The term *marital trust* in recent years has come to have, almost exclusively, a tax connotation. But now we are using the term to describe any trust that a husband creates for his wife, or a wife for her husband. Such a trust may be either a living trust or a trust under will.

a. Living trust. It is not at all uncommon for a husband to create a living trust and put into it property sufficient for the needs of his wife both during her lifetime and after his death. As pointed out earlier in this chapter, payments of income, of principal, or of both out of this trust may provide her living expenses while the estate is in process of settlement. Unless this trust was created in fraud of creditors, the trust would stand even though the property owner's general estate should turn out to be insolvent.

b. Under will. As pointed out in the preceding chapter, the property owner can leave in trust for his wife up to one-half of his adjusted gross estate without the property in this trust being subject to federal estate tax in his estate; but whatever is left of it will be subject to estate tax on her estate, added to and made a part of her own estate-taxable estate. But even where tax consequences may not be a point of serious consideration, the property owner, nevertheless, may desire to create under his will a separate trust for his wife. He may give her a special or general power of appointment over the property in her trust, or he himself may say how what is left of the property shall go after her death.

c. Remarriage. In his trust for her, whether living or under will, he may or may not provide that, upon her remarriage, the trust shall terminate or, if continued, that her benefits under the trust shall be diminished. However, in making any remarriage provision, he should be informed that, if his wife should be displeased with the provision for her, she might dissent from his will and take her share under the law. To the husband conscious of remarriage it is well to say that if he wants his wife to abide by and not dissent from his will, he had better leave her under his will more than she would get if she dissented from it.

3. *Family trust.* Instead of creating during his lifetime or under his will a separate trust for his wife, he may create a family trust of which she is one of the beneficiaries. Or, even though he has created a separate trust for her—even one to take full advantage of the marital deduction under the current tax laws—he still may wish to leave his residuary estate in a family trust and make her one of the beneficiaries. In doing so, he may provide for her to receive for herself a stated amount or percentage of the income or principal for her own use, or he may provide for her to receive all of the income "for the support of herself and the support and schooling of the children," as the provision frequently is worded.

Certainly in one or another or even in a combination of these ways, if the estate is large enough, the property owner can provide adequately for his wife during his lifetime and for her as his widow after his death.

Children

In much the same way as in providing for his wife, the property owner can provide for his children by outright gifts during his lifetime or under his will, by separate trusts, living or under will, for each of them, or by a family trust in which each of them is a beneficiary.

1. *Outright gifts.* As pointed out in the preceding chapter there may be tax advantages in making outright gifts to each of his children during his lifetime. But, tax consequences aside, he may prefer to make outright gifts to them under his will. Unless a given child lacks one of the elements essential to the management of property—namely, physical capacity, mental competency, providence, maturity, experience, interest, and prudence—the presumption should be in favor of an outright gift rather than a gift in trust.

2. *Separate trusts.* In a given family, some of the children, for some sound reason, should receive their share of the parent's estate outright while others should receive their share in trust. Those children who possess all of the elements essential to the management of property, as outlined in the preceding paragraph, should receive their share outright; while those who lack one of these elements should receive their share in trust. The son who already is a successful businessman or professional man, the daughter who

already is well married to a successful man, the daughter who is married to a spendthrift playboy, the daughter who is a victim of polio, the son or daughter who still is in school—each of these should be considered separately as to its needs on its own merits in deciding between outright gifts or gifts in trust and, if in trust, the duration and terms of the trust.

a. Duration of trust. This leaves us face-to-face with an unanswerable question: How long should a trust for a child continue? The easy answer is: as long and only as long as the child lacks any of the abovementioned elements essential to the proper care and management of property. But this is one of those general answers that is not very helpful in everyday trust administration. In Chapter 6, on trusts under will, we have discussed the different ages and conditions determining the termination of trusts for children; and it will be well for the student now to turn back and reread that section of that chapter in the light of its place in planning the disposition of property.

3. *Family trusts.* It is quite the common practice now, immediately following the marital trust under will, to leave the residue in trust for the family, and happily, the common name for them is "family trusts." In planning for these family trusts numerous questions will arise which will have to be answered before the estate plan can be completed, among them: (1) Shall all of the income be paid to the widow for herself and the children? (2) Shall she be required to account to the trustee for the way she expends payments to her as between herself and the children? (3) Must each of the children receive the same share of the payments? (4) Should principal, in addition to income, be paid to, or applied for, the members of the family?

a. All income to widow. In the normal case, when the widow is frugal and economical and the children are minors, all the income is paid to her and she uses it as her own judgment dictates as between herself and the children and as among the children themselves. This would seem to be the ideal arrangement. However, it might be upset by her remarriage, so it might be advisable to make some other arrangement in the event of her remarriage. Then, too, there might be undesirable tax consequences of having all of the income paid to her. Suppose she, herself, had a substantial independent estate; suppose she was the sole beneficiary of a marital trust; then suppose, in addition to all the income from these other two sources, she received all of the income from the family trust. That might cast too heavy an income-tax burden upon her. Consequently, tax considerations have led many persons leaving substantial estates to provide under the family trust that the widow and each of the children should be a separate beneficiary and, therefore, a separate income-tax payer.

b. Accounting by widow. Should the widow-and-mother be required to account to the trustee for the way she divides payments of income or of principal to her as between herself and children? It is regarded generally as being highly inadvisable to require any such accounting by her. If she cannot be trusted to do right for herself and her own children, a separate trust should be created for her and for each child. Besides, should there ever be flagrant abuse by the widow-and-mother regarding making all the payments to her and her using them for herself to the neglect of her children, the court of equity, when and if called upon by the children, would intervene and see that she did right by her children. To require her to make accountings to the trustee may cast an undue burden upon her and may embarrass the trustee.

c. Equalization of children's shares. It is possible, of course, to provide that each child shall receive an equal share of the income and ultimately of the principal of the family trust. This means that the widow-and-mother would have to keep books and account for each overpayment of income or principal to a given child. If this is what the husband-and-father really desires, he had better create a separate trust each for his widow and for each of his children.

The inadvisability of this plan has led to what commonly has come to be called a "sprinkling" family trust. This means simply that the income or the principal shall be applied for each child, not equally, but according to his needs. In view of the ever-changing needs of children as they advance in years, the sprinkling trust is the best, if not the only, arrangement whereby the trustee or the mother can do what is best for the child as an individual and for the family of which the child is a member at every stage of administration of the trust and development of the children.

d. Consumption of principal. Within the past half-century there has been a major change in the attitude of estate-planning specialists and, upon their advice, in that of property owners themselves toward the consumption of principal, in addition to income, for immediate beneficiaries, that is, in many cases for members of the family. In 1896, when Augustus Peabody Loring's *A Trustee's Handbook* was published, the presumption was that the principal of a trust should be preserved and held intact at almost all hazards. In 1944, forty-eight years later, when the author of this text made and published a study, *The Preferred Beneficiaries of Trusts*, he found that in the vast majority of cases the immediate beneficiaries were the preferred beneficiaries of trusts and that, if the income should not be sufficient for the needs of those beneficiaries, the creator of the trust would want the trustee to pay over or apply enough of the principal, in addition to the income, to meet those needs.

The fluctuating purchasing power of the dollar and the changing needs of beneficiaries make it highly advisable, in most cases, for the trustee to have power to consume principal, in addition to income, should income alone ever be insufficient for the needs of the beneficiary.

Grandchildren

At the present time it is not at all uncommon for a property owner of wealth to bypass his children and make gifts directly to their children, his grandchildren. By taking advantage of the present annual exclusions of $6,000, as explained in the preceding chapter, he and his wife together can give each of their grandchildren, no matter how many there may be, $6,000 a year and, thereby, not incur any present federal gift-tax liability or any ultimate estate-tax liability on the gifts. It would seem that indiscriminate gifts to grandchildren, primarily for tax-avoidance purposes, without due consideration of the respective needs, present or prospective, of those grandchildren, might, in the long run, do them more harm than good.

There are many cases, of course, in which the grandparent should make his gift directly to or for a grandchild. The grandchild already may have developed to the point where the grandparent can sense and judge his characteristics and his needs. The grandchild may be mentally or physically handicapped in some way or the parents of the grandchild may not be fit persons through whom to channel the grandparents' gifts.

But apart from these tax-saving considerations and the possible inadvisability of channeling gifts to grandchildren through their own parents, it would seem better in most cases to take advantage of special powers of appointment as the dispositive device adopted for grandchildren.

1. *Special power of appointment.* Let us assume that the property owner's son or daughter is a fit person through whom to channel his gifts to their children. The grandparent may know his grandchildren only as infants or, at most, as minors. There may be grandchildren born long after his own death whom he would want to share equally with their older brothers and sisters.

In all such cases it would seem to be advisable for the grandparent to leave the property in trust for his son or daughter and give his child a special power to appoint the property to and among their children, his grandchildren by them. As explained in Chapter 12, he can make the power exclusive, so that the son or daughter, if so minded, might exclude one or more of the grandchildren from sharing in the property, or he can make it nonexclusive, meaning that his son or daughter must have each of their children share substantially, even though unequally, in their grandparent's gift to him. Thus, special powers of appointment seem to be admirably adapted to grandparents' provisions for their grandchildren.

There are many other individuals or classes of individuals, such as parents, in-laws, brothers and sisters and nieces and nephews, employees, and former benefactors, to or for whom the property owner would desire to make some provision either by outright legacy, devise, or in trust. However, the foregoing suggestions about provisions for members of his family illustrate many of the points that would arise for consideration and decision in planning for these others. Furthermore, he may wish to make gifts to or for charitable objects, such as his college, a hospital, his church or his denomination, his community foundation, either as direct gifts or gifts in trust, either as vested or contingent, either as present or future gifts. By referring back to Chapter 10, the student will find the discussion of the points to be considered in making such gifts to or for charitable objects.

PROTECTIVE PROVISIONS

When a property owner makes a direct, outright gift to another person, either during his lifetime or under his will, he fully realizes that that person can do with the property so given what he pleases: waste it, give it away, hoard it, use it wisely or unwisely. He cannot make any such outright gift and then, as the lawyer would say, put any restraint on its alienation.

But when he puts property in trust during his lifetime or leaves it in trust under his will, he indicates by that very act that he thinks that there should be some restraint upon the alienation of that property by the person for whose benefit he creates the trust.

This leads us to inquire: What, if any, provision can he make for the protection of the property so given in trust? There are four groups of such protective provisions, three of which are well known in our country and the fourth largely confined to England and Wales. They are: (1) trusts for support, (2) discretionary trusts, (3) spendthrift trusts, and (4) protective trusts.

Trusts for Support

The property owner can provide in his trust agreement or will that the income or principal shall be paid over or applied by the trustee for the support and schooling of the beneficiary. In that case, the beneficiary cannot assign his interest in the trust, nor can his creditors reach it.[1]

Discretionary Trusts

The property owner can provide that the trustee shall pay over or apply so much and only so much of the income or principal as, in the trustee's uncontrolled discretion, he shall see fit to pay over to or apply for the beneficiary. In that case, the beneficiary cannot assign his interest in the trust nor can his creditors reach it unless or until the income or principal actually has been paid over to the beneficiary.[2]

[1] Scott on *Trusts*, Secs. 770–771.
[2] *Ibid.*, Sec. 774.

Spendthrift Trusts

By statute in most states, but not all, a property owner can provide that the beneficiary of a trust cannot assign his interest in the trust nor can his creditors reach it by any legal or equitable process. These spendthrift-trust statutes vary widely from state to state. The student has no other recourse than to find and study the spendthrift-trust statutes of the individual states.

The name of this type of trust, *spendthrift,* is indeed unfortunate. It is derived from the conception that any beneficiary of a trust who needed to be protected against the alienation of the trust created for his benefit must be a spendthrift—that is, one who, if he were free to do so, would waste his estate. A dictionary definition of *spendthrift* is "a person who, by drinking, gambling, idleness, or debauchery, so spends his estate as to expose himself or his family to want or suffering or to becoming a charge on the public." Yet, in fact, the vast majority of the beneficiaries of trusts do not belong in any of these questionable categories; they need to be protected for other, equally valid reasons.

The flagrant abuse of spendthrift-trust provisions has brought them into disfavor. For example, the beneficiary of a spendthrift trust, possibly capitalizing on the family name, will buy on credit and, when the bill is presented, take refuge in the nonalienability of the trust. Such abuses have led to attempts to so modify the spendthrift-trust statutes that a limit will be put upon the nonalienability of such trusts.[3]

However, it is the common belief of estate-planning specialists that more good than harm is done by the protection provided by the spendthrift trust and they, as a rule, encourage the inclusion of such a provision in the trust agreement or will.

Protective Trusts

In 1925, the British Parliament adopted the English Trustee Act of that year which contains a protective-trust provision.[4] The substance of this statutory provision is that, if the beneficiary does or attempts to do anything that would deprive him of the income of his trust, the trustee shall cease paying it to him and, thereafter, shall apply it not only for his benefit but also for the benefit of the beneficiary's husband or wife or children or more distant issue or, if there should be none of them, for the benefit of the ultimate, principal beneficiaries.

In England or Wales, all that the draftsman of the trust instrument has to do to take advantage of the statutory protection is to provide that the property shall be placed in *protective trust,* and that phrase, in effect, in-

[3] Griswold, *Spendthrift Trusts,* 2–3.
[4] For a copy of the Act, including this provision, see Stephenson, *Drafting Wills and Trust Agreements,* Vol. II, 373–376.

corporates the statute and affords the statutory protection. By careful draftsmanship, the same may be accomplished in this country, but the British statute serves to make the protection uniform and to make the drafting of the instrument much simpler.

In this chapter, no attempt whatever has been made to plan an estate—any estate. It has been an attempt only to suggest some of the points that should be considered in planning the disposition of a family man's property. Perhaps the student will be interested in the dispositive check list which is in Chapter 22 of the author's *Drafting Wills and Trust Agreements—Dispositive Provisions*. Following the precedent of the preceding chapter, this chapter well might have been entitled "Dispositive Considerations" and the chapter that follows this one, "Administrative Considerations."

COLLATERAL READING

Note: For complete citations, see Bibliography, pp. 417–428.
MacNeill, *Making the Most of Your Estate.*
Stephenson, *Drafting Wills and Trust Agreements,* Vol. II.

24

Planning Administration
of Property

$\mathcal{A}$s WAS BROUGHT OUT at the beginning of the preceding chapter, planning the disposition and planning the administration of property in estates and trusts are not separate nor independent activities. As soon as the property owner decides to make a will and, then, decides how he will dispose of his property, he faces these two questions: (1) Whom shall I have for my executor and trustee? and (2) What powers shall I give the one I select?

SELECTION OF EXECUTOR AND TRUSTEE

In the selection of his executor and trustee, the first thing that will impress the property owner is his freedom of choice.

Freedom of Choice

Within certain reasonable limits, he has complete freedom of choice. He would not be able to have for his executor or trustee an individual under legal disability of age or mental competence. He might not have an out-of-state trust institution. He could name them, but they might not be able to serve.

Outside of these and other minor restrictions, he can name (1) one or more individuals, (2) one or more individuals *and* a trust institution, or (3) a trust institution alone as executor or coexecutors, trustee or cotrustees. He can name one person or institution executor and another trustee. He can name a different trustee for each of several parts of his estate.

This freedom of choice casts upon him the duty to exercise extreme care in the selection of his executor and trustee. The best plan of disposition cannot overcome the administrative deficiencies of his executor or trustee.

The following are some of the qualities or qualifications he should look for in his executor or trustee.

Qualities or Qualifications

Among the qualities and qualifications he should seek are: (1) continuity of existence, (2) continuity of capacity, (3) specialization, (4) collective knowledge, (5) group judgment, (6) government supervision, and (7) financial responsibility and responsiveness to financial obligations.

1. *Continuity of existence.* Although an executorship is a comparatively short activity, it may be a long-postponed one. The property owner may live on many years after he makes his will, never change it, and leave his estate to be settled by an executor named many years before his death. Although a living trusteeship is an immediate activity, the administration of the trust may extend throughout a first and a second and over into a third generation. Although a trusteeship under will does not become operative until after the death of the property owner, it may extend over into the third generation after his death.

It would be highly desirable, of course, for the property owner to feel assured that the executor he names today will be in existence and prepared to settle his estate whenever he dies, and that the trustee he names today will be in existence and prepared to serve his beneficiaries of the second or even the third generation. Although he cannot have any such absolute assurance, by proper planning he can approximate it. If he names an individual, he can name one much younger than himself; he can name one or more successors, one of whom is likely to survive him to settle his estate. But he hardly can name an individual trustee who will survive unto the third generation. If he names a trust institution, he can provide for its succession, resulting from mergers, consolidations, change of name, or the like, to carry on with all the powers of the original executor or trustee.

2. *Continuity of capacity.* The property owner should look for continuity of capacity as well as of existence. This it will be easier for him to find in a trust institution than in an individual. In the trust institution continuity of capacity is to be found in the succession of trust officers. In the case of the individual, the power of removal can be given to the beneficiaries and the power of substitution rests in the court. But removal or substitution of an individual executor or trustee on the ground of incapacity is a drastic step that will be taken only in an extreme case.

3. *Specialization.* The settlement of an estate or administration of a trust is the work, not of one, but of several specialists. There must be specialists, for example, in the investment of funds; in the management of businesses and farms; in bookkeeping and accounting; in tax work; in property insurance.

The individual, no less than the trust institution, must have specialists. No one person, whether he is the individual executor or trustee or a trust officer of a trust institution, can be a specialist in every phase of executorship or trusteeship. In either case, in one way or another, he must rely upon specialists.

4. *Collective knowledge.* Collective knowledge, of course, goes along with specialization. Each specialist brings to bear upon the settlement of the estate or administration of the trust his own specialized knowledge.

5. *Group judgment.* In the settlement of a small estate or administration of even a small trust problems arise—investment problems, property-management problems, tax problems, personal problems of beneficiaries—for the solution of which the executor or trustee, whether individual or corporate, will need more than specialization and collective knowledge. He will need also the advice and judgment of persons who, although not specialists in any phase of executorship or trusteeship, have sound judgment. The individual executor or trustee supplements his own judgment by advising with other persons. The trust institution obtains the group judgment of its officers, its trust committees, and its board of directors.

6. *Government supervision.* In this one respect the individual executor or trustee does not share advantages with the trust institution. The latter is under constant and continuous government regulation, examination, and supervision designed to keep it from going wrong and to get it back on the right track, should it start going wrong, before any substantial damage has been done to the beneficiaries. The individual and the corporate executor or trustee are subject alike to the corrective and remedial supervision of the court.

7. *Financial responsibility and responsiveness.* Responsibility and responsiveness are different things. To be responsible is to be able to meet financial obligations; to be responsive is to be ready and willing, as well as able, to meet them as soon as they are determined. The individual executor or trustee is financially responsible by reason of his own solvency and his bond with surety; the corporate executor or trustee, by its own capital and surplus and by its deposit of securities to protect its estate and trust accounts.

Financial responsiveness, on the other hand, is a matter of attitude and spirit. The individual, as the Boston trustee, (who makes a business or profession of serving in fiduciary capacities), as well as the trust institution, realizes that he must convince people of his responsiveness to obligations or else, sooner or later, forfeit the patronage of thoughtful people seeking fiduciary service.

In planning the administration as well as the disposition of his property the property owner should consider and weigh each of the qualities or qualifications and select the executor or trustee that will be most likely to possess them to the greatest degree.

GRANT OF POWERS

Next in importance to the selection of the executor and trustee is the granting of powers to the one selected.

Amplitude of Powers

One thing the property owner may need to have impressed upon himself is the importance of his granting to the executor or trustee he selects powers ample to settle his estate and administer his trusts to the best possible advantage of his beneficiaries. It may not be easy for him to realize that twenty years or more may pass before his trustee will have completed the administration of his trusts and that within that twenty-year or longer period major economic and personal changes will probably have taken place calling for the exercise of powers he did not anticipate at the time he made his will or created his trusts.

So far as it is humanly possible a property owner never should allow his executor or trustee truly to say, "I know that I should have done that but I did not have, nor could I get, the power to do so," or "I know that I should not have done that, but under the terms of the will I had to do it." Furthermore, a property owner should not name an executor or trustee, whether individual or corporate, to whom or to which he is not willing to grant ample powers.

Separation of Executor's and Trustee's Powers

Where, as would be true in most cases, a property owner names the same individual or trust institution both executor and trustee under his will, he should not separate the duties of the two. Especially during the first years after his death, it may be difficult to say whether the individual or the institution is acting as executor or as trustee as regards the performance of a given duty.

Sources of Powers

The two main sources of the executor's or the trustee's powers are (1) the statutes of the state in which the estate is being settled or the trust administered and (2) the will or trust agreement itself. There are, of course, common-law powers and orders of court, but discussion of these would lead us too far afield.

1. *Statutes.* There is little uniformity in the statutory powers granted executors and trustees. In some states they are expressed in detail in statutes; in other states, the executor or trustee must rely upon judicial decisions or orders of court. In Florida, for example, under a statute known

as the Uniform Trust Administration Act, adopted in 1941[1] eighteen express powers are granted trustees. At this point it will be well for the student to inquire into the statutory powers of executors and trustees in individual states.

2. *Will or trust agreement.* The draftsmen of modern wills and trust agreements do not rely upon statutory powers but write into the will or trust agreement powers, whether or not already included in statutes, which, they think, the executor or trustee *will* or even *may* need. No harm will come of having unexercised powers; irreparable harm may come of not having enough.

SUGGESTED POWERS

In recent years, as just indicated, there has been a notable expansion of the express powers of executors and trustees. For example, the following is a list of the headings of twenty-eight administrative powers in one recently drawn will: (1) to postpone distribution; (2) to retain orginal investments; (3) to make new investments; (4) to carry on businesses; (5) to carry on farms; (6) to manage real property; (7) to receive additional property; (8) to sell or exchange property; (9) to deal with other trusts; (10) to borrow money; (11) to register property in the name of a nominee; (12) to vote shares of stock; (13) to exercise options, rights, and privileges; (14) to participate in reorganizations; (15) to reduce interest rates; (16) to modify or release guaranties; (17) to renew or extend mortgages; (18) to foreclose on and bid in mortgaged property; (19) to retain property so bid in or taken over; (20) to insure property; (21) to collect income; (22) to compromise claims; (23) to employ and compensate agents and other representatives; (24) to hold property in two or more trusts undivided; (25) to establish and maintain reserves; (26) to make distributions in cash or kind; (27) to allocate or apportion receipts and expenses; and (28) to rely upon evidence.

The wording of the above powers as it appeared in the will is given in the illustrative will which is Form I in Part IV.

Many of the foregoing powers are well-established common-law or statutory powers. To collect, receive, and receipt for rents, profits, and income of all kinds are common-law powers. In quite a number of states to carry property in the name of a nominee is a statutory power. The draftsmen who include in their instruments these common-law and statutory powers reason that the expression of the already-existing power may prevent any question about its existence ever being raised, may prevent litigation over it, and may expedite administration.

[1] Statutes, 1941, Secs. 691.01 *et seq.*

Postpone Distribution

This is primarily a power for executors to exercise. Yet, even for a trustee, it may be a legal or physical impossibility to distribute the trust property the day in course for termination of the trust. Since activities in the trust may continue up to and even during the day of its termination, the trustee may need additional time within which to make the final accounting and the necessary transfers of property to the ultimate beneficiaries.

Retain Original Investments

In some, but not all, states the prudent-man rule is made expressly applicable to original as well as to new investments. In the absence of a statute on retention the trustee may need power under the instrument to retain property which, but for the power in the instrument, might be an unauthorized investment and have to be disposed of within a reasonable time.

The trustee may need power for a time to disregard the doctrine of diversification, to retain cash uninvested for a considerable period, and to retain national bank stock. As to the last item, if the trustee should be a national bank and if the testator or settlor should be a stockholder in that bank, it would be necessary, if the stock is to be retained, for the trustee to have express power to retain it.

Make New Investments

In most states the prudent-man rule for investment has been adopted by statute or judicial decision, and this would seem to cover the requirements as to new investments. This, however, is not the case. There may be need for the trustee to go beyond the limits of the rule. For example, if the trustee is a national bank and the property owner one of its stockholders, it may be advisable to grant the trustee power to exercise stock rights in the acquisition of additional stock. If the trustee is near a state line, it may be advisable to grant it power to invest trust funds in mortgages on property outside the state. In some states, life insurance and annuity contracts are authorized trust investments. In the states that do not have such a statute, it may be advisable to grant the trustee power to invest in insurance on the life not only of the beneficiary but also of anyone in whose life the beneficiary has an insurable interest and to purchase with trust funds annuity contracts of its own selection. Whether or not the trustee has a common trust fund at the time the instrument is being drawn, it may have one later, and, therefore, it may be advisable to grant the trustee power to purchase participations in any common trust fund it should establish later. Circumstances may arise in which it would be advisable to invest trust funds in property temporarily unproductive.

Carry on Businesses

In recent years there has been a remarkable change in the attitude of both property owners and trust institutions towards the retention and carrying on of businesses for an extended period of time. As indicated in Chapter 18, until recently, trust institutions were disposed as a rule to get rid of small, family-owned or family-controlled businesses as soon as they reasonably could do so. And businessmen were not disposed to leave their business in trust to be carried on by a trustee. At the present time, on the contrary, many owners of small, closely-held businesses want them carried on for an indefinite period, usually until a son, a minor, is old enough to take over and carry on the family business. Trust institutions, on their part, are much more hospitable than they used to be to taking over and carrying on businesses in trust.

Where there is a probability that the property owner may have a going business at his death and may want it carried on beyond the reasonable period for its liquidation, sale, or distribution, the trustee should insist upon its having at least these powers with respect to the business: (1) to incorporate it as to limit liability; (2) to decide about putting additional capital into the business; and, in every case, (3) to close out, liquidate, or sell the business if, in its judgment, it would be unwise, imprudent, or purposeless to carry it on longer. A going business should not be allowed to become and to remain a millstone around the neck of the beneficiary.

Carry on Farms

Likewise, there has been a noticeable change of attitude towards a trustee's carrying on farms. The reasoning therefor is similar to that for going businesses. In many agricultural areas, up-to-date, mechanized farming has been profitable in recent years. A farmer with a fertile and productive farm and with a family of growing children may want his farm retained and operated by his trustee at least until his sons are old enough to take over and carry on. In response to this demand, trust institutions in agricultural areas are establishing farm-management divisions in their trust department.

If the trustee is to carry on farms successfully, it must have and it must exercise all of the powers common to good farm practices. However, there can be no standard nor even near-standard provision for carrying on farms. The provisions that would be appropriate for carrying on a farm in New England, in up-state New York, in the South, in the Middle West, in the West, or in the Southwest, would not be appropriate in all respects for any other section of the country. It would seem, therefore, to be advisable for draftsmen in each agricultural area, with the aid of practical farmers or farm-managers themselves, to work out more or less standard provisions for carrying on farms in the area. In Form I in Part IV, there is a suggested provision for carrying on farms in the northeastern section of North Carolina where the principal crops are cotton, peanuts, tobacco, and dairy products. This provision was worked out by the author with the aid, not only of lawyers in general practice in that area, but also of men who themselves had large farming interests.

Manage Real Property

Where the property owner already has or is likely to acquire real property, business or residential, the trustee should have broad powers of management. It should have power to deal with such property as a prudent man as the outright owner of similar property would do.

Lease beyond duration of trust. One of the powers that, by all means, should be included in nearly all trust instruments is the power to lease business property for a period that may extend beyond the duration of the trust. For example, the beneficiary is a nineteen-year-old daughter. The trust is to terminate when she is twenty-one. The lease expires when she is nineteen. The lessee, which is an entirely satisfactory tenant, offers to re-lease the property at an increased rental and to make certain needed additions and improvements at its own expense, provided it can obtain a new lease for ten or fifteen years. In such a case the trustee, in the absence of power to lease for a period beyond the duration of the trust, would be obliged to say that it could re-lease the property for only the two remaining years of the trust. The lessee would say that it would not be willing to take a two-year lease, that, if it cannot get a ten- or fifteen-year lease, it would have to look for another location. Thereupon, the building would be left unoccupied the last two years of the trust and be turned over to the daughter at twenty-one, untenanted and, therefore, unproductive.

In Form I in Part IV, the student will find a provision for managing real property which is, virtually, the provision suggested by a real estate and trust company in the Middle West which has had, perhaps, the most experience of any trust institution in our country in the management of real property in trust.

Receive Additional Property

There seems to be little, if any, doubt that a property owner himself can add property to his own trust, provided his doing so is agreeable to the trustee. But there is a great deal of doubt about anyone else doing so and about the power of the trustee to receive it. But there are cases in which a wife, let us say, wants to add her own property to a trust created for her by her husband. The trustee ordinarily should have power to receive that property. There may be some, perhaps rare cases in which the property owner might not want anyone—not even his wife nor a member of his family—to add property to his trust lest it upset his own estate plan. Therefore, the will or trust agreement should leave no doubt as to the power of the trustee to receive additional property nor as to the source of that property.

Along with the right reserved to add property, there should be the power granted to the trustee to decline to receive it unless certain conditions are met. In most additional-property provisions, it is stated that the trustee shall not be required to receive additional property from anyone unless satisfactory arrangement is made for its administration. Otherwise, the trustee might be required to receive additional property that it would not have received as original property, and to continue to administer the trust so augmented without its compensation being readjusted.

This provision about additional property is more important for an irrevocable trust agreement or a will than for a revocable agreement. If the trust is revocable, the property owner and trustee can make an amendment to the agreement or work out some satisfactory arrangement about the additional property.

Sell or Exchange Property

In most states a trustee has common-law power to sell personal property for cash to pay debts, taxes, and administration expenses or to improve the investment status of the trust. But in most states, in the absence of express power under the instrument or an order of court, the trustee cannot sell real property. In either case, there may be doubt as to the trustee's power to sell on time or to exchange instead of sell. Yet in everyday, practical administration it is very advantageous for the trustee to have express power to sell or exchange all kinds of property, real as well as personal, for cash or on time, with or without an order of court.

Deal with Other Trusts

It is common practice now for an estate plan to call for the creation of several trusts for members of the family—husband and wife, for instance—each to create one or more trusts. As was brought out in Chapter 22, it may be highly advisable for these trusts to make purchases from or loans to one another to raise funds without sacrificing the estate as a whole in a time of economic depression.

All such intertrust dealings, especially where the same individual or trust institution is both executor and trustee, are scrutinized carefully to see that there is no divided loyalty as between the beneficiaries of one trust and those of another trust.

Borrow Money

In most states a trustee has common-law power to borrow for the trust and to secure the loan by assignment of stocks, bonds, mortgages, and other personal property. But, in the absence of express power in the instrument, the trustee does not have power, except under an order of court, to encumber real property. Yet there are cases in which it would be easier and better for all concerned to borrow on mortgage of real property than on assignment of securities. The trustee should have power to borrow upon such terms as to rates, maturities, and renewals, as will, in its judgment, serve the best interests of the beneficiaries.

From itself. Where the trustee is both a bank *and* a trust company, it may be to the advantage of the beneficiaries for the trustee to be able to borrow from its own banking department, provided, of course, it can obtain the money on as good terms as it could from any other source. However, there is unavoidably an element of self-dealing in such borrowing which would be the subject of close scrutiny by the courts and the supervisory offices.

Register Property in Name of Nominee

In a slight majority of states trustees are authorized by statute to carry property in the name of a nominee. In some states this privilege extends to stocks only, not to bonds nor other property.

The use of a nominee facilitates the transfer of property in that it obviates the necessity of supplying the supporting documents and the consequent delay. Where the executor and trustee are a trust institution, even in states that do not have a nominee-registration statute, as well as in those that do, it is advisable to grant the executor and the trustee power to register all kinds of property—stocks, bonds, real property—in the name of its nominee.

Vote Shares of Stock

For a long time there was serious doubt as to the power of a trustee to vote stock by proxy. Giving a third person, who was not a responsible officer or director of the corporate trustee, power to vote trusteed shares was regarded as a delegation of duty. The trustee's giving anyone else power to do what it was under a duty itself to do was frowned upon. The practical result of this doubt was that many banks and trust companies were advised by their counsel not to vote shares at all unless they could vote them in person through their responsible officers or directors.

Yet, in practice, it may be fully as much a breach of duty for the trustee not to vote the shares at all as to vote them by proxy.

Within recent years there has been a noticeable trend toward applying the principle of the prudent-man rule to voting shares. If a prudent man as a stockholder would vote his shares in person only, or if he would give a general proxy, or if he would give a special proxy, or if he would not vote them at all, the trustee should have power to do the same.

The Trust Division of the American Bankers Association has worked out, approved, and recommended to banks and trust companies for adoption a statement of policies as to voting shares in estates and trusts.[2] The Uniform Trusts Act, which, however, has been adopted in only a few states, authorizes a trustee to vote shares by proxy.

In the absence of an enabling statute, draftsmen are granting executors and trustees power to vote shares in all the ways that a prudent man would vote his own shares.

If the shares to be voted are those in a national bank which is also trustee, the provision about voting should go on to say who is to instruct the trustee as to voting shares for directors of the bank. Except for the election of directors, the corporate trustee, granted general power in the instrument to vote, can vote the bank stock as it can any other stock.

Exercise Options, Rights, and Privileges

Stockholders, bondholders, mortgages, and other security holders frequently have acquired options, rights, and privileges with respect to their holdings from the beginning or later. The outright owner of such holdings as a prudent man would exercise or not exercise a given option, right, or privilege as his own judgment dictated. It would seem altogether logical that a trustee should have similar power. Modern wills and trust agreements contain a provision to this effect.

In exercising a given option, right, or privilege, the trustee may come into ownership of property which, under the law or the instrument, is not an authorized investment for that trust. To provide against such an eventuality the trustee should be granted power to retain such an unauthorized investment so long as, in its judgment, it should retain it. This is logical; it would be futile to authorize the trustee to receive such unauthorized property and then require it forthwith to get rid of that property.

Participate in Reorganizations

Trustees hold in trust stocks, bonds, and notes of corporations that go through all sorts of organic changes such as mergers, consolidations, reincorporations, foreclosures, sales, leases, re-leases. It stands to reason that for the protection of its trust property the trustee should have as much power as any other investor does to participate actively in any and all such changes. It should not have to sit on the sideline while others do the work and perhaps make decisions of which it disapproves. A representative of the corporate trustee should have the power to serve on protective committees of stockholders or bondholders of corporations going through reorganization.

[2] 34 *Trust Bulletin* (October, 1954), 16.

Moreover, if out of the reorganization there should come new stocks, bonds, or notes, the trustee should have express power to retain or dispose of them as it thought best. Since expenses must be incurred in serving on protective committees or taking any other protective action, the trustee should have express power to incur these expenses payable out of the trust.

Reduce Interest Rates

During the past quarter-century we have been in a period of easy money. Property owners have been able to borrow on mortgage at ever-decreasing interest rates—from six to five, to four, even to three per cent. Borrowers at six per cent have been going to trustees and saying that, unless the interest rate is reduced, they will pay off their loan and refinance at a lower rate. Trustees know that, if the six per cent loan is paid off, they will not be able to lend the money again at any such rate. Any prudent businessman or investor would reduce the interest rate rather than lose the mortgage. Yet, unless the power to reduce interest rates is expressed in the will or trust agreement, some thoughtless or unreasonable beneficiary, upon learning that the rate has been reduced, may claim that the trustee has given away income which, but for the reduction, would have been his. The power to reduce the rate only puts the trustee into a more reasonable and logical position in dealing with current economic and financial realities.

Modify or Release Guaranties

There was a period, just before the depression of 1929 and the early 1930's, when special safety was thought to attach to guaranteed mortgages as trust investments. But after the depression came, holders of these guaranteed mortgages soon found that the safety of their investment depended more upon the market value of the underlying property than the guaranty. They learned that it was better to have an unsecured and unguaranteed obligation of a solvent obligor than the secured and guaranteed obligation of an insolvent one. So, after the depression, there came a period during which trustees, in common with other investors in guaranteed mortgages, were willing and, in fact, eager to substitute unguaranteed for guaranteed obligations. In communities in which guaranteed mortgages had turned out to be so unsatisfactory, draftsmen began to grant trustees power to modify or even to release guaranties if by so doing they might improve the investment.

Renew or Extend Mortgages

At the present time a mortgage to be amortized on a ten-, fifteen- or twenty-year basis is much more common and popular than one payable in lump-sum on a specified date. Yet, there are cases in which the trustee prefers to accept a one-year mortgage so as to be in a position, if need be, to call it at maturity. If, however, the trustee and the mortgagor desired to continue the mortgage in whole or in part after maturity, the trustee should have power to renew or extend as it thought best.

Suppose at the time the mortgage was accepted the debt was only 50, 60, or, at most, 75 per cent of the appraised value of the property. Then suppose that, on account of general economic conditions or of some major change for the worse in real-property values in the community, a re-appraisal of the property would be 90 per cent or even 100 per cent of the amount of the mortgage. The trustee could not make a new loan on any such basis. But under the circumstances can it renew or extend the present loan? If it forecloses, it may have to take a substantial loss or buy in the property itself. A prudent man would renew or extend the loan and try to work out the debt with the help of the mortgagor. The trustee should have power to do as much.

Foreclose and Bid in Mortgaged Property

Under the terms of the mortgage, the mortgagee has the power, and it may be under a duty, to foreclose a mortgage in default. But does it have the power to bid in the property under the foreclosure sale? If not, the property may go for a song and the mortgagee take a big loss. If the trustee does bid in the property, it may be able, eventually, to work out the debt and save the trust any loss. Or the mortgagor may say to the trustee, "You take the property for the debt." This power, even though granted by the mortgagor, should not be exercised by the trustee except upon the advice of counsel in any given state. In some states, a trustee taking over property for the debt remains trustee and upon the sale of the property must account to the mortgagor or his estate for any and all surplus over and above the debt, interest, and expenses of sale.

Retain Property Bid in or Taken Over

Suppose the property bid in or taken over by the trustee should not be an authorized investment for the trust. It would be futile to take over or bid in property and then have to dispose of it immediately. So, coupled with the power to bid in or take over, there should be the power to retain the property as though it were an authorized investment.

Insure

In the United States a trustee is under a duty to carry the amounts and kinds of insurance coverage that a prudent man would carry on similar property. In England and Wales, on the contrary, the trustee *may*, not *must*, insure against loss by *fire* up to three-fourths of the value of the property.

However, there are two kinds of insurance to which some reference should be made in the trust instrument—public liability and insurance in mutual companies.

1. Public liability. Public liability insurance really is for the protection of the executor or trustee. Why should the estate or trust pay premiums on that kind of insurance? Because, if it did not, the executor or trustee would, properly, add the premium to its compensation so that the end result would be the same.

2. Insurance in mutual company. In a mutual insurance company the members of the company insure one another's property. Why should an executor or trustee insure other people's property in return for their insuring the property it controls? Because many of the mutual companies have as low or lower assessments as the stock companies have premiums and have as good records of service. Prudent men insure lives and property alike in mutual companies. Why should not executors and trustees have the same power?

Collect Income

One of the inherent powers of an executor or trustee is to collect income from all estate or trust property. Why then add to the already long list of administrative powers the power to collect? Only to put to rest any question that ever may be raised by anyone—and, given time, someone will raise it—about the power of the executor or trustee to receive and receipt for a given kind of property.

Compromise Claims

The common law gives an executor or trustee power, within reason, to compromise, adjust, arbitrate, sue on, or defend, and, even, to abandon claims. But prudent men, dealing with difficult debtors and creditors, try not to throw good money after bad by litigation. Executors and trustees should have power to do what prudent men do under similar circumstances.

Employ and Compensate Agents and Other Representatives

An executor or trustee has the common-law power to employ agents and other representatives to do for it what it cannot do or cannot reasonably be expected to do itself. Yet, when an item of expense for the employment and compensation of any such agent or representative appears in the account, some beneficiary is likely to ask why the executor or the trustee itself did not do the thing and save the estate or trust that expense. Then it is that the executor or trustee can point to a provision in the instrument and remind the beneficiary that the property owner himself realized that there might be need for such employment. Among the agents or other representatives usually specified are: accountants, brokers, attorneys at law, attorneys in fact, realtors, rental agents, and tax specialists.

Hold Property in Two or More Trusts Undivided

Sometimes, instead of creating a single family trust, a property owner will create a separate trust for his widow and each child. As brought out in Chapter 22, the tax consequences may lead him to create separate trusts. However, if the estate is of modest size or consists of undivided interests in real property, it may be overly expensive administratively to keep the trusts separated. No additional risk will be taken by giving the trustee power to carry the several trusts undivided and to show the respective shares on the books of the trustee.

Establish and Maintain Reserves

A trustee has the common-law power to establish and maintain reserves for the equalization of payments to beneficiaries and, perhaps, for some other purposes. But where nothing is said in the instrument about reserves, the importunate beneficiary may hound the trustee into paying out all of the income as it is received and run the risk later of having drastically to reduce the payments or even to stop them for a time in order to pay necessary expenses immediately chargeable to income.

Distribute in Cash or Kind

An estate or trust usually consists of many kinds of property. The executor or trustee must be absolutely impartial as among the distributees or beneficiaries. When time comes for the distribution of the estate or termination of the trust, some of the distributees or beneficiaries may want certain property, two or more may want the same property, and still others may want their share in cash. It may be, economically, an unpropitious time to sell the property, and converting it into cash would cause a tragic loss to most of the distributees or beneficiaries. Then it is that express power to distribute in cash or kind and to determine values enables the executor or trustee to treat the distributees or beneficiaries inpartially and yet, in a measure, to respect their preferences in making the distributions.

Apportion or Allocate Receipts and Expenses

One of the most vexatious problems of administration is the allocation or apportionment of a given item of receipt or expense. There is no way of telling whether a given receipt—a stock dividend, for example—should be credited to principal or income or apportioned between the two and, if apportioned, in what proportions. Similarly, there is no way of telling how a given item of expense—one incurred for the protection alike of the income and principal—shall be charged, whether all to income, all to principal, or apportioned. The Uniform Principal and Income Act, which is the law in some states, has helped a great deal, but even in those states in which it has been adopted, it has not answered all of the problems of apportionment and allocation. There still is need for a provision in the instrument empowering the trustee to use its own judgment in making such allocations and apportionments.

Rely upon Evidence

In the transaction of its business an executor or trustee must employ and rely upon the same mediums of communication as any businessman does, that is, upon letters, telegrams, and telephone conversations, as well as affidavits and certificates. If it had to insist upon and wait for the *best evidence* (a legal term) in every case, the wheels of trust administration would come to a stop. Therefore, in the interest of practical, common-sense administration, an executor or trustee should have power to rely and act upon any medium of communication reasonably regarded by it as genuine and, in the absence of any negligence on its part, to be protected in so doing.

Continuing payments. Where a trust is to terminate or change upon the happening of a specified event—as the remarriage of a beneficiary in a distant state—the trustee, in complete absence of negligence on its part, should not be liable for continuing the payments thereunder until it does receive notice of the event terminating or changing the trust.

POURING-OVER IN AID OF ADMINISTRATION

In recent years a dispositive device, commonly known as *pouring-over*, has come into general use.

What Pouring-Over Means

Pouring-over simply means taking property out of one estate or trust and putting it into another estate or trust. The process may arise in several ways. A property owner may create a living trust and make a will, and in his trust agreement he may provide that his trustee may receive additional property; he may provide in his will that upon the settlement of his estate and distribution of the property, certain property, possibly his whole residuary estate, shall be poured over into his living trust and, thereafter, administered as a part thereof. Or the other way round, he may direct in his living trust agreement that upon his death the property in the trust shall ꞌe poured over into his estate and, thereafter, administered as a part of his residuary trust under will. The administrative advantage of this pouring-over device is that it it provides for the consolidation of property for both dispositive and administrative purposes and saves administrative expense alike to the trustee and the beneficiary.

However, no sooner had pouring-over achieved a measure of popularity than lawyers began to raise two pertinent questions; one related to the legal requirement that the pouring-over be into existing instruments only; the other, to the effect of the amendment of a pre-existing instrument.

Into Existing Instrument

As the common law stood, pouring-over, to be effective, had to be into a pre-existing instrument. A property owner could not, effectively, make his will today, create his living trust tomorrow, and provide for the property under his will to be poured over into his living trust; this, because his living trust agreement was not an existing instrument at the time he made his will. If, however, he had made his trust today, his will, tomorrow, and provided in his will that his property should be poured over into his trust, identifying his trust agreement, that would have been all right. It was not long before it became, more or less, common knowledge among estate-planning advisers that pouring-over, to be effective, had to be done into existing instruments.

Into Amended Instrument

Then, this question arose: suppose the property owner makes a revocable living trust today, makes his will tomorrow, and amends his trust agreement the next day. The trust agreement was an existing instrument when the will was made and, therefore, suitable as a receptacle for the poured-over property. But the amendment to the trust agreement was not an existing instrument when the will was made and, therefore, was not a proper receptacle for the poured-over property. This gave rise to the possibility that in employing the pouring-over device the property owner might be pouring over into an instrument—the original, unamended trust agreement—that might provide for the disposition of his property entirely contrary to his wishes and to his later plans as revealed in the amendment to the agreement.

This situation now is being met, apparently successfully, by the adoption of a statute authorizing pouring-over into an amended trust agreement provided the trust agreement itself was in existence at the time the pouring-over was provided for under the will, even though the amendment itself was not made until after the will had been executed. This legislation is comparatively recent and only a few states have adopted it as yet. The student is advised to look up the pouring-over statutes, if there are any, of individual states for accurate information.

COLLATERAL READING

Note: For complete citations, see Bibliography, pp. 417–428.

BOGERT on *Trusts and Trustees*, Secs. 163A–196.

HYERT and RACHLIN, "Pour-over Trusts: Consequences of Applying the Doctrine of Incorporation by Reference and Facts of Independent Significance."

POLASKY, "Pour-over Wills—and the Statutory Blessing."

SCOTT on *Trusts*, Secs. 551–570.

———, "Pouring-over."

STEPHENSON on *Drafting Wills and Trust Agreements*, Vol. I.

part IV

ILLUSTRATIVE INSTRUMENTS OF
DISPOSITION AND ADMINISTRATION

Part IV presents four hypothetical instruments of disposition and administration of property—a will, a living trust agreement, a personal insurance trust agreement, and a business insurance trust agreement. They illustrate many of the points discussed in the three preceding Parts of this text.

All four of these instruments are built around the estate of A which has been used for illustration in the preceding Parts. However, names have now been given to A and to the members of his family. Details about the members of his immediate family and several other persons and some charitable objects have been added. Mr. Joseph Henry Barnes (formerly A) has been given a large and variegated estate in order to illustrate several points that might not be illustrated so well in a smaller and simpler estate.

ESTATE

Persons and Objects to Be Provided For

The testator, Joseph Henry Barnes, 53 years old, is a businessman, a resident of Pendleton, Northampton County, North Carolina, in good health, and still insurable.

His wife, Edith Bryant Barnes, 50, in good health, and has had little experience with and shown little interest in business or financial matters.

They have five children: (1) Thomas, a son, 26, a graduate of the School of Medicine of Duke University, has completed his internship, and recently entered upon the general practice of medicine in Ahoskie, Hertford County, North Carolina; married to Rachel Boone; they have one son, named for his paternal grandfather, two years old; (2) Dorothy, a daughter, 24, married to Walter Askew, a merchant employed in Barnes Brothers store in Pendleton; they have a daughter, Eugenia, one year old; (3) Martha, a daughter, 21, recently married to Thomas Davis, a lawyer, residing in Norfolk, Virginia, no children yet; (4) William, a son, 18, freshman in the University of North Carolina, has not decided upon his business or profession; and (5) Mable, a daughter, 15, a high school student, expecting to enter Randolph-Macon Woman's College, who was stricken with paralytic polio when she was seven, and is now a cripple but mentally alert and socially attractive.

In addition to providing for his wife, these five children, and two grandchildren, Mr. Barnes wishes also to make some provision for his mother, Anna Davis Barnes, 75, who has no substantial income except that provided for her by Joseph Barnes and his younger brother, William. She has a modest home in Raleigh, North Carolina; her competent and faithful housekeeper and companion is Mrs. Joan Carter, for whom he wishes to leave a token gift in appreciation of her service and loyalty to his mother. Joseph Barnes is interested also in Chowan College, Murfreesboro, North Carolina, of which his mother is an alumna; in Roanoke-Chowan Hospital, Ahoskie, North Carolina, in which his son, Thomas, will probably practice;

and in Pine Forest Rest Home, Potecasi, North Carolina, a rest home for the aging, in the development of which his wife is active and interested. He has several friends to whom he wishes to make token gifts, and several faithful employees at his and William's farm and store whom he wishes to remember in his will.

Property to Be Disposed Of

Joseph Barnes's present estate, at its estimated current market value, consists of the following items:

Residence in Pendleton, standing in Joseph's name valued at ... $	50,000
Household goods and personal effects, including two automobiles for personal and family use, valued at	10,000
A building lot in Pendleton adjoining Joseph's own residence lot, valued at	5,000
One-half interest, with his brother, William, in a plantation known as Barnes Place, two miles from Pendleton, consisting of 1,000 acres—300 in cultivation and 700 in woodland—under the general management of his brother William; Joseph's interest valued at	50,000
One-half interest, with his brother, William, in the livestock, machinery and equipment on the plantation; Joseph's interest valued at	10,000
One-half interest, with his brother, William, in their mother's residence in Raleigh, North Carolina, subject to her life estate; Joseph's remainder interest valued at	10,000
Joint checking account with his wife, Edith, in The Pendleton National Bank and Trust Company; present and average balance	5,000
Joint savings account with his wife, Edith, in same bank	5,000
Insurance on Joseph's life, presently payable one-half to his wife and one-half to his estate	200,000
Listed and readily marketable stocks and bonds (not related to his businesses) including $25,000 in the capital stock of The Pendleton National Bank and Trust Company of which Joseph is a stockholder and director; yielding, on the average, 4% on cost price	500,000
One-half interest, with his brother, William, in a farm-supply store in Pendleton, a partnership, in the name Barnes Brothers; Joseph's one-half interest valued at	150,000
Thirty-three and a third per cent of the stock of Meherrin Agricultural Company, a close corporation at Severn, North Caro-	

lina, engaged in the processing, manufacturing, and marketing
of peanuts, grain, cotton, cattle and other farm and dairy products; the only other stockholders, each with a one-third interest
in the corporation, are Walter Woodard, another businessman
in Pendleton, and Walter Askew, Joseph's son-in-law; the key-
man in the operation of the business is Walter Askew; Joseph's
stock valued at   100,000
                                                           ———————

Present estimated value of Joseph Barnes's estate: $1,095,000

Other pertinent facts about Joseph Barnes and his affairs are: Edith
Barnes, his wife, has no separate property except her personal effects and a
few items of household goods. His mother has no other property than her
life estate in the residence in Raleigh, her household goods, and personal
effects, and about $10,000 in securities yielding about $400 a year. Over the
past five years Joseph Barnes's net income, after taxes, has been about $30,-
000 a year. He does not have and does not expect to have any substantial
debts other than for current living expenses. Up to this time he has not made
any substantial gifts that would consume or reduce his gift-tax exemption
and exclusions. He wishes to take advantage of every proper tax-saving,
but not at the expense of the best interests of his beneficiaries.

FORM I

WILL

Beginning

I, Joseph Henry Barnes (commonly known as Joe Barnes), a resident of Pendleton, Northampton County, North Carolina, declare this to be my last will and revoke any will or codicil thereto heretofore made by me.

Family Situation

My immediate family consists of: my wife, Edith Bryant Barnes; a son, Thomas; a daughter, Dorothy, married to Walter Askew; a daughter, Martha, married to Thomas Davis; a son, William, unmarried; a daughter, Mable, unmarried; my mother, Anna Davis Barnes; one grandson, Joseph Henry Barnes, Jr., and one granddaughter, Eugenia Askew. However, in mentioning these grandchildren I do not mean to exclude any grandchildren born or adopted hereafter.

Throughout this will, when I say "wife" or "my wife", I mean my present wife; and when I say "children" or "grandchildren", I mean legally adopted children as well as those of the blood of myself and my children.

Household Goods and Personal Effects

ITEM I. Section 1. *To wife, if she survives.* I bequeath to my wife, if she shall survive me by as many as thirty days, all of my personal effects, household furniture, library, jewelry, works of art (other than the portrait of my father hereinafter bequeathed to my son, Thomas), chinaware, silverware, automobiles for personal or family use, and all other tangible personal property in, around, about, and used in connection with my main residence at the time of my death; not including stocks, bonds, or other intangible personal property, nor tangible personal property (although in, around, or about our residence) used for business purposes, of which purposes the executor shall be judge and its decision shall be conclusive.

Section 2. *Reference to items belonging to wife.* My wife owns certain items of tangible personal property, such as, heirlooms and other items which, from time to time, I have given her. I have suggested to her that she prepare a memorandum listing the items that belong to her and attach it to her copy of my will. But if she fails to prepare or to attach such a memorandum, I trust that her word will be accepted as to the items that belong to her.

Section 3. *To children, if wife does not survive.* If my wife shall predecease me or not survive me by as many as thirty days, I bequeath all of the abovementioned property, share and share alike, to my children, the issue of a deceased child representing and taking the deceased parent's share. In the division into equal shares, if any of my children or issue of deceased children shall be a minor, I direct that the executor shall represent such minor. In making such division, if there should be any disagreement among my children or issue of deceased children, I direct that the executor shall determine and put into effect the method of settling any such disagreement, and the result of the method so determined shall be conclusive.

Statement about Provision for Mother

ITEM II. In my will I am not making any provision for my mother. I am not doing so because I already have provided for her by means of a living trust created on the 16th day of May, 1960, of which The Pendleton National Bank and Trust Company is trustee.

Provision for Mother's Housekeeper and Companion

ITEM III. As a token of my appreciation of the excellent service she, as housekeeper and companion, has rendered my mother over the past ten years, I bequeath the sum of Five Thousand ($5,000) Dollars in cash or its equivalent to Mrs. Joan Carter if she shall survive me and if she shall be in my mother's employment at the time of my death or if, although surviving me, she shall have left my mother's employment because of her own illness or incapacity longer to care for my mother, of which illness or incapacity my executor shall be judge and its decision shall be conclusive.

Gifts to Employees

ITEM IV. As a token of appreciation of their faithful service, I direct that, as soon as practicable after my death, my executor shall divide and distribute the sum of Twenty Thousand ($20,000) Dollars or two (2) per cent of my taxable estate for federal estate tax purposes, whichever shall be the larger amount, in equal shares among employees on the Barnes Place and the Barnes Brothers store who survive me and who shall have been in our employment either on the plantation or in the store three (3) years (a major fraction being counted as a year) prior to my death, of which employment and term of employment my executor shall be judge and its decision shall be conclusive.

Specific Legacy

ITEM V. I bequeath the portrait of my father, William Henry Barnes, painted by Francis Speight and now hanging in the living room of our residence in Pendleton, North Carolina, to my son, Thomas, if he shall survive me; if not, I bequeath the same to my daughter, Dorothy, if she shall survive me; if not, the next of my children who survives me in the order of his or her age; hoping thus to keep this cherished portrait of my father in our family.

Specific Devise

ITEM VI. I devise to my daughter, Dorothy, if she shall survive me, the building lot, about 200 feet front and 300 feet deep, adjoining the lot on which my own residence stands, known on the map of Pendleton as Number 206 Kirby Street. If she shall not survive me, I direct that this lot shall be disposed of under Item XI as a part of my residuary estate.

Demonstrative Legacy

ITEM VII. I bequeath the sum of One Thousand ($1,000) Dollars in cash to my lifelong friend, Roger Davis, if he shall survive me, payable out of my joint savings account in The Pendleton National Bank and Trust Company; but, if the joint savings account shall not be sufficient, or shall not be available, to satisfy this legacy, I direct that any deficiency shall be made up out of my general estate.

Pecuniary Legacy

ITEM VIII. I bequeath the sum of One Thousand ($1,000) Dollars in cash to my former teacher, Mrs. Bessie Draper, if she shall survive me.

Gifts to Charity

ITEM IX. Section 1. I bequeath and devise one-tenth of my net taxable estate as determined for federal estate tax purposes to The Pendleton National Bank and Trust Company, trustee of the Pendleton Community Foundation, created by declaration of trust of the board of directors of the said bank on the first day of January, 1956, by the said trustee or its sucessor to be held in trust in perpetuity to pay the net income annually, one-third each to Chowan College, Murfreesboro, North Carolina; Roanoke-Chowan

Hospital, Ahoskie, North Carolina; and Pine Forest Rest Home, Potecasi, North Carolina.

Provision for Wife through Marital-Deduction Trust

ITEM X. Section 1. *Formula fractional gift.* If my wife shall survive me, I give to the trustee hereinafter named, as a separate trust to be known as my marital-deduction trust, property equal in value to one-half of my adjusted gross estate as defined in the Internal Revenue Code of 1954, reduced by the value as finally determined for federal estate tax purposes of all other items of my gross estate qualifying for the marital deduction under the said Revenue Code which pass or have passed to my wife outright under other provisions of this will or outside this will by operation of law or otherwise. It is my intention to place in this trust the maximum value in property, but no more, that may be deducted from my estate as the marital deduction under the applicable Internal Revenue Code.

Since the exact value of the allowable marital deduction cannot be determined until my federal estate tax return has been audited, I direct the executor, after such audit shall have been made and final tax values established, either to withdraw property from this trust and add it to my residuary trust under Item XI of this will, or to withdraw property from my residuary trust and add it to this trust so that the property in this trust will be the maximum allowable marital deduction but no more.

Section 2. *Selection of property.* I authorize the executor to pay over, deliver, assign, transfer, or convey to the trustee in satisfaction of this gift cash or property in kind; to select and designate the property whether cash or securities or real property (other than my main residence at the time of my death) or interests in real property, which shall be placed in this trust, but only at the values thereof as finally determined for federal estate tax purposes. In no event shall there be included in this trust any unproductive property within the meaning of the applicable tax laws nor other property, such, for example, as terminable interestates, with respect to which the marital deduction would not be allowed if it were included.

Section 3. *Protection of executor in excluding property.* If the executor shall decide that there is uncertainty as to the inclusion of particular property in my adjusted gross estate for federal estate tax purposes, it shall exclude such property from my gross estate in the estate tax return. The executor shall not be liable for any loss to my estate nor to any beneficiary resulting from its decision made in the exercise of due care that there is uncertainty as to the inclusion of that property and the consequent exclusion and later inclusion of that property.

Section 4. *Selection of valuation date.* If the executor shall have a choice of dates in valuing property in my gross estate, it shall elect the date that causes the lowest federal estate tax on my estate, and I give my executor that choice of dates as far as I shall have the right to do so.

Section 5. *Valuation of marital deduction.* I intend that the value for federal estate tax purposes of the property in this trust shall be available for and applicable to the marital deduction allowed by the federal estate tax law applicable to my estate; and all questions pertaining to this trust shall be resolved according to this expressed intention. Furthermore, I direct that the powers of the executor and trustee hereinafter set forth with respect to the property in this trust shall not be exercised nor be exercisable except for a purpose consistent with this intention.

Section 6. *Definition of terms* adjusted gross estate *and* marital deduction. If the terms *adjusted gross estate* and *marital deduction* shall not have determinable meanings in this will at the time of my death, I declare that the term *adjusted gross estate* shall mean my gross estate less all indebtedness and expenses but before the payment of estate, inheritance, or succession taxes that may be assessed against my estate; and I give to my wife in trust as hereinafter set forth one-half of my *adjusted gross estate* as so defined.

Section 7. *Abatement of gift in excess of marital deduction.* This gift shall abate to the extent, if any, to which it cannot be satisfied in the manner herein provided.

Section 8. *Presumption of wife's survival.* In the event that my wife and I shall be killed in a common accident or as a result of a common disaster or under such circumstances that it will be impossible, in the judgment of the executor, whose decision shall be conclusive, to determine which of us died first, it shall be presumed that she survived me; and this presumption shall apply throughout this will.

Section 9. *Income to or for wife for life.* Calculated from the date of my death, the trustee shall pay over to or apply for the sole benefit of my wife in convenient installments as nearly equal as practicable, at least quarter-annually, all of the net income of this trust, to the end that all of the net income shall be paid to her or applied for her benefit at least annually.

Section 10. *Consumption of principal for wife.* In addition to all of the net income, the trustee, in the exercise of its uncontrolled discretion, shall pay over to or apply for the sole benefit of my wife as much of the principal of this trust as shall be needful or desirable for her comfortable support and maintenance, including medical, surgical, hospital, or other institutional care, having in mind both the standard of living to which she has been accustomed and her income from other sources and adjusting the payment or application of principal accordingly to the end that consumption of principal shall supplement, not substitute for, income from other sources.

Section 11. *Right of wife to demand principal.* In addition to all of the income in any event and to so much of the principal as the trustee shall see fit from time to time to pay over to or apply for her, my wife shall have the right to demand and receive from the trustee during any one year up to but not over Two Thousand ($2,000) Dollars of principal, and her receipt shall be complete acquittance to the trustee. However, this right of my wife to demand principal shall not be accumulative.

Section 12. *Wife's special power of appointment.* During the lifetime of my wife, she shall have the right, by specific reference to this power in an instrument or instruments in writing filed with the trustee, to direct the trustee to distribute to or apply for the benefit of any one or more of our children or issue of deceased children so much of the principal of this trust, up to but not exceeding the aggregate of one-half thereof as appraised at the time of the creation of this trust, as my wife shall direct by such instrument or instruments. Any such appointment or appointments by my wife shall be of such estates and interests and upon such terms, trusts, conditions, and powers as she shall determine. If the exercise or exercises of this special power of appointment shall impose a federal estate or gift tax upon my wife, I direct that the trustee shall pay to her out of the principal of this trust an amount or amounts sufficient to cover the tax or taxes so imposed upon her. My intention is to give my wife the right to exercise this special power of appointment as often as she shall see fit to do so, and her exercise of it once shall not preclude her exercising it again. However, it is my intention also that in the exercise or exercises of this power she shall not dispose of more than one-half in value of this trust estate as originally appraised.

Section 13. *Wife's general power of appointment.* Upon the death of my wife, the entire remaining principal and the uncollected or undistributed income of this trust shall be paid over, delivered, assigned, transferred, or conveyed to and among such appointee or appointees (including her own estate), and upon such terms and in such proportions as she shall direct by her will made either before or after my death making specific reference to this power. In distributing this property, the trustee shall be protected in relying upon an instrument admitted to probate in any jurisdiction as the will of my wife or in acting upon the asumption that, if the trustee shall not have received notice of the existence of any will left by her within three months after her death, she died intestate and had not exercised this power of appointment.

Section 14. *Gift in default of appointment.* Upon the death of my wife, any property remaining in this trust as to which she shall not have exercised her power of appointment shall be added to and administered and ultimately distributed as a part of my residuary estate as set forth in Item XI of this will.

Section 15. *Taxes on property in marital-deduction trust.* None of the property in this trust shall be used for the payment of estate, inheritance, transfer, succession, legacy, or other taxes that may become payable upon or by reason of my death, except to the extent, if any, that all other property of my estate shall not be sufficient for the payment of such taxes.

Disposition of Residuary Estate

ITEM XI. I direct that the residue of my estate of every nature and wherever situated (including real, personal, or mixed property, lapsed or void legacies or devises, and property over which I may, now or hereafter, have a general power of appointment by will) shall be divided by the executor into as many equal shares as I shall have children then living or children dead with issue surviving, and I dispose of the several shares as follows:

Section 1. *Provision for children twenty-five years of age or over or their issue.* I give one equal share to my son, Thomas, who already is over twenty-five years of age and an equal share to each of my other children, if any, who shall be twenty-five years of age at my death. If any child shall have died before attaining the age of twenty-five years, I direct that his share shall be disposed of at my death as he or she shall have appointed by will and, in default of appointment by him or her, that his or her share shall be held in trust by the trustee hereinafter named until the oldest of such child's children shall be twenty-one years of age and, as each of them shall attain the age of twenty-one years, pay over, deliver, assign, transfer, or convey to such child an equal part of such child's parent's share of my estate. The trustee shall dispose of the income from the property so held in trust for the benefit of the issue of a child of mine so dying before attaining the age of twenty-five years not necessarily to be in the same amount or amounts for each of such issue but to or for each according to his or her needs in the judgment of the trustee. If any child of mine shall have died before attaining the age of twenty-five years without issue surviving and without having exercised the power of appointment herein provided for, such child's share shall be added to, administered, and ultimately distributed as a part of my other children's or issue of deceased children's shares.

Section 2. *Provision for children under twenty-five years of age, including a family home for them and their mother.* I direct that the shares of my residuary estate not distributed outright to such of my children as shall be twenty-five years of age at the time of my death and the issue of such children as provided for in the preceding section shall be held in trust, the several shares being undivided, by the trustee hereinafter named and administered as a single trust as follows:

a. Family home. To retain my main residence at the time of my death (my main residence at present is 208 Kirby Street, Pendleton, North Carolina; but I mean my main residence wherever it may be at the time of my death) as a family home for my wife and such of our children and grandchildren (whose parents may be dead) as shall desire and as she shall desire to have make their home with her and to retain it as long as she shall desire to have it retained as a family home; out of this trust estate to pay taxes, insurance premiums, repair bills, and all other expenses of upkeep and maintenance of the residence so retained; to sell the residence publicly or privately, for cash or on time, without an order of court, if at any time my wife shall express in writing to the trustee her desire not to have it retained any longer as a family home or if, in the judgment of the trustee, it no longer should be retained for that purpose, and the purchaser shall be under no duty to inquire into her expression of desire or the trustee's judgment as to the sale of the residence; to convert the residence into apartments or to make any other changes in it so as better to adapt it to the needs of my wife and children at and after my death; to use the proceeds of the sale of the residence for the purchase, exchange, or construction of another residence suitable to the wishes of my wife, augmenting, if need be, the proceeds of the sale by funds from this trust estate and adding any surplus funds resulting from the sale to this trust estate; and, considering the size and nature of my estate and the needs of my wife and children, to do all other things that, in the uncontrolled discretion of the trustee, shall be needed for the retention, adaptation, acquisition, substitution, maintenance, and upkeep of a suitable residence for my wife and children so long as she shall desire and, in the judgment of the trustee, so long as she shall be able to hold the family home intact. In the interest of providing a suitable residence for my wife and children at all times and under all circumstances, I intend and desire that the trustee shall give a liberal construction to the foregoing powers.

b. Disposition of income and principal during wife's lifetime. During my wife's lifetime to pay to my wife the share of the income of each child then under twenty-one years of age to be used by her for the support and schooling (including college, university, graduate, and professional training and internship) or if or when my wife shall so direct on writing, to make payments of income monthly or quarterly direct to such child; between twenty-one and twenty-five years of age, to pay such income direct to such child; and as each child becomes twenty-five years of age, to pay over, deliver, assign, transfer, or convey to such child, discharged of trust, a child's share of this trust estate; to apply the income of the issue of a child dying before attaining the age of twenty-five years for the benefit of such issue until the oldest of them shall be twenty-one years of age, not necessarily in equal amounts but for each according to his or her respective needs, in the judgment of the trustee, and as each of them shall become twenty-one years of age, to pay over to him or her an equal part of the deceased parent's share of the estate and to continue to apply the income of the part of the estate remaining in trust for the benefit of the issue still under twenty-one years of age; and when the youngest of such issue shall be twenty-one years of age, to terminate this portion of the trust.

c. Disposition of estate after wife's death. After the death of my wife, to divide this trust estate (including the family home at a fair valuation if that still should be a part of the trust estate) into as many equal parts as I shall have children under twenty-five years of age at the time of my wife's death or children of that age then dead but with issue surviving; to pay over, deliver, assign, transfer, and convey an equal share of the trust estate, discharged of trust, to each child upon attaining twenty-five years of age; to continue to hold in trust and pay the income of the share of each child under twenty-five years of age to such child and when he or she shall attain that age, pay over, deliver, assign, transfer, or convey the share of that child, discharged of trust, to that child; and to hold in trust the share of the issue of a deceased child until the oldest of such issue shall attain the age of twenty-one years and, as each of such issue shall attain that age, pay over, deliver, assign, transfer, and convey to such issue his or her part of the deceased parent's share of my trust estate, holding the part or parts of one under twenty-one years of age in trust for the support and schooling of that one until he or she shall be twenty-one years of age.

Spendthrift-Trust Provision

ITEM XII. So far as permissible by law, the interest of any beneficiary in the principal or in the income of any trust under my will shall not be subject to either voluntary or involuntary alienation nor to the control of the beneficiary's husband or wife.

Vesting Provision

ITEM XIII. The interest of every beneficiary, whether created by me directly or under a power of appointment granted by me in this will, shall vest, anything else in this will or in the exercise of a power of appointment to the contrary notwithstanding, within twenty-one years after the death of the last survivor of beneficiaries of my estate who were in being at the time of my death. Upon such vesting the principal shall be distributed among those who theretofore had been income beneficiaries and in the proportions that each had received income or had it applied for his benefit. If at the time of the vesting of an interest the beneficiary shall be a minor, the trustee shall continue to hold his share in trust for his benefit, paying over or applying income and as much of the principal as the trustee shall deem advisable, until such beneficiary shall be twenty-one years of age and then distribute his share of the trust property to him, discharged of the trust. And, if at the time of vesting, the person entitled to the interest is a beneficiary of a trust under my will and his interest under that trust is vested, his share shall be added to that trust and thereafter administered as a part thereof.

Tax Provision

ITEM XIV. I direct that the executor shall pay out of my residuary estate as defined in the first paragraph of Item XI of this will (without any right of reimbursement) all estate, inheritance, legacy, and succession taxes which may be assessed against any gift made by me under this will and which may be determined to be due against any property owned by me and any other persons as joint owners with right of survivorship and passing at my death to the survivor and all such taxes as shall be assessed against any insurance on my life. It is my intention that all property passing under this will, except that passing under Item XI hereof as my residuary estate, and all property transferred by me in trust during my lifetime and all jointly owned property passing to the survivor and all proceeds of insurance on my life shall pass undiminished by any such taxes.

Accounting Provision

ITEM XV. The executor and trustee shall make accountings to the appropriate court or courts as required by law. In addition to these court accountings, the trustees shall account once each twelve months to each adult, competent beneficiary and to the guardian or legal representative of each minor or incompetent beneficiary then receiving or entitled to receive income from any trust under this will. Each account shall show the receipts, disbursements, and distributions of principal and income since the last annual accounting and the invested and uninvested principal and undisturbed income on hand at the time of the accounting.

Compensation Provision

ITEM XVI. Section 1. For its services as executor and as trustee, The Pendleton National Bank and Trust Company or its successor shall receive the compensation stipulated in its regularly adopted schedules of compensation in effect and applicable at the time such compensation shall become payable.

Section 2. If the executor or trustee shall not have regularly adopted schedules of compensation in effect and applicable at that time, it shall receive reasonable compensation for the service rendered.

Legal Counsel

ITEM XVII. I suggest that the executor and trustee employ Garland S. Ricks, of the firm of Ricks, Davis, and Johnson, Jackson, North Carolina, as counsel for any legal service in connection with the settlement of my estate or the administration of my trusts, provided he shall be engaged in the practice of law at the time. I make this suggestion, and it is intended to be a suggestion only, because of his intimate acquaintance with my affairs over a long period of time and my high regard for him as a lawyer and as a friend. He, as the draftsman of my will, is incorporating this provision, not at his own suggestion, but at my direction. However, I intend that this shall be a suggestion and nothing more, and that the executor and trustee shall be free to employ other or additional counsel at any time and from time to time as it may deem advisable.

Advisers to Executor and Trustee

ITEM XVIII. I suggest that from time to time, as occasion in its judgment shall call for it, the executor and the trustee shall consult with my brother, William, particularly as to matters related to our farming operations and our store; with my son-in-law, Walter Askew, as to matters related to our corporation, Meherrin Agricultural Company at Severn, North Carolina; and with my wife as to personal matters, particularly with those related to the schooling and careers of our two minor children. In making this suggestion I do not intend to impose any legal obligation upon the executor or the trustee; nor do I intend to relieve it of any of its duties or responsibilities with respect to the settlement of my estate or administration of my trusts; nor do I intend to impose any legal obligation upon my brother, my said son-in-law, nor my wife. I do not name my wife executrix or coexecutrix or trustee or cotrustee because I desire to relieve her of any and all business or financial responsibility regarding my estate and to leave her free to maintain our home and give her attention to our two minor children. I do not name my son, Thomas, although he is twenty-six years of age, in any of these capacities because I wish not to distract him from his own profession of medicine. I am confident that, whether named or not, my wife, my brother, my son in-law, as well as our children, will be of all help possible to the executor in settling my estate and to the trustee in administering the several trusts under my will.

Appointment and Succession of Executor and Trustee

ITEM XIX. Section 1. *Appointment.* I appoint The Pendleton National Bank and Trust Company of Pendleton, North Carolina, the executor and trustee and request that it be permitted to serve without surety on its bond.

Section 2. *Succession.* If The Pendleton National Bank and Trust Company, either before or during the settlement of my estate or the administration of my trusts, shall (by sale, merger, conversion, consolidation, reorganization, or otherwise) be changed into another corporation, under the same or another name, whether a state bank or a national bank, authorized to serve as executor and trustee, such successor or resulting corporation shall succeed to all of the powers and be entitled to all of the compensation of The Pendleton National Bank and Trust Company. This is supplementary to and not in limitation of any law on this subject now existing or hereafter enacted. Throughout this will the term *executor*, or *trustee*, includes either the original or the successor or substitute executor or trustee unless the wording of the will in a given provision or context shows clearly a different intention.

Powers of Executor and Trustee

ITEM XX. Without distinguishing between its or its successor's or sub-stitute's powers as executor and as trustee, and by way of illustration and not of limitation and in addition to any inherent or implied or statutory powers it may have now or hereafter acquire in either capacity, I grant the following powers to the executor and the trustee and its successor or sub-stitute. However, none of these powers shall be exercised nor be exercisable if the exercise of it would or might defeat my intention regarding my marital-deduction trust as set forth in Item X of this will.

Section 1. *Postpone distribution.* To postpone the settlement, distribu-tion, and accounting with respect to my estate for a period of five years or any portion thereof from the date of its qualification, if, in the judgment of the executor, it shall need additional time for the payment or adjustment of debts, taxes, or other charges against my estate or to reorganize, sell, or liquidate any business in which I shall be engaged or financially interested at the time of my death, or for any other reason, in the judgment of the executor, making such postponement advisable; likewise and for any similar reason to postpone the distribution in a trust for a period of two years for the time in course of such termination.

Section 2. *Retain original investments.* To retain any of the original property in my estate, including my stock in The Pendleton National Bank and Trust Company or its successor, regardless of the character of such property or whether it shall be such as then will be authorized by law for trust investment or whether it shall leave a disproportionately large share of my estate invested in one type of property or even in cash uninvested, and to dispose of such property by sale, exchange, or otherwise as and when it shall deem advisable.

Section 3. *Make new investments.* To invest and reinvest in stocks (common or preferred) including stock and stock-rights in The Pendleton National Bank and Trust Company or its successor; in bonds, notes, or mortgages on property in or outside the State of North Carolina; in insur-ance contracts of the type selected by the executor or trustee on the life of any beneficiary or of any person in whom a beneficiary has an insurable interest or in annuity contracts for any beneficiary; in real property, whether or not it is productive at the time of investment; in participations in common trust funds established by The Pendleton National Bank and Trust Company or its successor for the use of its own estates and trusts; and, generally, in such property as it shall deem advisable, even though such investments shall not be of the character nor in the proportion approved by applicable law or regulation but for this provision.

Section 4. *Carry on businesses.* To continue and operate any business which I shall own or in which I shall be financially interested at the time of my death and to do any and all things deemed needful by the executor or trustee, including the power to incorporate or to participate with others in the incorporation of the business; to put additional capital into the business for such time and in such amount or amounts as to it shall seem advisable, without liability for loss from continuance of the business except for its own negligence; and to close, liquidate, sell, or otherwise dispose of the business or interests at such time or times and upon such terms as to it shall seem advisable.

Section 5. *Carry on farms.* To continue and carry on any farming operation in which I shall be financially interested at the time of my death and to operate alone or as partner or stockholder any other farm or farms which may be acquired by the trust or trusts and, in doing so, by way of illustration and not limitation of its powers, to operate the farm or farms with hired labor, tenants, or sharecroppers; to lease or rent the farm or farms for cash or for a share of the crop or crops; to determine whether cash received shall be allocated to income or to principal or apportioned and, if apportioned, in what proportions; to purchase or otherwise acquire farm machinery and equipment and livestock; to construct, repair, and improve farm buildings of all kinds needed, in its judgment, for the operation of the farm or farms; to make or obtain loans or advances at the prevailing rates of interest for farm purposes, such as, production, harvesting, or marketing, or for the construction, repair, or improvement of farm buildings, or for the purchase of farm machinery or equipment or livestock; to employ approved soil-conservation practices in order to conserve, improve, and maintain the fertility and productivity of the soil; to protect, manage, and improve the timber and forests on the farm or farms and sell the timber and forest products as and when, in its judgment, it will be to the best interest of my estate; to ditch and drain damp or wet lands when and where needed; to install irrigation systems; to engage in livestock production or in dairying, if it shall be deemed advisable, and to construct such fences, buildings, and plant and cultivate such pastures and crops as shall be deemed necessary or advisable to carry on such a livestock program; and, in general, to employ the method or methods of carrying on the farming operation and farm practices that are, in its judgment, in common use by other landowners and farmers in the community or communities in which the farm or farms are located.

Section 6. *Manage real property.* To improve, manage, protect, and subdivide any real property in my estate or trusts; to dedicate parks, streets, highways, or alleys; to vacate any subdivision or part thereof or to sub-divide the same as often as desired; to contract to sell; to grant options to purchase; to sell or exchange on any terms it shall deem advisable; to convey either with or without consideration; to mortgage or otherwise encumber any such real property or part thereof, from time to time, in possession or reversion, by lease to commence at the present or in the future, and upon any terms and for any period or periods of time, although such period or periods may extend beyond the duration of the trust in which the property is held; to renew or extend leases and options; to renew leases and options to purchase the whole or any part of the reversion and to contract with respect to the manner of fixing the amount of present or future rentals; to employ agents to rent and collect rents whenever and to the extent that it shall deem advisable; to partition or exchange property or any part thereof for other real property or personal property; to grant easements or charges of any kind; to release, convey, or assign any right, title, or interest in or about any easement to any property or part thereof; and to deal with any such property and every part thereof in all other ways and for such other purposes or considerations as it would be lawful for any person owning the same to deal with such property either in the same or in different ways from those specified above at any time or times hereafter.

Section 7. *Receive additional property*. To receive additional property from any source, including any living trust or insurance trust created by me or my wife or any child of mine, and administer such additional property as a portion of the appropriate trust under my will; provided, the trustee shall not be required to receive without its consent such additional property involving additional or different duties or to receive it without satisfactory adjustment of its compensation.

Section 8. *Sell or exchange property*. To sell and exchange property, real or personal, for cash or on time, with or without an order of court, at such times and upon such terms and conditions as it shall deem advisable; and the purchaser shall be under no duty to follow the proceeds of the sale.

Section 9. *Deal with other trusts*. To sell property, real or personal, to or to exchange property with the trustee of any other trust I or my wife or any of our children shall have created or shall create, upon such terms and conditions as to sale price, payment, and security as to it shall seem advisable; and it shall not be under a duty to follow the proceeds of such sale or exchange.

Section 10. *Borrow money*. To borrow money for such periods of time and upon such terms and conditions as to rates, maturities, renewals, and security as to it shall seem advisable, including the power to borrow from its own banking department or from any trust created by me or my wife or any of our children, for the purpose of paying debts, taxes, or other charges against my estate or any trust under this will, and to mortgage or pledge such portion of my estate or trust property as may be required to secure such loan or loans; and to renew existing loans either as maker or endorser.

Section 11. *Register property in name of nominee*. To hold any and all stocks, bonds, notes, mortgages, or other property, real or personal, in bearer form, in its own name, in my name, in the name of any other person, partnership, or corporation, or in the name of its nominee, with or without disclosing the fiduciary relationship, and its liability shall not be increased nor decreased thereby; but it shall be liable for any loss to my estate or trusts for any negligent or wrongful act or omission of its nominee in connection with such property so held in the name of its nominee.

Section 12. *Vote shares.* To vote shares of stock owned by my estate or trusts at stockholders' meetings in person or by special, limited, or general proxy, but without power of substitution; and to vote shares of my stock in The Pendleton National Bank and Trust Company, if any be held as sole executor or trustee, in the election of directors in the manner directed by my son, Thomas, if living or, if not, by my son-in-law, Walter Askew, if living, and, if not, by my daughter Dorothy, if living, as provided in the National Banking Act and, except for the election of directors, to vote or not vote such bank stock and, if voted, to vote in such way as its own judgment dictates.

Section 13. *Exercise options, rights, and privileges.* To exercise all options, rights, and privileges to convert stock, bonds, notes, mortgages, or other property into other stock, bonds, notes, mortgages, or other property; to subscribe for other or additional stock, bonds, notes, mortgages, or other property; and to hold such stock, bonds, notes, mortgages, or other property so acquired as investments of my estate or trust so long as it shall deem it advisable to do so.

Section 14. *Paricipate in reorganizations.* To unite with other owners of property similar to any which may be held at any time in my estate or trusts in carrying out any plan for the consolidation or merger, dissolution or liquidation, foreclosure, lease, or sale of the property, incorporation or reincorporation, reorganization or readjustment of the capital or financial structure of any corporation, company, or association the securities of which may form any portion of my estate or trusts; to become and serve as a member of a stockholders' or bondholders' protective committee; to deposit securities in accordance with any plan agreed upon; to pay any assessments, expenses, or sums of money that may be required for the protection or furtherance of the interests of my estate or trusts; and to retain, so long as it shall deem advisable, any securities issued as a result of the execution of such plan, whether or not they would be authorized investments but for this provision.

Section 15. *Reduce interest rates.* To reduce the interest rate at any time and from time to time on any mortgage constituting a part of my estate or trusts.

Section 16. *Modify or release guaranties.* To consent to the modification or release of any guaranty of any mortgage in my estate or trusts or in which my estate or trusts may have a partial interest.

Section 17. *Renew and extend mortgages.* To continue mortgages upon and after maturity with or without renewal or extension upon such terms as may seem advisable to the exeutor or trustee, without reference to the value of the security at the time of such continuance.

Section 18. *Foreclose and bid in mortgaged property.* To foreclose, as an incident to the collection of any bond or note, any mortgage or deed of trust securing such bond or note and bid in the property at such foreclosure sale, or to acquire the property by deed from the mortgagor or obligor without foreclosure; and to retain as a trust investment property so bid in or taken over without foreclosure.

Section 19. *Insure.* To carry such insurance coverage, including public liability, for such hazards and in such amounts either in stock companies or in mutual companies as the executor or trustee shall deem advisable.

Section 20. *Collect.* To collect, receive, and receipt for rents, issues, profits, and other of my estate or trusts.

Section 21. *Compromise.* To compromise, adjust, arbitrate, sue on or defend, abandon, or otherwise deal with and settle claims in favor of or against my estate or trusts as to the executor or trustee shall seem advisable, and its decision shall be conclusive.

Section 22. *Employ and compensate agents and other representatives.* To employ and compensate, out of income or principal or both and in such proportion as to the executor or trustee shall seem proper, agents and other representatives, such as, accountants, attorneys at law, attorneys in fact, investment brokers, realtors, rental agents, tax specialists, and other assistants and advisers deemed by the executor or trustee to be needful for the proper settlement of my estate or administration of my trusts; and to do so without liability for any neglect, omission, misconduct, or default of such agent or other representative provided he was selected, retained, and supervised with due care by the executor or trustee.

Section 23. *Hold property in two or more trusts undivided.* To hold and retain the principal of several trusts undivided until division shall become necessary in order to make distributions; to hold, manage, invest, and account for the several shares or parts of shares by appropriate entries in the trustee's books of account, and to allocate to each share or part of share its proportionate part of all receipts and expenses; provided, however, the carrying of several trusts undivided shall not defer the vesting of the interest of any share or part of share of my estate or trusts.

Section 24. *Establish and maintain reserves.* Out of rents, interest, dividends, profits, or other income, to set up and maintain reserves for taxes, assessments, insurance premiums, repairs, improvements, depreciation, obsolescence, and general maintenance of buildings or other property; and to set up reserves for the equalization of payments to or for beneficiaries of my trusts.

Section 25. *Distribute in cash or kind.* To make distributions in cash or in kind at valuations to be determined by the executor or trustee, whose decisions as to values shall be conclusive.

Section 26. *Pay to or for minors.* To make payments to or for a minor in any one or more of the following ways: (*a*) directly to such minor; (*b*) directly by the trustee in payment for the support, maintenance, schooling, and medical, surgical, or other institutional care of such minor; (*c*) to the legal or natural guardian of such minor; or (*d*) to any other person, whether or not appointed guardian of the person by any court, who shall, in fact, have the care and custody of the person of such minor; the trustee shall not be under a duty to see to the application of the payments so made, provided it exercised due care in the selection of the person to whom such payments were made, and the receipts of such person shall be full acquittance to the trustee.

Section 27. *Apportion and allocate receipts and expenses.* To determine what is principal and what is income of any trust and to allocate or apportion receipts and expenses as between principal and income, in the exercise of its uncontrolled discretion; and, by way of illustration and not limitation of its discretion, to charge premiums on securities purchased at a premium against principal or income or partly against each; to determine what expenses, costs, taxes (other than estate, inheritance, legacy, and succession taxes) shall be charged against principal or income or apportioned between principal and income and in what proportions; and to change its plan of allocation or apportionment of receipts and expenses at any time and from time to time as it shall deem advisable, and its allocation or apportionment shall be conclusive.

Section 28. *Rely upon evidence.* To rely upon any affidavit, certificate, letter, notice, telegram, or other paper-writing, or upon any telephone conversation believed by it to be genuine and upon any other evidence believed by it to be sufficient; and to be protected and saved harmless in all payments or distributions required to be made hereunder if made in good faith and without actual notice of any changed condition or status of any person receiving payments or other distributions upon a condition.

Execution

ITEM XXI. In witness whereof, I hereunto have set my hand and affixed my seal this the first day of January, 1961.

Joseph Henry Barnes

_____(Seal)

Attestation:

Signed, sealed, published and declared by the said JOSEPH HENRY BARNES as his will in the presence of each of us who at his request and in his presence and in the presence of one another subscribe our names hereto as witnesses.

NAME: *Charles K. Maddrey*
ADDRESS: *110 Francis St., Pendleton, N.C.*

NAME: *Robert R. Edwards*
ADDRESS: *120 Woodard St., Pendleton, N.C.*

NAME: *Roger W. Layton*
ADDRESS: *221 Burgess St., Pendleton, N.C.*

FORM II

LIVING TRUST AGREEMENT

Beginning

This agreement, made this the 16th day of May, 1960, and executed in duplicate, between Joseph Henry Barnes of Pendleton, North Carolina, hereinafter referred to as the settlor, and The Pendleton National Bank and Trust Company, a national bank with its head office at Pendleton, North Carolina, hereinafter referred to as the trustee, witnesses that:

Property Trusteed

ITEM I. The settlor has paid over, delivered, assigned, transferred, or conveyed to the trustee the property itemized on Schedule A attached to this agreement as a part hereof which, together with other property which hereafter may be added to this trust, shall be held and administered by the trustee for the purposes hereinafter set forth.

Dispositive Provisions

ITEM II. The trustee or its successor shall administer this trust for the following purposes:

Section 1. *Income to settlor's mother for her life.* To pay the income quarterly or monthly or as often as she shall desire but at least once a year to the settlor's mother, Anna Davis Barnes, now a resident of Raleigh, North Carolina;

Section 2. *Consumption of principal.* If, in the judgment of the trustee, the income from this trust, together with her income from other sources, should not be sufficient to meet the needs for the comfortable support and maintenance of his mother, including medical, surgical, hospital, or institu-

392

tional care, to pay over to his mother or apply for this purpose any portion of the principal of this trust up to the whole thereof;

Section 3. *Application of income or principal.* If at any time or from time to time the trustee shall deem it inadvisable to make payments direct to the settlor's mother, then to apply the income and the needful part of the principal, in the judgment of the trustee, for her support, maintenance, and medical, surgical, hospital, or institutional care, taking into consideration both the standard of living to which she has been accustomed and the income or principal available to or for her from other sources;

Section 4. *Expenses of last illness, funeral, and burial.* Upon the death of the settlor's mother, to pay the expenses, out of income or principal or partly out of each as to the trustee shall seem advisable, of the last illness, the funeral, and the burial of the settlor's mother;

Section 5. *Termination of trust.* Upon the death of the settlor's mother, to terminate this trust and pay over, deliver, assign, transfer, or convey whatever principal or undistributed income remains to The Pendleton National Bank and Trust Company, trustee of the Pendleton Community Foundation created by declaration of trust of the board of directors of the said bank on the first day of January, 1956, by the said trustee or its successor to be held in trust in perpetuity to pay the net income annually to Chowan College, Murfreesboro, North Carolina.

Trust Declared Irrevocable

ITEM III. The settlor has been advised as to the legal effect of his execution of this trust agreement and informed as to the amount and character of the property placed in trust. He has given consideration to the revocability of this trust, and he has decided to make it irrevocable. He therefore declares that this trust is irrevocable, and he hereby divests himself of any power whatsoever to revoke this trust or to modify its terms or to amend this trust agreement in any respect whatsoever.

Note: If the trust were revocable, Item III might be:

The settlor reserves the following rights: (1) to withdraw property from this trust in any amount and at any time upon giving reasonable notice in writing to the trustee; (2) to add other property to the trust; (3) to change the beneficiaries, their respective shares, and the plan of distribution; (4) to amend this agreement in any other respect; (5) to revoke this trust in its entirety by an instrument in writing filed with the trustee; provided, however, that the duties or responsibility of the trustee shall not be enlarged without the trustee's consent nor without satisfactory adjustment of the trustee's compensation.

If the trust were revocable, the trustee might, on its part, wish to reserve the power to resign during the settlor's lifetime. If so, there might be an additional item as follows:

The trustee may resign this trusteeship during the settlor's lifetime by giving him thirty (30) days' notice in writing delivered to the settlor in person or mailed to his last known address, the resignation to become effective at the end of the thirty (30) days from the time the notice was delivered in person or mailed to the settlor. After the settlor's death, the trustee may resign only upon an order of court.

Spendthrift-Trust Provision

ITEM IV. So far as permissible by law, the interest of any beneficiary in the principal or in the income of any trust under this agreement shall not be subject either to voluntary or involuntary alienation nor to the control of the beneficiary's husband or wife.

Accounting Provision

ITEM V. The trustee shall render to the settlor during his lifetime and after his death to his mother during her lifetime a statement of account showing receipts, disbursements, and distributions of both principal and income of the trust estate during the period covered by the accounting.

Compensation Provision

ITEM VI. Section 1. For its services as trustee The Pendleton National Bank and Trust Company or its successor shall receive the compensation stipulated in its regularly adopted schedules of compensation in effect and applicable at the time such compensation shall become payable.

Section 2. If the trustee shall not have regularly adopted schedules of compensation in effect and applicable at that time, it shall receive reasonable compensation for the service rendered.

Legal Counsel

ITEM VII. The settlor suggests that the trustee employ Garland S. Ricks of the firm of Ricks, Davis, and Johnson, Jackson, North Carolina, for any legal service in connection with the administration of this trust, provided he shall be engaged in the practice of law at the time. He makes this suggestion, and it is intended to be a suggestion only, because of Mr. Ricks's intimate acquaintance with his affairs over a long period of time and the settlor's high regard for him as a lawyer and as a friend. He, as the draftsman of this trust agreement, is incorporating this provision, not at his own suggestion, but at the settlor's direction. However, the settlor intends that this shall be a suggestion and nothing more, and that the trustee shall be free to employ other or additional counsel at any time and from time to time as it may deem advisable.

Advisers to Trustee

ITEM VIII. The settlor suggests that from time to time, as occasion in its judgment shall call for it, the trustee shall consult and advise with the settlor's wife and with his brother, William, and his son, Thomas, about the comfort and welfare of his mother. In making this suggestion he does not intend to impose any legal obligation on the trustee to consult or advise with any of them, nor does he intend to relieve the trustee of any of its duty or responsibility regarding the administration of this trust.

Successor Trustee

ITEM IX. If The Pendleton National Bank and Trust Company, either before or during the administration of this trust, shall (by sale, merger, conversion, consolidation, reorganization, or otherwise) be changed into another corporation, under the same or another name, whether a state bank or a national bank, authorized to serve as trustee, such successor or resulting corporation shall succeed to all of the powers and be entitled to all of the compensation of The Pendleton National Bank and Trust Company. This is supplementary to and not in limitation of any law on this subject now existing or hereafter enacted. Throughout this trust agreement the term *trustee* includes either the original or the successor trustee unless the wording of the agreement in a given provision or context clearly shows a different intention.

Powers of Trustee

ITEM X. By way of illustration and not of limitation and in addition to any inherent or implied or statutory powers the trustee or its successor may have or hereafter acquire, the settlor grants the following powers to his trustee or its successor:

Section 1. *Postpone distribution.* To postpone the distribution and accounting with respect to this trust for a period of one year or any portion thereof from the date of the settlor's mother's death if, in the judgment of the trustee or its successor, such postponement shall be necessary or advisable.

Section 2. *Retain original investments.* To retain any of the original property in this trust regardless of the character of such property or whether it shall be such as then will be authorized by law for trust investment or whether it shall leave a disproportionately large share of the trust invested in one type of property or, in case of cash, uninvested, and to dispose of such property by sale, exchange, or otherwise as to it shall seem advisable.

Section 3. *Make new investments.* To invest and reinvest in stocks (common or preferred); in bonds, notes, or mortgages on property in or outside the State of North Carolina; in real property whether or not it is productive at the time of investment; in participations in common trust funds established by The Pendleton National Bank and Trust Company or its successor for the use of its own estates and trusts; and, generally, in such property as it shall deem advisable, even though such investment shall not be of the character nor in the proportion approved by applicable law or regulation but for this provision.

Section 4. *Receive additional property.* To receive additional property from any source, including any living trust or insurance trust created by the settlor or his wife or any child of his, and administer such additional property as a portion of this trust; provided, the trustee shall not be required to receive without its consent such additional property involving additional or different duties without satisfactory adjustment of its compensation.

Section 5. *Sell or exchange property.* To sell or exchange property real or personal, for cash or on time, with or without an order of court, at such times and upon such terms and conditions as it shall deem advisable; and the purchaser shall be under no duty to follow the proceeds of the sale.

Section 6. *Purchase property from estate.* To purchase property, real or personal, from the settlor's general estate upon such terms and conditions as to price and terms of payment as the settlor's executor or administrator and the trustee shall agree, to hold the property so purchased in this trust although it may not qualify as an authorized trust investment but for this provision, and to dispose of such property as and when the trustee shall deem advisable.

Section 7. *Lend to estate.* To lend funds to the settlor's general estate upon such terms and conditions as to interest rates, maturities, and security as the settlor's executor or administrator and the trustee shall agree.

Section 8. *Borrow money.* To borrow money for such periods of time and upon such terms and conditions as to rates, maturities, renewals, and security as to it shall seem advisable, including the power to borrow from its own banking department or from any trust created by the settlor, his wife, or any of his children, for the purpose of paying debts, taxes, or other charges against this trust, and to mortgage or pledge such portion of this trust estate as may be required to secure such loan or loans; and to renew existing loans.

Section 9. *Register property in name of nominee.* To hold any and all stocks, bonds, notes, mortgages, or other property, real or personal, in bearer form, in its own name, in the settlor's name, in the name of any other person, partnership, or corporation, or in the name of its nominee, with or without disclosing the fiduciary relationship, and its liability shall not be increased nor decreased thereby; but it shall be liable for any loss to this trust estate for any negligent or wrongful act or omission of its nominee in connection with such property so held in the name of its nominee.

Section 10. *Vote shares.* To vote shares of stock owned by this trust at stockholders' meetings in person or by special, limited, or general proxy, but without power of substitution.

Section 11. *Exercise options, rights, and privileges.* To exercise all options, rights, and privileges to convert stocks, bonds, notes, mortgages, or other property into other stocks, bonds, notes, or other property; to subscribe for other or additional stock, bonds, notes, mortgages, or other property; and to hold such stock, bonds, notes, mortgages, or other property so acquired as investments of this trust so long as it shall deem it advisable to do so.

Section 12. *Participate in reorganizations.* To unite with other owners of property similar to any which may be held at any time in this trust in carrying out any plan for the consolidation or merger, dissolution or liquidation, foreclosure, lease, or sale of the property, incorporation or reincorporation, reorganization or readjustment of the capital or financial structure of any corporation, company, or association the securities of which may form any portion of this trust; to become and serve as a member of a stockholders' or bondholders' protective committee; to deposit securities in accordance with any plan agreed upon; to pay any assessments, expenses, or sums of money that may be required for the protection or furtherance of the interests of this trust; and to retain, so long as it shall deem advisable, any securities issued as a result of the execution of such plan, whether or not they would be authorized investments but for this provision.

Section 13. *Reduce interest rates.* To reduce the interest rate at any time and from time to time on any mortgage constituting a part of this trust.

Section 14. *Modify or release guaranties.* To consent to the modification or release of any guaranty of any mortgage in this trust or in which this trust may have a partial interest.

Section 15. *Renew and extend mortgages.* To continue mortgages upon and after maturity with or without renewal or extension upon such terms as may seem advisable to the trustee, without reference to the value of the security at the time of such continuance.

Section 16. *Foreclose and bid in property.* To foreclose, as an incident to the collection of any bond or note, any mortgage or deed of trust securing such bond or note and bid in the property at such foreclosure sale, or to acquire the property by deed from the mortgagor or obligor without foreclosure; and to retain as a trust investment property so bid in or taken over without foreclosure.

Section 17. *Insure.* To carry such insurance coverage, including public liability, for such hazards and in such amounts either in stock companies or in mutual companies as the trustee shall deem advisable.

Section 18. *Collect.* To collect, receive, and receipt for rents, issues, profits, and other income of this trust.

Section 19. *Compromise.* To compromise, adjust, arbitrate, sue on or defend, abandon, or otherwise deal with and settle claims in favor of or against this trust as to the trustee shall seem advisable and its decision shall be conclusive.

Section 20. *Employ and compensate agents and other representatives.* To employ and compensate, out of income or principal or both and in such proportion as to the trustee shall seem proper, agents and other representatives, such as accountants, attorneys at law, attorneys in fact, investment brokers, realtors, rental agents, tax specialists, and other assistants and advisers deemed by the trustee to be needful for the proper administration of this trust; and to do so without liability for any neglect, omission, misconduct, or default of such agent or other representatives provided he was selected, retained, and supervised with due care by the trustee.

Section 21. *Establish and maintain reserves.* Out of rents, interest, dividends, profits, or other income, to set up and maintain reserves for taxes, assessments, insurance premiums, repairs, improvements, depreciation, obsolescence, and general maintenance of buildings or other property; and to set up reserves for the equalization of payments to or for beneficiaries of this trust.

Section 22. *Apportion and allocate receipts and expenses.* To determine what is principal and what is income of this trust and to allocate or apportion receipts and expenses as between principal and income, in the exercise of its uncontrolled discretion; and, by way of illustration and not limitation of its discretion, to charge premiums on securities purchased at a premium against principal or income or partly against each; to determine what expenses, costs, taxes (other than estate, inheritance, legacy, and succession taxes) shall be charged against principal or income or apportioned between principal and income and in what proportions; and to change its plan of allocation or apportionment of receipts and expenses at any time and from time to time as it shall deem advisable, and its allocation or apportionment shall be conclusive.

Section 23. *Rely upon evidence.* To rely upon any affidavit, certificate, letter, notice, telegram, or other paper-writing, or upon any telephone conversation believed by it to be genuine and upon any other evidence believed by it to be sufficient.

Situs of Trust

ITEM XI. This trust has been created under the laws of the State of North Carolina, and its validity, construction, and administration shall be determined by the laws of that state.

In Testimonium Clause

In witness whereof, the settlor has set his hand and affixed his seal, and the trustee, in acceptance of the trust, has caused these presents to be executed and attested by its appropriate officers and its corporate seal affixed.

WITNESS:

Randolph Phillips   *Joseph Henry Barnes*
_____   _____
ATTEST: SETTLOR

                                            THE PENDLETON NATIONAL BANK AND
Harvey Davis   TRUST COMPANY
_____   BY   *Norris Boone*
SECRETARY   _____
(CORPORATE SEAL OF BANK AFFIXED)   VICE PRESIDENT

SCHEDULE A

Schedule A is a separate sheet attached to the Trust Agreement listing and acknowledging receipt of listed and readily marketable securities of the current market value of Seventy-five Thousand ($75,000) Dollars.

FORM III

PERSONAL INSURANCE TRUST AGREEMENT

Beginning

This agreement, made this the 16th day of May, 1960, and executed in duplicate, between Joseph Henry Barnes of Pendleton, North Carolina, hereinafter referred to as the insured, and The Pendleton National Bank and Trust Company, a national bank with its head office at Pendleton, North Carolina, hereinafter referred to as the trustee, witnesses that:

Property Trusteed

ITEM I. The insured has caused certain policies of life insurance to be issued on his life, as set forth in Schedule A attached hereto as a part of this agreement. The proceeds of these policies now are or hereafter will be made payable to the trustee either upon the death of the insured or upon the occurrence of some event before or after his death. The insured may bring still other policies under the operation of this agreement.

Note: The above provision is appropriate for an unfunded insurance trust agreement. If it is a funded agreement, the following paragraph should be added after Item I and numbered as a separate item.

The insured also has delivered to the trustee certain property itemized on Schedule B attached hereto as a part of this agreement. This property, together with other property which hereafter may be brought within the operation of this trust, and the life insurance policies mentioned above shall constitute the trust estate and shall be held and administered by the trustee for the uses and purposes hereinafter set forth.

400

Payment of Premiums

ITEM II. The trustee shall be under no duty or obligation to pay any of the premiums, assessments, or other charges or to keep itself informed with respect to them or with respect to the performance of any act necessary to keep the said policies in force. The trustee shall not be liable to anyone if for any reason the policies, or any of them, shall lapse or otherwise be uncollectible. The trustee shall have no duties or obligations hereunder until the maturity of the policies or the death of the insured.

Note: The foregoing provision would be appropriate only for an unfunded insurance trust agreement. If it were a funded trust, the following would be the appropriate provision in place of the foregoing one:

ITEM II. Out of the net income of the trust estate and out of the principal to the extent to which it may be necessary, the trustee shall pay the premiums and assessments and other charges on the above-described policies and additions thereto as they fall due. Unless herein otherwise provided, any surplus income shall be added to and be reinvested as a part of the principal of the trust estate. The trustee may apply the dividends on such policies or may use the loan or other values under the policies for the payment of premiums, assessments, and other charges, all in accordance with the terms of the respective policies. If, however, the trustee shall not have in the trust estate sufficient income or principal, including the above-mentioned dividends and loan and other values under the policies themselves, to pay the premiums, assessments, and other charges then due upon the policies or any of them, it shall proceed to take the necessary steps to divest itself of all rights under the policies whether by release or assignment or otherwise, and then shall mail the policy or policies to the last known address of the insured; whereupon the trustee shall be relieved of all liability for lapse of the policy or policies for failure to pay the premiums, assessments, or other charges thereon, and the trust thereupon shall terminate with respect to such policies.

This item must be drawn in the light of the applicable rule against accumulations. In some states adding unexpended income to principal might be a violation of the rule; in most states it would not.

Rights Reserved by Insured

ITEM III. During his lifetime all rights of every nature accruing to the insured hereby are reserved by him, to be exercised in accordance with the terms of the respective policies; but, if the consent of the trustee is necessary at any time, the trustee agrees to give its consent, which consent shall bind all the beneficiaries of this trust. By way of illustration but not of limitation, the insured reserves the following rights: (1) to add other insurance to the trust by making the policy payable to the trustee; (2) to receive or apply dividends or distributive shares of surplus, disability benefits, surrender values, or the proceeds of matured endowments; (3) to obtain and receive from the respective insurance companies such advances or loans on account of a policy as may be available; (4) to sell, assign, or pledge a policy; (5) to change the beneficiary of a policy; and (6) to withdraw a policy in order to exercise a reserved right or for any other purpose.

Note: The foregoing provision would be appropriate for a revocable insurance trust agreement only.

Collection of Insurance Proceeds

ITEM IV. As soon as practicable after the death of the insured, the trustee shall make proofs of death and shall collect all moneys due under the policies then within the operation of this agreement and then payable to the trustee. Likewise, as soon as practicable after the occurrence of any event before or after the death of the insured which may cause any policy or policies then within the operation of this agreement to become payable to the trustee, the trustee shall make proper proofs and shall collect all moneys then due under such policy or policies. The trustee may institute any proceeding at law or in equity in order to enforce the payment of any policy and may do and perform any and all acts and things which may be necessary or proper for the purpose of collecting any sums which may be due and payable under the terms of such policy. But the trustee shall not be required to maintain any litigation to enforce the payment of any of the policies unless it is indemnified to its satisfaction against all expense and liability arising on account of such litigation. If the trustee shall elect to demand indemnity, it shall make such a demand in writing upon each of the beneficiaries under this agreement whose interest is vested by mailing or delivering the same to his last known address. If satisfactory indemnity is not furnished within thirty (30) days thereafter, the trustee shall assign all its rights under the policy in question to the beneficiaries under this agreement and thereupon its liability with respect to such policy shall cease and the trust hereunder shall terminate with respect to such policy. The trustee is authorized to compromise and adjust claims arising out of the insurance policies or any of them upon such terms and conditions as it may deem just, and the decisions of the trustee shall be binding and conclusive upon all persons interested therein.

Dispositive Provisions

ITEM V. The trustee or its successor shall administer this trust for the following purposes:

Section 1. *Income to insured's daughter, Mable, for her life.* To pay the income quarterly or monthly or as often as she shall desire but at least once a year to the insured's daughter, Mable, during her lifetime;

Section 2. *Consumption of principal.* If, in the judgment of the trustee, the income from this trust, together with the income from other sources, including the insured's general estate, should not be sufficient to meet the needs for her comfortable support and maintenance, including medical, surgical, hospital, or institutional care, to pay over to his daughter or apply for this purpose any portion of the principal of this trust up to the whole thereof;

Section 3. *Application of income or principal.* If at any time or from time to time the trustee should deem it inadvisable to make payments direct to the insured's said daughter, then to apply the income and the needful part of the principal, in the judgment of the trustee, for her support, maintenance, and medical, surgical, hospital, or institutional care, taking into account the standard of living to which she will have been accustomed and the income or principal available to or for her from other sources;

Section 4. *Termination of trust.* Upon the death of the insured's said daughter, to dispose of the property remaining in this trust as she shall direct by her will; but, in the event of her failure effectively to exercise this power of appointment, at her death to pay over, deliver, assign, transfer, or convey the property remaining in the trust to The Pendleton National Bank and Trust Company, trustee of the Pendleton Community Foundation created by declaration of trust of the board of directors of the said bank on the first day of January, 1956, by the said trustee or its successor to be held in perpetual trust to pay the net income anually or oftener to the Roanoke-Chowan Hospital, Ahoskie, North Carolina.

Powers of Trustee

ITEM VI. By way of illustration and not of limitation and in addition to any inherent or implied or statutory powers the trustee or its successor may have or hereafter acquire, the insured grants the following powers to his trustee or its successor:

Section 1. *Postpone distribution.* To postpone distribution and accounting with respect to this trust for a period of one year or any portion thereof from the date of the insured's daughter's death if, in the judgment of the trustee or its successor, such postponement shall be necessary or advisable.

Section 2. *Retain original investments.* To retain any of the original property in this trust regardless of the character of such property or whether it shall be such as then will be authorized by law for trust investment or whether it shall leave a disproportionately large share of the trust invested in one type of property or, in case of cash, uninvested, and to dispose of such property by sale, exchange, or otherwise as to it shall seem advisable.

Section 3. *Make new investments.* To invest and reinvest in stocks (common or preferred); in bonds, notes, or mortgages on property in or outside the State of North Carolina; in real property whether or not it is productive at the time of investment; in participations in common trust funds established by The Pendleton National Bank and Trust Company or its successor for the use of its own estates and trusts; and, generally, in such property as it shall deem advisable, even though such investment shall not be of the character nor in the proportion approved by applicable law or regulation but for this provision.

Section 4. *Receive additional property*. To receive additional property from any source, including any living trust or insurance trust created by the insured or his wife or any child of his, and administer such additional property as a portion of this trust: provided, the trustee shall not be required to receive without its consent such additional property involving additional or different duties without satisfactory adjustment of its compensation.

Section 5. *Sell or exchange property*. To sell and exchange property, real or personal, for cash or on time, with or without an order of court, at such times and upon such terms and conditions as it shall deem advisable; and the purchaser shall be under no duty to follow the proceeds of the sale.

Section 6. *Purchase property from estate*. To purchase property, real or personal, from the insured's general estate upon such terms and conditions as to price and terms of payment as the insured's executor or administrator and the trustee shall agree, to hold the property so purchased in this trust although it may not qualify as an authorized trust investment but for this provision, and to dispose of such property as and when the trustee shall deem advisable.

Section 7. *Lend to estate*. To lend funds to the insured's general estate upon such terms and conditions as to interest rates, maturities, and security as the insured's executor or administrator and the trustee shall agree.

Section 8. *Borrow money*. To borrow money for such periods of time and upon such terms and conditions as to rates, maturities, renewals, and security as to it shall seem advisable, including the power to borrow from its own banking department or from any trust created by the insured, his wife, or any of his children, for the purpose of paying debts, taxes, or other charges against this trust, and to mortgage or pledge such portion of this trust estate as may be required to secure such loan or loans; and to renew existing loans.

Section 9. *Register property in name of nominee*. To hold any and all stocks, bonds, notes, mortgages, or other property, real or personal, in bearer form, in its own name, in the insured's name, in the name of any other person, partnership, or corporation, or in the name of its nominee, with or without disclosing the fiduciary relationship, and its liability shall not be increased nor decreased thereby; but it shall be liable for any loss to this trust estate for any negligent or wrongful act or omission of its nominee in connection with such property so held in the name of its nominee.

Section 10. *Vote shares*. To vote shares of stock owned by this trust at stockholders' meetings in person or by special, limited, or general proxy, but without power of substitution.

Section 11. *Exercise options, rights, and privileges.* To exercise all options, rights, and privileges to convert stocks, bonds, notes, mortgages, or other property into other stocks, bonds, notes, or other property; to subscribe for other or additional stock, bonds, notes, mortgages, or other property; and to hold such stock, bonds, notes, mortgages, or other property so acquired as investments of this trust so long as it shall deem it advisable to do so.

Section 12. *Participate in reorganizations.* To unite with other owners of property similar to any which may be held at any time in this trust in carrying out any plan for the consolidation or, merger, dissolution or liquidation, foreclosure, lease, or sale of the property, incorporation or reincorporation, reorganization or readjustment of the capital or financial structure of any corporation, company, or association the securities of which may form any portion of this trust; to become and serve as a member of a stockholders' or bondholders' protective committee; to deposit securities in accordance with any plan agreed upon; to pay any assessments, expenses, or sums of money that may be required for the protection or furtherance of the interests of this trust; and to retain, so long as it shall deem advisable, any securities issued as a result of the execution of such plan, whether or not they would be authorized investments but for this provision.

Section 13. *Reduce interest rates.* To reduce the interest rate at any time and from time to time on any mortgage constituting a part of this trust.

Section 14. *Modify or release guaranties.* To consent to the modification or release of any guaranty of any mortgage in this trust or in which this trust may have a partial interest.

Section 15. *Renew and extend mortgages.* To continue mortgages upon and after maturity with or without renewal or extension upon such terms as may seem advisable to the trustee, without reference to the value of the security at the time of such continuance.

Section 16. *Foreclose and bid in property.* To foreclose, as an incident to the collection of any bond or note, any mortgage or deed of trust securing such bond or note and bid in the property at such foreclosure sale, or to acquire the property by deed from the mortgagor or obligor without foreclosure; and to retain as a trust investment property so bid in or taken over without foreclosure.

Section 17. *Insure.* To carry such insurance coverage, including public liability, for such hazards and in such amounts either in stock companies or in mutual companies as the trustee shall deem advisable.

Section 18. *Collect.* To collect, receive, and receipt for rents, issues, profits, and other income of this trust.

Section 19. *Compromise.* To compromise, adjust, arbitrate, sue on or defend, abandon, or otherwise deal with and settle claims in favor of or against this trust as to the trustee shall seem advisable and its decision shall be conclusive.

Section 20. *Employ and compensate agents and other representatives.* To employ and compensate, out of income or principal or both and in such proportion as to the trustee shall seem proper, agents and other representatives, such as accountants, attorneys at law, attorneys in fact, investment brokers, realtors, rental agents, tax specialists, and other assistants and advisers deemed by the trustee to be needful for the proper administration of this trust; and to do so without liability for any neglect, omission, misconduct, or default of such agent or other representatives provided he was selected, retained, and supervised with due care by the trustee.

Section 21. *Establish and maintain reserves.* Out of rents, interest, dividends, profits, or other income, to set up and maintain reserves for taxes, assessments, insurance premiums, repairs, improvements, depreciation, obsolescence, and general maintenance of buildings or other property; and to set up reserves for the equalization of payments to or for beneficiaries of this trust.

Section 22. *Apportion and allocate receipts and expenses.* To determine what is principal and what is income of this trust and to allocate or apportion receipts and expenses as between principal and income, in the exercise of its uncontrolled discretion; and, by way of illustration and not limitation of its discretion, to charge premiums on securities purchased at a premium against principal or income or partly against each; to determine what expenses, costs, taxes (other than estate, inheritance, legacy, and succession taxes) shall be charged against principal or income or apportioned between principal and income and in what proportions; and to change its plan of allocation or apportionment of receipts and expenses at any time and from time to time as it shall deem advisable, and its allocation or apportionment shall be conclusive.

Section 23. *Rely upon evidence.* To rely upon any affidavit, certificate, letter, notice, telegram, or other paper-writing, or upon any telephone conversation believed by it to be genuine and upon any other evidence believed by it to be sufficient.

Section 24. *Exercise options of settlement.* If any company issuing a policy or policies in this trust will hold the proceeds of such policy or policies under any of the options of settlement contained in the policy or policies, the trustee, in the exercise of its discretion, is authorized to permit the proceeds of such policy to remain with the insurance company or companies under any option of settlement available to the trustee under the terms of the policy or policies.

Spendthrift Trust Provision

ITEM VII. So far as permissible by law, the interest of any beneficiary in the principal or in the income of any trust under this agreement shall not be subject either to voluntary or involuntary alienation nor to the control of the beneficiary's husband or wife.

Vesting Provision

ITEM VIII. The interest of every beneficiary shall vest, anything else in this agreement to the contrary notwithstanding, within twenty-one years after the death of the last survivor of beneficiaries of this trust who were in being at the time of insured's death. Upon such vesting the principal shall be distributed among those who theretofore had been income beneficiaries and in the proportions that each had received income or had it applied for his benefit. If, at the time of the vesting of an interest, the beneficiary shall be a minor, the trustee, shall continue to hold his share in trust for his benefit, paying over or applying income and as much of the principal as the trustee shall deem advisable, until such beneficiary shall be twenty-one years of age and then distribute his share of the trust property to him, discharged of the trust. And, if at the time of vesting, the person is entitlee of a trust under the insured's will and his interest under that trust is vested, his share shall be added to that trust and thereafter administered as a part thereof.

Accounting Provision

ITEM IX. The trustee shall render to the insured during his lifetime and after his death to his daughter, Mable, during her lifetime a statement of account showing receipts, disbursements, and distributions of both principal and income of the trust estate during the period covered by the accounting.

Compensation Provision

ITEM X. Section 1. For its services as trustee The Pendleton National Bank and Trust Company or its successor shall receive the compensation stipulated in its regularly adopted schedules of compensation in effect and applicable at the time such compensation shall become payable.

Section 2. If the trustee shall not have regularly adopted schedules of compensation in effect and applicable at that time, it shall receive reasonable compensation for the service rendered.

Legal Counsel

ITEM XI. The insured suggests that the trustee employ Garland S. Ricks of the firm of Ricks, Davis, and Johnson, of Jackson, North Carolina, for any legal service in connection with the administration of this trust, provided he shall be engaged in the practice of law at the time. He makes this suggestion, and it is intended to be a suggestion only, because of Mr. Ricks's intimate acquaintance with his affairs over a long period of time and the insured's high regard for him as a lawyer and as a friend. He, as the drafts-man of this trust agreement, is incorporating this provision, not at his sug-gestion, but at the insured's direction. However, the insured intends that this shall be a suggestion and nothing more, and that the trustee shall be free to employ other or additional counsel at any time and from time to time as it may deem advisable.

Successor Trustee

ITEM XII. If The Pendleton National Bank and Trust Company, either before or during the administration of this trust, shall (by sale, merger, con-version, consolidation, reorganization, or otherwise) be changed into an-other corporation, under the same or another name, whether a state bank or a national bank, authorized to serve as trustee, such successor or resulting corporation shall succeed to all of the powers and be entitled to all of the compensation of The Pendleton National Bank and Trust Company. This is supplementary to and not in limitation of any law on this subject now existing or hereafter enacted. Throughout this trust agreement the term *trustee* includes either the original or the successor trustee unless the word-ing of the agreement in a given provision or context shows clearly a differ-ent intention.

Situs of Trust

ITEM XIII. This trust has been created under the laws of the State of North Carolina, and its validity, construction, and administration shall be determined by the laws of that State.

Protection of Insurance Company

ITEM XIV. The insurance company or companies issuing any of the policies in this trust now or hereafter shall not be held nor bound in any manner nor to any extent nor be responsible for the application by the trus-tee of the proceeds of any policy or policies paid to the trustee, nor for any act or omission of the trustee regarding the policies now or hereafter in this trust either during the lifetime of the insured or after his death nor as to any policy maturing before his death. The receipt of the trustee for the proceeds of any policy or policies shall be full acquittance to the insurance company or companies.

Protection of Trustee

ITEM XV. The trustee accepts this trust without any responsibility for the validity of any policy now or hereafter in this trust or for the legality or effectiveness of any assignment, designation, or change of beneficiary of any policy in this trust.

In Testimonium Clause

In witness whereof, the insured has set his hand and affixed his seal and the trustee, in acceptance of this trust, has caused these presents to be executed and attested by its appropriate officers and its corporate seal affixed.

WITNESS:

Randolph Phillips

Joseph Henry Barnes

INSURED

ATTEST:

THE PENDLETON NATIONAL BANK AND TRUST COMPANY

Harvey Davis

BY   *Norris Boone*

SECRETARY

VICE PRESIDENT

(CORPORATE SEAL OF BANK AFFIXED)

TRUSTEE

SCHEDULES

Schedule A is a list of the insurance policies of the face value of One Hundred Thousand ($100,000) Dollars.

If the trust were funded, *Schedule B* would consist of an itemization of the funding securities for the policies. (See Item I, Note.)

FORM IV

BUSINESS INSURANCE TRUST AGREEMENT

Beginning

This agreement, made this the 16th day of May, 1960, by Joseph Henry Barnes, Walter Woodard, and Walter Askew, all of Pendleton, North Carolina, hereinafter referred to as stockholders wherever appropriate, and The Pendleton National Bank and Trust Company, a national bank with its head office at Pendleton, North Carolina, hereinafter referred to as the trustee, witnesses that:

Statement of Purpose

Whereas, stock of Meherrin Agricultural Company, hereinafter referred to as the company, is held by the above-named stockholders who are actively engaged in the management of the company and in order to insure continuity of management, it is considered advisable to arrange so that on the death of any one of the stockholders, his stock may be acquired by the survivors; and

Whereas, for the purpose of providing the cash so to acquire the stock of a deceased stockholder, the life of each of the stockholders is being insured by the other stockholders under policies listed on *Schedule A* attached and made a part of this agreement, to be made payable to and deposited with trustee;

Now, therefore, in consideration of the mutual covenants and agreements herein contained, it is agreed by and among the parties hereto as follows:

410

Payment of Premiums

ITEM I. Section 1. The duty and responsibility concerning the payment of premiums, assessments, and other charges on such policies shall rest solely upon the respective stockholders.

Section 2. It is understood that each stockholder shall contribute to the payment of the premiums, assessments, and other charges on the policies on the life of every other stockholder in proportion to the stock of such contributing stockholder in the company.

Duties of Trustee as to Collection of Insurance

ITEM II. As soon as practicable after the death of the insured, the trustee shall make proofs of death and shall collect all moneys due under the policies then within the operation of this agreement and then payable to the trustee. Likewise, as soon as practicable after the occurrence of any event before or after the death of the insured which may cause any policy or policies then within the operation of this agreement to become payable to the trustee, the trustee shall make proper proofs and shall collect all moneys then due under such policy or policies. The trustee may institute any proceeding at law or in equity in order to enforce the payment of any policy and may do and perform any and all acts and things which may be necessary or proper for the purpose of collecting any sums which may be due and payable under the terms of such policy. But the trustee shall not be required to maintain any litigation to enforce the payment of any of the policies unless it is indemnified to its satisfaction against all expense and liability arising on account of such litigation. If the trustee shall elect to demand indemnity, it shall make such a demand in writing upon each of the beneficiaries under this agreement whose interest is vested by mailing or deivering the same to his last known address. If satisfactory indemnity is not furnished within thirty (30) days thereafter, the trustee shall assign all its rights under the policy in question to the beneficiaries under this agreement and thereupon its liability with respect to such policy shall cease and the trust hereunder shall terminate with respect to such policy. The trustee is authorized to compromise and adjust claims arising out of the insurance policies or any of them upon such terms and conditions as it may deem just, and the decisions of the trustee shall be binding and conclusive upon all persons interested therein.

Rights Reserved by Stockholders

ITEM III. Section 1. This agreement shall be operative only with respect to the net proceeds of such policies as may be due and payable upon the death of any of the stockholders; and during the lifetime of the insured under any of said policies, stockholders, acting in concert, may in accord-

ance with the terms of the respective policies and without the consent of
the trustee, except as required by an insurance company, exercise every
privilege and receive every benefit granted under any of said policies, assign,
pledge, release, or surrender said policies or any of them, and the trustee
shall be bound thereby.

Note: The stockholders may specify the rights under the policies reserved by them as in the Personal Insurance Trust Agreement Item III.

Section 2. The stockholders jointly but not singly may revoke this
trust in whole or in part; may withdraw any of the policies held hereunder
at any time or from time to time; may change the terms of this trust without
limitation; may change any or all of the beneficiaries hereunder, divesting
them or any of them wholly or partly of rights created hereunder; may add
other policies to this agreement; but none of such changes shall be effective
to increase or enlarge the duties, powers, or liabilities or change the compensation of the trustee without having first obtained its written consent
thereto.

Deposit of Stock

ITEM IV. Section 1. The stockholders agree immediately upon the execution of this agreement to deposit with the trustee, endorsed in blank or
accompanied by an irrevocable power of attorney, all their stock and any
additional or other stock which they may acquire from time to time in the
company either as stock dividends or otherwise, transferring to the trustee
legal title to such stock and the shares represented thereby.

Section 2. The stockholders reserve the right to vote and to receive all
dividends paid on the stock; to have the stock held in their respective names
on the books of the company and not transferred into the name of the trustee; and to have all or any part of the stock standing in the name of any one
of the stockholders to be transferred on the books of the company to one or
more of the other stockholders.

Purchase of Stock

ITEM V. Section 1. On the death of any stockholder, the trustee, upon
receiving the net proceeds of the insurance, shall deliver to the surviving
stockholders, pro rata (that is, pro rata to the contribution of each surviving
stockholder towards premiums, assessments, and other charges on the policies on the life of the deceased stockholder) such number of shares of stock
standing in the name of the deceased stockholder as such proceeds suffice to
purchase at the price hereinafter fixed.

Section 2. The surviving stockholders shall have the right at any time
within sixty (60) days from the death of the deceased stockholder to purchase at the same price any part or all of his shares of stock which the proceeds of the policies on his life shall be insufficient to purchase.

Section 3. If the surviving stockholders desire to purchase stock in the company in excess of the number of shares so held by the trustee, the shares shall be allotted pro rata to the contribution of each stockholder to the premiums, assessments, and other charges on the policies of the deceased stockholder.

Section 4. If the cash received by the trustee is in excess of the amount necessary to purchase such stock of the deceased stockholder, the surplus shall be divided pro rata among the surviving stockholders.

Section 5. Any payment to be made by a surviving stockholder to the trustee under any of the provisions of this agreement may be made in notes secured to the satisfaction of the trustee maturing in not more than three years, bearing interest from date at 5 per cent per annum, payable semi-annually.

Fixing Value of Stock

ITEM VI. The purchase price of the stock of a deceased stockholder shall be the price determined by the book value of said stock at the time of the last annual inventory preceding the death of such stockholder. The proceeds of the insurance shall not be included in the valuation. But if an inventory shall not have been made within one year of the death of the deceased stock-holder, the value of the stock shall be determined by a committee of appraisers, one of whom shall be chosen by the surviving stockholders, one by the executor or administrator of the deceased stockholder, and the third by the other two, and the decision of two shall govern and shall be binding on all parties.

Note: This is only one of several ways of fixing the value of the stock. Each type of business has its appropriate method of valuation and its method should be prescribed. It is highly important that some *workable* method be specified in the agreement. In determining the method of fixing the value of the stock, the draftsman should have in mind that the market for the stock would be restricted largely to the surviving stockholders themselves and their competitors.

Cash Surrender Value of Insurance on Life of Surviving Stockholders

ITEM VII. The interest of a deceased stockholder in any insurance on the life of the surviving stockholders may be purchased by the surviving stockholders at any time within sixty (60) days from the date of the death of the deceased stockholder. The value of such deceased stockholder's interest in the cash surrender value of the policies on the lives of the surviving stockholders shall be the part of the cash surrender value that represents the proportion that the deceased stockholder contributed to the payment of the premiums, assessments, and other charges on the policies on the lives of the

surviving stockholders. If, however, such interest of the deceased stockholder shall not be purchased, the surviving stockholders agree to take whatever steps may be appropriate or required by life insurance companies to
enable the estate of the deceased stockholder to realize his interest in the cash
surrender value of such policies.

Note: The wording of this item should be considered in the light of
the transfer-for-value provision of the Internal Revenue Code of 1954.

Distribution to Deceased Stockholder's Beneficiaries

ITEM VIII. The proceeds of the sale of the deceased stockholder's stock
in the company, together with any portion of his stock not purchased by
the surviving stockholders, and the cash surrender value of his interest in
the policies on the life of the surviving stockholders shall be held by the
trustee free of this trust but subject to a trust agreement of even date between The Pendleton National Bank and Trust Company and the deceased
stockholder.

Note: This contemplates that the proceeds of insurance, after having
been paid over for the purchase of the stock, will be poured-over into a
living trust created by the deceased stockholder. But the proceeds might be
added to the deceased stockholder's general estate or distributed direct to
his beneficiaries. This provision must be drawn in the light of the applicable
state law regarding the nontestamentary disposition of property or disposition by an instrument other than a will.

Right of Trustee to Resign

ITEM IX. Trustee reserves the right to resign this trusteeship at any time
during the joint lifetime of the stockholders by giving them thirty (30) days
notice in writing; but after the death of any stockholder only for cause
shown to the satisfaction of the probate court of the county in which is
located the principal office of the company, which court shall have
authority, if it deem advisable, to accept the resignation and appoint a successor trustee clothed with all the powers of the original trustee.

Termination of Trust

ITEM X. Section 1. If all the policies on the life of any stockholder shall
be cancelled or surrendered before maturity, this trust shall terminate as
to such policies and as to all stock in the name of the stockholder, and such
stock shall forthwith be delivered to him.

Section 2. When only one of the stockholders who were then parties
hereto shall survive, this agreement shall terminate as to his stock, which
shall forthwith be delivered to him, and his interest in the policies on his
life shall be assigned to him.

Note: Other possibilities which in a given case might be covered are suggested by these questions: What would happen should all three of the stockholders be killed simultaneously in a common accident? What would happen if one of the stockholders should sever his connection with the company while retaining his stock?

Compensation of Trustee

ITEM XI. Section 1. For its services as trustee The Pendleton National Bank and Trust Company or its successor shall receive the compensation stipulated in its regularly adopted schedules of compensation in effect and applicable at the time such compensation shall become payable.

Section 2. If the trustee shall not have regularly adopted schedules of compensation in effect and applicable at that time, it shall receive reasonable compensation for the service rendered.

Situs of Trust

ITEM XII. This trust has been created under the laws of the State of North Carolina, and its validity, construction, and administration shall be determined by the laws of that State.

Successor Trustee

ITEM XIII. If The Pendleton National Bank and Trust Company during the administration of this trust, shall (by sale, merger, conversion, consolidation, reorganization, or otherwise) be changed into another corporation, under the same or another name, whether a state bank or a national bank, authorized to serve as executor and trustee, such successor or resulting corporation shall succeed to all of the powers and be entitled to all of the compensation of The Pendleton National Bank and Trust Company. This is supplementary to and not in limitation of any law on this subject now existing or hereafter enacted. Throughout this trust agreement the term *executor* or *trustee* includes either the original or the successor or substitute executor or trustee unless the wording of the agreement in a given provision or context shows clearly a different intention.

In Testimonium Clause

In Witness Whereof, the stockholders have set their hands and affixed their seals; and the trustee, in acceptance of the trusts herein created, has caused these presents to be executed and attested by its authorized officers and its corporate seal affixed on the date stated above.

WITNESSES:

Horace Outland	*Joseph Henry Barnes*	(Seal)
Louis Johnson	*Walter Woodard*	(Seal)
Hinton Smith	*Walter Askew*	(Seal)

STOCKHOLDERS

THE PENDLETON NATIONAL BANK AND
TRUST COMPANY

ATTEST:

Harvey Davis   BY   *Norris Boone*

SECRETARY   VICE PRESIDENT
(CORPORATE SEAL OF BANK AFFIXED)   TRUSTEE

SCHEDULE A

Schedule A is a list of the policies trusteed by each stockholder, giving the name of the insurance company and the amount of each policy, with provision for receipt for policies by the trustee.

BIBLIOGRAPHY

In this edition the bibliography contains many more items than appeared in either of the preceding editions. They are included primarily for the sake of the student who wishes to go further in the study of the disposition and administration of property than the text alone carries him.

As stated in the Preface to the first edition, this is not a handbook on the law of estates and trusts. Nonetheless, as a practical matter, it has been impossible to avoid some discussion of principles of law governing disposition and administration of property. Consequently, this bibliography contains a number of well-known treatises and books and a few articles on legal aspects of estates and trusts.

Most of the current discussion of disposition and administration of property in estates and trusts from the practical as distinguished from the purely legal point of view is to be found in two monthly publications; namely, *The Trust Bulletin,* which is the official organ of the Trust Division of the American Bankers Association (12 East 36 Street, New York 16, N.Y.) and *Trusts and Estates* (50 East 42 Street, New York 17, N.Y.), which has been in continuous publication since 1904. In the numerous citations to these two publications, *The Trust Bulletin* is abbreviated *TB* and *Trusts and Estates, TE.*

In the field of trusts, two of the most recent developments have been the handling of businesses in trust and employees trusts. In order that the student may be apprised of these developments, the bibliography contains an unusually large number of citations of articles on these two subjects.

Treatises

American Jurisprudence (San Francisco, Bancroft-Whitney Company, and New York, The Lawyers Cooperative Company), cited *American Jurisprudence.*

Bogert, George Gleason, *The Law of Trusts and Trustees* (Kansas City, Mo., Vernon Law Book Company; and St. Paul, Minn., West Publishing Company), cited Bogert on *Trusts and Trustees.*

CASNER, A. James, Editor in Chief, *American Law of Property* (Boston, Little, Brown & Co.), cited Casner, *American Law of Property*.

Corpus Juris (New York, American Law Book Company), cited *Corpus Juris*.

NOSSAMAN, Walter L., *Trust Administration and Taxation* (Albany, N.Y., Matthew Bender and Company, Inc.), cited Nossaman on *Administration and Taxation*.

POWELL, Richard R., *Real Property Law* (Albany, N.Y., Matthew Bender and Company, Inc.), cited Powell on *Real Property*.

Restatement of the Law of Property (Philadelphia, The American Law Institute), cited *Restatement of the Law of Property*.

Restatement of the Law of Trusts (Philadelphia, The American Law Institute), cited *Restatement of Law of Trusts*.

Ruling Case Law (Northport, N.Y., Edward Thompson Book Company; San Francisco, Bancroft-Whitney Company; and New York, The Lawyers Co-operative Publishing Company), cited *Ruling Case Law*.

SCOTT, Austin Wakeman, *The Law of Trusts* (Albany, N.Y., Matthew Bender and Company, Inc., and Boston, Little, Brown & Co.), cited Scott on *Trusts*.

Books

American Bankers Association, *Glossary of Fiduciary Terms* (New York, Trust Division, 1959).

———, *Handbook on Handling Businesses in Trust* (New York, Trust Division).

———, *The Prudent-Man Rule for Trust Investment* (New York, Trust Division, 1942).

———, *Common Trust Funds, A Handbook on Their Purposes, Establishment, and Operation*, 3d ed. (New York, Trust Division, 1956).

A Statement of Principles of Trust Institutions (New York, Trust Division, 1933; also in 23 *TB*, June, 1944; and appended to *Regulation F—Trust Powers of National Banks*).

American Institute of Banking, Textbook Vol. I, Ch. 1 (New York, Trust Department Services).

ANDREWS, F. Emerson, *Philanthropic Foundations* (New York, Russell Sage Foundation).

APPLEMAN, John Alan, *Basic Estate Planning* (Indianapolis, The Bobbs-Merrill Company, Inc.).

ATKINSON, Thomas E., *Law of Wills and Administration of Decedents' Estates including Principles of Intestate Succession* (St. Paul, Minn., West Publishing Company), cited Atkinson on *Wills and Administration*.

Board of Governors, Federal Reserve System, *Regulation F—Trust Powers of National Banks* (Washington, D.C.).

BOGERT, George Gleason, *Handbook on the Law of Trusts* (St. Paul, Minn., West Publishing Company), cited Bogert's *Handbook*.

BOWE, William J., *Estate Planning and Taxation* (Buffalo, N.Y., Dennis and Company).

———, *Tax Planning for Estates* (Nashville, Tenn., Vanderbilt University Press).

CASNER, A. James, *Estate Planning* (Boston, Little, Brown and Co.).

COLLINS, Basil L., *The ABC of Business Insurance Trusts* (Boston, Bruce Humphries, Inc.).

DODGE, Chester J., and SULLIVAN, John F., *Estate Administration and Accounting* (New York, Clark Boardman Company, Ltd., New York, 1940).

FLIPPO, Edwin B., *Profit-Sharing in American Business* (Columbus, Ohio, Ohio State University Press).

GORDON, George Byron, *Profit-Sharing in Business and Estate Planning* (New York, Farnsworth Publishing Company).

GRANGE, W. J., STAUB, W. A., and BLACKFORD, E. G., *Wills, Executors and Trustees* (New York, The Ronald Press Company).

GRISWOLD, Erwin N., *Spendthrift Trusts,* 2d ed. (Albany, N.Y., Matthew Bender and Company), cited Griswold on *Spendthrift Trusts.*

GUTKIN, Sydney A., and BECK, David, *Tax Avoidance* vs. *Tax Evasion* (New York, The Ronald Press Company).

HARRIS, Homer, *Family Estate Planning Guide* (Mount Kisco, N.Y., Baker, Voorhis and Co., Inc.).

HORTON, Guy B., *Some Legal Aspects of Life Insurance Trusts* (Montpelier, Vt., pub. by author).

————, *Life Insurance Trusts—A Handbook for the Draftsman* (Montpelier, Vt., pub. by author).

————, *Making the Best Use of Your Life Insurance* (Montpelier, Vt., pub. by author).

HOWE, Mark deW., ed., *The Letters of Oliver Wendell Holmes and Harold J. Laski,* (Cambridge, Harvard University Press, 1953), 1247.

KIRKBRIDE, Franklin, STERRETT, J. E., and WILLIS, H. Parker, *The Modern Trust Company* (New York, The Macmillan Co.).

LEACH, W. Barton, *Cases and Text on the Law of Wills,* 2nd ed. (Boston, Little Brown & Co., 1949).

————, and TUDOR, Owen, *The Common-Law Rule against Perpetuities* (Boston, Little, Brown & Co.).

LORING, Augustus Peabody, *A Trustee's Handbook,* Shattuck rev. (Boston, Little, Brown & Co.), cited Loring's *Trustee's Handbook.*

McGILL, D. M., *Fundamentals of Private Pensions* (Homewood, Ill., R. D. Irwin Company, Inc.).

————, *Life Insurance* (Homewood, Ill., R. D. Irwin Company, Inc.).

MacNEILL, Earl S., *Making the Most of Your Estate* (New York, Harper and Brothers).

————, *What Women Want to Know about Wills* (New York, Harper and Brothers).

REMSEN, Daniel S., BURTON-SMITH, R. H., and REMSEN, Gerard T., *Preparation of Wills and Trusts* (Mount Kisco, N.Y., Baker, Voorhis and Co., Inc.).

RHEINSTEIN, Max, *The Law of Decedents' Estates* (Indianapolis, The Bobbs-Merrill Company, Inc.).

RICH, Wilmer Shields, *American Foundations and Their Fields* (New York, American Foundation Information Service).

SHATTUCK, Mayo Adams, and FARR, James F., *An Estate Planner's Handbook* (Boston, Little, Brown & Co.).

SIME, Lewis M., and BAYSE, Paul E., *Problems in Probate Law: Model Probate Code* (Ann Arbor, University of Michigan, 1946).

SMITH, Allen, *Insurance Trusts* (Albany, N.Y., Matthew Bender and Company).

STEPHENSON, Gilbert T., *Trust Business in Common-Law Countries* (New York, Research Council, American Bankers Association).

————, *Drafting Wills and Trust Agreements*—I. Administrative Provisions; II. Dispositive Provisions (Boston, Little, Brown & Co.).

————, *Studies in Trust Business*, 1st, 2d, 3d, and 4th ser. (New York, Trust Division, American Bankers Association), cited Stephenson's *Studies*.

————,*Reflections of a Trustman* (New York, Trust Division, American Bankers Association)

TRACHTMAN, Joseph, *Estate Planning*, ann. ed. (New York, Practicing Law Institute).

WHITESIDE, Horace E., *Statutory Rules against Perpetuities and Accumulations* (Boston, Little, Brown & Co.).

WORMSER, René A., *Your Will and What Not to Do About It* (New York, Simon and Schuster, Inc.).

————, *Preserving the Family Enterprise*, (Philadelphia, The Practicing Lawyer).

————, *The Theory and Practice of Estate Planning* (Chicago, Callaghan and Company).

————, *Personal Estate Planning in a Changing World*, (New York, Simon and Schuster, Inc.).

————, *A Guide to Estate Planning*, (Englewood Cliffs, N.J., Prentice-Hall, Inc.).

WYATT, Birchard E., BJORN, Walter, WILLIAMSON, William Rulon, and BRONSON, Dorrance C., *Employee Retirement Plans*, (Washington, D.C., Graphic Arts Press, Inc.).

ZUBER, John M., *Life Insurance Trusts* (Richmond, Va., D. D. Staples Associates, 1959).

Articles

ACKERMAN, L. J., "Financing Pension Benefits," *Harvard Business Review* (September-October, 1956), 63.

ANDREWS, J. B., "Farm Management Service," 95 *TE* (May, 1956), 436.

APPLEMAN, John Alan, "Don'ts and Why Not's in Estate Planning," *The Spectator* (December, 1954).

ARTHUR, Robert N., "Renegotiation of Agency and Custody Fees," 38 *TB* (January, 1959), 40.

ATHERTON, Frederick W., "Investment Aspects of Oil Industry," 95 *TE* (March, 1956), 239.

BAKER, Walter C., "Are We Caring for Assets or People?" 96 *TE* (May, 1957), 432.

BARCLAY, George C., "Uses of Living Trusts," 35 *TB* (November, 1955), 11; 94 *TE* (November, 1955), 920.

BECKWITH, S. Vilas, "The Registrar—To Be or Not to Be," 37 *TB* (May, 1958), 5.

BETHEL, Carlysle A., "The Case for the Trustee in Funding Pension and Profit-Sharing Trusts," 38 *TB* (December, 1958), 23; 97 *TE* (December, 1958), 1107.

BIEGEL, Herman C., "Pension, Profit-Sharing, and Bonus Plans," 93 *TE* (August, 1954), 731.

BLAKE, Mrs. Bruce, "Trusts and the Family," 21 *TB* (September, 1941), 5.

BORLAND, John Jay, "How a City Bank Handles Farms in Trust," 36 *TB* (September, 1956), 18.

BOULET, O. E., "Trust Services for Corporations," 38 *TB* (June, 1959), 23; 98 *TE* (June, 1959), 610.

BROCKENBROUGH, Henry W., "Termination of Trusts for Children," 97 *TE* (February, 1958), 108.

BRONSON, Cecil P., "Collective Investment of Funds in Employees Trusts," 96 *TE* (March, 1957), 259.

———, "This Business of Employees Trusts," 37 *TB* (March, 1958), 62.

———, "Current Developments in Employee Benefit Trusts," 38 *TB* (April, 1959), 11.

BROWN, Leon B., "By Gifts to Charity," 97 *TE* (December, 1958), 1168.

BUEK, Charles W., "New York's Bank Fiduciary Fund," 34 *TB* (March, 1955), 28; 94 *TE* (February, 1955), 143.

———, "Recent Developments in New York Bank Fiduciary Fund," 35 *TB* (April, 1956), 50.

BURFORD, Albert L., Jr., "Basis of Business Assets—Effect of Death on Partnership Interest and Close Corporation Stock," 97 *TB* (February, 1958), 149.

BURY, W. J., "Ranch Management as a Trust Service in the Southwest," 36 *TB* (December, 1956), 13.

CAMERON, Juan, "Whose Authority?," 204 *Atlantic Monthly* (August, 1959), 38.

CASNER, A. James, "Fractional Share Marital Deduction Gifts," 39 *TB* (March, 1960), 42; 99 *TE* (March, 1960), 190.

CHADWICK, Mary L., "Problems of the Almost-Incompetent Incompetent," 36 *TB* (June, 1957), 42.

CHAPMAN, Douglas G., Jr., "Uses of Life Insurance Trusts," 98 *TE* (September, 1959), 834.

CHAPMAN, Richard P., "Business Interests," 94 *TE* (December, 1955), 1020; 35 *TB* (December, 1955), 6.

———, "Widening Horizons for Management of Property in Trust," 35 *TB* (December, 1955), 6.

CHRISTY, Francis T., "The Transfer of Stock Suggestions for Simplification and Definition," 94 *TE* (April, 1955), 315.

———, "The Model Fiduciaries' Securities Transfer Act," 37 *TB* (April, 1958), 10.

———, "Why Fiduciaries Should Support Model Securities Transfer Act," 97.

COBURN, Arthur L., Jr., "Investment Policy in Pension and Profit-Sharing Trusts," 95 *TE* (March, 1956), 227; 96 *TE* (March, 1957), 255.

COFFIN, Vincent B., "Estate Creation and Conservation," 96 *TE* (May, 1957), 449.

CONKLIN, Maynard D., "Opportunities and Responsibilities in Estate Planning and Trust Administration," 39 *TB* (January, 1960), 32.

CONRAD, Alfred F., "Simplification of Security Transfers by Fiduciaries," 93 *TE* (October, 1954), 953; 94 *TE* (October, 1955), 835; 95 *TE* (October, 1956), 904; *TE* (September, 1957), 861.

COOK, Cecil N., "Disposition of Oil and Gas Interests," 96 *TE* (September, 1957), 846.

COWDERY, Clarence D., "Basis of Compensation for Handling Businesses in Trust," 36 *TB* (June, 1957), 2.

———, "Business Interests in Trust," 95 *TE* (November, 1956), 1023.

———, "Handling Businesses in Trusts," 93 *TE* (February, 1954), 105; 34 *TB* (June, 1955), 20; 94 *TE* (June, 1955), 484.

———, "Making the Most of a Business Interest," 38 *TB* (December, 1958), 30, 97 *TE* (December, 1958), 1106.

———, "When a Trustee Has a Business to Handle," 37 *TB* (June, 1958), 14.

COYLE, Hugh F., "Oil and Gas Properties," 97 *TE* (November, 1958), 1026.

DOHERTY, James E., "Joint Tenancy—Objectives *vs.* Results," 37 *TB* (May, 1958), 9.

DURAND, Harrison F., "Exercise of Power of Appointment," 95 *TE* (May, 1956), 424.

———, "Which State's Law Governs Exercise of Power of Appointment?" 22 *TB* (May, 1956), 424.

EARLY, Albert D., and KIRKPATRICK, Laniel N., "Oil and Gas Interests—Avoiding Estate Problems by Adequate Drafting," 97 *TE* (July, 1958), 620.

EGGER, Roscoe L., Jr., "Liquidation and Valuation of Business Interests in Estates," 95 *TE* (February, 1956), 104.

ELLISON, David E., "Continuous Review Service for Business Interests," 97 *TE* (May, 1958), 486.

FOSTER, F. Perry, "Simplification of Fiduciary Security Transfers Achieved," 39 *TB* (October, 1959), 2.

FRIEDMAN, Nelson, "Patterns in Estate Planning," 99 *TE* (January, 1960), 67.

FREYBURGER, Walter D., "Gifts of Life Insurance," 94 *TE* (June, 1955), 476.

GRIFFIN, Frank L., Jr., *Funding Pension Plans under Today's Economy*, 39 *TB* (April, 1960), 38.

GRISWOLD, Erwin N., "Tax Problems Involved in the Exercise and Release of Powers of Appointment," 22 *TB* (March, 1943), 7.

HANES, Robert M., "Going the Second Mile—How a Foundation Has Helped Its Community," 94 *TE* (August, 1955), 644.

HARRIS, Reese H., Jr., "The Estate Planning Team—Its Duties and Functions," 38 *TB* (March, 1959), 56; 98 *TE* (March, 1959), 189.

HARVEY, Warren M., "Supplemental Unemployment Benefit Plans," 36 *TB* (April, 1957), 57; 96 *TE* (March, 1957), 263.

———, "Employee Saving and Investment Plans," 98 *TE* (February, 1959), 92.

HAYES, Ralph, "The Community Foundation," 35 *TB* (October, 1955), 9.

———, "Corporate Charitable Giving—Community Trusts as Solution of Dilemma," 91 *TE* (July, 1952), 492 at 493.

HEADLEY, Louis S., "The Community Foundation," 96 *TE* (April, 1957), 328.

———, "The Transforming Power of a Will," 38 *TB* (June, 1959), 38; 98 *TE* (June, 1959), 603.

HEALY, Joseph L., "Corporate Services–Multiemployer-Employee Benefit Plans," 38 *TB* (November, 1958), 21; 97 *TE* (November, 1958), 1033.

HENDERSON, Curtis R., "Balanced Retirement Programs," 93 *TE* (May, 1954), 440.

HINES, J. M., "The Changing Role of Insurance Companies in the Pension Field," *Journal*, American Society of Chartered Underwriters, 10, 240–249.

HOBBS, G. Warfield, III, "Whither Pensions?," 93 *TE* (July, 54), 612.

HOLMES, Roy A., "Real Estate Management," 97 *TE* (April, 1958), 318.

HOOVER, Earl R., "Basic Principles Underlying Duty of Loyalty," *Cleveland-Marshall Law Review* (Spring, 1956).

HOWES, Alfred S., "Employee Benefit Plans," 97 *TE* (August, 1958), 717.

HYAM, "Public Auction of Personal Property," 96 *TE* (December, 1957), 1184.

HYERT, Martin D., and RACHLIN, Paula, "Pour-over Trusts: Consequences of Applying the Doctrines of Incorporation by Reference and Facts of Independent Significance," 39 *TB* (October, 1959), 23; *New York University Law Review*, (June, 1959).

JENNETT, Clarence B., "The Prudent-Man Rule Today," 35 *TB* (June, 1956), 12.

JOHNSON, Aurie I., "Handling Businesses in Trust," 93 *TE* (February, 1954), 105.

JOHNSON, Richard L., "Federal and State Legislation Regulating Employee Welfare and Pension Funds," 39 *TB* (January, 1960), 45.

JOLLS, Thomas H., "Security Transfer Simplification," 96 *TE* (July, 1957), 641.

KELLEY, Elliot G., "Security Transfers Eased," 98 *TE* (February, 1959), 94.

KENNEDY, Walter, "The Statement of Principles–A Guide to Sound Management," 37 *TB* (June, 1958), 4.

KIMBALL, Ronald M., "Administration of Corporate Trusts," 35 *TB* (April, 1956), 28; 95 *TE* (March, 1956), 247.

KING, Edward C., "Reappraisal of the Revocable Trust–Cautions in Face of Spouse's Rights," 26 *TB* (January, 1947), 11; 83 *TE* (December, 1946), 649.

KNIGHTON, R. A., "Investment Powers Re-examined," 98 *TE* (May, 1959), 471.

KOPP, Charles L., "Insurance in Estate Planning," 95 *TE* (September, 1956), 772.

LACKMAN, William F., "Streamlining Administration and Operation of Employee Benefit Trusts," 35 *TB* (April, 1956), 12; 95 *TE* (March, 1956), 230.

———, "Investment Relations with Company in Employees Trusts," 96 *TE* (March, 1957), 258.

LAURITZEN, Christian M., II, "Pour-Over Wills," 95 *TE* (November, 1956), 992.

LLOYD, R. McAllister, "CREF and TIAA–A Variable Annuity Plan in Action," 35 *TB* (March, 1956), 50.

LOCKTON, John D., "Investing for Pension Trusts," 39 *TB* (November, 1959), 46.

LOUTHAN, Carter T., "Trusts for Minors," 35 *TB* (October, 1955), 24.

Luick, David J., "The Actuary's Functions in Trusteed Pension Plans," 35 *TB* (April, 1956), 1; 95 *TE* (March, 1956), 224.

McIlwain, John F., "Avoiding Pitfalls for Executors," 97 *TE* (February, 1958), 100.

McIntyre, Raymond A., "Practical Questions on Gifts to Minors," 97 *TE* (April, 1958), 320.

McKenney, W. Gibbs, "Some Estate Planning Considerations Involving Business Interests," 35 *TB* (March, 1956), 55; 95 *TE* (March, 1956), 212.

McLean, Archie W., and Draper, E. V. S., "Handling Farms in Trust in the Southeast," 35 *TB* (June, 1956), 20.

McLucas, Don H., "Discretionary Trusts," 97 *TE* (March, 1958), 210; 37 *TB* (April, 1958), 17.

McNeill, Charles R., "Registration of Pension Plans," 97 *TE* (March, 1958), 196.

MacNeill, Earl S., "Giving to Minors Made Easy—in Eight States," 35 *TB* (November, 1955), 28.

———, "Stock Gifts to Minors Act—Ten Months Later," 36 *TB* (September, 1956), 10.

Maduro, Denis Brandon, "Stock Perpetuation—An Approach to Continuing Closely Held Business Interests," 95 *TE* (November, 1956), 1000.

Mallory, Frank L., "Charitable Gifts in Estate Planning," 94 *TE* (May, 1955), 434.

Mannerheimer, Albert, "Sprinkling Trusts," 95 *TE* (October, 1956), 919.

Marks, Albert A. Jr., "Easing Security Transfers," 96 *TE* (December, 1957), 1234.

Mason, Vernon, "A Lawyer Looks at Estate Planning," 94 *TE* (July, 1955), 572.

Meyers, Edward F., "Composite Trust for Separate Employer Retirement Plans," 95 *TE* (December, 1956), 1098.

Moore, A. F., "Insurance Aspects of Estate Planning," 95 *TE* (July, 1956), 616.

Morris, Joseph W., "Oil and Gas Interests in a Decedent's Estates," 93 *TE* (October, 1954), 890.

Mudge, Norman E., "The Simplification of Corporate Fiduciary Transfers," 35 *TB* (February, 1956), 20.

Niles, Russell, D., "Two Lives Down—and Goal to Go," 98 *TE* (February, 1959), 104.

Nolan, William, J., Jr., "Pension and Profit-Sharing Trusts," 98 *TE* (October, 1959), 1006.

Olswang, Charles H., "Management of Real Property in Trusts and Estates," 37 *TB* (November, 1957), 33; 96 *TE* (November, 1957), 1095.

Partridge, David, III, "Simplification of Security Transfers by Fiduciaries," 97 *TE* (October. 1958), 906; 98 *TE* (October, 1959), 1019.

Pfleiderer, Arthur B., "Handling Businesses in Trust," 93 *TE* (February, 1954), 105.

———, "What to Do about Business Interests," 93 *TE* (November, 1954), 1010.

———, "Value of Estate Planning when Handling Business in Trust," 34 *TB* (December, 1954), 7.

PIERCE, Lovick, "Has Your Town a Nest Egg?," *Together* (February, 1958).

POHL, Frank J., "The Administration of Trust Indentures by Corporate Trustees," 36 *TB* (April, 1957), 19; 96 *TE* (March, 1957), 247.

POINDEXTER, C. W., "Estate Planning with Short-Term Trusts," 39 *TB* (February, 1960), 9.

POLASKY, Alan N., "Pour-over Wills—and the Statutory Blessing," 98 *TE* (October, 1959), 949.

PORTER, James Kenneth, "Trusts—Duration and Indestructibility," *Tennessee Law Review* (Spring, 1957).

REED, David, "Drafting Wills for Oil and Gas Interests," 94 *TE* (November, 1955), 966.

———, "Supervision of Oil and Gas Interests by Corporate Trustees," 35 *TB* (November, 1955), 18.

RHYNE, Charles S., "Folkways and New Ways of Writing Wills," 38 *TB* (October, 1958), 56.

RIEGE, John H., "Pension and Profit-Sharing Trusts," 94 *TE* (March, 1955), 200.

ROBB, Paul B., "Corporate Trust Services," 96 *TE* (February, 1957), 126.

ROBINSON, Noel T., "Handling Farms in Trust in the Midwest," 35 *TB* (May, 1956), 3.

———, "Trustee's Responsibility and Suggested Procedure for Voting Stock Held in Fiduciary Accounts," 37 *TB* (September, 1957), 4.

RUSS, Lillian M., "What Women Should Know about Trust Services," 94 *TE* (August, 1955), 640.

SANDWEG, G. K., "Corporate Trusteeship," 96 *TE* (April, 1957), 340.

SAVIDGE, Edgar T., "Farm and Ranch Operations in Trust," 37 *TB* (November, 1957), 27.

SCOTT, Austin W., "Pouring-Over," 37 *TB* (March, 1958), 25; 97 *TE* (March, 1958), 189; 38 *TB* (December, 1958), 41.

———, "Liability for Participation in Breach of Trust," 97 *TE* (December, 1958), 1114.

———, "Trusts and the Conflict of Laws," 39 *TB* (March, 1960), 28; 99 *TE* (March, 1960), 186.

SEAL, Hilary L., "Pension Trusts—Some Current Aspects," 38 *TB* (June, 1959), 10; 98 *TE* (June, 1959), 600.

SEUFFERT, Charles F., "Business Estate Planning," 99 *TE* (February, 1960), 156.

SHATTUCK, Mayo Adams, "The Revocable Trust: Its Manifold Uses in Times of War and Peace," 22 *TB* (March, 1943), 25; 76 *TE* (February, 1943), 189.

SHORT, R. C., "When Should a Trust End?," 96 *TE* (November, 1957), 1084.

———, "The Family Trust," 98 *TE* (May, 1959), 418.

SMITH, Craig R., "Philanthropy and Estate Planning," 35 *TB* (September, 1955), 30.

———, "Philanthropic Services of a Modern Trust Department," 97 *TE* (January, 1958), 20.

SMITH, Frances M., "Operation of Businesses by Corporate Executors and Trustees," 39 *TB* (December, 1959), 44.

STEPHENSON, Gilbert T., "Cotrustees or Several Trustees?" 14 *Temple University Law Quarterly* (April, 1942), 249.

————, "Trusts in the Everyday Affairs of People," 24 *TB* (October, 1944), 27; *Studies*, 3d ser., 1.

————, "The Preferred Beneficiaries of Trusts," *Studies*, 2d ser. (1944), 289.

————, "Transfer of Securities Held in Trust Accounts," 24 *TB* (June, 1945), 9; *Studies*, 3d ser., 79.

————, "A Bank's or Trust Company's Own Shares in Its Trust Accounts," 24 *TB* (June, 1945), 5.

————, "Cofiduciary or Consultant?," 96 *TE* (August, 1957), 741.

————, "Fiduciary Principles and Policies," 37 *TB* (February, 1958), 29. (May, 1958), 22; and 38 *TB* (September, 1958), 36.

————, "The Trustman in Perspective—as a Social Man," 38 TB (January, 1959), 13.

STOCK, David, "Employee Death Benefits," 96 *TE* (October, 1957), 972.

STRATFORD, Ralph B., "Handling Businesses in Trust, 37 *TB* (December, 1957), 38.

SWAIM, Robert S., "Recent Developments in Employee Benefit Funds," 35 *TB* (April, 1956), 17; 95 *TE* (March, 1956), 233.

————, "Retirement Trusts—A Challenge to the Smaller Trust Departments," 37 *TB* (January, 1958), 40; 96 *TE* (December, 1957), 1224.

TIERNEY, Joseph F., "New York's Bank Fiduciary Fund—Advantages, Objections, and Pitfalls," 35 *TB* (October, 1955), 34.

TOMLINSON, Eustace W., "Support Trusts and Gifts to Minors," 97 *TE* (October, 1958), 929.

TORP, Frederick H., "The ABC's of Pension and Profit-Sharing Plans," 37 *TB* (November, 1957), 16.

TRACHTMAN, Joseph, "Handling Businesses in Trust," 93 *TE* (February, 1954), 105.

————, "Pour-overs," 97 *TE* (May, 1958), 416.

TREMAN, C. E., Jr., "A Bank Fiduciary Fund for Multiple Bank Participations," 38 *TB* (March, 1959), 44; 98 *TE* (March, 1959), 244.

TREMAYNE, Bertram W., "Estate Planning for a Man with a Business," *Washington University Law Quarterly* (February, 1955).

TROWBRIDGE, John F., "Farm Property Problems in the Pacific Northwest," 37 *TB* (October, 1957), 32.

TURK, Richard J., Jr., "Powers of Appointment," 93 *TE* (September, 1954), 752.

VESTAL, Alan D., "Critical Revaluation of the Charitable Trusts as a Giving Device," *Washington University Law Quarterly* (June, 1957).

WALLIS, Gordon T., "Pension and Profit-Sharing Trusts," 93 *TE* (October, 1954), 942; 94 *TE* (October, 1955), 841; 95 *TE* (October, 1956), 915; 96 *TE* (September, 1957), 868.

WANDA, C. P. Bartos, "The Voting Trust," *New York University Law Review* (February, 1959).

WARNER, Paul A., "Superiority of Trusteed over Insured Pension Plans," 38 *TB* (November, 1958), 28; 97 *TE* (November, 1958), 1030.

WEYHER, Harry F., "Pension and Profit-Sharing Trusts," 97 *TE* (October, 1958), 920.

WHIPPLE, Wade R., "Who Should Be Property Guardian for a Minor?," 96 *TE* (November, 1957), 1125.

WHITE, Joseph W., "Handling Businesses in Trust," 93 *TE* (February, 1954), 105.

WIDMARK, G. Norman, "Security Gifts to Minors," 95 *TE* (August, 1956), 698.

WILLCOX, Donald S., "Valuation of Close Held Business Interest," 35 *TB* (September, 1955), 36.

———, "Blueprint for Handling Business Interests," 98 *TE* (July, 1959), 662.

WILLIAMS, Joseph E., "Easing Problems of Stock Transfer," 35 *TB* (April, 1956), 34; 95 *TE* (March, 1956), 278.

WINDLE, William T. "Principles and Policies Applicable to Direction Trusts," 38 *TB* (February, 1959), 2.

WIRTH, Conrad L., "Trusts for Public and Civic Uses," 96 *TE* (August, 1957), 748.

WOLF, G. Van Velsor, "Twenty Pointers on Liquidation of Business Interests," 97 *TE* (January, 1958), 24.

———, "Drafting Insurance Trust with Pour-over Will," 98 *TE* (October, 1959), 997.

WORMSER, René A., "The Age of Discretion," 95 *TE* (January, 1956), 8.

WYNN, James O., "Management of Property of Infants and Incompetents," 95 *TE* (October, 1956), 924; 97 *TE* (October, 1958), 921.

YOUNG, George A., "Planning and Management of Charitable Foundations," 35 *TB* (February, 1956), 36.

———, "Individual Deferred Compensation," 95 *TE* (August, 1956).

ZAUGG, John V. W., "Recent Developments in the Pension Trust Field," 36 *TB* (October, 1956), 32; 95 *TE* (September, 1956), 797.

ZUBER, John M., "Life Insurance and Estate Planning," 3 *Journal*, American Society of Life Underwriters (1949), 212.

Miscellaneous

"Farm Management by Banks," 35 *TB* (October, 1955), 8. A manual.

"Management and Retention of Small Businesses," 96 *TE* (September, 1957), 882. A committee report.

"Standard of Care for Corporate and Professional Trustees," *Virginia Law Review* (June, 1956). A note.

Panel Discussions

"Pension and Profit-Sharing Trusts," 95 *TE* (March, 1956), 224.

"Employees Trusts," 96 *TE* (March, 1957), 255.

"Handling Businesses in Trust," 93 *TE* (February, 1954), 105.

In addition, see the articles about estates and trusts in *The Trust Bulletin* and in *Estates and Trusts*, of which the foregoing are only a few selections; *American Banker*, 32 Stone Street, New York City, a daily newspaper, has a section on estate and trust subjects.

Loose-Leaf Services on Estates and Trusts

Commerce Clearing House Trust and Estate Law Reporter, 214 North Michigan
    Avenue, Chicago, and 420 Lexington Avenue, New York 17, N.Y., cited
    Estate Law Reporter.
Prentice-Hall Wills, Estates, and Trusts, Prentice-Hall, Inc., Englewood Cliffs,
    N.J., cited *Wills, Estates, and Trusts*.

Other Bibliographies

The June issue of *The Trust Bulletin* and the December issue of *Trusts
and Estates* each carries an index to current estate and trust literature.
Trusts and Estates has a department entitled "Literature Notes." Each
autumn, following the annual meeting of the Probate and Trust Law Division of the American Bar Association, *Trusts and Estates* carries the "Report
of the Committee on Trust and Probate Literature" which is an annotated
bibliography of estates and trusts during the preceding year. Also, Shattuck
and Farr's *An Estate Planner's Handbook* carries an eighteen-page bibliography covering material up to 1953.

Index